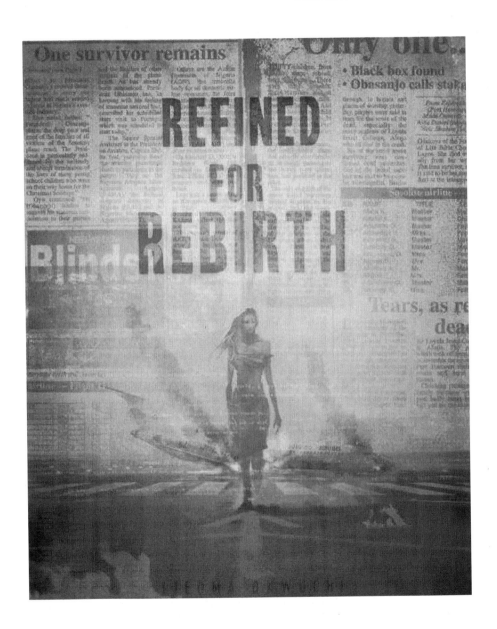

Refined for Rebirth

Ijeoma Okwuchi

Refined for Rebirth

Published in 2014 by Customer Centricity Limited
15, Biaduo Road, Off Keffi Street,
SW Ikoyi, Lagos, Nigeria.
www.customercentricityltd.com

Copyright © Ijeoma Okwuchi 2014
Cover art copyright © DuksArt 2014

All rights reserved. No part of this publication may be reproduced, stored in or introduced into a retrieval system, or transmitted, in any form, or by any means (electronic, mechanical, photocopying, recording or otherwise) without the express prior written permission of the publisher.
This book is sold subject to the condition that it shall not, by way of trade or otherwise, be lent, re-sold, hired out, or otherwise circulated without the publisher's prior consent in any form of binding or cover other than that in which it is published and without a similar condition including this condition being imposed on the subsequent purchaser.

ISBN: 1500838861
ISBN-13: 9781500838867

DEDICATION

To the sixty Loyola Jesuit College, Abuja students, lovingly referred to as "The 60 Angels," who went home to be with The Lord on December 10th, 2005.
…..never forgotten.

ACKNOWLEDGMENTS

All glory, of course, goes to God for His immense grace that not only saved Kechi, but kept her alive against all odds.

-To Gabriel, a rescue worker who seeing Kechi move at the crash site, obeyed a prompting from God and put her in one of the ambulances.

-To my family, whose constant prayers and support sustained, and still sustains, us.

-To Shell Petroleum Development Company, especially the former MD, Engineer Basil Omiyi, and the Senior Medical Director, Dr. Moses Ohiosimuan whose decision to take over Kechi's treatment set in motion a chain of events that are still unfolding.

-To the Shell nurses, Sister Jane, Sister Tokunbo and the rest of the dedicated staff in Shell Hospital, Port Harcourt.

-To Betty, Ike, Lanre, Ifeoma, Layi, Media, Bro Dotun and his lovely wife, Michelle and her girls, and to Deidre, who all took such exceptional care of me in Johannesburg.

-To my church family in Nigeria who never stopped praying.

-To my friends all over the world who with constant phone calls, assured me that they were praying round the clock for Kechi.

-To the exceptional medical staff at Milpark Hospital: Dr. Plani, Dr. Nel, Dr. Pahad, Dr. Opolot. The wonderful nurses, Hilda, Rochelle, Maureen, Primrose, Thandi, Tchidi, Mr. X, to name a few.

-To the bereaved families who, though they had lost their children, still reached out to us to encourage us.

Sometimes, "Thank you" seems very inadequate, but from the bottom of my heart, "Thank You, and may God continue to bless you all."

DECEMBER 10, 2005

"Behold, I have refined thee, but not with silver; I have chosen thee in the furnace of affliction. For mine own sake, even for mine own sake, will I do it: for how should my name be polluted? and I will not give my glory unto another."
Isaiah 48: 10 & 11(KJV)

There was no feeling of foreboding that morning. Nothing went wrong to signal the beginning of a lousy day. For my household, it started as a perfectly ordinary Saturday. The only difference was that Kechi was coming home from school for Christmas holidays. This was always a cause for joy in our house. The house came alive, became vibrant and noisy, when Kechi came home.

I woke a bit late and as usual, took my bible to the sitting room for my morning devotions. My husband, Mike, and I were in different places spiritually and he still could not understand why I felt the need to pray so much, so I usually just took myself off to the sitting room to pray. On that morning, I prayed as I did every time Kechi was coming home; for journey mercies for all in the aircraft. I was later to wonder if, had I devoted more time to that particular prayer, things could have turned out differently.

The flight was supposed to be on ground at about 11.00am. Chigozie, my husband's driver, and I left Aba around 9.00am to give plenty of time for the police checks on the road between Aba and Port Harcourt. Sure enough, a few miles down the road leading to the airport, inside Port Harcourt, we fell victim to a police roadblock and made their day when it turned out that Chigozie did not have his driving license. It cost me =N=3000.00.

We finally made it to the airport on time. I rushed to the arrival gate, thinking that the plane had landed, only to be told by some other parents that there was Environmental Sanitation in Abuja and since the kids could not be at the airport before 7.00am, when the exercise began, they would now come home with the 1.00pm flight.

This was disappointing but I decided to use the time to drive into town and buy chocolates and other goodies for Kechi, our usual practice whenever she came home.

When I got back to the airport at about 2.00pm, the plane was said to be 10 minutes from landing. This was when I got my first feeling of unease. It came from nowhere. I called my sister in Lagos whose son, Ugochukwu was also in Loyola Jesuit College, Kechi's school, and asked if he was home yet. She said yes, though she had not seen him as she was still in Lagos Business School, where she was studying for her MBA. He had been met and taken home from the airport. She asked if Kechi had come home and I said I was at the airport waiting for the plane to land. By this time the weather had changed and I told her I would call her back.

At about 2.15pm, the storm started. The winds were crazy, lightening flashed, the rain was fierce. It lasted about 15 minutes. Meanwhile, there was no news of the plane that was to have been on the ground by then. I had disquiet in my spirit and I moved close to some of the parents intending to ask them for us to pray but I overhead them saying to each other that they had prayed extensively and that the kids were going to be okay. I moved to one side and began to pray. My main concern was for the pilot not to attempt to land in that weather.

Suddenly, there was a lot of activity, cars driving very fast to and from the tarmac, general pandemonium. Some parents enquired, and were told that a helicopter had crashed on the tarmac. With the benefit of hindsight, one can only think of the chances of a helicopter crash at the same time a plane was supposed to land. But frankly, the very idea of what happened next could never have been contemplated by anyone.

A private car raced by and I could see that there was someone lying on the back seat. In fact, the person was tall and the door could not be closed fully. Several more cars sped by and then ambulances followed.

At about the same time, the officials at the airport had closed and locked the arrival doors and were not answering any questions. Then suddenly, one man rushed to the front of the arrival gate where most of the parents were now asking questions about the flight.

I will see that man's face and the expression on it for the rest of my life.

His eyes were opened wide to their fullest extent. His hands were crossed in front of him, left hand in right armpit, and right hand in left armpit. His mouth was squeezed shut, lips pulled into his mouth. He was clearly horrified!

And I knew!

In my heart I knew at once that a helicopter had not crashed. It was Sosoliso Flight 1145 that was carrying our children that had crashed. At this point, the man was being questioned by parents, "What's going on? What is it?" He said nothing and took off running.

I turned to the mother beside me and said to her, "That plane has crashed". She agreed with me and we took off to find Sosoliso staff and make enquiries. On our way, news of the crash filtered down to us and we took off running to the tarmac.

It seemed that while most of us were at the arrival gate waiting for the plane, those who were closer to the tarmac had seen the plane go down and had rushed to the tarmac.

In the distance, I could see the smoking body of an airplane but it looked small and crushed and the wings were not attached to it. Also, where that part of the plane was lying was a distance from where the crowd was running to, further up. As I ran towards the site, I was praying that the plane, having crashed so close to the tarmac, had survivors. As I ran, I was trying to get Mike on the phone. I was not getting through to him, so I called my father. I remember telling him that Kechi's plane had crashed and that they should pray. Then I finally got through to Mike. His scream of anguish still rings in my ear to this day. I asked him to hurry to the airport, that I needed him and he should get someone to drive him. I was worried because Kechi was, still is, the apple of Mike's eye, his princess, and I was concerned that he might not concentrate on his driving during the journey to Port Harcourt.

I continued past what used to be the body of the airplane, still smoldering, on my left and followed the crowd to a field further down, also to the left where a fire truck and other vehicles were parked. As I got closer to this place, I could smell burning flesh and I knew it was all over. Twisted metal and other aircraft parts were strewn here and there. I got to the edge of the field and I looked out at an array of human bodies strewn all over the field our babies, our hopes and dreams, tossed out like handfuls of stones flung from a giant's hands, motionless, lifeless.

It was as if the fuselage of the plane had upended the bodies before going on to land somewhere else. I went closer, thinking, "my baby is so light complexioned, I will be able to pick her out and get someone to pick her up and carry her out of that field." But that was not to be, because every single body on that field was completely white from having the skin completely stripped off by fire. I saw a big woman lying on her belly, skin stripped off. Then I saw kids. One still had a workman or iPod ear phone in his/her ear. There was also a cluster of 3 bodies lying close together. One had my daughter's build and I thought, "Oh that must be Kechi". Their clothes had been burnt off but their underwear was still on them. I could look no further, could go no further. I turned back, heading towards the airport building, walking slowly, trying to get Mike on the phone.

At this point, I found that I could not cry. I did not even try to. I was very unnaturally calm, strangely detached. My heart had gone beyond breaking. I tried and failed to think of my world without Kechi. I did not even think of being upset with God because He is my everything. I turned to Him now and started to speak.

"Okay, Lord. My baby is gone. But you know what? You are still God. You are still sovereign. I still love You. Thank You for sixteen wonderful years with her. But promise me one thing. That I will be with Kechi again one day."

Then I wanted to die right then so I could be with Kechi again, but then I remembered Chizitara, my miracle daughter, so called because I had her eleven years after Kechi, when I had given up hope of having another child.

"So, okay, Lord, this is why You gave me Chizitara, so I won't be left without a child. I thank You."

Then, knowing the strength of Kechi's love for me, I knew that she would not be happy, even in heaven, if she thought I would be inconsolable. I looked up to the sky and said,

"Kechi, it's okay, baby. Go with Jesus. Mommy will be fine, I promise you.

Sweetheart, you know we will be together again one day. I promise you right now that I will live the rest of my life in such a way that when the end comes, I will be in heaven with you. Go on, love. I love you". Then I started to sing,

"Because He lives, I can face tomorrow
Because He lives, all fear is gone
Because I know He holds my future
My life is worth a-living
Just because He lives"

As I was singing, I was walking back to the airport building. I passed many parents expressing their sorrow and grief in different ways. The two memories that still stick out in my mind during that walk from the tarmac to the airport building were of two women. One was just rolling on the ground, first one way, and then the other way, screaming and crying and calling her child's name. Another woman was screaming at her husband, "Where is my son? Go and get my son for me. I told you that he should take the bus back but you said he should fly with his schoolmates. Oya, where is he? Where is my son?" The poor, confused man, tears streaming from his eyes, was trying to hold her but she beat him off, slapping him, out of her mind with pain.

At this point, I still had not shed a single tear. Some part of me knew this was unusual and unnatural so I called Chigozie, who had stuck beside me during my race to the tarmac, and told him that he should stay nearby because I feared that I was not myself. When I wondered about my lack of tears, I felt that I was waiting for Mike to come before I could collapse.

I got to the airport building near the departure lounge where most of the parents were gathered. At this point we had all passed from the state of disbelief and shock to thinking, "It's really true, our kids are gone". We held on to each other. Men were weeping like children. I noticed one particular woman who was talking to the rest of the parents, even as tears were pouring out of her eyes. She was telling us not to mourn like unbelievers and to believe that our children have gone to heaven. I was later to learn that her name was Mary, and two of her children had been inside that aircraft. From Mary, I found the courage to try and console some kids that were among us, siblings of the kids on the aircraft, who had come with their parents to the airport to welcome their sisters and brothers. The poor kids were crying, bewildered, wondering if it was true that their siblings were gone. Mostly, the sight of their parents weeping with abandon was probably the most frightening thing they had ever seen in their young lives.

Another woman was kneeling on the ground, wailing into her phone, "Yes, it's true. My angels are gone. Three of them are gone." A man, who I later identified as her husband was sitting on the ground, weeping. They had three children in Loyola Jesuit College. All three kids had been in that plane.

It was at this point that I remembered to call Uzoma, my friend, who was taking care of Chizitara for me that day. The plan had been for Tara to go to a birthday party with Uzoma's daughter, Kamara, and then when Kechi and I got to Aba, we would pick her up on our way home. I called Uzo and said to her that she would have to keep Tara for some days. I told her I was still at the airport and there had been a plane crash and Kechi was gone.

"Gone where?" Uzo asked me, sounding puzzled.

"Gone to heaven", I replied "The plane crashed". When she started to scream, I switched off my phone, knowing she would call back when she calmed down and also knowing that Tara was safe with Uzo, and I did not need to worry about her just then.

Mom called and told me to be strong. She said that God had given us sixteen beautiful years with Kechi and we would always be grateful to Him. She assured me that she and my brother, Chinedu, would leave Lagos that night for Port Harcourt to be with me. I heard her but I was not fooled. I knew my Mom was trying to sound strong for me. Kechi occupied a special place in their hearts because she was their first grandchild.

Dad called me and asked me if there were any survivors. I had actually heard two guys talking on that fateful walk from the tarmac and they were saying that some people were alive and had been rushed to hospitals. One of the men said that there was one particular woman he hoped would survive. I asked him what the woman looked like and he said she was big but could not go into detail. I did not dare to even go there. I mean, what were the odds?

I told Dad what I had overheard and that they said the survivors were adults. My Dad said to me that Kechi could be mistaken for an adult. He then went on to state very clearly,

"If there are any survivors in that plane, then Kechi is one of them".

I thought to myself that my Dad was in denial and this was the way he could handle the trauma. I was quite worried about him and Mom and asked him how Mom was doing. He confirmed my fears. Mom was totally gone. He was worried about how she was taking the news.

It was the strangest call I have ever received. An urgent pleading call from Ijeoma urging, 'Daddy! Daddy! Daddy, pray, pray, pray!'

I asked her, 'Pray for what? What's the matter?'

She said, 'Oh Daddy, please pray, there is a plane crash and Kechi is on that flight!'

'How do you know she was on that flight?'

'Daddy I am sure, I spoke to her in the plane before they took off'

'Okay Ije calm down, there must be survivors, and if only one person survives, that one person will be Kechi'.

'Oh Daddy, it is a terrible sight, Kechi is gone'.

'Impossible ' I thundered, 'Kechi cannot die' Are there no survivors at all?

Ije responded in a broken tone, 'Yes Daddy, they said they carried out three women to a hospital'.

'Then one of those women is Kechi', I hollered.

But Ije replied, 'Daddy they said three women, not girls!'

'Kechi is a big girl and can be mistaken for a woman. She is one of the three,' I insisted.

Meanwhile hell was let loose in my house. Uncontrollable weeping and lamentation rent the air. Family members were rolling themselves on the floor crying like little babies! My telling them that all hope was not lost fell on deaf and hopeless ears. I left the wailing crowd in the living room and went to my bedroom upstairs to pray.

Then Ijeoma called again. This time excitedly with the news 'Kechi is alive!!' The expression of joy that rent the air was only comparable to the wailing that preceded it. Wow! That joy was palpable. What was hidden from the joy-drenched family was that this was the beginning of a long repair and healing process.

But we give all the glory to God.

……..Account of that day by my Dad, Chris Duru

RESURRECTION

I kept calling Mike to make sure he was okay and to monitor his journey to Port Harcourt. I felt myself coming apart and I needed his strength. My friend, Lizzie and her husband, Jeff called me to sit with them on a bench. I remember asking her if was possible that we were about to bury our children. Meanwhile my phone was ringing off the hook. The news had spread and family and friends were calling to find out if it was true and to pray with me.

Then my phone rang one more time and a male voice asked, "Is this Mrs. Ijeoma Okwuchi?"

"Yes"

"Do you know any Nkechi Okwuchi?"

I said yes, while thinking, what can this be about, at this time? "She's my daughter"

"Madam, your daughter survived the plane crash. She is at Braithwaite Memorial Hospital. Please rush there as fast as you can".

I flew up from the bench, screaming, "Did you say my daughter is alive?" Next thing I knew, I fell on the ground. The man was still speaking very urgently in the phone.

"Madam, where are you?"

"By the departure hall", I answered.

"Please hurry directly to the front of the departure hall. You will see some people wearing blue overalls".

I took off running. I was aware as I ran that other parents were running with me, praying that their kids were also among the survivors.

My driver, pursuing me, then shouted, "Aunty, see Oga!" Mike had just driven through the gates of the airport car park.

I called Mike, babbling, "Mike, Kechi is alive! Kechi is alive!

Come to the front of the departure hall."

Meanwhile, the rescue staff asked to use my phone to inform the relatives of other survivors and I willingly gave it to them.

Mike rushed up to me and we both got into his car and took off for the hospital. We were both shaking. I was hyperventilating. I could not catch my breath.

I tried to call Dad but could not reach him. I called Ulo and screamed into the phone, "Ulo, Kechi is alive. Pray. Pray. Pray."

There was loud screaming in the background and I switched off. I began to pray.

Having just finished lunch at about 2pm on that terrible Saturday afternoon, I went upstairs to rest. Chris was already reading something, a newspaper, I think. Then his phone rang and he repeated what he was hearing, 'Daddy pray, pray, pray.' I looked at him and he looked puzzled and worried at the same time. I asked what was happening and he said Ije asked us to pray. I told him to ask for the prayer-point and he said Kechi's plane had crashed!

That's all I remember.

They said I was thrashing all over the room telling them I could not take it and that God should take me and leave Kechi. But when I came to, Chris and two others were pinning me down to the floor. I was wailing and was uncontrollable. It was then that I understood what is meant by 'the heart being cut in two'. It was like a saw was being used to hack at my chest or is it heart? Some one came up to say the whole house is filled with people and that we should come downstairs. When did all these people get here? Many more were outside crying and wailing. It was a heart-breaking sight.

Then I heard Chris saying 'if seven people are alive, Kechi is one of them' Then ' if only three people are alive, Kechi is one of them'. The next call was "Kechi is alive." The whole gathering shouted in unison as you hear in a football game when there's a goal!

Then prayers began from every angle the church, the family, friends, strangers, everyone.

My life has not been the same again seeing God's mercies.
…..My Mom, Floy Duru's account

My husband said to me,

"Ije, if it is true that Kechi is alive, if she survives this…"

I cut him off and said to him that the fact that Kechi was alive meant that she was going to be okay.

One of the rescuers kept calling me to ask if I was at the hospital yet. Port Harcourt is known for traffic jams but that day was truly horrible. We were barely moving and were getting very frustrated. I was praying ceaselessly with Mike concurring. I made a vow to God that because He had saved Kechi's life, my family and I would serve him forever. Mike said a big "Amen" to that.

The next time the rescuer called he was impatient. 'Madam, you are not there yet? Your daughter is calling for you. Please rush."

Mike called his sisters who lived in Port Harcourt, and his friends, and told them where Kechi had been taken. Kate, my sister-in-law called us and told us to hurry. She had been to the hospital and had seen Kechi and was not sure she would be alive for much longer. I had seen the bodies at the airport and knew what to expect.

At this time, I also got several text messages that I now know were from one of the parents telling me to rush to the hospital.

Mike said then, "Maybe Kechi is just hanging on to see you one last time; you know how close she is to you".

I rejected that at once, in the name of Jesus, and told Mike that the God I served would not keep Kechi alive only to take her away. The traffic became so bad that Mike asked me to take a commercial bike to the hospital because they were able to weave in between cars and would get me there faster. This was a mode of transportation he usually forbade us to take for safety reasons.

This was not a normal day.

I quickly jumped out of the jeep and got on the first motorbike I could stop. The man asked for =N=300.00. I asked him to step on it. The nearest way was blocked by a wedding party and he turned to go through Trans Amadi. After stopping to buy gas, we got to the hospital and he asked for =N=500.00. I gave him =N=600 and hurried inside.

Ikenna and Patty, Mike's brother and sister, were waiting at the hospital gates and rushed me to the emergency room. On a stretcher lay my baby, so badly burned.

I rushed to her side and said to her, "Kechi, Mommy is here".

She turned her head in my direction and opened her eyes, "Mommy, Mommy".

I said, "I'm here, darling". "Mommy, I love you"

"I love you too, baby. I love you. You are going to be okay".

December 10, 2005 is a day I cannot forget in spite of a natural propensity not to indulge in unpleasant memories. Here was a day that began like every other day before it, no unusual expectations except that I planned to surprise my wife, Ijeoma and the kids, Kechi and Tara with an announcement later that day in Port Harcourt. Ije and the kids would be in Port Harcourt that day because Kechi was coming in from her school in Abuja, and Ije was picking her from the airport. I was going to tell them that we were moving house from Aba to Port Harcourt, something I had been discussing with Ije for a while.

So on this seemingly regular day, I had concluded my preparations for departure to Port Harcourt from our residence in Aba, put my stuff in the car and was standing by the car in the court yard chatting and sharing a coke with my brother, Ikenna, prior to driving off when a call came through to my mobile. It was my wife and there was a note of panic and near hysteria in her voice.

"Mike I don't know what is happening, I don't understand what they are saying. They say Kechi's plane is in trouble, it's like its going to crash ..."

It was a crazy, bizarre and frightening call all at once. I was trying to calm her down, "calm down, woman, slow down, what exactly is the problem?" when she trailed off and the line cut off. I turned to narrate this strange call from Ije to

Ikenna and had barely started when she called again this time to confirm that the plane had crashed.

I truly cannot recall clearly my immediate reaction. All I remember was that soon after I found myself on the high way speeding towards Port Harcourt. On reflection, however, I dimly recall smashing the coke bottle against the fence of my court yard, spinning into my car and telling Ikenna I must get to the airport at once. I suspect Ikenna offered to drive but I would not hear of it, my mind was a complex of confusion, anger and fear. Not the best state to drive in, but I probably would have gone mad en route, were I not driving.

It was simply insane. This was not supposed to happen, not to a plane load of growing innocent children coming home for Christmas. Barely weeks before, a Belleview plane had crashed en route Abuja from Lagos. This was an outrage.

That was the state of my mind. I was angry, even furious at the indifferent fate that would let this happen but there was also an inescapable knot of cold fear at the back of my mind grimly acknowledging the inevitable reality of my wife's phone call and the fact of tragedy and death as part of our lives.

I imagine that was where I was emotionally when I started calling my friends asking them to arrange for an ambulance for the airport. In fact, Ezigbo and Patrick(Sule) were unaware of the crash before I called them.

From them, and a few others I had called, came the uncertain assurance that plane crashes can be survived and this was probably a crash landing which was even less fatal, hence an ambulance might be a little hasty. George, on the other hand, provoked spiritual assurance. He simply said, ' No it's not true, Mike, Kechi can't die! I will put it in prayer right now and I am joining you in Port Harcourt.'

Perhaps it was the confidence with which he said it or his apparent faith in prayers but in that drive to the airport I found myself actually praying silently for a miracle, for a reality less tragic than the message I got and making every kind of promise to God should I get my miracle. One promise I remember making was that if God saved Kechi, I was going to become a born-again Christian.

To this day I frankly cannot figure out how I drove over 65 miles of rough and tumble turnpike to get to the airport in less than an hour and a half on a busy Saturday. Perhaps it was all part of the miracle I prayed for, because I got my miracle, and Kechi lived and lives on today as a testimony that miracles still happen and a memorial to her colleagues, that we may never forget that December 10, 2005 happened.

When Ije called to say that Kechi was alive, there was an immediate loosening of the cold knot of fear inside me. I remember that Ikenna said to me, 'Well, it looks like you are about to become born-again.'

Then the fear came back and I was thinking that sometimes people survive accidents only to die later, then I thought maybe the crash was not so bad. In the midst of these see-saw of emotions, I arrived at the airport, and Ije and I began the mad dash to Braithwaite Memorial Hospital. The traffic was insane, and I remember I told Ije to take a commercial motor bike which would get there faster, I would meet up with her.

At the hospital, my friends were already there, crowded around the ER doors. Ody, Ezigbo's wife, rushed up to me and gave me a hug and I immediately thought, 'Oh Kechi is dead'. I thought she was comforting me.

That's when I lost it. I broke down and wept like a baby.

Ody said, "No, no, Mike. She is not dead. She is alive'.

From there, it was off to Shell, where we met with Dr. Moses, a man who was going to become very important to us.

I want to forget, because several years down the line, the memories are still very painful, but I cannot and hopefully the Nigerian nation will not also, for in not forgetting, we may ensure prevention of, or life-saving response to, future accidents.

As for me, I am still striving to keep the promises I made to God and in time I will.

….Account by Mike, Kechi's Dad, my husband.

The doctors then converged on Kechi, and I stayed by her head, talking to her. They were desperately looking for a vein. I saw them cut into several places in her skin to find a vein; all her veins had collapsed. She was in severe shock. They found one by cutting into her right foot and started an infusion. I have never seen anyone infused that quickly. One of the doctors was squeezing the IV bag with his hand. When that one finished he would quickly replace it and continue squeezing. They were obviously trying to hydrate her as fast as possible. Kechi was losing fluids at an alarming rate. The gurney where she lay was full of liquid draining from her burns.

One of the doctors inserted a catheter to drain her urine. My baby screamed when the catheter was inserted. The urine that came out was black. I saw the doctors glance at each other and I knew it was serious. I resumed my prayers, all the while talking to Kechi.

I was in my shop with customers, two ladies, I can't remember who they were now, when I received a phone call from Dad saying Kechi's plane was in trouble and that we should pray. I stared praying quietly.

I knew the kids were vacating that day for Christmas. We were expecting Ugo and I thought Kechi was coming to Lagos, so I was kind of expecting Kechi in Lagos.

Then I got another call from Dad saying Kechi's plane went down..... I didn't hear the rest. My phone dropped......I think I froze and I couldn't breathe!

I kept hearing "Aunty! Aunty! What is it?" It was the two ladies in my shop.

I couldn't breathe. I couldn't talk. I just stared at them. Then I started struggling to breathe! The most important thing then seemed to be to fight for air! Which I was doing noisily! I think I was hyperventilating. They laid me on the long chair and were trying to fan me.

After some time I was able to say "Kechi....plane crash...."

Everything became a blur. I remember telling Miriam who lived with me then and she started crying! I wasn't crying. I think I was in shock. I made some calls to Ned and Ulo and said that we should go to Apapa, to my parent's house. Mom was on my mind.

How we got to Apapa, I don't remember. I think I rode with Ned. When we got there, just as we feared, it took three people to restrain Mom from harming her self. She had been throwing her self all over the place in her grief!

It was a horrible meeting with everybody crying and plans were being made to buy tickets to go to PH.

Suddenly there was a phone call. Dad, I think answered and announced that Kechi survived! I think there was the incredulous few seconds of silence before the crying turned to laughter! And then straight into praise worship!

….My sister, Nkechi's account.

After a while Kechi asked me why everyone was telling her that she would survive. I explained that she had been in an accident but that she would be okay. She had no recollection of the plane crash.

At one point she started complaining of pressure in her hands and legs. She said her fingers were numb and the skin on her hands and legs felt like they were going to explode. I relayed this to the doctors and they said they would give her something for the pain, which they did. They opened up her hand; they called it a "cut down", from her wrist to her elbow. At that time I did not know why they did that but at that point I was all for anything that would save her life. They were relieving the pressure build up in her arms.

I now took a closer look at Kechi's injuries. She was still wearing her school uniform and the doctors now cut this away from her body. They also cut out her pants but her bra was intact. They took this off and handed it to me. From what they were saying, it appeared that she had third degree burns on forty per cent of her body. Half of her face had peeled off, the skin on her hands were peeling off and were hanging in strips. I saw her raise her hands to look at them. Her thighs and legs were badly burned too. None of this meant much to me. Kechi was alive. That was all that mattered to me.

I now noticed the presence of our friends outside the emergency room. They were not allowed inside so I went out to thank them for their support. Mike arrived and came in to stay with me and to see Kechi for the first time.

I don't remember very clear details of that day, but I remember the emotions vividly. I remember that my wife, Karin, the girls and I were at home. I received a

phone call from Mom and she wailed the news that Kechi's plane had gone down and that Kechi was gone. Those were her exact words, 'Kechi is gone'. After a stunned moment of shock, I asked her to repeat it and she did and then I screamed loud. Karin rushed out of the room to find out what was wrong and I told her. I did not become very emotional then. I went very quiet, then I told Mom I was coming to Apapa right away. By then, Ulo and some others were already gathered in Apapa, Mom was wailing continuously.

Before I left, I sat Chisa and Jaachi down and explained to them what had happened. Chisa understood immediately, because she was old enough to, and started to weep. Jaachi did not fully grasp what was going on at that time, as she was quite young then. Karin was in total shock, and she had not reacted yet. I cannot remember, but I think I picked Nkechi up and we rushed to Apapa.

We walked into the house and there was major mourning going on in the house. Mom was being restrained, so she would not hurt herself. That picture has never left me - the level of grief that was in that room. At that point I fell on the floor and started crying. I cried and wailed, and then just sat quietly. I remember that Dad never accepted the idea of Kechi's death. I remember that he would come into the living room where we were all gathered to say one or two things and go away, but he never once accepted that Kechi was gone.

Then after a while, more and more people gathered and we were all inconsolable, then the other news came! Kechi was alive!

I have never seen anything like that. How all that level of grief and mourning turned into magnificent joy and praise. We all started praising God and dancing and worshipping God, thanking Him. There was an explosion of joy that Kechi was alive. It was in the midst of that rejoicing that I got a nudging in my spirit to separate myself a bit, so I left the scene of rejoicing and I immediately went to one of the rooms upstairs and knelt down and began to receive a very clear and vivid ministration.

"Yes, indeed Kechi is alive. She will be okay. She will be fine, but it will take time.

The recovery will be long, but she will be restored fully. It will take time, but it will be complete."

After I shared the ministration, there was rejoicing, and then we started discussing logistics, who was to leave immediately to be with Ije, what was the best hospital to take Kechi to etc. But God soon showed us that He was in full control of the situation and the rest is history.

….My brother, Chinedu's account.

Then God began to move………………..

A tall, dark and slim, well-dressed woman approached me and introduced herself as the Permanent Secretary, Ministry of Health. She told me that they were making plans to move Kechi to Shell Hospital, and I thanked her profusely.

The Consultant at the Braithwaite Memorial Hospital was on the phone with Shell and soon concluded arrangements to move Kechi. The doctors continued to work on Kechi, even after the ambulance from Shell arrived, trying to stabilize her before moving her. She was then wheeled outside. I remember that there were so many people crowded at the hospital entrance. It was when some people started to take pictures that I realized that they were the press and sure enough, a picture of Kechi lying on the gurney soon made headlines everywhere.

She was transferred to the ambulance and we all took off for Shell Hospital, accompanied by one of the doctors from BMH.

After a very fast ride, we arrived at the Shell Hospital and Kechi was whisked off to the emergency room. One of the drivers on duty was sent off to fetch the doctor on duty and Mike asked to go with him. Meanwhile, the staff on duty started work on Kechi. We were asked to wait outside and soon after, the Senior Medical Officer of Shell Hospital arrived.

I did not know it then, but this man was going to be instrumental in laying the foundations of Kechi's future. He went inside the emergency room and after some time, came out with the doctor from BMH. They talked a bit and then the other doctor took leave of us. I hugged him and thanked him for all he had done for Kechi. He said that Kechi's life fully depended on God at this point and he would pray for her.

By this time, Mike was back with the doctor on call, whom I remember was a Dutchman.

I asked to see Kechi and they allowed me in. She had been given drugs for the pain and more IV lines were attached. There was concern about her urine, which was still very dark in color, indicating possible renal failure, a major concern in such extreme burn cases as Kechi's. After a while, the urine started to clear up.

We waited outside, praying, while they worked on Kechi. She, at every point in the procedure, was co-operating with the medical team, lifting her limbs when told to and so on. They were very impressed with her and kept saying how strong she was.

It was high noon in Lagos. Outside, the tropical sun had crested and it seemed as if the world was a furnace. But I was ensconced in a climate-controlled, elegantly-furnished corporate Boardroom in downtown Lagos. Although a Saturday, the matter at hand was serious. My employers had a four week deadline to close an M&A deal or risk going out of business all together. Together with a group of colleagues and consultants, we were furiously working against time and at great odds to make the deal happen.

It was a high octane, testosterone-charged environment as counter parties strove to get the best possible deals for their respective corporations. I was midstream in the course of one such submissions when the persistence beeping of my cell phone compelled me to excuse myself and reach for it in annoyance. As I made to notify the caller to call back at a more auspicious time; I literally stopped dead on my tracks. To the onlookers, as I would later be told, my facial expressions morphed from panic, disbelief, shock, and horror all in one split second. They were all transfixed and watched as the phone fell from my hands in dreamlike fashion. My hard-nosed negotiator reputation rapidly peeled away as I cried uncontrollably like a baby.

The phone call was from Daddy and he had given me the news as he got it: there had been a plane crash at the Port Harcourt Airport. Kechi and about 60 other school mates of hers had all perished. The news was irrefutable as Ije and other parents who were at the airport saw the plane disintegrate into a ball of fire.

Random thoughts ran through my mind as I grieved. I remembered the day Kechi was born and how her Dad and I anxiously paced the corridors of First Consultant Hospital and the sheer joy that followed her birth. Till this day, Kechi remains the prettiest baby I ever saw. To have watched her grow in beauty, brains and manners and to see her plucked away at the threshold of womanhood was a personal blow, too cruel for me to fathom. Strikingly, she reminded me of Ify, her cousin, another Jewel whose death finds root in our country's intractable inability to place regard and value to the lives of it's citizenry.

But with my Kechi story, the plane crash and the news of her 'death' was the high point of evil, grief and despair. Joy and amazing grace however followed swiftly. A few hours later another phone call from Daddy sowed a mustard seed of hope which incredibly blossomed into a full fledged confirmation that Kechi had somehow defied death and was tenaciously clinging to life in a Port Harcourt hospital. Apparently someone had found her with three-quarters of her entire body burnt near the crash site and in that condition she was still able to give this individual her mum's phone numbers.

That was our reconnection with Kechi and the commencement of her incredible story of God's love, favor and amazing grace.

My Uncle Eze's account.

The outpouring of love, concern and prayers that came our way that night as we waited in the parking lot of the Shell Hospital was incredible. Apart from family members, friends from all over the country and all over the world were calling us. People I had not spoken to for more than 20 years were calling me from London, U.S, Canada, everywhere. Everyone wanted to know how Kechi was doing and also assuring us of their prayers. By this time I had called my brethren and church members and everyone was praying. This was about the time I also heard that Pastor Bimbo Odukoya had been in the aircraft.

I also heard that there were so many people at the Shell gates that it was almost becoming a security issue. In fact, while we were there, the Head of Security was called in. The few family members and friends who had been allowed in kept vigil with us, praying with us.

At around 12.30am, 10 hours after the accident, she was wheeled into the ICU and I went with her. She was conscious and I was talking to her, praying over her, reading verses of the bible to her. She was communicating. She kept complaining about the pressure in her hands and legs, and I kept reassuring her that she was going to be okay. I was advised not to stay the night in her room because of the risk of infection since most of her body was open and raw.

We talked with the Senior Medical Officer (SMO), who assured us that they were doing everything they could and a lot depended on whether she survived the night. He came across as a very kind man and we felt that we could trust that he was telling us the truth.

We had no idea at the time just how kind he was.

I was still doing my MBA at Lagos Business School. It was a Saturday morning. First time Ugochukwu was coming home from school and I could not go to the airport to pick him, because I had to be in school.

So Chidi, my husband, went to pick him. I finished my lectures by about 12pm and was rushing back to the house when Chidi called me, asking if I had heard anything from LJC. In my usual breezy manner, I said yes, I knew the children were all back. Chidi said, 'No, no. Have you heard anything from Ijeoma?'

'Ah ah, there is nothing to hear. Kechi is heading back just as Ugochukwu is heading back.' And he dropped the phone.

I got back to the house and noticed that he was very uneasy. And then he told me to call Dad because there was something about Kechi's plane not having landed, and I was very irritated because I did not understand why he did not have the whole message.

But I called Ije anyway, and Ijeoma announced to me in a very uncomplicated manner that 'there has been a plane crash and Kechi is dead'.

I did not recognize who I became. I remember throwing myself on the floor. I had seen and heard of people doing this and I always felt, 'come on'. And then I started rolling myself uncontrollably on the floor around my room, yelling at the top of my voice.

I remember the boys running up to my room. I especially remember Bube, my youngest, because he was the one who asked me, crying already, 'Mommy, what is it, what's wrong?'

I said to him, 'Kechi is dead. Kechi had a plane crash and she is dead'. And so he was the person told everyone that came running up that Kechi was dead.

The first person that came up was Aunty Cook. When she asked me what the problem was, Bube said "Kechi is dead'. Everyone started crying.

I remember Ugochukwu's face. He was so confused. He had just come back from school for the first time and he was so confused. He had left Kechi at the airport in Abuja.

There was nothing left to do. Everyone started calling us to confirm and as if it was announced, everyone started converging in my parent's house in Apapa.

By the time I got there, Nkechi and Chinedu were already there, and in no time at all, the place was full. Even Ngozi Nzekwe, my friend who was supposed to be hosting a party for her friend from the US that day, cancelled the party, and was in Apapa with us.

I'm not sure why we gathered really, except to feed off each other's pain and disbelief and loss. I was on the phone a lot with Ije. I was calling her every two minutes. I really wanted so much to be in Port Harcourt with her. I knew I could not bring Kechi back, but it just seemed so unfair that she was alone there and we were all in Lagos. Even Mike was not with her because she had gone to the airport without him.

We started making plans on who was going to go to Aba the next day to be with Ije and Mike. Mom was a mess, a total wreck, saying all sorts of things that I'm sure she cannot remember saying. Some of them may have been blasphemous, because I remember Dad saying once or twice, 'Florence, shut up!'

I have never seen the display of faith my Dad showed that day ever or since. The man was silent. Before we came he had gone and prayed and came back and was silent. In one of the phone calls Ije had said that there were a few survivors.. This meant nothing to most of us because I just thought 'ah well'. Nothing prepared me for us being one of the survivors and Dad just made a simple statement. He said, 'If there are any survivors in that plane, then Kechi is one of them'. I pitied him that day. I thought 'Oh poor man, he is still in denial. He does not know Kechi is dead'.

Ije called and said she heard about three woman survived. My Dad said, 'they will think Kechi is a woman because she is fully mature.' He said again, 'If there is any survivor in that plane, Kechi is one of them'.

Then we heard there were eight, then five, then three survivors, and at each number, Dad said that Kechi was one of them. The rest is history.

When we got that call......When Ijeoma called and said that they had called her to rush down to that hospital, that Kechi was alive, never have I felt that kind of euphoria. It was like all of a sudden, life started again. But I guess that's what happened, wasn't it? It was like all of a sudden we......O my God.. we were hugging each other, we were praising God, thanking Jesus, praying and praying and praying and praising Him.

By the time we had determined that it was indeed Kechi, Ije had met up with her, it was incredible. Then the journey started. The minute by minute phone calls did not ever stop, I'm not even sure they have to this day.

It was a horrible day and it was a beautiful day all in one. I also remember calling Obinna and I remember when Chinedu said what he had gotten from the Lord concerning Kechi, that she was going to be fine.

Oh, we needed that word…that she was going to be fine. It was the word that we held unto throughout her entire healing process, because she was so touch and go. We did not even realize how touch and go Kechi was until the pictures started coming.

We thank God and we praise Him. God is awesome.

….My sister, Uloma's account.

We left Kechi around 1.00am and went to a nearby hotel owned by my brother-in-law's friend. The owner offered us a room to stay as long as necessary. When I got inside the room, I prostrated myself on the floor to my Creator. I could not pray, I could only wail and give thanks to God.

After a while, a waiter brought in a malt drink from my husband. It was only then I realized that I had not had even a drop of water since Saturday morning when I had rushed out of my house, almost late for the airport.

Mike came in and we knelt down to pray. In all the years I had known my husband, we had never knelt down together to pray. Awesome God!

I asked Mike to lead the prayer and He told God that because He had spared Kechi, he and his family would worship Him forever. Alleluya!

We lay down and drifted off for a couple of hours. Kate had packed an overnight bag for me and by 4.00am, we woke, prayed and dressed up and left for the hospital.

It was the 10th of December. It was a weekend, and I was at work with Pardeep Gupta. It was getting late, nothing happening, same old stuff and I was tired. Then I get a phone call from Uloma. All I remember was her just saying,

"Obinna, Obinna, start praying, start praying, start praying."

I knew immediately that there was a problem, and it was something serious. Now the scale, I had no clue.

I said, 'Uloma, what's wrong? What's going on?" How bad is it?" 'Obinna start praying, plane crash, plane crash'.

'Ulo, who was in the plane?'

'Obinna, the plane crashed. Ijeoma was at the airport to pick Kechi. The plane just crashed in front of her. It was very fatal. The plane exploded. At that point, the worst case scenario crossed my mind and I thought, "Oh no. Plane crash at its descent into Port Harcourt airport. No emergency services. So my first reaction was 'No this cannot be. Ulo must be mistaken'. Ulo had dropped the phone at that point. I could imagine the millions of phone calls going on here and there and all

she was doing was putting me in the loop. I had left my desk to take the call, so I rushed back to my desk and told Pardeep that there had been a plane crash and my niece was in that plane. We rushed to Sky news and confirmed that indeed there had been a plane crash. Gosh, my heart sank. I thought the worst had happened. I did not think anything at all would come out of this. So I packed my bags and called Op, my wife, immediately. I told her what was going on and that I was heading home immediately. Op panicked, we were very agitated. I called Ulo back. "What's going on, update please!"

"Ijeoma is still at the airport and there is no news". I was still thinking the worst. I got downstairs, got into my car, and started driving home, had my hands-free on. Ulo called me back and said she heard there were some survivors, so I called Op, and we started praying again for the survivors. At that point, even while praying, I was thinking, 'Is it possible?' I had heard that there were ten or so survivors, and I began to question if it was possible that Kechi was one of them. I knew in my heart of hearts, that I had given up. My faith was not strong enough. I was thinking, what are the chances, what are the odds? This was me using logic again.

Meanwhile I was still driving home. It was the hardest drive I had ever made because I had to concentrate on driving when what I really wanted to do was to close my eyes, open them and be in Port Harcourt. I wanted to be involved. Ulo and I kept on calling each other continuously all the way from the city to my house, and I was calling Op from time to time to update her.

I cannot remember now whether I was still driving or if I had gotten home when Uloma called to say, 'Obinna, start praising God, start praising God. Kechi survived!'

I asked, 'how?'

'Kechi is in a hospital somewhere in Port Harcourt. They found her!' I have never been that overwhelmed with joy in my life. Nothing has come close since then. It was like someone had been given a new lease of life. It was like God said, 'You guys had complete faith in the face of such a disaster, so I'm giving you a fresh start. Let's see what you do with it. ' That was the way I felt at that moment.

At this point, I cannot put the time line together because the news was coming in fragments and I could not really get Uloma to be very articulate because I knew she was also going through a lot, but the way I understood it, Ije had already been to the crash site and was waiting with other parents when someone called her, 'Are you Ijeoma Okwuchi? Your daughter is alive. Come to the hospital."

There was still news coming out of Nigeria that the remaining survivors were dying one at a time, and I was praying, "God please. You can't do this again. You have given her back her life. Please don't take it again".

The next news I heard was that Kechi was going to be moved from that hospital to a different one. I think Mike had come to join her at that point, and then the news got very sketchy again, but then we understood that Kechi was transferred to Shell Hospital. Then the rest is history.

….My brother, Obinna's account.

I was driving to Northolt with my friend, Chioma, for a business meeting, when my sister, Kate, called me on my cell phone. "Dorothy, Kechi's plane crashed. Kechi is dead". I hit the brakes, right there in the middle of the highway. I remember that cars were honking all around us, but I was oblivious, filled with the deepest, darkest despair. The bottom had just fallen out of my world and the pain was overwhelming.

I remember that Chioma took over the driving, while I wailed, 'Why Kechi, why Kechi, God? Why did You take her and not me? I have lived a good life, she is just a baby, why, why didn't you take me instead?' Kechi was a girl I loved with all my life. Right from the day she was born, she and I were very close. I was in a daze until we got to the meeting. I remember the client was very understanding, and even tried to console me; of course the meeting was cancelled.

On our way back to London, I had composed myself a bit, and was driving, until Kate called me again and gave me the most unbelievable news of all! Kechi had been found and was alive.

Right there and then in front of God and the whole world, I stopped my car by the side of the road, and fell to my knees, thanking and worshipping God. Everyone that passed us must have thought I was bonkers! Meanwhile, Chioma went into action and immediately started calling members of her church to start a prayer chain, constantly updating them with every development and new prayer requests.

By the time I got my house, all my friends were there. They had all heard the news and came to comfort me. I remember that I went into the kitchen to make tea for everyone, and while I was there, everything suddenly became too much and I burst into tears. I was particularly sad because Tonia's kids were coming home from the States for the first time that Christmas and they were very excited that they were finally going to meet their cousin, Kechi. It was a double blow to them.

Remembering that day still gives me the shivers. It is an open wound that just never seems to heal.

….My sister-in-law, Dorothy Okwuchi's account.

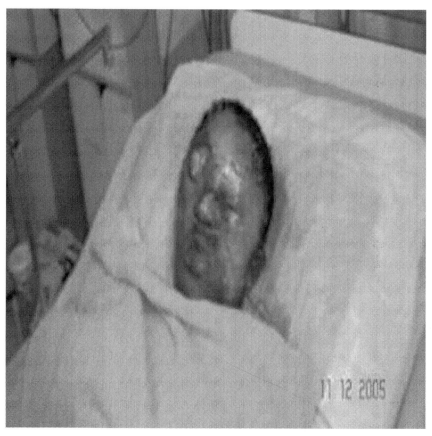

First picture taken of Kechi after the plane crash. Location: Shell Hospital, Port Harcourt, Nigeria.

CHAPTER TWO

"Behold, I am the Lord, the God of all flesh: Is there anything too hard for Me?"
Jeremiah 32:27 (KJV)

Mike and I got to the clinic at 6.00am and went straight to the ICU. Sister Tokunbo was still on duty and told us that Kechi was holding her own. But by this time her appearance had greatly changed. Her face had swollen so much that her eyes were squeezed shut. But she was still alive!

I called her name and she turned her head towards me. I told her not to try and open her eyes because it was swollen shut due to her accident. She was by this time on morphine and so was drifting in and out. She was also muttering things that were hard to understand. Her mind was clearly drifting. At one point she said she wanted water and when she was given a sip she complained that it was not cold. She said she wanted cold water and asked us to go to the fountain and get cold water. I could only surmise that she was referring to the water fountains in her school.

She then asked for Milo, a hot cocoa drink, and it was provided for her. She then started to mumble that she was in prison, behind bars, because she could not see. She was sedated again and I left the room.

Then I was informed that the first responders to the scene of the crash were asking to see me. A young man named Gabriel came to me and told me that he was with the Virgin Nigeria emergency crew and that they were among the first to arrive on the scene. By the time they got there, there were already some people there and the sight that met his eyes shocked him to the core. Apparently, there had been quite a lot of cash on board the aircraft, and it was strewn all over the crash site. Gabriel said to me, "Madam, I'm talking about millions of Naira all over the place."

People at the scene were busy, not rescuing survivors, but stuffing as much money as they could into their clothes, with bodies lying all around them, people dying or dead within reach. At this point, Gabriel said the urge to join them was almost overwhelming, but a voice came to him saying, "If you touch even one of those notes, you will be destitute for the rest of your life."

This stopped him in his tracks and he began to entreat the others to stop so they could check if anyone was alive.

At that point, he said he heard someone moan and move a little. That was how he saw that a lady, who turned out to be Kechi, was alive. He quickly raised an alarm and Kechi was placed in one of the first vehicles that rushed to the hospital.

Then he asked if Kechi survived. I told him yes and then just hugged him for a long time. I told him that God would surely bless him for what he did and would reward him for heeding His command.

I did not dwell on those who can strip dead bodies of cash and valuables because I knew that the Lord I serve is not mocked and what a man sows, he reaps.

I went back to the car park where Mike was. By this time, family members and friends who could get through the rigorous security screening at the Shell gates were gathered together. My husband's close friend, George had come from Aba, which I found touching since it was not quite 7.00am. He had been trying without success to persuade Mike to go into town with him to buy food for us. I asked Mike to go because I felt it would do him good to be outside the hospital environment for a while. Mike never did too well in such situations and I knew what seeing Kechi that way was doing to him.

My friend, Carol, had also come from Aba and it was obvious from her swollen eyes that she had spent the night crying. She held me and we prayed together.

Then God started again to reveal His plans for Kechi........

The Senior Medical Officer, whose name I now knew to be Dr. Moses Ohiosimuan had also come in early and had been inside the ICU to see Kechi. He came to where we were and called me aside. He told me that while they were giving Kechi the best care possible, they felt that she would benefit from more specialized care and were thinking that, if we agreed, they wanted to make arrangements to fly her out of the country immediately to a South African hospital. He wanted to know if that was okay with us. I said yes at once, (thinking, are you kidding me?) "Of course it's okay with us."

He said he would get back to me once he had reported back to the MD of Shell that we were okay with the plan. He then said I should call Mike.

As soon as Mike drove in, I gave him the news and he rushed off to find Dr. Moses.

I called Uloma at once and told her of the new development. By this time she was in church and of course Kechi was the main prayer point.

Mike came out looking stunned. I asked him if everything was okay and he said that Dr. Moses was arranging for an air ambulance to fly out from South Africa and pick Kechi and I up. The ambulance will leave within the hour and should be in Nigeria by 8.00pm that night, and we would leave as soon as they landed.

Mike said he told Dr. Moses that he should please go ahead and make the arrangements and he would find a way to pay them back for all the expenses.

That was when Dr. Moses told Mike that Shell was taking full responsibility for all the expenses!

I fell on my knees and began to thank God and to praise His Holy Name.

We were then told that Kechi would need to travel with one of us. I quickly said it would have to be me and I was told to get our passports ready and pack a bag.

I called my friend, Uzoma, who had earlier called to say she was about to leave Aba to see us. Luckily, I caught her on her way out and told her to swing by my house and get our passports and pack a small bag for me.

Then we were faced with the issue of funds. It was Sunday morning, all banks were closed. Mike and I had been in Port Harcourt since the previous day and no one had thought about money or any such thing!

By God's grace, one of our friends, Meche, called from Abuja and when he heard about the money problem, he told Mike to call their friend, Kenneth Yellowe, a man who would later play a very critical role in Kechi's recovery process. Kenneth lived in America but was in Port Harcourt for business. Mike called Kenneth, who was horrified that Mike's daughter was one of the victims of the crash. He said he had GBP410.00 on him and Mike was welcome to it.

Mike rushed off to get the money and then Kate, my sister-in- law, also gave me $100.00 and Mike promised to send me more money as soon as he could.

I then went in to see Kechi, and the nurses were cleaning her wounds. She was actually sitting up in bed, and obeying their instructions to lift her hands, bend her leg etc. It was at that point that she asked me, "Mommy, was I the only one that survived?"

"Survived what?" I answered carefully, my mind busily sorting out how to answer without distressing her further.

"The plane crash" "No", I said.

Then she asked the question I was dreading.

"What of my friends, Toke and the rest?"

Toke was one of her best friends and much later when she could recall the plane trip, she remembered that they had been sitting on the same row, across the aisle from each other.

"Toke is fine", I said. "Everyone is fine". In my mind I was justifying to myself, 'They are fine in the bosom of the Lord'. But I knew there was no way I could tell Kechi this. Not yet.

My daughter heaved a huge sigh of relief and said, "O, thank You, Jesus. Jesus I love You".

She drifted off to sleep again.

Uzoma arrived at the Shell gate but the security detail would not let her in, so Mike had to go to the gate to explain to them that she was family and she came back to the hospital with them.

Other groups of people came but I had to go outside the gates to meet with them. My boss, Benjamin, came with Chioma, a colleague, and I was pleased because I could tell Benjamin about the trip and how I would need an extended leave.

The brethren from my church group in Aba also came and prayed with me. One of my church members from the Port Harcourt fellowship, Brother Amos, who incidentally was a staff of Shell, had also been contacted and he never left Mike's side throughout that day.

Then we were reminded that we were battling against principalities and powers that were not pleased to see Kechi alive. In order to come inside the Shell compound with Mike, Uzoma had to leave her car outside the gate and so she put the bag she had packed for me, which contained not just my clothes, but also our passports, in George's car. When George left for Aba, he forgot to remove the bag from his car. Communication became impossible, as we could not get through to him. By the time we finally got through, he was already in Aba. This was at 4.00pm, and we were to leave at 8.30pm. He said he would give the bag to Mike's brother, Duru, to bring to Port Harcourt.

Dr. Moses sent for me and told me that there were two people that wanted to see Kechi, and he wanted to make sure we were okay with it. One of them was a high-ranking officer at the Nigeria Airport Authority and the other was the Managing Director of Sosoliso Airlines. I gave my permission. The airport had been closed to all traffic since the disaster and so Dr. Moses told them that the plan was for the air ambulance to land at the Owerri airport, and then we would be transported by helicopter to Owerri and leave from there.

After seeing Kechi, the NAA official told Dr. Moses that here was no need to subject Kechi to all that, the Port Harcourt Airport would be opened for the air ambulance to land and take off!

Dr. Moses was in the hospital monitoring Kechi's progress and making arrangements for our trip throughout that Sunday. He was truly amazing. I felt so safe knowing that he was in charge of Kechi's well being. Our gratitude knew no bounds but each time we tried to express it to him, he told us that we should focus on praying to God for Kechi's life to be spared as she was far from out of the woods.

I think that as a doctor, he knew the gravity of her situation and that so much could still go wrong. All I knew was that Kechi was alive and was going to stay that way. Looking back, I think I was probably in denial as to the extent of her injuries. I just focused on living from one minute to the next, trusting God all the way.

Mike and I went in to tell her about the trip to South Africa and with her usual forthrightness she said,

"I don't like the sound of that". I explained her need for further treatment than could be provided at Shell hospital. She seemed to accept that and asked," So by the time I wake up, I'll be in South Africa?"

"Yes", I replied. And she slept off.

Mike's friend, Sule and his wife, Helen, insisted that I should go to their house to shower, change and have lunch before the trip, and Uzoma and Carol went with me. When we got back to the hospital, I went to the ICU to be with Kechi.

The nurses were dressing her wounds, wrapping them up for the flight. This meant that most of her body was covered in bandages. By this time she was crying out loud at the pressure in her hands and wondering for how long she would be able to stand the pain. I was later to know that this swelling was normal for deep tissue burns. The swelling could only be released by making cuts in the skin. The nurses assured her that the pain would go away soon but she kept crying, obviously in a lot of pain. The nurses at Shell hospital were very professional, but very kind and obviously very affected by Kechi's condition. I left knowing that they would be praying for her.

She was transferred from the hospital bed to a stretcher and we started the journey. By the time we got outside, the sedative she was given had started to take effect and she was out. I went into the ambulance with Kechi and Sister Jane, one of the kindest nurses I have ever met. Mike, Brother Amos, Dr. Moses and some other staff of Shell followed in their cars and the procession left for the airport. Jane talked to me all the way to the airport, reassuring me of God's grace and telling me never to stop trusting God.

We got to the airport by 8.30pm. The S.O.S. plane was supposed to arrive at 9.00pm. We waited for about 30 minutes and the plane arrived on schedule.

As soon as the plane taxied to a stop, a doctor and a paramedic disembarked and were met by Dr. Moses and the other doctors from Shell. They immediately came to the ambulance and I left to give them room to work. They set to work on Kechi, started an IV from a vein they located in her chest. After that, they asked for help to load her into the air ambulance, the smallest plane I had ever seen. Inside the plane, there was hardly any space because it was full of equipment one would usually see in a hospital. Kechi was strapped onto a narrow cot and was soon connected to a lot of lines and leads, and instruments began beeping and humming.

I was asked to board and I gave Mike a hug before taking my bag and bible from him. I thanked everyone and boarded the aircraft. There was hardly any space left to sit as there were about three other people apart from the pilot and the doctor and paramedic. I was sitting at the rear of the plane, but the good thing was that Kechi was directly opposite me.

During taxing and takeoff, her heart rate went up alarmingly. George, the paramedic said she was anxious, probably at some sub-conscious level remembering the crash. Every time she looked as if she was waking up, she was sedated.

I slept for the first two or three hours, waking up as we were about to land in Angola to refuel. When we took off for Johannesburg, reaction set in for me. I had been strong because of Mike. I had to let him take strength from me because it was killing him to see his precious princess suffer.

Suddenly, it all washed over me and for the first time since the horrific experience, I started to sob. I cried for a long time, for my daughter, for all those parents I had left behind to bury their kids, for the children that died, I cried in gratitude that I was the recipient of this grace, I cried until the tears stopped coming. I vaguely remembered George handing me some tissues and trying to comfort me. After my crying jag, he gave me some food but I could hardly swallow anything. I was emotionally and physically spent.

I was awake for the rest of the flight, reading my bible, praying, and keeping an eye on Kechi, wondering what was in store for her, for me, for all of us.

I wondered about the other survivors. How many other kids had made it? Had the ones that had gone to Jesus been in any pain before they died? How could any of this be possible? Was I in some kind of cruel dream that would not let me wake up? Could that plane have really crashed? Was any of this real? Was I really in a plane racing across Africa in order to save my daughter's life?

CHAPTER THREE

"And he said unto them, I beheld Satan as lightening fall from heaven. Behold I give unto you power to tread on serpents and scorpions, and over all the power of the enemy: and nothing shall by any means hurt you."
Luke 10: 18&19 (KJV)

We arrived Johannesburg around 6.00 am and I was assisted through Customs by a representative of International S.O.S., the organization in charge of the whole hospital process for Kechi, and we were issued visas there and then.

Kechi was taken straight to an ambulance that was waiting on the tarmac and we took off for the hospital.

There was a lot of traffic and I remember wondering why and then recalling that it was Monday morning and life was going on as usual for everyone else.

We were crawling at snail's speed. By this time, Kechi's face had swollen alarmingly. I began to perceive an odor from the ambulance, as if something was burning, like the brakes or some other mechanical part. I also noticed that the ambulance was not moving smoothly and the driver was getting agitated.

Thirty to forty five minutes into the trip, the driver pulled over on the side of the road, came out of the ambulance, opened the bonnet and then came back to inform us that the gear box had burnt.

I recognized the hand of our old adversary, the devil. I laughed inwardly and told him I knew what he was trying to do and that he would surely fail.

Then I began to pray, or should I say, resumed my prayers, because I had never really stopped praying since the plane crash.

Another ambulance was called and we spent another twenty minutes waiting by the side of the road, in the heat, with a child that was in critical condition, until the replacement ambulance came. Kechi was transferred, and we continued our journey.

By this time, I noticed that the doctor that had travelled with us from Nigeria was very, very concerned and was now on the phone with the hospital, giving them minute by minute reports on Kechi's condition.

This time we drove very fast with lights flashing until we arrived at Milpark Hospital.

The emergency crew raced out as soon as we got there and Kechi was whisked in while I was told where to sit and wait.

I was in a daze by then, not knowing what to feel and feeling everything.

Then a very nice lady came to me and introduced herself to me. Her name was Annarie, and she was one of the hospital counselors. She had actually come out, asking if I was the wife of the man that came in from Nigeria. I did not blame her at all because by the time we arrived at the hospital, Kechi had swollen to more than twice her size, and her skin, naturally very fair complexioned, had darkened to almost black. Also, she had very short hair, because her school did not allow girls to grow their hair.

After apologizing for her mistake, Annarie took me to a more private room and talked to me, assuring me that Kechi was in the best hospital for the kind of injuries that she sustained. She then asked me where I was staying.

I had not even thought of that!

I told her I did not know but I supposed that Int'l S.O.S. should be handling that. She gave them a call and after a while they called back and told her that they had booked me into the Garden Suite Hotel, which was a stone throw from the hospital.

Annarie also introduced me to another Nigerian lady named Linda whose husband had sustained serious burns on an oil rig in Port Harcourt and was also being treated at Milpark.

Then a big, tall man came in and introduced himself as Dr. Plani, the trauma surgeon. He had a brusque attitude and a gruff voice. Not exactly friendly, but I got an immediate sense of someone who was very good at his job, and I relaxed a bit.

He told me that they were about to do a tracheotomy on Kechi. I did not know what this was and I must have looked puzzled because he explained that they were going to make a cut in her throat and insert a tube into her trachea and connect it to a lung machine because her airways were swollen shut and she could no longer breathe on her own. Also they were going to begin to scrape off the burnt skin to minimize infection.

He left and came back shortly to tell me to go and see Kechi before they wheeled her into the Operating Room.

I went in and saw Kechi on a gurney, her face all swollen and raw, attached to tubes and what appeared to be an inflatable blanket. She was deeply sedated.

I walked up beside her and told her that I loved her very much, and she was going to be fine. I prayed over her and asked God to keep her safe during the surgery.

I signed consent forms both for the surgery and for blood transfusions.

When I came out, Annarie and Linda were waiting for me.

Linda told me that she and her husband had been in the hospital for six weeks and would be returning to Nigeria in two weeks.

I naively hoped it would be the same for us!

Linda gave me some very useful details about the hospital routines then proceeded to loan me R1000, while making arrangements for the guy who assisted her in changing her currency to Rand, the South African currency, to come to the hospital and change the little money I had brought with me. She also made arrangements for Franz, the taxi guy she used, to come later and take me to buy a SIM card and airtime, and also to take me to the hotel so I could check in.

Annarie took me to the Intensive Care Unit where Kechi would be taken after surgery, and introduced me to Glory, the Nursing Sister on duty. This was my first introduction to the very wonderful men and women who nursed Kechi back to life. I filled out some more forms and then went to the waiting room to wait for Kechi to come out from surgery. After a couple of hours, as I waited in prayer, a word came to me from the Lord,

"Be still, my daughter, for I am with you. I will never let anything happen to you. Righteousness is My grace, which I have given to you. Be still, my daughter."

I was also directed to read Psalm 1.

On "righteousness" I was a bit confused until I read the Psalm, and on further discussion with Ulo, she pointed out that righteousness is indeed God's grace which He gives to whom He pleases. That is why our own righteousness is like a filthy rag to Him. We cannot get it by ourselves. It is only by His grace.

Kechi was in the Operating Room (OR) for four hours!

When she was wheeled into the Trauma Intensive Care Unit (TICU), Sister Glory came and led me to where Kechi was lying. What a sight!

She was completely covered, with a sheet up to her neck. Her whole body was wrapped with bandages under the sheet. She was connected to about ten different machines, including one that was breathing for her!

Her body was considerably swollen. She didn't even look as if she was alive. But I knew that inside that body, Kechi was alive and fighting for her life. I leaned over and said directly into her ear,

"Kechi, This is Mom. You are going to have to fight, sweetheart. I will not leave you. We will go through this valley of the shadow of death together. You are alive and you will remain that way because that is God's plan for you. He saved you and will save you to the uttermost. Hang in there."

Then God started to send His angels………………..

Uloma contacted Lanre, her colleague at Microsoft, who was, at that time, based in their Johannesburg office, and he came to the hospital. Ulo had made arrangements for him to give me R1000. He also put R500 worth of airtime in my phone.

Lanre insisted on taking me to eat even when I insisted that I was not hungry. After that, he took me back to the hotel.

Another angel was waiting for me in the hotel. Betty, whose husband and my brother's wife are siblings. I had even forgotten that Betty and Ike lived in Johannesburg!

She had traced me through the hospital and had been frantic when I was not at the hotel, wondering where I was, and knowing that I did not know anyone in Johannesburg. She went with me to my room and told me that she was available any time I needed her, day or night.

When she took her leave, I unpacked, had a shower, and lay down, knowing that with all going on in my head, I would never be able to sleep.

I did drop off, but as soon as I did, I found myself in the aircraft and felt all the shock and terror of the children.

I saw kids crying.

I saw Toke, in particular and I comforted her. I was crying and encouraging the children to go home with Jesus.

I got up and begged God to give me rest from the anguish and finally slept.

I woke up with a heavy burden to pray for healing for the hearts of the parents of the kids that had been called home to Jesus.

When I got out of bed, I took a good look at the room and saw that it was a really nice hotel. After taking a shower, I got dressed and went downstairs to the taxi park and headed for the hospital.

After getting lost a number of times, (it was a huge hospital), I made my way to the (T)ICU and asked to see Kechi.

In the ICU, it was one nurse per patient, and I introduced myself to the nurse taking care of Kechi and was informed that her blood pressure had dropped because her body was going into septic shock. She had been immediately placed on adrenaline drugs to bring up her blood pressure and antibiotics for the infection. She assured me that the doctor said this was not unusual in burn patients.

I stood over Kechi and took a good look at her.

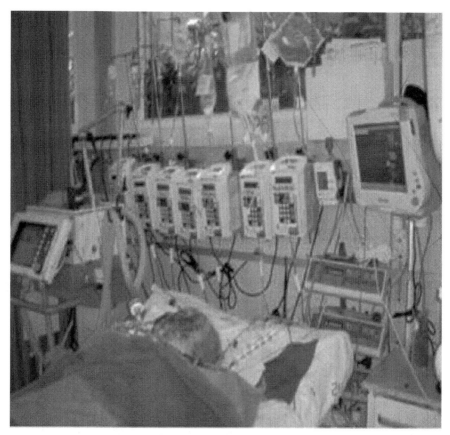

Kechi in deep hospital-induced coma. Location: Milpark Hospital, Johannesburg.

Her body was so swollen that she did not look like herself at all. Her face was very dark, one side burnt away. Her left ear was black and I knew that was going to be a problem later. Her body was losing a lot of fluids and the sheets were soaked.

Looking back at it now, I realize that throughout Kechi's stay in South Africa, I never saw what everyone saw when they looked at her. Other people saw a broken body that could not possibly survive the injuries to it. I saw Kechi. And I knew she was going to be fine. There was a complete lack of doubt in my mind that God would see her through. Later, my family would accuse me of not telling them the full story about

Kechi's injuries, because I would always say Kechi was fine when they asked me.

After looking her over that morning, I sat down and began what would become a daily routine of praying and reading portions of the bible to her. That morning, Mom sent me a text that I should read Psalm 91 to Kechi and use it as my prayer focus. Then I started to talk to her. I told her of how much she was loved, calling out the names of everyone that sent their love to her.

I stayed until the morning visit was over, then I sat in the waiting room to wait for the evening visit. They were quite strict about visiting times at Milpark.

Kechi's accident brought out the best in people. I got so many calls and had so many visitors that I was overwhelmed with kindness.

Most of the people who reached out to me were people I either did not know well, or had never met before. It was an incredible experience.

Betty came by and sat with me for quite a while. We had not been very close in Nigeria and thus I had missed out on knowing a wonderful human being.

She said she was going to get me flats or sneakers so I would be more comfortable. She also insisted on bringing cooked food for me. I still could not stand the idea of eating food, and asked for fruits instead.

She left, promising to come back in the evening with her church elders who wanted to pray for Kechi.

I got a call from Pat, my friend Stella's friend from London. She had contacted her pastor friend in Johannesburg, Noni, who called to also say she would come later to pray with me. Pat called constantly from London to ask after Kechi.

My sister-in-law, Chi's, friend, Sade and her husband had just come in from Nigeria and brought money from Mom and from Chi, and Eze, my brother. I was truly touched. But then I was to be even more shocked and overwhelmed.

Sade and her husband, people I had just met, insisted on shopping for clothes for me since I left Nigeria with very little. They did not let me thank them. Sade said that I did not understand how privileged they felt to be able to do something for someone that God had touched so directly. The love expressed was incredible.

Later that afternoon, I had to sign a consent form for Kechi to go in for surgery. They were going to scrape off more of her burnt skin. My mind refused to delve deeply into what that entailed. All I knew was that she was being taken care of. The matron of the unit informed me that the third survivor of the crash had been flown in from Nigeria. She also had 60% burns like Kechi, and was in her 20s. Apparently, the younger you are, the better your chances are of pulling through.

Kechi came in from surgery about 5.30pm. She was "stable", a word I became very familiar with. When the staff told you a patient was stable, they were actually saying that nothing had changed since the last time you asked, five seconds ago!

Her blood pressure was okay. My baby was holding her own. Her face did not look so bloated to me, but when I mentioned it to the nurse, she told me Kechi would still swell some more.

Sade and her husband came back with loads and loads of clothes and underwear for me. It was a humbling experience. Then Betty brought jackets and sneakers for me, because I was complaining that I was cold.

Betty's pastors came in later and prayed for Kechi, and I also asked them to pray for Pauline, the other survivor. Some other Nigerians resident in South Africa, also came to the waiting room to wish Kechi well.

I could not wait for Kechi to open her eyes so she could see me. I spoke to her over and over again, prayed over her, sang to her because I believed she needed to know that I was close by, and I believed she could hear me.

I was content with the way she was resting because I knew that her body needed rest to recover from the trauma of being thrown from a burning plane.

It still seemed like a dream, like it did not happen in real life. I was so overwhelmed by the awesomeness of God and I now realized that I had really made Him small in my eyes.

❖

I had not seen Dr. Plani since the first day we came, and the nurses advised me to come early so I could catch him after his early morning rounds. I got there pretty early the next day, but I could not see him because new patients had come in from a bus accident in Nigeria. Matron informed me that the hospital staff were now calling Trauma ICU 'Nigeria ward.'

Distressingly, Matron also informed me Pauline's condition was deteriorating and that they had called the family to inform them. My heart was breaking. "God", I prayed, "please do that which You are known for and give her a miracle also".

MY FEELINGS

God is sovereign! That much is clear and incontrovertible. There is a certainty and an assurance deep within me that this is an established fact. He is mighty and awesome and He is my father. He loves me and all He wants from me is an acceptance of who He is and an unfailing, blind, total, unwavering trust in Him, no matter the situation.

He wants me to love Him back.

Unconditional love is not a helpless kind of love, like saying, 'I have no choice but to love You, after all, You are God and You do whatever You want'.

It is more of a certainty, a conviction deep within you that you have been created to love and trust God.

That the Creator loves His creation you so much that He sent His son to die when it appeared that if He did not intervene, His creation - you - will perish forever.

You have the assurance that one day you will be with God for eternity and that life on earth is just a preparation for eternity with your Creator.

That this Creator is willing to forgive His creation - you - just about anything just to ensure that you get back to heaven.

That everything in His Word points to one thing - Return to Me!

He is truly an awesome God.

Pauline passed away!

I was truly distressed. I had prayed hard that she would make it. I hurt so much for the family that had pinned their hopes on the fact that her coming to South Africa was a sign that she would be fine.

Pat sent some of her friends to visit me - Gbemi, Layi and Magdalene. Magdalene was also my friend, Ijeoma Udensi's sister-in-law, and she was a cancer survivor. She gave me her testimony and I lapped it up because at the moment, anyone that had survived anything life-threatening was an inspiration to me.

Layi informed me that she had been in touch with the Nigerian High Commissioner and had told him about Kechi's presence in Johannesburg.

CHAPTER FOUR

"For I am the Lord that healeth thee"
Exodus 15 : 26 (KJV)

By day four, I had started to develop a routine. I usually left for the hospital between 7am and 7.30am. In the ICU, there was a white board just inside the door on which all the names of the patients were written. A patient's name was rubbed out if he or she was transferred to another ward or if they passed away.

So every morning, I would go to the ICU, peer inside the room to look at the board, frantically search for Kechi's name, find it, exhale, and then go to the waiting room to stay until the first visit of the day which was from 11am to 12pm.

On this particular day (day 4), I noticed during my visit that Kechi's breathing seemed to be a bit unstable. It seemed as if the respirator was halting and restarting.

When I mentioned it to the nurse looking after Kechi that day, she said that this had happened through the night and they had in fact called in the people that installed the machine to take a look. Meanwhile, they had replaced the one Kechi was hooked up to. This was not exactly the kind of news I wanted to hear but I was told not to worry, they were on top of things.

I left everything in God's hands and continued my usual pattern of praying over Kechi, reading to her from the bible, and singing to her.

Visitors continued to stream in. Brother Dotun, of the South African brethren of our fellowship group came to visit with me, to encourage me, and to pray with me.

I also had a visit from the Nigerian High Commissioner and his entourage. I took him into the ICU to see Kechi. He was very kind and they all said they would pray for Kechi.

I met Pauline's cousin who came in from Nigeria. Apparently he knew before boarding the plane in Abuja that she had passed away but still decided to come and take her body back home. It was really hard to know what to tell someone in that kind of situation but I did my best to comfort him.

The next day, I was informed that Kechi was stable during the night and the respirator problems did not repeat themselves. She had been scheduled for surgery that day for debridement of the right arm. This meant that they would scrape away dead tissue so as to prevent infection and also prepare the area for skin grafting.

The anesthetist was there to inform me that they were spacing the surgery out a bit so that they did not destabilize Kechi and lower her body temperature for too long. Again, I shut my mind to what was going to happen to Kechi in the OR, and just focused on the fact that every trip to the OR was a step towards her total recovery. This kept me sane.

Pauline's cousin sought me out in the visiting room to tell me that he was going back to Nigeria. He would not wait to take his cousin's body with him after all because an autopsy had to be performed on her at a different hospital and then her body would be flown back.

Then he shocked me by giving me quite a bit of money to help defray my expenses. Even in his pain, he reached out to me. I was truly humbled. I cried as I hugged him and he comforted me and told me he would continue to pray for Kechi. When he left, I went to pieces. Luckily, I was alone in the waiting room.

I called Ulo, told her what happened, and asked her to please tell me something I could do for God. There must be something more than just praising Him and giving thanks. Ulo told me to just bask in His love and to praise Him.

When I had settled down a bit, Uloma asked me to please not call her to cry on the phone, or had I forgotten that I was there with a very sick child?

This made me laugh because I realized that when I called Ulo and was crying on the phone, she assumed that the worst had happened, that Kechi had passed away. I apologized but told her that Kechi was not going anywhere.

Ulo spread the news like I expected her to and soon Mom and Dad called me to remind me that God is Jehovah Jireh, the God that provides all our needs, and He would continue to provide even before I asked.

God is awesome and mighty!

Lanre came to drag me off to eat lunch but I asked him to wait until Kechi came out of surgery. The surgery went well and when she was settled in the ICU, I went with Lanre to have lunch. Between him and Betty, I was getting fed, whether I felt like it or not. They also showed me around some parts of Johannesburg. It really was a lovely place but my heart was back in the ICU of Milpark Hospital with Kechi, and I could not really appreciate the sights.

That day my usual prayers over Kechi felt like a fellowship because the sister on duty was also a believer and kept giving me bible references to read to Kechi. I felt a breakthrough, that for the first time, Kechi had participated in the prayers and at the end when I asked God to open up the windows of heaven and rain down His anointing on Kechi, I felt an assurance in my spirit that the worst was over.

That night, the sister on night duty told me that Kechi was responding to my voice. She encouraged me to continue letting her hear my voice because the nurses believe that even in a coma, patients respond to the voices of their loved ones and it encourages them to hang on and fight their way back.

One week after the plane crash, on the 17th of December, I decided to remove the weave in my hair and wash it.

This was a major move on my part because it indicated that I was relaxed enough to actually look at myself in the mirror and decide to take better care of myself. Of course, this did not run to make up or any sort of primping. It just did not seem important to do any more than basic hygiene and then rush off to the hospital. But my hair was a mess, and I was beginning to look like a crazy person so I decided to fix that and felt so much better.

In order to speak to any of the doctors, I had to get to the hospital early and this time I wanted to catch up with the plastic surgeon that was handling Kechi's surgeries so far.

He was a young South African named Dr. Nel, and he took the time to explain to me what exactly they were doing. So far, they had done the debridement on her two arms. They were moving slowly so as not to cause her undue stress and the surgeries would be done every forty eight hours.

The next surgery was slated for the following day, Sunday, on one leg, and the next one on the following Tuesday. He also said they would check on the first arm and see if it was ready for grafting and if so, they would begin grafting on Tuesday. They would not be able to graft until they were sure they removed all of the dead and infected skin unless the graft would "fail". This meant that the skin used to graft onto the wound would become infected and will not be integrated into the site.

I now had another prayer point, 'Lord, please let the graft 'take'!

The procedure was thus:

- The affected area, or the site, would be scraped down until they get to healthy tissue.
- A strip of artificial skin would be placed on the site, and stapled or sewn on.
- It was watched for a few days to see if the body would reject it.
- If all went well, a strip of her own skin would be grafted on top of the artificial one, and left to heal.

Dr. Nel stressed that this was a very slow process. He also warned that there will be scar tissue from the grafting which might be corrected with reconstructive surgery and pressure garments, six months to a year down the line. He also said that the last person that had Kechi's kind of burns needed more than seventeen surgeries!

This seemed so much to me at the time. Little did I know that Kechi was going to have almost fifty surgeries before we left South Africa!

Also, Kechi's face would likely need debridement and require grafting. At this point, I was praying that her face would be spared.

I was very grateful that Dr. Nel took the time to explain in detail what was going on with Kechi. He did not make any promises, indeed he stressed that Kechi was a very, very sick girl and that they were all praying that she pulled through.

After my session with him, I sought out Dr. Plani, the trauma surgeon. In his gruff, but kind manner, he assured me that Kechi was doing well so far, and in response to my questions, said that she would be on the respirator and sedated for a while.

I then retired to the visiting room to wait for visiting time and also used the opportunity to ruminate over the reports I had got from the doctors. Then I began to pray. It was beginning to dawn on me that this was not going to be a short hospital stay.

After I visited with Kechi, Layi and her husband came by and brought me chicken salad for lunch. After they left, I felt very weary and decided to go and catch a nap in the hotel.

Brother Dotun and his wife visited me at the hotel, brought me food and also gave me R200. At this point, my fridge in the hotel was overflowing with food people kept bringing me. I was very grateful for this because I did not have to buy food and could save money that way.

Brother Dotun and his wife dropped me off at the hospital and soon after, Lanre came with his friends, Mike and Vicki, and insisted I go out with them.

He was furnishing his house because he was expecting his family to move down from Nigeria and we all went with him to shop for bargains in beds and mattresses. I knew Lanre was trying to give me a break from the hospital and I really appreciated it, but when it got close to visiting time I told him I needed to be with Kechi.

When we got to the hospital, they actually waited for me to visit with Kechi and it took a little longer that time because she was running a fever and was being kept cool. She was shivering a little as her bandages were being kept moist. I spent the whole visit praying, and rebuking the fever. When I looked up, I saw Lanre standing just inside the door of the ICU, head bowed, obviously praying. I was so touched.

Lanre was an incredibly genuine, caring kind of person. Very rare. It was clear why Ulo called him a friend. I was so glad there were still people like him in this world, and so proud he was a Nigerian.

I had seen the best in human beings since Kechi's accident.

Sade and her husband are other examples of fantastic human beings. After my visit with Kechi, Lanre took us to a place in Randburg for dinner. Sade and her husband had come to the hospital to see me and when they called me, they found out where we were having dinner and drove thirty minutes to see me. They were leaving the next day and had to see me before going. I will miss them so much. Sade actually bought two outfits for Tara, my baby girl in Nigeria.

I was very fortunate to have met the most selfless, incredible people during this trying period. It was indeed true that God would not allow a burden too hard for us to bear.

He surrounded me with the love and support of the most wonderful people.

CHAPTER FIVE

"My soul melteth for heaviness: strengthen thou me according unto thy word."
Psalm 119 : 28 (KJV)

Since Kechi was going in for surgery on Sunday, I decided to go in early so I would see her before she got wheeled into the OR. I was pleased to see that she was stable and the fever of the previous day had subsided. Also, her mouth did not seem to be as swollen as before. I took this as a good sign and prayed over her before leaving the nurses to prepare her for surgery. These preparations were quite elaborate because Kechi had to be unhooked from about ten different machines and then hooked up to others that would take her into the OR.

When I peeked into her room at 11.30am, she had returned from surgery. I waited a while because it was also an elaborate process to hook her back on the different machines all around her bed. Although it was way past visiting time, I was allowed to have a quick visit and prayer before going back to the hotel to rest.

First Breakthrough..............................

I had been sitting been sitting beside Kechi, reading some bible passages from Psalms to her when it seemed to me that I heard a gurgling sound from the respirator. Then it started to beep. I was alarmed and thought the machine was defective again. I ran out to get the sister, who had just stepped out, and she brought out a long tube connected to a machine and proceeded to suction

Kechi's mouth and nose. Apparently, saliva and mucus sometimes filled the patient's mouth and nose and had to be suctioned off.

Then she said to Kechi, "Come on, darling, open your mouth". AND KECHI MOVED HER MOUTH!

I exclaimed, "Can she hear you?" "Oh yes", replied the nurse.

She asked Kechi again to open her mouth and Kechi moved her eyelids.

"No, darling, not your eyes", the nurse laughed, "your mouth".

I could not believe it. All these days, Kechi had lain unmoving.

It was very startling to see her respond to anyone.

"So……has she been hearing me all this while?" I asked the nurse. She said yes.

Then Kechi moved her mouth some more and sounds came from her throat.

She was trying to speak!

The nurse calmed her down and explained to her she would not be able to speak because she had a tube down her throat. I also came round to the side of her bed and told her to calm down, and that I would sing for her. I started singing one of her favorite songs The Woodpecker's Song.

The second verse had always been a problem to me because I had somehow never been able to memorize it. Kechi always used to correct me when I got there. As I got to the second verse, she shook her head slightly and I said, "I know, I'm messing it up. Please bear with me, okay?"

She actually shook her head!

I almost lost it then, but I pulled myself together because I knew my crying would upset her.

I sang more songs to her until it was past visiting time.

I was overwhelmed and needed to call my family and spread the news.

When I returned later that night, the nurse explained that sometimes the sedation was not very deep and that Kechi responded to her every time she asked her to open her mouth or do some other thing.

Right then, though, she appeared to be in deep slumber so I just sat quietly and sang to her.

Betty's husband, Ike, had returned from Nigeria and he came into the ICU to see Kechi. He encouraged me by saying that she did not look as bad as he thought. Layi and her husband also came and we all visited for a while in the waiting room.

Ike and Betty dropped me back at the hotel just as Lanre came in to check on me. Lanre would be going to Nigeria soon and promised to take me to shop for Tara so he would take stuff back for her.

He also said that Ulo was arranging to send me some more money through him. I was really so grateful to Ulo. With her I could go into detail about Kechi's condition that others could not handle at that time. Everyone was saying that I was so strong but the truth was that Ulo was the strong one because she always had just the right words to lift me up. For all I knew, she probably went to pieces after calling or texting me, but at those moments when I needed strength, she gave it to me through God's word. As anyone who knows Ulo is aware of, God has imbued her with uncommon wisdom and I drew from her when I needed it. I thanked God every day for her.

Ike had come with letters and newspaper clippings from my family and when I got back to my room that night, I started to go through the letters from my sister, Nkechi's, kids for Kechi. I broke down crying as I read those letters because for the first time I was seeing the whole situation from their point of view. If Kechi had gone to be with Jesus last Saturday, those boys' lives would never have been the same because she was so close to those cousins of hers that at times it seemed that her spirit was connected to theirs. Bichu especially would have been devastated. They all wrote that they saw that there was a calling on Kechi's life and that they loved her very much.

My crying jag set the mood for the next few hours as I went through the newspaper cuttings Mom had enclosed.

I was sinking into gloom and despair, looking at pictures of parents grieving. The last straw was seeing the pictures of some of the students, including my friend, Angela Ubah's son, Ifeanyi.

Mom and Nkechi called just then and I told them what I was doing and that I could no longer handle it. Mom immediately told me to pack them up and put them at the bottom of the box and forget all about them. They spoke with me until midnight, consoling me and encouraging me to remain strong. I told them to pray for a little girl, a baby, really, Erin, who had been brought into the ICU for burns. She was so little and it broke my heart to see her burns and hear her cry.

After the phone call, I felt better but still had a feeling of heaviness as I prayed for the hurting families.

I called the hospital before going to bed and was told that Kechi was stable.

I woke up feeling blue but felt better after praying and reading Psalms 138 and 139.

I was physically weak and I decided then and there to take better care of myself, force myself to eat and rest more. I could not afford to be ill.

Not at this time.

When I went in to see Kechi, I notice that her temperature was down but her face was bleeding in some places. It appeared that this was because of the cleaning of her facial burns. This bleeding was supposed to be a good sign. I remember the plastic surgeon saying that they would debride her face because they wanted it to bleed. I was quite sure he told me why, but at that point, for the life of me, I could not remember why Kechi's face bleeding was a good thing. I had trusted them thus far and resolved to continue to trust them.

The nurse on duty said that Kechi had had those breathing problems again the previous night. They had called in her doctor, who gave her a muscle relaxant which put her in an even deeper sleep so they could control her. Personally, I think Kechi was just fed up with the tube in her throat and wanted it out.

I sat by her and prayed until one of the nurses came to sit by me and encourage me to hang in there. She said she had noticed that I was not looking my best that morning and told me to stay strong. I was very touched. One thing I noticed in Milpark Hospital was that all the staff, not just the nurses, were very empathetic. They genuinely cared about, not just their patients, but also the families. Here I saw that nursing is a calling, not just a job.

I had been warned that there would be ups and downs in Kechi's recovery process. I just needed to stay strong.

"Dear Lord", I prayed, "Please infuse me with Your joy. Joy belongs to You and Your joy is my strength. Amen."

It appeared that Erin, the little girl, was also doing well. Thank God.

During the afternoon visit later that day, Kechi again reacted to the sound of my voice. She tried to open her eyes and started to move her lips. I could sense her frustration and tried to calm her down. Eventually, the nurse had to give her the muscle relaxant and she calmed down. I sang to her again as always before leaving.

Pat's friend, Noni, visited when I was in the waiting room and assured me that she and the rest of her church were praying for Kechi and she promised to visit again soon.

There was a certain calmness I felt about Kechi's condition that day. It was very reassuring to me that she recognized my voice, although she got agitated. When I spoke to Ulo later, she said I should reassure Kechi that even when she did not hear my voice, she should know that I was nearby, ready to be with her the second visiting time came around. She also suggested I should tell Kechi the visiting times and start each visit by telling her, "It's 4pm and I'm here". That way, Kechi would know that sometimes I was in the room with her and at other times, I was nearby. This made a lot of sense to me and I adopted it from the very next visit.

Lanre came and took me shopping for Tara, like he promised he would. He also gave me R2500 from Ulo, who would not let me thank her for it. I bought clothes, shoes, underwear and some toys for her and for the children of my friend, Uzoma, who was looking after Tara in my absence.

The trauma physician, Dr. Plani, had informed me that he was handing Kechi over to another physician who would now take care of her since she was now out of immediate danger, and thus no longer a trauma patient. Dr. Pahad was an internal medicine physician and I took to him as soon as we were introduced because there was a certain calmness about him that soothed me. I trusted him immediately. He was with Kechi when I returned to her room to visit. In response to my enquiries about her healing, he said that her lungs and kidneys are fine and he was pleased with her progress. He said that Kechi was in a much better state than she was when she came in, but I should talk to the plastic surgeon for details about the condition of her burns.

Needless to say, this was good news for me. I was happy that her doctor was pleased with her recovery. I just wanted to prostrate and thank God and tell Him that indeed my eyes had seen, my ears had heard, and my mouth would talk about His goodness for the rest of my life and unto eternity! He is an awesome God.

I was getting very worried about my accommodation arrangements as the hotel had informed me that Int'l SOS had not extended my stay past Saturday the 17th. I called ISOS several times and they kept promising to call back but they never did. When I called yet again, they said they had called the hotel and spoken to a lady called Pauline.

When I got home that night, Pauline had left, but had noted that my stay was only extended to the next day.

I called Mike and asked him to call Dr. Moses and find out what he situation was. I also called Mom and Ulo and we were throwing ideas back and forth when suddenly it hit me! Everything had been done by God so far, with no input by any of us. Why were we now getting involved? Were we trying to help Him? I immediately repented of my sin of lack of trust and sent texts to Ulo and Mom to do the same.

Then I let go and let God.

CHAPTER SIX

"...for the Lord will go before you, the God of Israel will be your rear guard."
Isaiah 52 : 12b (NKJV)

The next day, December 20th (day 9 after the plane crash), I got out of bed later than usual. It had rained in the night and was quite chilly that morning. I had not realized how chilly until I went outside and discovered that my denim jacket was inadequate.

On my way past the front desk that morning, I spoke to Pauline and she said that ISOS had extended my stay and that the lady who called from their office said Pauline should tell me not to panic, my welfare was their responsibility. I immediately bowed my head and thanked God for His grace. I had disobeyed by doubting; repenting, I asked for forgiveness and His grace filled me.

So why was I still feeling this heaviness that should not have existed? I sent up a prayer for the Lord to fill me with His joy. I was still feeling shaky when, a few minutes into my visit with Kechi, a lady in the room next to Kechi tapped on the glass partition and signed for me that she was praying for me. She was there to visit the patient in the room who was probably her husband and who, as far as I know, had been either unconscious or sedated since he was brought in.

I was moved to tears at her compassion for a stranger even though she was in a similar situation but I managed to hold on to some control until I got to the waiting room. Once I got there, especially when I saw other patient's relatives surrounded by their families and friends, I sobbed my eyes out.

For the first time, I felt alone and far from my family.

After I finally managed to pull myself together, I finished my visit (they had asked me to leave so they could take some x-rays).

But I needed help so I sent Ulo a text. As if on cue, Obi called from London and when I told him how I was feeling, he told me to look for ways to distract myself. (How like a man to think that all I needed to do was to go out and play ball or something!). I assured him that I would not let myself get so low again.

Ulo called me and really ministered to me telling me this:

- God, In His infinite mercy, chose Kechi, my child, for what He is doing at this time, and has strengthened me so that others will draw strength from me.
- This situation is bigger than Kechi and I. It is a whole new birthing process and God is showing, through everything that has happened, that His hand is in this and His name WILL be glorified.
- I would have to remain deep in the womb of prayer and supplication, abiding in his Word, and drawing strength from Him. I could not waver, could not afford to.
- We should realize that we were privileged to be a part of this move of God.
- Every birthing comes with pain, which is what we were going through then. But sorrow only endures through the night and joy comes in the morning.
- It was understandable that I felt low looking at Kechi just lying there, unmoving, but I would have to look beyond what I was seeing and look forward to the glory of God that will be revealed through her when her work in God begins.

Ulo said so many other things that ministered to my soul, and I was calm. I thanked God for the uncommon wisdom He had bestowed on Ulo. I knew that it was right to tell her what I was feeling.

After Ulo's call, I received a call from someone who identified himself as the Managing Director of Sosoliso Airlines. He said that they would like to support us in any way they could. I told him that my focus for now was praying for my daughter and that he should speak to my husband on any other matters.

As far as I was concerned, if the company wanted to help us out, they would call and say, "this is how we want to help, how do you feel about it?", not to call me and say they would like to help. What did he expect me to say? "Okay, send me $1m so I can pay bills?" I did not want any distractions. I was focused on God and Kechi and did not wish to be disturbed.

Many people had been visiting me to find out how Kechi was doing and some of them gave me money to help pay for food and transportation, many of them people I had never met before. None of them called to tell me that they would like to support me in any way they can. They just obeyed the prompting of The Spirit and gave. That was how God worked.

Shortly after this upsetting call, I received a call from one of my brothers in law, Patrick. Apparently he was with the governor of Imo State (my home state), Governor Achike Udenwa, who wanted to speak to me. The Governor spoke words of encouragement and told me to also take care of myself to be strong for Kechi.

Susan, Elsie's friend who had helped Mike get his visa from the South African embassy in Nigeria, paid me a visit all the way from Pretoria. Very pretty and petite, she had the lovely accent most South Africans have. We had a lovely visit and she promised to keep in touch.

Ulo called after Susan left. She was with Chinedu, our brother, and in discussion with him about the things she had said to me, it turned out that Chinedu received that same word for me and had in fact shared it with his friend, William, that morning. He also received word that I should minister to others in the hospital. A bit scary, but I prayed that God would make a way. I trusted absolutely in Him.

I sat waiting for Kechi to come out of surgery. She went in at 6.30pm, and when I peeked in her room at 7.50pm, she was there, and the nurses were re-attaching her to tubes and lines. Kechi was now having surgery every forty eight hours because the doctors were trying very hard to remove all the dead skin as soon as they could to minimize infection.

When I was finally allowed to see her, I could see that her face was now fully bandaged. They had done the debridement of her face and the remaining leg. I wondered what this meant for the future of her face and whether her beautiful face would ever be the same after so much of it had been scraped away. I quickly pulled myself back from those thoughts, reminding myself that surgery can only be performed on the living and that by God's grace, she would be fully restored, as He promised.

She seemed peaceful, not agitated as she sometimes was after surgery, so I sat by her, sang and prayed.

As I was getting ready for bed, a text message came from Chinedu. He had received two messages from the Holy Spirit for me and they went thus:

"I have surrounded her with My presence, and My servants are ever present, encamped around them.
They are instruments of My purpose, My purpose, so she must not fear or be discouraged.
She need only to open the eye of her heart to see Me afresh in all this. I have ministered peace to her soul; she only has to receive it.
I am her God".

And then,

"It is My intention for her own strength to fail. I want her to depend entirely on me.
The strength she had thus far was of Me. I want it to remain so."

I bowed my head, full of praise and thanksgiving, awed at the privilege and honor to be a part of this move of God.

`What an exhausting day it had been. I was so completely drained that I fell asleep while kneeling to pray. I woke up and dragged myself onto the bed and slept very soundly till morning. I kind of knew God would understand.

I woke up with a bible verse resonating through my being,
"My grace is sufficient for thee:
For my strength is made perfect in weakness."
This was from Second Corinthians, chapter 12, verse 9. I had always been very familiar with that verse, but never had it had so much meaning to me.

Total dependence, that was what God wanted from me.

I would give it to Him and watch as miracle upon miracle overtook me. The arm of man will fail. God cannot, because it is not in His nature to fail. When I am weak, He is strong, and His strength is made perfect when I am completely leaning on Him, completely trusting in Him.

I read the rest of that verse and it went,

"Most gladly therefore will I rather glory in my infirmities, that the power of Christ may rest upon me."

I spent some time meditating on these words and resolving to make them a part of my life henceforth.

I discovered that my "quiet times" with God were quite different from what I had been used to before the plane crash. God had always been a very significant part of my life, way before I got born again in 1998, and fellowship with Him, whether in church, with family, or alone, had always brought me joy and peace. But there was something different now. It was as if God was sitting beside me as I prayed or read the bible. Things became clearer to understand. I felt more peaceful and fulfilled after meditating on His Word. I felt much closer to Him. And the best thing was, I could not wait to be in His presence.

There were some other patients here from Nigeria. One of them was a lady well known to Ulo and her husband, Chidi. She had been in an accident with her son and they were both flown to Milpark Hospital from Nigeria. I understood that her son passed away, and she was in critical condition. I made enquiries and went and introduced myself to her husband. He said he had suspected I was related to Ulo because of our resemblance to each other. I gave him Ulo's message that his wife was in their prayers and offered my condolences for his son.

I also met another lady whose daughter had kidney complications due to lupus. The family had been through so much, but they were trusting in God for a miracle. According to man's knowledge, their child should not even be alive. But because of God's grace, He had kept her to testify of His goodness, and therefore God was going to be glorified through her, even if it was just because of her mother's unshakable faith.

I knew there was a reason that God led me to hear this remarkable woman's story, and I was learning to make use of every opportunity He brought to glimpse into His heart and see what lesson lay there.

This lady and her daughter had been in Milpark for two months and she had not given up for one day. Such faith, even when the girl had no blood pressure at all and her white blood cell count was below zero. Incredible! God would reward such faith, I knew He would.

I met with the plastic surgeon and he gave me details on Kechi's progress. What he said hit me very hard because I had been expecting that Kechi's wounds would heal much quicker than this, forgetting that the Lord had revealed that the recovery would be long.

First of all, contrary to my thinking, the debridement was far from over. They had just done her face and parts of her legs. The surgeon said that all her wounds were infected and there was a particular bacterium that she had contracted in the ICU which they were very concerned about.

The debridement would continue until there was no more infection. She was on antibiotics and would remain on them. She may need grafting on her forehead as the burns there were deep. The burns in her hands were also deep.

I knew she had been having fevers from infections but for the first time, I was actually realizing that things were a lot more serious than I realized. The doctor's tone put me on alert. It was as if he was telling me that things were pretty serious.

Now, it was not that I did not realize how serious Kechi's condition was, it was just that I was so sure that God was in control that I was not paying attention to the details. My mind was focused on the end, when I would take my fully healed child and go home. Maybe this was how I was keeping sane, I do not know. Thinking back to those days in Milpark, and looking at photographs, I know now that I held it together purely by God's grace.

I left a message for Ulo for a prayer request against the infection. When Mom called, I gave her the doctor's update and I know she was upset although she tried to be strong. Ulo and Dad called to reassure me, and I prayed for strength and peace.

At the end of the day, I got visits from Ike and Betty and also from Don and his wife and the Nigerian Ambassador.

I received a call from our friend, Chike Onyenso, from America. Apparently, someone had blogged that Kechi had passed away. I assured him that Kechi was alive and well.

I got ready to leave and was concerned that the sister on night duty was a bit elderly and I was worried that she might not be alert, especially with Kechi's fever. But I surrendered Kechi to God and left.

At 2.00 a.m., Eunice, my sister-in-law, called me frantically from America, saying that someone had said the papers reported that Kechi had passed away. I figured it must be the same news that Chike referred to. I reassured her that Kechi was fine, but she was frantic, telling me to find a Mountain of Fire church and get anointing oil to put on Kechi and make pronouncements to her that she will not die. Realizing how upset she was, I promised to make enquiries.

I rebuked Satan, covered Kechi with the blood of Jesus, and went back to sleep.

CHAPTER SEVEN

"Trust in the Lord with all thine heart; and lean not unto thine own understanding. In all thy ways acknowledge Him, and He shall direct thy paths"
Proverbs 3:5 & 6 (KJV)

I woke up determined not to rush to the hospital, or phone them in reaction to Eunice's call the previous night. I had made the decision to trust Him and lean on Him completely, and I trusted Him to keep His word concerning Kechi. I would leave for the hospital at the normal time, have breakfast in the hospital cafeteria, as usual, then visit Kechi at 11.00am, as usual.

This was harder than I thought, and it was not made easier when Eunice called again around 9.00am. I knew she thought I had seen Kechi already and without telling her that I had not, I assured her that Kechi was fine. She was very relieved and told me to still go ahead and look for anointing oil.

God had placed it in my heart to approach the couple with the little baby and ask her name so that the church back home would pray for her, and I was determined to do it that day.

I spoke to the Nigerian lady whose daughter was so ill on my way to Kechi's room. Her surname was familiar and when I enquired, it turned out she is married to Mike's friend's oldest brother. Small world. I asked her for her daughter's name so the church at home could also pray for her.

When I went in to see Kechi, her temperature was high again, due to the infection. Her blood pressure was also quite low. This was definitely one of the "down" periods we were warned about in burns patients. The infection was raging through her body but I was not moved because the blood of Jesus was also all over and inside her. I was trusting in the Lord.

When I spoke with Dr. Pahad, he admitted that this was the period they got most concerned about in burns patients when the infection has grabbed a hold. But he was also confident that they were dealing with it.

As soon as I walked into Kechi's room, I got the urge to say the Psalm that begins thus over Kechi,

Give thanks to the Lord; for He is good: Because His mercy endureth forever.

After praying, I got out my bible and asked God for help in locating the Psalm. I flipped open the bible to Psalms, turned a page and there it was, Psalm 118.

I would like to note here that by this time, I was no longer surprised at this sort of thing happening. I was daily feeling closer and closer to God and without much thought, I was relying on Him to make things happen for me not just the big stuff, even little stuff like helping me find exactly where relevant verses were located in the bible. This happened very often and has continued till today. Sometimes, I woke with a verse in my heart, opened my bible, and there it was!

Back to that day, I recited the whole Psalm aloud while standing over Kechi, and it ministered greatly to me. I loved verse 4,

"Let them now that fear the Lord say, that His mercy endureth forever"

and Verse 17, I declared to Kechi every day since the plane crash,

"I shall not die, but live, and declare the works of the Lord."

I did not get a chance to speak to the parents of the baby. I think that the fear of rejection was holding me back.

Back at the hotel, Mom and Chinedu called me and we spent time talking about depending fully and totally on God. Chinedu also asked me to pray for the grace to minister God's love to others in the hospital. He stressed that it should be led by God and therefore be totally natural, not forced. If God wanted to, He would present the opportunity.

As I walked into the hospital for the afternoon visit, I found myself face to face with the baby's mother in the corridor. I stopped her and told her I was praying for her baby. She smiled and said she appreciated that. I went on to tell her that I wanted my church family back home to also pray, so would she mind giving me her baby's name?

"Marlee", she said, and thanked me again.

Not so hard to obey the Lord, after all.

Kechi had been given two pints of blood to bring up her blood pressure but it remained low. Her temperature and heart rate went down slightly, and the sister on duty had sent for the doctor to take a look at Kechi.

I noticed that Kechi's eyes were slightly open. I sang to her and read from the scriptures to her. As I prayed, I told her to keep fighting, we all loved her, Jesus loved her, and she should believe that she would not die, but would live and testify of the goodness of God.

I "spoke" to her blood pressure and commanded it to rise to normal by the authority contained in the name of Jesus. I knew this would be the case by the time I came for the night visit.

God did not fail me. When I came back at night, the blood pressure was normal and her temperature had come down even more. Wasn't God awesome?

I bowed my head in thanksgiving and praise.

Then God started to move again………………..

Upon getting back to the hotel, Elsie called to inform me that her friend, Susan, had called the South African Embassy in Nigeria to arrange for Mike's visa.

She asked me for Mike's phone number so she could tell him how to go about it. After about thirty minutes, Elsie called back to say that both she and Susan had called Mike and that the Charge d'Affairs of the embassy had also called Mike and told him to forget about getting any letter from Shell for his visa and instead to get to the embassy before 12noon the next day, Friday, December 23rd and collect his visa.

They eventually agreed for Tuesday 27th, since Mike would be unable to make it into Lagos before noon because of the Christmas weekend rush at the airports, and Monday 26th was a public holiday.

I was amazed. Mike had been trying so hard to get a letter from Shell that he would take to the embassy to get his visa, and now he was being offered the visa. Could God be any more awesome?

Later as I was praying, I admitted to God that it was very painful seeing Kechi lying there, broken and bruised. Just then I was reminded of His Son on the cross, broken and bruised. I heaved a huge sigh and went to bed.

CHAPTER EIGHT

"There hath no temptation taken you but such as is common to man: but God is faithful, who will not suffer you to be tempted above that ye are able; but will with the temptation also make a way to escape, that ye may be able to bear it."
1 Cor. 10:13 (KJV)

Dorothy, my sister-in-law, arrived in Johannesburg on the morning of December 23rd. I directed her to the hotel and decided to wait for her so that we could go to the hospital together. As soon as Dorothy saw me, she collapsed into tears. It was quite an emotional moment as we both cried for a while. When she freshened up, we went off to the hospital.

Kechi appeared to have passed a peaceful night. Her blood pressure was fine, temperature normal. Dorothy was wonderful. She immediately began to talk to Kechi, reading scripture to her, and even making jokes to her. Kechi responded by moving her head from side to side and we calmed her down.

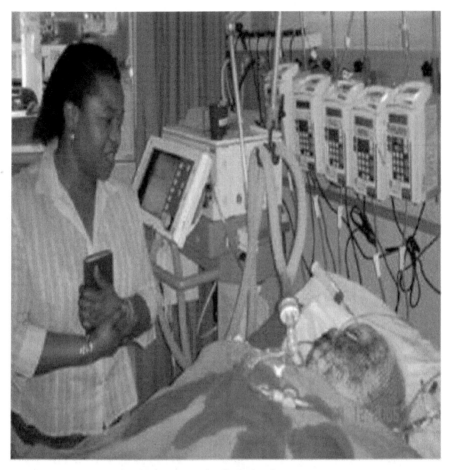

Dorothy praying by Kechi's bedside Christmas eve, 2005.

The sister came in to inform me that Kechi's surgery had been moved up to the afternoon and I had to sign yet another consent form. I noticed that her face and arms were bleeding.

When we left the ICU, we met Kathryn, Sarah's mother. Sarah and Erin and others were in the bus that had an accident in Port Harcourt. We prayed together and encouraged each other.

When we got back to the hotel, God moved again.

The front desk called to tell me that they wanted to move me into a room with two beds at the same price, because of Dorothy, and would move me back into a single room when Dorothy left. This was pretty overwhelming to me. I did not know what to say. We moved to the room next door and I simply knelt down and thanked God for His favors.

After a nap, we went back to the hospital for the 4pm visit. As usual, we prayed and sang to Kechi. It did not look as if she would go into surgery that day, after all. The doctor had two patients before her and the nurses thought that she would probably go in the next day. Her temperature has gone up a bit as her poor body battled infection. But I held on to God, believing Him to still be firmly in control.

I called Ulo and told her of the hotel room change and we reaffirmed that what God was doing was bigger than we realized. But I think that at that point we were beginning to know that the work ahead which God was preparing for was an awesome one.

When Dorothy and I returned for the night visit, Kechi had been taken to the theatre. They wheeled her in around 8.00pm. Dorothy was in tears when she came to the waiting room to tell me that Kechi was back in her room. She had gone to a more private waiting room to pray, a room they called the "grieving room". I had resolved when I heard the name of that room never to go there again. I would never grieve I would only thank God.

Anyway, on her way out of the room, she saw them wheeling Kechi back to the ICU. I jokingly told her that she should go back home if she was going to cry every time Kechi went to the theatre and she assured me that they were tears of relief and thankfulness, not fear. I totally understood. She was trying so hard to be strong and I know it was not easy for her seeing Kechi like that. After two weeks, it was still hard for me to see Kechi like that.

When we were allowed to see her, I noticed they had changed the dressings on her face. The dressings were still soaked through with blood, but God had given me the strength to look upon Kechi in that state without falling into despair.

Her blood pressure was fine, but her body temperature was below normal, and they covered her with a warm air blanket.

We prayed over Kechi and left.

Ike and Betty came over to the hotel to visit and Betty insisted on coming to take me out after my morning visit with Kechi.

My prayers that night were full of praises and thanksgiving to my Awesome God!

Magdalene called the next morning to pray with me and said also that she and her family were planning to visit us the next day.

When we saw Kechi, I noticed that the swelling on her face had reduced significantly. I took my first picture of her since we arrived in Milpark. It had not even occurred to me to take pictures of her before then. The gauze was bloody and her lips and ears appeared black with dried blood, but my spirits were lifted up because her face was not as puffy as it used to be. The blisters on her upper arms and chest seemed to be healing and peeling, but her shoulders were still puffed up and swollen. She looked much bigger that she really was.

We spoke to Doctor Pahad and he said the plastic surgeon had to go quite deep on her left leg to remove the dead and infected tissue. The other wounds were also cleaned. Also, it was likely Kechi would go back to the OR the next day, Sunday, or on Monday.

Doctor Pahad reminded us that we still had a long way to go, but I was already reconciled to that because God had revealed that the recovery would be long.

Betty picked me up as she promised and took me to a steak place called Spur in Bryanston. We spent some time window shopping at the mall.

During the afternoon visit, Kechi was running a fever. She was shivering and her heart was racing. They gave her something for it and by the time we left, she had stabilized a bit. I rebuked her fever and also pronounced healing on the blood pressure, which was a bit low. Not surprisingly, her blood pressure began to inch up almost immediately and I reminded myself that the sooner I start realizing who I was in Christ Jesus, and the authority I had in His Name, the better prepared I would be for the work ahead.

Christmas Day! December 25th 2005.

I spent my praying time thanking God for the best Christmas gift He could have given me - my daughter's life. But I also had a burden in my heart and in my spirit for all the families with grief instead of joy on that day. I prayed for God to continue to comfort them and my mind kept going back to the seconds before the impact, when they must have realized that the plane was going to crash. I was probably punishing myself, but I kept praying that they went to Jesus without pain and agony. I even asked Jesus to promise me that they were all with Him. By this time, I was quite upset and melancholic, and went downstairs for breakfast with a heavy heart.

I was now missing Mike in earnest and was glad he would be coming soon. I prayed that Kechi would look better so that he would be able to handle seeing her.

I had been dehydrated for a few days, following a bout of diarrhea, which explained why I was feeling so weak, so I forced myself to eat, took some drugs I got from the pharmacy, as well as the multivitamins Betty had bought for me since the previous week, which I had ignored. I gave myself a serious talking-to. I could not afford to fall ill, so I prayed for healing for myself.

When Dorothy and I went in to see Kechi, her temperature was fine, her pulse and blood pressure were fine and she was stable. That magic word.

The plastic surgeon, Dr. Slabbert, (Dr. Nel was on vacation) had seen her and was going to have her back in the OR the next day to clean her wounds and check on their state.

The physician, Dr. Pahad, examined her and said she was better than the day before and the infection finally seemed to be under control. God be praised!

Kechi was super-responsive that day, moving her legs when we talked to her, moving her head, and even trying to open her left eye.

I asked permission to touch her and the nurse said yes. So I had to kit up - disposable apron, gloves - and look for a patch of uninjured skin to touch. I finally settled on a spot on her shoulder and stroked it gently.

It was such an awesome moment for me.

That was the first time I had touched Kechi since the accident.

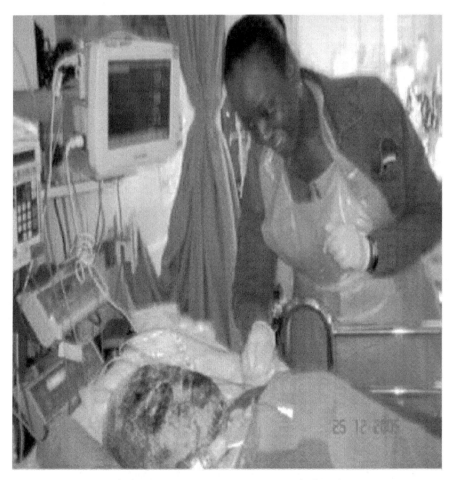

Christmas Day, 2005. First time I touched Kechi.

Kechi was such a tactile person that she always used to hug and hold onto me as often as she could throughout the day. To be with her and not be able to touch and hug her had been so hard for me and I really cherished that moment.

She responded by moving her legs. I remembered that she is very ticklish, though, and after some time I stopped because her pulse rate was going up. It was beyond thrilling to be able to touch Kechi even a little, when I yearned to hold her in my arms and soothe away her pains. I gave God glory for that opportunity. Dorothy jokingly said that she hoped I was not going to faint from touching Kechi. It was a special moment.

When we got back to the hotel, Dorothy treated us to Christmas lunch. It was a buffet and we had far too much to eat.

After lunch, Magdalene, Layi and her husband, Francis, Ifeoma Nwosa and her husband, along with two of their friends from Zambia and Zimbabwe came for a visit. We all sat at the hotel lobby, praying and singing. It was wonderful.

Ifeoma and Magdalene brought food which we kept for supper.

Then Magdalene took me aside.

"Ijeoma, "she asked me, "Are you mourning your daughter?" I was startled. "No!"

"Then why do you go around looking like you are? Why don't you do up your hair nicely? Why are you not wearing lipstick? Why are you not looking like a woman who is celebrating God's gift to her?"

She reminded me that she had cancer and yet people who did not already know would never guess. She told me to powder my face, put on my make up, and celebrate God, Who had done so much for me.

I was deeply moved and thanked her.

When we went back to the hospital that evening, Dorothy and I were wearing makeup.

Kechi appeared to be much more aware, opening her left eye, obviously trying to focus, and mouthing something that, knowing Kechi, looked like "Mummy".

I responded at once, telling her I was there.

Then it occurred to me that if Kechi was coming out of sedation, she would be very confused, and would be wondering where she was, and what was going on with her body. I began to explain to her where she was, why she was not able to talk and how she had been in an accident. This was the start of something I continued until Kechi came off the coma. Besides, Kechi was always the kind of person who needed to know exactly what was going on.

Later that evening, Brother Dotun and his family came and took me to their fellowship at Hillbrow. I had not heard good things about that area of Johannesburg, but it was nice to fellowship among the brethren once again.

I was fifteen minutes late for the evening visit, but Kechi appeared to be fine and was still moving her legs and eyes. I asked the matron on duty if that would cause her any harm and she said no, it was actually a good sign. It meant that she would find it easier to move at the end of her stay in ICU, or when she had to be weaned off the heavy-duty drugs she was on at that time.

Mom called that night and she had Chizitara with her for the Christmas holidays.

We had all agreed not to tell her anything about Kechi so she believed that Kechi and I had to travel to Lagos together for Kechi to take an exam. But people talked around her and she was beginning to piece things together. Mom decided it was time to tell her the truth, especially since neither Kechi nor I were in Lagos when she got there.

Mom said she told her that Kechi had an accident and was badly hurt and so I had to take her to a big hospital in South Africa. Tara then wanted to speak with Kechi and Mom told her Kechi was still too weak but she could speak to her later.

I spoke to Tara then and she thanked me for the things I bought for her. I reassured her that her sister was going to be fine. Mom told me not to worry about Tara.

But something that could only be of God had been happening. It was as if God wiped Tara out from my mind. If I ever dwelt on her for a single moment, the pain of leaving her behind would have be too much. So it was as if God was saying to me, concentrate all your energies on Kechi, I am taking care of Tara.

I did not for one moment worry about Tara.

Mike was staying at Ulo's and I spoke to him. He said that he had been surrounded with love from my family and he was very grateful. He told me that the MD of Sosoliso Airlines had asked for a private meeting and that Chidi, Ulo's husband would go with him.

It had been a long, eventful day and I thanked God at the end of it.

CHAPTER NINE

"O give thanks unto the LORD; for he is good; for his mercy endureth forever."
I Chronicles 16:34 (KJV)

The day after Christmas, December 26th, I woke up around 4am with severe stomach cramps. I had no idea what was going on, so I just prayed and tried to go back to sleep. Apparently, I succeeded because next thing I knew, it was morning and I woke up with a calm stomach and a song on my lips. Then followed a period of praise, worship and thanksgiving. Dorothy joined me and gratitude just poured out of us. It was wonderful. We marveled at the grace of God and how He is lifted up, exalted and magnified through the miracle of Kechi's life.

I received a call from my mom as we left for the hospital. She told me that she was going to take Tara and her best friend, Kamara, to the cinema. I was so grateful to my family. They had been with me from the word go, an awesome support group.

When we got to the hospital, we were told that Kechi's surgery had been moved to the next day. Kechi was even more active that morning, moving her legs and head around. The sister told us that Kechi had started to resist them when they tried to turn her over to clean her. They believed that it was because she was in pain. They had also noticed that she kept moving her lips, trying to say something, as if she was aware of what was going on around her.

This made me even more determined to continue to explain to her in detail everything going on with her body.

At some point during the visit, Dorothy became very concerned about the noise the nurses in the ICU were making. They constantly gathered to talk quite loudly, making the unit very noisy. We agreed that this was probably not the way any ICU should be run. Dorothy decided to write about it and drop it in the suggestion box but I did not intend to complain until I saw negligence in the way Kechi was being cared for, and I had not seen that yet. The way I saw it, medical staff had to have some kind of armor against all the death and near-death they saw constantly. So long as Kechi was being well taken care of and they answered my numerous questions, even when I was sure they thought I was being a nuisance, I was fine.

I had handed everything over to God, including the care-givers, and I knew He was in control of Kechi's life.

Ifeoma Nwosa and her husband, Ody, came to take us to their house for Ifeoma's birthday party. (I should probably not refer to her as Nwosa, which is her maiden name, but I could not remember Ody's surname). We met their lovely children. The first girl was very elegant and when I commented on that, Ifeoma told me that she attended a modeling school. We also met their friends, mostly white people, and we had a very good time. I met Moyo again. Nice lady. She and Ifeoma dropped us off in the hospital in time for the 4.00pm visit.

Kechi seemed to be deeply asleep, although her facial muscles were moving, as though her face was itching. We prayed and then sang to her and talked about anything we could think of.

Ifeoma picked us up again after the visit and we rejoined the party. This time everyone was outside for a barbeque, which is called braai in South Africa. We ate too much, as usual, and left laden with a lot of takeaway.

Back at the hospital, Kechi's blood pressure gave me some concern. It was high for her at 153/84. The sister agreed with me that it was high for her age, but nothing to worry about as long as it remained under 160. Her heart rate was fluctuating between 120 and 150 and the sisters said that was because of when they moved her or turned her, and when she heard my voice. I decided to be quiet. I just sang some of the songs she liked very softly and I knew she was listening to me.

I noticed that her stomach appeared to be distended and I brought it to the notice of the sisters. They said that they were keeping an eye on it, and suspected that it was because she had not stooled for about two days.

Kechi was given a blood transfusion earlier that day because her HB level was low and the doctor was awaiting the result of her blood test before deciding whether she would need more blood or not.

At some point during the visit, one of the equipment for IV infusion of antibiotics started to malfunction. They got a new one, installed it, and it continued to beep. They changed the line itself, and it continued to beep. At this point, I bowed my head and prayed. The bible says that the earth is the Lord's and everything in it. That included that machine. While the sisters were working on the line, baffled as to what could be the problem, I spoke to the machine and commanded it in the name of Jesus to cease its malfunction and do its job.

As I was praying, the sister put in the line, switched it on and it started working. I gave glory to God at once. The nurses, not having heard me as I prayed under my breath, were relieved, because at this point, three of them had tried and had not succeeded.

To skeptics, it may simply be a simple matter of a malfunctioning machine that was properly fixed. But to me, it was just more evidence of the awesome resurrection power of Jesus within me. If this power could raise the dead, then what was a machine? Brother Bisong once said that we have a power greater than atomic or nuclear power within us and I believe it.

I started to pray very hard that Kechi would have improved remarkably by the time Mike came. I was afraid of what seeing her in her current state would do to him. But on second thoughts, I felt that maybe it was important that he saw how sick she was in order to appreciate just how great a miracle God wrought in our lives.

When we got back to the hotel, a man called me and said he was supposedly from the Nigerian Embassy and that he was waiting at the hospital to see Kechi. I had no idea of who he was and I called the ICU and told them that absolutely no one could see Kechi if I was not there. I had to be very careful and protect my child. Already, rumors were circulating about interviews I was supposed to have given and I did not really need the distraction.

The man called back and said he could not see Kechi but wanted to come and see me. He came to the hotel and told me that he was a Catholic and would book masses for Kechi. I thanked him and he left.

Dorothy had already told me that if he asked what help the embassy could render, I should ask for transportation to and from the hospital, which was proving quite expensive. But the man never asked what I needed. On the other hand, he may have just come on his own.

I thanked the Lord for the lessons I had been learning from Him. I was learning to depend entirely on Him. He was making provision for all my needs and He was going to continue to do so.

Dorothy was livid that the Nigerian government had not made any effort to help out in any way.

It was really very strange and disconcerting, but I refused to dwell on it because the bible says in Philippians 4:v19,

But my God shall supply all your need according to his riches in glory by Christ Jesus. (KJV)

So, like the bible says, it is well.

Anyway, Mike and I agreed that we did not want anyone getting political mileage out of Kechi's situation. It is God that will be glorified and not man, no governor or president. God alone! So I absolutely refused to be bitter.

The following day, December 27th was my younger brother,

Obi's birthday. I hoped he would call so I could wish him a happy birthday. I would have loved to call him but he and his family were in the States for Christmas.

Kechi was looking fine that morning. She was definitely aware of our presence and was moving her legs. She had also started scrunching up her face whenever we came in to see her. I spoke to her and she calmed down, and I began to minister to her spirit the love of Jesus.

She was due to for surgery that afternoon for wound cleaning and dressing. I prayed that there were no new infections.

When we got back to the hotel, there was the, now usual, accommodation mix up between ISOS and the hotel regarding my departure date and so we could not get into the room. I called ISOS and they promised to resolve the problem. Meanwhile, the hotel reprogrammed my key card and we gained access.

While we were getting some rest, I got a call from a Mrs. Obi from the South African embassy in Lagos. She wanted to know where Mike would stay when he came and I gave her the name and address of the hotel. Mike later called from the embassy and informed me that he might be leaving for Johannesburg the next day. Apparently, the Office of the Presidency in South Africa called the South African Embassy in Lagos and paved the way for a speedy issuance of his visa.

It turned out to be a day of good calls because soon after, ISOS called me to say that they had sorted out my accommodation problems and I should not worry about it. They also wanted to know when my visa was going to expire so that they would arrange for its renewal.

By this time, I was so overwhelmed with God's continuous grace to me that I just fell on my bed and gave Him praises. One of the songs of praise we had sang while praying came to me:

"All the glory must be to The Lord
Only He is worthy of our praise
No man on earth should take glory to himself
All the glory must be to The Lord."

It was very obvious to me that this was God moving in all His glory.

Upon getting to the hospital for the 4.00pm visit and were told that Kechi was just wheeled into surgery and so we waited. As we were waiting, I felt the need to go into worship and this went on for about thirty minutes. At the end of it, Mom called me to say that she and Mike had been issued with 60 day visas. Mom had gone to the embassy with Mike and had insisted that she should also be issued with a visa as Kechi's grandmother. After many phone calls and consultations, they obliged her.

I went into another round of praise and thanksgiving.

Kechi was returned to the ICU at 5.00pm and after her tubes and wires were re-attached, we were allowed to see her briefly. They had covered up her face completely with a dark material, which I later learnt was called Acticote silver burn dressing, and bandages. The Acticote contains an antibiotic which is released into the skin when moistened. Kechi appeared to be okay and still deeply anaesthetized, but the sister told us that she was aware of her surroundings and opened her mouth and such when asked. I hoped that did not mean that she was feeling pain. I mean, she was supposed to be in a hospital-induced coma, so how come she was that aware of her surroundings? I made a mental note to talk it over with Dr. Pahad the next day.

Dorothy was not feeling very well by now. She had a stomach upset and I prayed for God to heal her. She had been such a rock for me and I really did not want her to fall ill.

Kechi was still out of it, so we just prayed and left for the night. Betty, the angel that she is, came by the hotel and whisked us off for dinner. It was a very eventful day and at the end of it we were pretty much wiped out.

CHAPTER TEN

"Let us therefore come boldly unto the throne of grace, that we may obtain mercy, and find grace to help in time of need."
Hebrews 4:16 (KJV)

I woke up the following morning, knowing I just had to call my cousin, Chinwe. There had been a certain distancing caused by family issues, but I now had a changed perspective on everything. The family rift was not important to me anymore; I wanted to get back to being close with my cousins again.

I called Ulo and she said Chinwe was in Lagos, and after praying for wisdom, I called her. She was surprised I called, but very sweet on the phone, and told me that she and her brothers had been praying for Kechi.

Like Ulo said, this was a time of reconciliation.

Dorothy and I asked to see Dr. Nel, the plastic surgeon, when we got to the hospital, and he gave us a rundown of what he had been doing so far. He had completed the debridement of the left leg and sent a sample of the tissue for lab investigation to see if there was still infection present. If they did not find any, Kechi's wounds would be prepared for grafting.

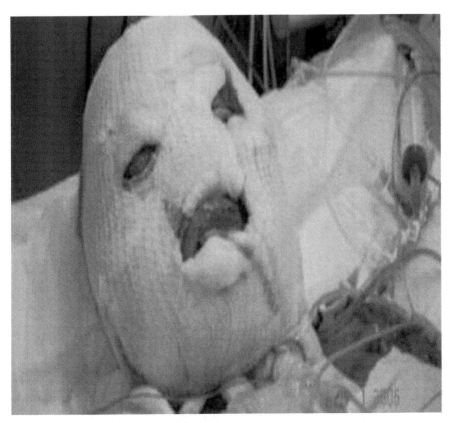

Kechi's first face surgery.

He had not removed all the dead tissue on the right leg because he did not want her to bleed too much from several places at the same time.

On her face, he said that due to the swelling, he put a dressing that could stay for three to five days at a time, so that it would not be dressed too often as there was a lot of bleeding on the face. He stressed that he was moving very slowly so as not to destabilize Kechi and reminded us that it was going to be a very long process, considering the extent and severity of her burns.

He however added that Kechi was making steady progress and that her physical state was much better than it had been when she was first brought to the hospital. He advised us to talk to her physician, Dr. Pahad for an update on how her body was doing.

We immediately sought Dr. Pahad out and he said that Kechi was doing well in terms of her vital signs, her blood pressure, lungs, kidneys and so on. Their main concerns were her burns,

and controlling the infection so that they could start grafting. They were quite anxious to start covering up her wounds with skin grafts, but they could not do that if there was infection present, which would cause the graft to fail. I learnt that graft failure meant that the grafted skin would fail to become incorporated into her body, and would be rejected.

Dorothy and I refused to be shaken by all these weighty issues. We were just going to be more specific in our prayers.

Ifeoma and Ody came and drove us to a Pick 'n' Pay Hyper Store in Northgate to buy a microwave for the room. Dorothy is really one-in-a-million! She paid for the microwave and other groceries, and then Ifeoma and Ody dropped us off in the hotel.

We received a shocker when we returned to the hospital. Kechi had been rushed back to the OR and had only just been returned to the ICU.

She had started bleeding at the site of the previous day's procedure, and the bleeding was so profuse that they had to send for Dr. Nel, who took her back to the OR to cauterize the blood vessels on her leg and stop the bleeding. Her HB level had become seriously compromised and she was given a blood transfusion also.

This was unexpected, but I pulled myself together and began to pray. The blood transfusion was followed by a plasma transfusion.

Dorothy and I stayed for a while and prayed by Kechi's bedside. I had been reading The Acts of the Apostles aloud to Kechi and we were now in Chapter 10. I read one chapter to her, but she seemed pretty much out of it, so we left her to rest.

We visited with the Nigerian lady and her daughter. The girl looked very ill, but I prayed that God would intervene in her situation, and that all of us mothers would walk out of Milpark Hospital with our children walking tall beside us.

In the night, Kechi was stable and still deeply asleep. Her stomach was still distended and the sister confirmed that she still had not stooled. When we enquired how the stool is taken care of, we were told that she passed stool on the bed and they cleaned her up.

Knowing Kechi, Ok Yuck! That was probably why she was holding back. Finicky, fastidious Kechi, poop on her bed? Nope!

But what did I think really? That they would have a tube pushed into her rectum that siphoned all her waste? I just was not thinking that far.

Dorothy just laughed because Kechi's excessive cleanliness gene is also in her. We talked to Kechi and told her it was okay to poop on the bed for now and she should not worry about making a mess. This was just temporary.

The sister assured us that if she did not poop that night, they would give her an enema in the morning. I prayed about the condition and I knew that by the next day, everything would be okay. I also prayed that her blood pressure would stabilize by morning.

On Thursday, December 29th, I called Ike after my morning devotions. He had offered to pick Mike from the airport and I wanted to remind him. He said he was just leaving and I figured that they would be back around 8.00am and settled down to read some scripture.

Less than 10 minutes later, Mike called me from the hotel lobby. He had not seen Ike when he came through Immigration and hopped into a taxi. I called Ike at once and told him Mike was already with me.

It was great to see Mike.

He told us that in the airplane, he was sitting near a man who after hearing Kechi's story, gave Mike some money and a rosary, which his Dad had given to him when he was going offshore on an oil rig.

As soon as Mike had a shower, we left for the hospital. I was very nervous about what his reaction was going to be when he saw Kechi because I knew that Kechi was Mike's one weakness. His Princess.

I was praying the whole way to the hospital.

When we arrived in the ICU, my worst fears materialized. Mike deflated before my eyes upon seeing Kechi. He visibly pulled himself together and managed to call her name. I asked him to go to the waiting room for a while but he refused. He calmed down after a while and began to talk to Kechi.

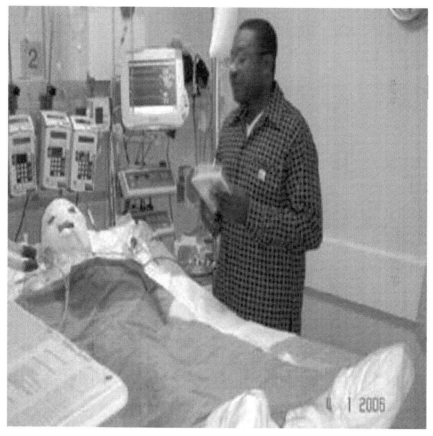

Mike praying by his daughter's bedside.

Meanwhile, upon hearing her father's voice, my daughter went crazy. Her eyes fluttered, she moved her head from side to side, moved her legs about and her pulse went haywire.

Oh yeah, she knew it was her Daddy, alright!

At the end of the visit, Mike asked to see Dr. Nel, who gave him all the details, including some I never knew, thank goodness. Like the fact that when we came, it was so touch and go as to whether Kechi would survive that she was given a 30% chance of survival.

According to them!

Mike was told that she now has a 70% chance of survival.

As for me, I knew that God had decided that she had 100% chance of survival, which is why we were in South Africa in the first place.

When we dropped Mike off at the hotel to sleep, Dorothy, Betty and I went to Cresta Mall to pick up a few things.

We picked Mike up for the 4.00pm visit and found that Kechi was still active and aware. Mike asked to see Dr. Pahad and went off to talk with him alone, because I was not in the mood to hear again that Kechi's life was being measured in percentages.

Mike returned to grill the sisters and matron on duty, and by the time we left for the night, he appeared to be more relaxed.

Betty and Ike picked us from the hotel and Ike probably took one look at Mike and decided that he needed a drink to take his mind off things. They left for a bar and Betty stayed with Dorothy and I in the room. Betty had brought dinner, which was really thoughtful of her.

I was saving a lot of money on food, as people were constantly bringing me things to eat. My support group was awesome.

Embarrassingly, I fell asleep before Ike and Mike came back, but it had been a full day. Luckily, Dorothy kept Betty company until Ike came back.

Dorothy left very early the next morning. Her flight was at 8.15am. I missed her terribly and thanked God Mike had come. I prayed for a while before waking Mike up for us to pray together.

For some reason, I found it hard to connect with God that morning. Distractions were clouding my mind and this scared me to death. I needed to remain a pure vessel so that I could receive from the Holy Spirit what God was ready to make available to me. I could not afford to lose focus now.

I fell prostrate before God and begged for forgiveness. There was a lifting in my spirit and I was able to pray. I resolved not to let this happen again.

When Mike and I prayed, he vowed that we would serve God and asked Him to make it clear to us what our roles at this time were.

We did not get to stay long with Kechi because she was being prepared for surgery. We prayed over her and left.

Mike then decided that since music had always been a major part of Kechi's life, it might help her if she listened to some of her favorite songs. Ike picked us up and we went to Makro to buy a small CD player and some CDs by Usher, Destiny's Child and Westlife.

When we got back to the hospital, Kechi was out of surgery and the nurse/sister gave us the great news that the wounds on her arms appeared to be clean enough for grafting to start on her next surgery day. I felt like dancing a jig.

I was still riding on this high when one of the sisters asked me to buy a toothbrush and paste for Kechi so she could start having her teeth cleaned.

It just then occurred to me that the doctors and sisters had gone from,

"You just have to keep praying for her" to "She's going to be okay" and "We've seen worse".

Suddenly, there was talk of a future. Alleluia!

But then all my elation disappeared in the blink of an eye when we got back to the hospital for the evening visit. The sister told us that Kechi had developed two new infections, one from her tracheotomy site.

Kechi was unable to cough up phlegm on her own, so the fluids had to be suctioned from her lungs constantly. This was quite distressing to watch because a pipe was pushed into her lungs and at the press of a button, fluids came up into the pipe and deposited in a container. Kechi always heaved during this procedure and her torso rose up from the bed, just like when one is coughing very hard in a reclined position. Anyway, these fluids were regularly tested and an infection was discovered there.

I just gave God all the glory that she was in a hospital where everything in her body was tested on a regular basis, and most of all, that she was in a place where the staff knew what to expect at every point.

An antibiotic IV was started immediately. We prayed over Kechi and left for the night.

NEW YEAR'S EVE, 2005......20 days after the plane crash

Ulo sent me a text saying that a fast had been declared for December 31stfor Nigeria. The text ran thus:

STOP! Our children must have a country to inherit.
Only God can ensure that something is left in Nigeria for posterity.
Join in a county-wide prayer and fast, 6am-6pm On December 31.
Let's believe God for a Divine intervention this season. 2006 MUST NOT be another pathetic year.
Do it for the children. Pass this on. Don't stop till it gets back to you.

Mike and I decided to join in the fast. If there was a country that needed saving, it was our dear country.

Kechi had been moved to an isolation unit within the ICU, away from the general room. The bacteria, or bug, as the doctors called it, was highly infectious and because of the one year old baby in the room, they felt it was safer to move Kechi out so she did not infect the others. They also did not want her to contract any new bugs.

Kechi was stable and was aware of our presence. She moved her mouth and tried to open her left eye. She seemed okay, but at some point, she turned down her lips like she was about to cry. I tried to bolster her spirits by talking about positive things, and she started to relax.

Hilda, the sister on duty and a very warm and nice lady, assured us that the bug Kechi had caught was one expected in burn patients and in fact, they had been expecting her to get it, though she caught it later than other patients in her experience. She said that they had the treatment for it and Kechi did not seem to be going into septic shock, which was when they would worry.

I sent out a text at once with the new information and prayers started going forth.

At night, I noticed that her temperature was higher than usual, also her blood pressure. We prayed about both things and handed them over to God before we left.

I noticed that Kathy, Erin's mother was a bit low so I comforted her. She was overwhelmed with keeping strong. I prayed for God to strengthen her. Erin was relying on that strength, and so was her husband.

A new patient came in today from Zambia, accompanied by his wife. He had been shot in the head, and we decided to add them to our prayers.

CHAPTER ELEVEN

"I will be glad and rejoice in thy mercy: for thou hast considered my trouble; thou hast known my soul in adversities;"
Psalm 31:7 (KJV)

At midnight on the first of January, 2006, Mike and I heard people yelling, "Happy New Year" and so we opened our window and looked out. Guests at the hotel had their windows open, heads stuck out, and were shouting New Year greetings to each other. We joined in the festivities for a while and then went back into the room to pray and dedicate our lives to the service of God.

It was truly amazing that between 2.00pm and 4.00pm on December 10th 2005, it had seemed like 2006 would be one without Kechi in it. But by God's grace, our daughter was spared and Mike and I were in Johannesburg with her, thanking God every minute for sparing her life and healing her. There was so much to be grateful to God for. We were blessed. Richly blessed indeed!

When we saw Kechi, we prayed again as a family, re- dedicating our lives to God. Kechi, as was now expected, moved her lids and mouth as we talked to her. All her vital signs were fine.

I was becoming quite good at reading medical equipment.

Dr. Nel came in to examine Kechi while we were there and told us that he intended to do a test graft on Kechi the following day and I immediately sent a text message to the church in Nigeria to pray concerning both the infection and the success of the skin grafting.

By the afternoon visit, however, the temperature had climbed to 38.6 degrees. We knew that this was as a result of her body's fight with the infection and remembering what Hilda said about septic shock, we went into warfare prayers. At the end of the prayers, I felt peace and I knew that Kechi was going to be fine.

I now applied myself to convincing Mike of the same. He was so scared for his princess, it was hard to watch.

I was relieved when Lanre and Remi, his wife, picked us up for a New Year's party at Moyo and Obi's. We met some other Nigerians there and hung out for a while before Lanre took us back to the hospital for the last visit. It was a good outing because it took Mike's mind off worrying about Kechi for a while.

She looked to be deeply asleep, so we just prayed over her concerning the coming surgery.

Ulo called me and I went into the waiting room to answer the call. They were very strict about cell phone use in the ICU.

She said was calling to tell me certain things I did not know that happened to Mike on the day of the accident.

Apparently, when Mike and his brother, Ikenna were on their way to Port Harcourt airport after I had called Mike to give him the news of the crash, Ikenna had heard that there were some survivors. Mike then said to Ikenna that if Kechi was among the survivors, he would become born again. Ulo told me that it was time to lead Mike through the prayer of salvation.

Every born again Christian knows that to become born again, you have to obey the dictates of Romans 10 v 9-10:

That if thou shalt confess with thy mouth the Lord Jesus, and shalt believe in thine heart that God hath raised him from the dead, thou shalt be saved.

For with the heart man believeth unto righteousness; and with the mouth confession is made unto salvation. (KJV)

Therefore, it was all well and good to decide to be born-again, but you had to go past believing to actually saying it out loud. I received confirmation of this when I was doing my daily reading of Scripture to Kechi later when I got back to her bedside. I was still on Acts of the Apostles. I was at the story in Acts 19, verses 13-17 of the seven sons of Sceva, rogue exorcists who were casting out demons in the name of "Jesus whom Paul preacheth". The demon said to them,

"Jesus I know, and Paul I know; but who are ye?" (KJV)

Mike needed a heavenly ID card that would separate him unto the kingdom of God and which could only come from obeying the injunction to get saved. I prayed for God to take authority and give me the opportunity to lead him through the prayer.

Kechi's temperature came down to 37.6 degrees before we left for the night and I was convinced that it would come down to normal before her surgery.

As Mike and I were praying the following morning, I got the prompting to ask him if he was ready to be born again and he said yes. I read Romans 10:8-10 to him and led him through the prayer of salvation as best as I knew how, with the help of the Holy Spirit. After that, I then went on to pray for him. I realized of course, what a momentous moment this was, but I dared not shout and jump for joy because I knew my husband very well, and I knew he still was not ready for a lot of things. I would just take things one step at a time, as the Spirit led. Inside though, I was leaping for joy.

Kechi had been taken into surgery by the time we got to the hospital. The sister on duty, Lungi, gave us a rundown of what had been done when they brought her back. They had finally started grafting and had done a patch on her upper arm. They also did some debridement on her leg. Some skin was taken from her inner right thigh for the grafting. This made her thigh the "donor site". (I was going to become very familiar with that term.)

We thanked God for the new direction in her healing, and Mike told Kechi that he gave his life to Jesus and that we would all start worshipping God together at the church in Aba when we went home. Mike then prayed for the first time as the head of the family and reminded God that he was now His son.

This was music to my ears. My daughters and I had prayed for so long for the day that Mike would accept Jesus as his Lord and Savior. At the start of every new year we prayed that that would be the year of Mike's salvation. It was enough for me that Mike was saved; that it took the accident for it to happen was something that only God could fathom and not for me to question. I could only accept it and bow down in adoration and praise.

Ike and Mike had earlier arranged to go to the bank and exchange Mike's dollars for rand, and by the afternoon visit, they were still not back. I called Mike and asked him to meet me at the hospital, only for me to spend the whole visiting hour in the waiting room because Kechi's dressings were being changed. As she had dressings on her whole body, this was always a long process.

Mike came in as I was begging to see Kechi even if for five minutes. Lungi was on duty and she agreed. When Mike asked whether the skin on Kechi's face was healing, Lungi pulled back the dressing on Kechi's upper lip to show us the fresh new skin growing there. We were encouraged when we saw the new skin, as we thought her whole face would heal that way. We would later learn that the upper lip was the only place on her face that would have that smooth soft skin. The other burns on her face were very deep and would form keloids.

In retrospect, it may have been silly to worry about her face when her life was at stake, but Kechi was so beautiful I could not help thinking ahead and pray that a scarred face was not one of the things she would have to deal with in the future.

Layi, during one of her visits had told me that she likened Kechi to Naaman from the bible story, and every surgery she went in for was like when he dipped his body into the river. She believed that like Naaman whose leprosy was fully cured when he dipped his body into the river for the last time, her body would also be fully restored at the end of the last surgery and also like Naaman, she will have the skin of a new born baby, fresh and perfect.

I liked that analogy.

The next visit was just an hour away, so we decided to wait. The last visit was more of the same. She was really out of it and so we talked to her, I sang, and we both prayed for her before leaving for the day. For some reason, that day had been a very tiring day and by the end of it, my muscles were tense. Mike tried to massage my shoulders but he really had no clue what to do. I made a mental note to buy some liniment the next day.

After we got ready for bed, I tried as gently as possible to tell Mike that we should read the scriptures as much as we could, but he did not respond, and I left the matter alone. Mike would need to know that his journey into Christianity was just starting, but I had to be patient because he had a lot of ground to cover.

I remember that when I left the Grail Movement to become a Christian, my Dad told everyone to leave me alone, and not inundate me with advice or lectures; the Holy Spirit would lead me. And He did. It was a learning experience I needed to go through and I was going to afford Mike the same courtesy.

One of the parents from the Loyola Jesuit College, Port Harcourt Parent/Teacher Association, Ada, called to tell me that that the Port Harcourt parents were praying for Kechi and holding on to her as a symbol of hope. This moved me deeply.

Then Ngozi Nnaji called, my friend from Aba, whose daughter, Chidera, had also been in the ill-fated Sosoliso flight. I told her that I had been praying for her and for all the other parents and she told me that she was fine. She went on to say that she knew that God was going to use Kechi to console her and all the other parents that lost their children on that day.

After Ngozi's call, I just lost it. I wept until I could not weep any more. Ngozi, who had lost her beautiful girl, was calling to encourage me to keep trusting God for Kechi's full recovery. Not only that, she told me that she and her family were also praying for Kechi. This was one more example of the selflessness I was seeing so much of since the accident.

People actually living Christianity!

I felt very blessed to be part of the group of people that called themselves followers of Christ. At this point, I knew that the prayers being said all over the world were the reason that Kechi was still alive and I was very grateful whenever anyone said they were praying for her. That was the reason I was praying without ceasing wherever I was, whatever I was doing. I was praying until prayer became a part of me.

I woke up the next day to the sound of Mike sneezing, coughing, and sniffling. He seemed to have caught a chill and he was not happy. He was wandering about the room, taking his supplements and grumbling about having a cold. After he had settled down a bit, I knelt down and began to give praises to God, a prelude to my morning prayers. Mike did not join me until I started to pray. That was when he got down from the bed to pray with me. We also included a prayer of healing for him.

Mike then recalled a dream he had about a garden full of snakes and how he got the idea of breeding eagles to prey on the snakes. I did not like the snake idea, and so I got down on my knees once again and we began to pray against evil spiritual attacks on Kechi. Mike ended the prayer by adding that because we wished no evil on others, no evil would ever come near us.

Kechi was stable and her vital signs were normal. The first thing we noticed was that her face was now completely bandaged. The swelling of her shoulders were considerably reduced, and the burns on her upper chest had begun to heal. Kechi had also lost weight, but the sisters had warned me that she would lose a lot of weight so I was not very surprised.

Mike was reading a book, "The Warrior" by Francine Rivers, out loud to Kechi and I just sat quietly, writing in my journal. Before we left, I told Kechi that a friend of hers, Subomi Aluko, had called the hotel earlier that day to ask after her.

We decided that Mike would stay out of Kechi's room until his cold cleared because we could not take the risk of Kechi picking up a new infection.

By that afternoon, I started to feel poorly myself but I knew there was no way my health could break down now. No way! I was not very happy with Mike for being ill, even if it was not his fault. I knew I was being irrational, but I did not care. I had my hands full with Kechi and I did not need to nurse Mike right then. And, like most men, my husband always turned back into a needy little boy whenever he was ill.

Uloma called just then and I was venting on her when she reminded me that even if I could not cope, God could, and I should just tell Him I could not do it alone and hand everything over to Him. I calmed down, took a deep breath and did what she asked.

We called all the Nigerians we knew in Johannesburg to ask for malaria medication, since we knew from experience that Mike's malaria presented first as cold and weakness. Luckily, Lanre had some and promised to bring some for Mike that night.

I visited Kechi alone that afternoon and her temperature was slightly high, but everything else was fine. I told her again that Subomi called and she moved her head a bit. The sister on duty came in to tell me that when she used mouthwash on Kechi that morning, she brought out her tongue and licked her lips! I was thrilled.

Later that night, Sister Magdalene told me that whenever they turned Kechi, which they had to do from time to time to prevent bed sores, she always tried to push away their hands, which meant that she was feeling pain. I noticed that she was bleeding, or oozing, as they called it, from her right hand. They had already called for the doctor to take a look. Dr. Nel was going on vacation, and his partner, Dr. Edwards was going to take over from him. By the time I left, the doctor had not arrived. Mike meanwhile, had been talking to Dr. Opolot, an East African physician, who sometimes took over from Dr. Pahad.

Dr. Opolot brought Mike down to earth on some of his expectations. Mike had actually hoped that by the time he left on Sunday, Kechi would be able to see him and talk to him. The doctor told him that Kechi was likely to be on the respirator for another three weeks. That was what I expected, but Mike was crushed.

When Lanre came with Fansidar and Panadol and Mike finally started the treatment, I was relieved. But by then, I knew that it was just the grace of God keeping me upright because I was definitely not feeling well. I took vitamins and Panadol and prayed for strength.

CHAPTER TWELVE

"For the weapons of our warfare are not carnal, but mighty through God to the pulling down of strong holds;"
2 Cor 10 : 4 (KJV)

It was day twenty-four of the plane crash and Mike was feeling better, but we felt that he should still hold off visiting Kechi until later that evening.

Kechi was stable. I read to her and also talked to her until the doctor came to examine her. When he came out, he sought me out in the waiting room to tell me basically the same thing he had told Mike the previous day she was doing well and at this time he expected her to make a full recovery. Plastic surgery could come later, but for now, he was happy with her progress. He also said that she had three things in her favor: Firstly, she was young, secondly she was strong and healthy, and thirdly she had a very supportive family. This was great news and meant that we had finally turned a corner. For the doctor to say that he was expecting a full recovery was a milestone and I went back to the hotel with a spring in my steps.

It was really, really hard, seeing Kechi lying there on the bed, all bandaged up from head to toe, but I thanked God for her life and for her being in Milpark Hospital. I thanked God for Shell. I thanked God that everyone He wanted to use made themselves available to Him. I just wanted to praise God continually forever and ever and unto eternity. The fact of the miracle of her life made it easier to go from day to day.

Just then I remembered that Mike had had another dream the previous night. He had this cloak protecting him from everything evil. Suddenly the cloak was snatched away from him by someone and when he gave chase, the ground opened up in front of the fleeing thief, and he fell in. Mike swooped down and grabbed the cloak before the ground closed back up and then he put the cloak back around himself.

I was no Joseph, interpreter of dreams, but it was pretty clear to me. Mike had just gone from "the world" into God's marvelous light. The evil one was not happy and would use every means at his disposal to return things to status quo.

To me, the cloak was the mantle of protection that Jesus had placed on Mike. Mike's doubts had caused his tenuous hold on Jesus to slip and Satan pounced. When Mike moved to regain the protection, God saw his heart and caused the enemy to be swallowed up so that Mike was able to once more grasp the mantle.

What a merciful God!

Ike was going to Nigeria soon, so I went with him to Sandton Mall to get some toys for Chizitara. We got back a little after visiting time, and Mike was already at the hospital. I noticed at once that he was looking flustered and distracted as a sister tried to explain something to him. It turned out that the sister was explaining about a new trial drug to be administered to Kechi. She had given Mike a consent form to sign which indemnified the hospital against any adverse effects arising from the drug. It was a trial antibiotic that had been used quite successfully in burns patients right there in Milpark. Mike did not like the idea of an experimental drug being administered to Kechi, but I had the conviction that God was firmly in control and there was no treatment of Kechi that did not have His permission. If it was going to harm her, He would simply not allow it. I tried to convey this to Mike and to remind him that God was in charge and in control.

Mike called Hilda to seek her opinion of the drug and she and the sister on duty did their best to reassure Mike that the antibiotic had been used with great success.

Ifeoma and Ody came in the evening, bringing jollof rice for us. This was a life saver, because we were fed up with the hotel food.

God, as far as I was concerned, sent Brother Dotun to visit us just before the night visit. The Holy Spirit guided him on what to say to Mike concerning fear. He ministered with 2 Cor 10 : 4-6 and explained that we were not battling with carnal weapons and we should learn to bring every thought into captivity. If not, the devil would hold sway and we would begin to entertain and build upon thoughts that may not even have been our own to start with.

This turned out to be exactly what Mike needed to hear and from someone other than me. The hand of God was everywhere and in everything, and I just bowed my head and gave thanks.

After prayers and scripture reading (we were now in John), Ulo called and we discussed her son's return to school. He was in Kechi's school, Loyola Jesuit College. She said that one of the members of our church had asked her to consider changing schools for him, his reasoning being that the children that died in the plane crash died a violent death and their spirits might roam the school. I told Ulo that I totally disagreed with that. I refused to believe that any of those kids was outside the loving arms of Christ at that moment. No way! I told her that Jesus had said, "suffer little children to come unto Him" and as far as I was concerned, they were with Him. Ulo also said that early reports coming in from the crash investigation indicated pilot error. Of course, I thought, they would blame the man that was dead and unable to defend himself. How convenient!

All the talk of the children had brought down my mood. They were constantly on my mind and when I dwelt too much on them, if they had been in pain, scared etc. before they died, it got too painful. I kept thinking of Toke and Chinenye, Kechi's friends. Then I started to think of the day Kechi would have to be told the whole truth about the crash and I quailed inside. What a burden she would have to bear! All that consoled me was my unshakable belief that God was in control and when that day came, He would still be in control. I was convinced that for the past twenty four days of her lying still, the Holy Spirit was ministering eternal things to her, preparing her for the work ahead, equipping her and strengthening her for her future responsibilities.

When we went in to see Kechi, we were told that Dr. Edwards, who was Dr. Nel's partner and said to be the best plastic surgeon in Milpark Hospital, had been in to see Kechi and had asked them to change all the dressings except the one on the left arm that was grafted. He would examine the graft in the theater the next day. Kechi's temperature and her blood pressure had been fluctuating all day, as if there was a battle raging inside her between the resistant bacteria and the new antibiotics that they started administering by 10.00pm the previous night.

Betty and her friends, Kathryn and Cherie, came by and prayed with Mike and I and then Betty took me to the hair salon to retouch my hair.

I was away for the afternoon visit, so Mike went alone. At the evening visit, we were told that her leg wounds still had sepsis on them. Her hands were clean, though. I prayed that they would debride her legs the next day in the OR, and that the grafting in her arm would have "taken" when they exposed it the next day, but I was really happy that the hands were free from sepsis. The ups and downs were very draining, but one had to just grab the little triumphs and hang onto them to mitigate the low points when they came. I was at that moment holding onto the fact that her hands were clean, that helped me to deal with the worry about her legs.

Mike, however, was a different story. He was extremely distressed about the sepsis on Kechi's legs. He became distracted and appeared confused as he visibly tried to pull himself together.

I was very worried about him and went off to pray quietly for God to give me the right words to minister to him.

I took Mike to the waiting room and reminded him of God's promises concerning Kechi. I reminded him of how far God had brought Kechi and how blessed we were. I reminded him of how essential it was that we let go of all our feeble attempts to control things and learn to rely entirely on God, and that by worrying we were being disrespectful and disobedient and the bible clearly stated that by worrying we cannot add even a second to our lives, so why bother?

I reminded him that he should take things one step at a time because he would discover that learning to leave things to God was going to be one of the most difficult things he could ever do, but that it was essential that he started to put it into practice because that was the will of God.

I must have made some inroads because he took a deep breath and said he was going to start trying. I further encouraged him by telling him that faith was very much like a muscle, the more one used it, the stronger it would get. He wanted to know how one could start to learn to have faith and I told him that the first step was trusting God. When he prayed next time, he should imagine a bucket, call all his concerns by name, and as he called each one, he should put it in the bucket. When he was done, he should place the bucket at God's feet, tell Him that he trusted God to take care of all his problems, and then leave them there. I told him that if he continued to worry about them after that, it would be as if he went back to God, told Him that he could do a better job by himself, and then carried the bucket away from God. I went on in this vein for a while until Mike seemed calmer.

We went back to Kechi's room and stayed until it was time to pray and leave. Later that night, I wrote a letter to the principal of Kechi's school, Fr. Peter and brought him up to date on Kechi's condition. I also told him that Kechi would not be returning to school that term. At that point I was naively thinking that Kechi may be able to return to school and graduate with her classmates. How wrong I was!

Kechi was very responsive the next day. Dr. Edwards had already been in to examine the grafting and said it appeared to be holding. He was going to do another grafting the next day and clean all the other wounds. I spent a lot of time that morning just talking to Kechi, reassuring her that she was going to be fine and telling her how much we loved her. Then I got a thrill when I said that Jesus loved her very much and she nodded. She was also fluttering her eyelids and moving her head from side to side. When I told her we were leaving, she got agitated and the ventilator started beeping. I calmed her down and stayed with her until she stopped being restless. I dragged Mike off with me to 4Ways Mall, which was close by.

R300 for transportation! South Africa is expensive!

We found a book store and Mike was thrilled to find several books by his favorite western novels author, Louis Lamour. I found quite a collection of Georgette Heyer novels.

I remembered Nora Roberts was one of Kechi's favorite authors and bought Black Rose to read to her.

Mom called when we got back to the hospital and said that my sisters were trying to stop her from coming until February when,

by God's grace, Kechi would look better and may be off the ventilator.

I tried to explain that maybe seeing Kechi might be more than she would be able to handle at that time. She insisted that she could handle anything and she was coming soon. I was just grateful for the company, especially since Mike was leaving soon and did not spend too much time trying to dissuade her. It was so much better having someone else to talk to.

I started reading the Nora Roberts novel to Kechi during our evening visit. At the end of the visit, I asked Mike to pray. He demurred at first, but I insisted, and he launched into this lovely prayer that came straight from his heart, and went straight up to heaven.

Bother Dotun came and pick us up as earlier agreed and we went to his home for a late lunch. Their home was very lovely and the lunch was delicious. We shared the word of God for a while and then I left the men talking on the dining table, and went to the living room to be with Brother Dotun's wife.

We were a few minutes late for the night visit and this time, Mike read the novel to Kechi. We rounded off the visit with the reading of one of my favorite psalms, Psalm 91, and then prayed for a successful surgery.

CHAPTER THIRTEEN

"Eye hath not seen, nor ear heard, neither have entered into the heart of man, the things which God hath prepared for them that love him."
1 Cor 2 : 9 (KJV)

It was exactly twenty eight days after the plane crash and our morning devotions that day consisted more of worship than any other thing and a firm commitment to wait upon the Lord for whatever work He had for us. When we got to the hospital, Kechi had already been wheeled off to surgery. We ran into Marlee's mom and she was crying. Apparently, the doctors had attempted to stitch Marlee's tongue but they doubted that the stitches would hold because she was really too young to stop herself from moving it around a lot so it could heal. If it did not heal, they said they might have to eventually cut off a part of her tongue. This was hard news for any parent to hear, so we comforted her as much as we could and assured her that Marlee would be in our prayers.

When Kechi got out of surgery, we learnt that skin was taken from her stomach to graft onto her right thigh which had the deepest wound. All the dressings were changed apart from the ones on her face. Dr. Edwards informed us that he had seen all the wounds and all of them seemed to be healing well. Then he went on to give us the most shocking news so far. He had been the plastic surgeon on duty the day Kechi was admitted and had in fact examined her the day she came in. He had gone on vacation the next day and had not expected that Kechi would still be there upon his return. In other words, her injuries were so bad he was convinced that she would not survive them! To say that we were shocked would be an understatement. This fully brought home to us the enormity of God's miracle concerning Kechi. When the doctors had told Mike that they had given Kechi a 30% chance of survival when she came in, somehow I did not fully grasp it all. This now was a testimony of how critical her condition was when we came to South Africa. Suddenly, opened up to us was the vastness, the extent, the enormity of God's grace and His mercy.

He practically raised Kechi from the dead!

I was so convinced of this. How else was it that in spite of the seriousness of her prognosis when she came to South Africa, all her internal organs were fine? (When her last x-rays came back, her lungs were so clear that the nurse called them "super lungs"). Her kidneys were functioning well, she did not break any bones. In fact, her physicians were very satisfied with her internal organs and their concentration was on controlling infection.

Dr. Edwards stressed that Kechi was in no way out of the woods yet and was in fact still in very critical condition, but her wounds were healing and the infections were under control. He also said that because Kechi had 60% burns, that left him with 40% of her skin from which to harvest for grafting, and he would harvest skin, allow the donor site to heal, and harvest it again. He thought that Kechi would need up to ten or more skin grafts.

It turned out to be more than double that!

Since Kechi was not South African, cadaver skin could not be used, according to their law. Mike asked if he could donate his skin and the doctor said that Mike's skin would only last for about twenty days on Kechi before her body rejected it. He then told us to just be prepared for a long stay but that he believed that she would pull through. This was a lot to absorb so we left Kechi as the nurses were still connecting tubes and connecting the warming machine to her bed. He temperature had dropped to below 34 degrees as a result of the frigid temperature of the OR which was that way because very cold temperatures inhibit the growth of germs on the exposed wounds.

When we visited Kechi later, her temperature was 36.7 but she was still under the effects of anesthesia and was sound asleep. We sat and prayed and thanked God for her life and healing. Later that night, she was opening and closing her right eye. We were not sure if she could see us but we talked to her anyway. Mike told her that he was leaving the next day but he would be back in two weeks or less.

The next day, since Mike's flight was at 2pm, we went to the hospital for his last visit. Kechi was a little aware and we mostly prayed and then I sang to her, but I spent much of the time just gazing at this miracle that was my daughter and marveling anew about God's mercies. It was beyond anything I could possibly imagine. Within me I was singing,

"My eyes have seen My ears have heard
My mouth will talk about the goodness of God"

This time last month, I was just plodding along, not imagining what God was going to do in our lives. I just kept glorifying His name over and over again. Then I remembered the parents that were in mourning and my heart bled again for them. In the two hours that I thought Kechi was dead, the feeling of helplessness almost crushed me. Nothing seemed real. But I knew that God was more than able to bring comfort to their souls.

Lanre came in as we prayed and joined in and then we left for the airport. Mike checked in, we said our goodbyes, and Lanre dropped me off in the hotel.

When I got back to the hospital for the evening visit, the sisters were excited. They had changed Kechi's face dressings and said she was healing very well and they wished I had been there to see it. They also said that she was a very pretty girl, and I was thinking that if they could see that she was pretty, then her skin must have been healing nice and smoothly. I was ecstatic and proceeded to whip out her picture from my purse. I started to praise God, He Who makes everything beautiful in His time. Maybe it was petty of me, in view of the great miracles we had already seen, to want her face to be unmarred. But Kechi was such a beautiful girl and I just wanted her to look like she did before the plane crash.

I sat down and started to read to her, (we had just started on Romans), then I prayed and went back to my now lonely hotel room.

That night, the sister told me that the plastic surgeon had been in to see Kechi and had said that the wounds should be exposed and then dressed the following day. She also told me that Dr. Edwards, who was the Head of Plastics, was very meticulous and fussy in his work, and expected the same out of everyone else; and so when the patient was his, everyone was on their toes. Wasn't it just like God, to provide the best for His own?

The sister, whose name I later learnt was Magdalene, also told me that the physician had discontinued the continuous sedation, and ordered that it should only be used when necessary.

In effect, Kechi was about to start to wake up. She was still on morphine, though. I got a glimpse of what lay ahead when I told Kechi that I had to go that night. She scrunched her lips up, her eyelids flickered, there were spasms in her shoulders and she became generally agitated. I immediately told her that I would stay and she calmed down. By the time I left, Kechi was still shuddering as if she was cold and I asked if the sedative was addictive and the spasms withdrawal symptoms. The sister said no, but I had my doubts. It seemed to me that Kechi was likely to get very restless now that she was about to wake up. I handed the next stage over to God and asked for His help, because I felt I was going to need it.

During the next visit, Kechi's pulse was 160/min and the nurse said it has been up to 170/min. When I started talking to her, it came down to 112/min. The sister said that maybe Kechi had thought that I was going home with Mike.

The blood tests and all other tests were scheduled for the next day. In my prayers, I ask God for negative results on "bugs", as they referred to infectious bacteria in the hospital. When I got to Kechi's room, the sister on duty was a bit flustered because Kechi's pulse rate was climbing steadily. When I asked why, she said that it was because Kechi was more active. I also discovered that Kechi was not on continuous morphine, on doctor's orders. It was only to be administered as needed. Kechi was also breathing on her own, with the machine as backup. She was taking ten breaths a minute, which was considered normal for a person in repose. I was not at all sure that the girl should be made to handle all these new developments at once. I made a mental note to ask to see the physician.

Meanwhile, Kechi was 100% aware that I was there. She nodded yes and shook her head no to my questions. I asked her if she was aware that she was in a hospital and she nodded. I then asked if she wanted me to sing to her and she nodded again. So I proceeded to sing my heart out, until she started to get agitated, moving her arms. The nurse told me to ask her if she was in pain and she nodded. They gave her a shot and after about five minutes I asked if she was still in pain, she shook her head no. I started to tell her all over again about why she is in hospital, told her about the bandages all over her body, that we had been in the hospital for over a month and that she was healing nicely. She drifted off after a while. Her pulse and temperature were a bit high, but the nurse said that it was because she was now a little more mobile and therefore, restless.

When Mike called, I gave him an update and he was concerned that Kechi was breathing by herself. I reassured him that that she was still on the respirator but that it was now a back up to take up the slack if she should fail to breathe.

All in all, I had peace in my spirit because I was sure God was still in control. I wanted to buy Christian music and novels for Kechi now that she was waking up. I called Betty and she said she would come by at 1.30pm to take me to Rhema Bookshop which Layi said would have all I need.

The Rhema Church in Randburg was huge place and the bookshop was well stocked. I bought several CDs by Don Moen and other artists and two Christian fiction novels for both of us. Betty dropped me off in time for the 4.00pm visit.

Kechi was awake when I got there. By awake, I meant that though her eyes were still firmly shut, she responded to questions I asked her by nodding or shaking her head. But this time when I asked if she wanted me to sing, she shook her head no, so I just talked to her instead. I told her how everyone sent their love to her, how Aunty Ulo called and sent love from Kechi's friends from school, from Sister Chika and Fr. Marc. But maybe I should not have mentioned school because her heart rate, already high, went up to 180/min. The sister went to the machine to check if that was really Kechi's pulse rate or if the machine was malfunctioning! I could see that they were worried. They gave her morphine because she nodded yes when I asked if she was in pain. They also gave her a muscle relaxant. I stayed with her until she drifted off. Her pulse rate was still fluctuating between 165 and 175 and the doctor was paged and he asked that Kechi be given fluids before he came. The sister explained that usually when the pulse was that high, it meant that there was not enough blood going to the heart and so the heart starts to overcompensate by pumping faster, so they add extra fluids to aid the blood flow. I just went off to the corner and began to pray. I knew that God was in control and I forced myself to stop going by what I was seeing in front of me. I prayed for God to bring enlightenment to the doctor so that he will make the right decision. I stayed way past visiting time to see if the pulse would go down, but it did not, so, trusting in God, I left.

I decided not to go to the hotel, but to get something to eat from the coffee shop, and wait until the next visiting period. I was reading this fantastic book, "When God doesn't make sense", by Dr. James Dobson. The title apart, this was a powerful faith- building book. I was sitting engrossed when the Nigerian Ambassador to South Africa walked in with his wife, Kehinde. I went into Kechi's room with Kehinde. The doctor had prescribed something to bring down the rapid heart rate.

Sister Magdalene told me that she believed that Kechi was not properly sedated before being moved around by those washing her and was therefore in a lot of pain, leading to the accelerated pulse. I agreed with her, although I still thought that I should probably not have mentioned her school, which must have reminded her of the crash, her friends, and gotten her worked up. Her pulse rate was now in the 130s and everything appeared to be fine except the temperature, which was 38.1 ° and climbing. Magdalene had a fan brought in as she did not want Kechi's temperature to go higher than that. The Ambassador and his wife left soon after and I thanked them so much for their kindness.

I put on one of the Don Moen CDs, sang along, and then prayed for Kechi before leaving. I surrendered everything to God. My prayer pattern was gradually changing. I no longer asked God to take control, because He had never let go of the control. Even to ask for healing appeared presumptuous because He was already doing that with no help from me. All He asked was that I should trust and believe in Him and have faith that He would do what He promised. I was learning to exercise my faith and it was tested earlier today as I fought not to give in to panic and to trust in Him.

I thought I did pretty okay in dealing with the situation only to get into the hotel room and after getting into bed, fell prey to heart palpitations. They lasted for more than quite a while. I did not time them but when they did not stop, I went on to do other things, drank coffee (which was the worst thing to do), did some reading, before my heart settled down. I could see that I still had a lot of work ahead in exercising my "faith muscle", because clearly my anxiety manifested in palpitations of which stress was a major cause. I prayed for forgiveness for not fully trusting God to be in charge of the situation.

Mom and Dad called me just before I dropped off to give me the details of Mike's Holy Ghost baptism. Honestly, God is mighty. Mike born again, baptized in the Holy Spirit! Was I dreaming? We were richly blessed indeed.

Nkechi and her boys were the last to call that night and I spoke to the boys one by one, assuring them that Kechi was going to be all right.

CHAPTER FOURTEEN

"I have blotted out, as a thick cloud, thy transgressions, and, as a cloud, thy sins: return to me, for I have redeemed thee."
Isaiah 44 : 22 (KJV)

I was beset by all kinds of troubling dreams and I knew that the devil wanted to destabilize me and shake my faith. I woke up and sternly admonished him to keep away from me. My morning devotion consisted of mostly worship and I was led to Isaiah 44 and 45 for bible reading. I had prayed for forgiveness the previous night for lack of faith and I found it interesting that Isaiah 44 and verse 22 states clearly that He has blotted out my transgressions! I bowed my head in gratitude for answered prayer.

But I was admonished quite thoroughly in Isaiah 45 and verses 9-11. It goes thus:

"Woe to him who quarrels with His Maker, to him who is but a potsherd among the potsherds on the ground.
Does the clay say to the potter, 'What are you making?' Does your work say, 'He has no hands'?
Woe to him who says to his father, 'What have you begotten?'
Or to his mother,
'What have you brought to birth?' "This is what the Lord says
The Holy One of Israel, and its Maker: Concerning things to come,
Do you question me about my children,
Or give Me orders about the work of My hands?"

I thought, "Ouch"!

But then I remembered that it says in Hebrews 12 that the Lord disciplines those He loves. Once again I marveled at the fact that the spirit of God was actually 'speaking' to me through the Word of God. Several places I had been brought to by the inner promptings of the Holy Spirit were places in my bible I had never read before.

I came to the conclusion that my prayer pattern had to change; I had to stop making demands or supplications because God had everything under control. I would now just give thanks, and have faith in Him and trust Him, and strive to deepen my relationship with Him by delving deep into His Word.

Having made this momentous decision, I called Mike and was very happy that he had arrived safely in Port Harcourt. I also called and spoke to Tara, then left for the hospital.

Kechi's temperature was still at 38.1 degrees. It did not appear to have gone down throughout the night. This was about to bother me until the nurse made a discovery that changed everything for me.

She noticed that Kechi's right eye was open and she asked

Kechi, 'Can you see me?'

Kechi nodded. I quickly raced over to that side of the bed and asked Kechi if she could see me. She nodded. Then she focused her eye and looked right at me. To this day, I cannot describe how I felt. Kechi had been somewhere I could not reach her for 30 days and now she was looking at me and she recognized me. But I could not give in to my emotions because I knew she would be feeling disoriented and confused and so I started talking to her. I told her that she was not dreaming, she was really looking at her Mummy. I told her where she was, and that I had been with her from the first day. I told her not to try to talk and explained about the tube down her throat. I spent the whole hour just talking non-stop.

Kechi did not appear to be in pain. Each time I asked if she was hurting, she would shake her head no. The sister on duty was amazed because Kechi had not been given morphine that morning and she concluded that it may be that her body had adjusted to a certain level of pain that it could tolerate.

I made an appointment to see Dr. Schleicher, who was standing in for Dr. Opolot, the physician. He said Kechi was stable and her vital signs were fine, but they were worried about the infections. He stressed that she might not be completely free of the infection that they christened 'the super bug' until she left the ICU, since that was where she picked it up from in the first place. They would simply keep treating it whenever it became aggressive with antibiotics. This was not comforting news to me at all and it seemed to me that the sooner Kechi left the ICU, the better.

I asked about the high pulse rate of the previous day and he said that arrhythmia is caused by extreme trauma. Sometime, the heart's electrical impulses go haywire from stress, and Kechi's had been corrected with the drug that was administered to lower her heart rate and it had not occurred again.

When I went back to Kechi's room, her temperature was 38.1 and climbing. The sister had left for lunch as soon as I came in, but when the temperature got up to 38.9, I asked the assistant to call her. When she came in, it was obvious that she was not pleased to have been disturbed. She very curtly told me that Kechi would not be given anything for the temperature until the blood samples that had been taken to the lab that morning were cultured and the results obtained in five days time! This was unacceptable to me and for the first time, I lost my temper. I asked her if we were going to sit down quietly for the next five days waiting for Kechi's temperature to reach 100 degrees while we waited for the lab results. I must have gotten through to her because she went out and came back shortly with Dr. Schleicher.

The doctor said it was obvious that the infection was back and that Kechi would be put back on the antibiotics. Now that I understood that we would have to live with this infection for a while, I was not too alarmed; I was just pleased that something was going to be done to bring down the temperature. It was disturbing that if I had not made a fuss, the doctor would not have been called.

I resolved to be more attentive. I was not going to take for granted that most of the sisters were dedicated and serious, after all, they were also human beings with families and problems. Someone having a bad day may not be as attentive as she should be.

Certainly I was not pleased with the sister on duty that afternoon. She did not appear to have her mind on the job. I had noticed earlier that she touched

Kechi without gloves. Her bad mood may have had something to do with my having pointed this out. No other sister had ever touched Kechi without gloves. I prayed that she would not handle Kechi after that day because she lacked empathy for her patient.

During the evening visit, I was told that Kechi was to be moved back to her former room. The shift leader, Bernice, tried to explain that she was moved out in the first place so as not to infect Baby Marlee. She said that the other two patients have the same bug anyway. It seemed to me that this meant that Kechi could get re-infected also. Nothing she said convinced me that this was a good decision, but I resolved to speak with the matron the following morning. And anyhow, Kechi did get re-infected in isolation, anyway. I decided that since God was in control, I would leave it up to Him. This was a bit hard because of the events of the day - the doctor's information, Kechi's re-infection, her spiking temperature. I prayed for the strength to hand it all over to God and leave it there.

I was having a bit of a letdown because the morning had started so well, with Kechi opening her eyes for the first time since the accident and actually recognizing me. We were warned of ups and downs, and I refused to give in to despair. That was the devil's snare, and I was not going to fall into it.

There was some drama in the later part of the visit, as Kechi kept yawning. Then she started heaving and threw up. She was suctioned and there was quite a bit of vomit. After she was cleaned up, she appeared to be a lot more relaxed and her temperature started to go down. She dropped off to sleep before I left. This was definitely a new phase - Kechi being awake.

The following morning, I woke with a heavy burden to pray for a miraculous healing for Kechi's skin. I prostrated myself before God and begged Him to astound the doctors. Yes, I had decided to change my prayer pattern from petition to thanksgiving, but after getting a good look at Kechi's body the previous night, when they exposed her in order to bring down her temperature, something gave way inside me. Not my faith in God for a complete healing, but a mother's anguish for the suffering of her child. I fell before God and begged for another miracle for my child- the restoration of her skin.

❖

Betty came to the hotel and picked me up for breakfast at Wimpy's before going to the hospital. She wanted to see Kechi. Luckily, Kechi was awake and I reminded her of who Betty was and the family connection. We stayed with her for the whole hour and then Betty dropped me off at the hotel. Kechi was still stable, her temperature had dropped to 37.9 and she was not in pain. She was a bit drowsy, though, as she had received a shot of morphine just before our visit.

When I got back for the afternoon visit, Layi was waiting for me and we went in together to see Kechi. As I spoke to her, she began to heave again and I asked if she was okay. She shook her head no so I called her nurse. He tried to suction her but nothing came out so he drained her stomach with a syringe-like thing attached to the tube in her mouth. In response to my questions, he explained that they were going to continue to drain her stomach over the course of that day and then start to feed her through the tube in her mouth from the next day. Up to that moment, her only sustenance was the IV. Also, Kechi was now breathing by herself; the lung machine was now a back up, though it still provided the oxygen she needed. This was good news.

During the night visit, Kechi's eyes were open, but she did not seem to be very alert. I asked if she had just got her morphine shot and the sister said her last shot had been at 3pm. I asked the usual 'are you in pain?' question and she shook her head no. Then her eyes opened wider and she began to retch. I called the attention of the sister who said that that there was a pipe in her stomach draining her stomach contents into a bag and this should take care of the vomit. But she also suctioned Kechi's lungs, in case she had fluid making her feel like coughing. After a while, Kechi calmed down and nodded yes when I asked if she was feeling okay.

I sang worship songs along with the Don Moen CDs and then I prayed.

I talked to Kechi and reassured her of God's love and my continuous presence in South Africa, as long as she was there. Then I took my leave and told her I would be back in the morning.

Leaving my daughter while she was wide-awake was one of the hardest things I had ever done.

Reading the book of Romans was such a revelation to me of the Word of God being so real. I was getting a new understanding of God's will through His Word and I was filled with joy. I left for the hospital thinking that Mike and I should buy a laptop for Kechi. It would keep her busy during recuperation and she would be able to play her games and watch her DVDs on it. I was not afraid to plan ahead because I trusted God.

When I saw Kechi, I could sense that all was not well. She was awake but very still. I asked if she was okay and she shook her head no. I asked if she was in pain and she nodded. I sent for the nurse and he said he had just given her a shot of morphine because he had just turned her. (They turned her from one side to the other regularly in order to prevent bed sores). I told her to remain calm because the drug would soon kick in. After a few minutes, I asked if she was still in pain and she shook her head no. Then she fell asleep. I put one of the Don Moen CDs on low while she slept. Her temperature was now 37.4 and her blood pressure and pulse rates were stable. She was still breathing on her own and everything appeared to be fine. The nurse assured me that for now, she appeared fine, but warned me that burn injuries were unpredictable. The doctors had stopped most of her drugs while they waited for the blood test results. The preliminary results were due the next day and the wounds would be exposed for Dr. Edwards' examination at 2pm.

I arranged for Herbert, the cab driver, to pick me up and take me to Auckland Park Mall just for a change of scene. I got a sweater and sneakers for myself because of the cold weather.

When I got back, all Kechi's wounds had been fully exposed and her body, even her face, covered with a sheet for assessment by the plastic surgeon, Dr. Edwards. Thomas, the nurse, opened her face for me to take a look. Kechi's face was always heavily bandaged so I was very happy to see it exposed. The healing seemed to be going well, and though the skin was very raw and red, I could still see my baby's face. I did not ask to see the other wounds, though. Thomas said they were healing, though there were still small patches of sepsis which would be removed at the next surgery.

After the examination, Dr. Edward said he was satisfied with the grafts, they were holding up well and he was going to harvest skin from her back to cover some of the wounds the following week. He was happy with her healing and this was great news for me. Kechi was sedated for the examination so I just read scripture aloud to her and then left so that they could bandage her wounds again.

That night, Kechi started to retch again and nodded yes when I asked if she wanted to throw up. The sister came in and suctioned her lungs, but she was still retching. The sister said it was irritation from the suction tube since they had stopped the drug that was causing her to throw up. I began to speak to her in a soothing voice and she slowly drifted off to sleep. Her face had been dressed again but her right cheek was left open as the healing seemed to be quite advanced there. It was wonderful to see that small patch of healed skin and it gave me hope that piece by piece, Kechi was going to be fully healed.

I noticed that Kechi has lost quite a bit of weight, but I decided that that was the least of our problems right then and went back to the hotel, full of praise and thanksgiving.

CHAPTER FIFTEEN

"But seek ye first the kingdom of God, and his righteousness; and all these things shall be added unto you." Matthew 6:33 (KJV)

I was now reading First Corinthians and being daily enriched by God's word. Kechi was awake for the morning visit, but kept drifting in and out. I assumed she must have been sedated, so I was not very worried at first, but things were about to change. The sister in charge of her was not at her usual place by Kechi's bed for most of the visiting hour and so she was absent when Kechi had apnea. This condition involved Kechi stopping to breathe for a while, at which point she had to be awakened and told to breathe. This was very distressing to watch because the ventilator was showing a flat line, meaning that there was no air going into her lungs. The nurse's aide came into the room and started to say, "Kechi, breathe", very loudly. I got agitated because her nurse was not there and the other nurse attending to the other patient in the room did not even glance over to see what was happening. I rushed over to the aide and asked her who I should call to attend to Kechi. At this point, the aide told me to calm down and to stop frightening Kechi, whose eyes were wide open, looking at me. She told me that Kechi was fine and reset the machine. Kechi gradually relaxed. I got myself together and as calmly as I could, I told Kechi to continue breathing. I thought the whole idea of her still being hooked up to the machine was so that it would kick in automatically in situations like this and spare the patient the trauma of gasping for breath. I decided to speak with someone in charge.

In the afternoon, Kechi was stable, although I noticed that her temperature was inching up again. She continued to drift in and out, appeared weak and lethargic, just barely managing to nod in response to my questions.

By the night visit, Kechi's pulse rate had gone way up to 160. This alarmed me, and the sister, Lyn, said she had informed the shift leader about it and had been asked to give Kechi extra fluids. I began to speak to Kechi, asking her to calm down and relax.

Kechi's pulse remained high for the whole hour of my visit and I spoke to the shift leader about it. She replied by telling me that Kechi was young, she had a temperature, and they were giving her fluids. I did not understand what this meant and did not like her attitude. I asked her to call the doctor. She said that even if they called the doctor, he would only say that they should watch her for now. I swallowed my irritation because these are the people who were watching over my girl when I had to leave, and I did not see the sense in antagonizing them. I asked her as humbly as I could to please keep an eye on Kechi and she said she would.

As I was leaving, I was thinking that it just brought home to me the fact that I could not trust in man at all. I could only trust in God to look after Kechi. The medical staff was great and all, but they were not personally involved. They were just doing their jobs to the best of their abilities. If the patient recovered, fine. If the patient died, they had seen it before. This realization made me bow my head and pray beside Kechi's bed. I told God that He knew what the situation was and that although I knew that He had said that Kechi's recovery would be slow, He should not be angry with me for asking for specific healing for Kechi. I was not telling Him what to do, (He had already chastised me for that) but my request flowed from the heart of an anguished mother seeing her child suffer.

I told Him that although to our own understanding, the fact that He has made all these arrangements for Kechi was to facilitate her healing, I recognized that He might still, if it was His will, call her home to Him. I assured Him (and myself) that He would still be God and I would still serve Him if that should happen. I surrendered my will to His and left Kechi in the most capable hands ever - God's.

Sister Lyn gave me a hug on my way out and told me that Kechi would be fine. I called Ulo on my way back to the hotel and our conversation was in line with the theme of letting God be God. We should just seek the kingdom of God and His righteousness, and all other things will be added on to us. Ulo and I were in agreement, and I shared my message about Isaiah 44 and 45 with her.

My prayer that night was that God should lead me to seek His kingdom through His word.

I woke up the next day with the burden of delving into God's word concerning seeking His kingdom. I read Matthew on the parables of Jesus on the kingdom of heaven and these raised questions that I gave up to the Holy Spirit to guide me through. The parables of the hidden treasure and the pearl of great value suggest that the kingdom of heaven is personal and within everyone. The parable of tares and seeds suggest something broader, based on Christ. The former suggests making effort after finding it to keep it within oneself and the other suggests that Christ chooses His own people and has prepared them for His kingdom so that at the end of the ages, His own will shine forth, and those of the enemy, the tares, will be burnt.

Mustard seed - the awareness starts small and blossoms into something large that will become useful to more than the initial possessor. The knowledge of the kingdom should be shared.

Leaven - yeast. Just a little of it makes a loaf of bread rise and feed many.

Knowledge of the kingdom cannot be hidden. It is a precious gift that comes at a great cost (selling all one's possessions to buy it being a symbol of getting something precious at great personal cost which could also be denying oneself, dying to self and the world etc.), but becomes the most precious possession of the owner. But it cannot be hidden. The mustard seed, though tiny, becomes the most beautiful plant in the garden and then grows into a mighty tree and birds come and nest. It bears fruit and gives shade and is shared to all.

The key to the kingdom of God is in His word. I prayed that the Holy Spirit should guide me into all truth in my search for His kingdom.

God sent Sister Hilda to take care of Kechi that day, and I spent a moment in thanksgiving when I realized that. Kechi was going through a particularly difficult time and she needed someone who not only did her job exceptionally, but also liked her. I thanked God again that I had trusted Him the night before to take care of Kechi and I know that was why He sent Hilda. He also knew I needed peace of mind.

Kechi was looking better the next morning. Her vital signs were fine, her temperature was down to 37.2 degrees, and her heart rate was between the range of 127-132. That was wonderful to see. Hilda said she had asked the doctor to prescribe a medicine that would calm Kechi down. Apparently after I left the previous night, her pulse rate had jumped even higher. I was thankful that Hilda used her initiative. Kechi was awake and I had the prompting to ask if she remembered the accident. She nodded yes. I told her she was injured and told her where. I also asked her if she knew where she was and she shook her head no. I told her we were in South Africa, that she had been asleep for five weeks. She just stared at me and I doubted that she understood me. I assured her that she was healing well and I had been with her from the beginning and would always be near her. I then told her to sleep and her eyes closed.

The sleep apnea happened again, but this time the machine kicked in. Hilda explained to me that the condition occurred when Kechi forgot to breathe due to very deep sleep usually caused by the morphine or other sedatives she had been given. I urged Kechi to remember to breathe and she calmed down and went back to sleep.

Dr. Edwards came in and scheduled Kechi for grafting and dressing of wounds the following Tuesday. Kechi received a lot of Nigerian visitors that evening. Layi and her husband came with a group of four men who belonged to a group called Patriots comprising of Nigerian professionals in South Africa. They came to offer their support and to pray for Kechi. I was very touched.

Betty and Cherie also visited, and Betty brought food for me, as usual. Brother Dotun and his family visited later at the hotel and we all prayed together.

Kechi was drowsy at the night visit as she had just been given a shot of morphine. Her vitals were fine and she was not in pain. It was a quiet visit because she was mostly asleep, and I just sat and prayed by her bed.

I woke late the next morning and as I lay in bed, I spent a considerable amount of time asking for God's forgiveness for being upset at two phone calls I received earlier that morning. A friend of mine called first from Nigeria and said that it seemed that there was no end to Kechi's issues. This friend has always blunt, but a little insensitive at times. She went on and on about after rejoicing that Kechi was alive, it was only to hear that she was seriously injured and needed prayers and then from there to the small issues in the hospital becoming big issues and needing even more prayers. I did not think I needed to hear that kind of thing at that time when Kechi was not out of the woods yet. It would have been more bearable if Kechi had been up and about and the hospital stay was a thing of the past. But to joke about this now to someone who was seeing Kechi every day, knowing that there were still numerous mountains to climb in the future was just unfair. I seriously failed to see the humor she saw in the situation.

Then I received a call from Ulo and she said that her son, Ugo, told her that the students of Loyola Jesuit College had more or less gotten over the deaths of the sixty students that died in the plane crash. I was angry at them, even though I knew it was irrational, because the kids had to get back to their lives and all of that. But it just hurt me so deeply that it did not take them very long to get over the deaths of their school mates, and also if Kechi had died, they would also have gotten over her death.

But even more upsetting was what I perceived as indifference on the part of the school authorities in not even bothering to enquire about Kechi's welfare since the accident. The president of the school did not respond to the email I sent him and to the letter Mike wrote to inform the school authorities that

Kechi would not be returning to the school that term. I decided I would write to the principal, Fr. Marc and see what happened.

When I caught myself wallowing in bitterness, I got up and prayed for forgiveness and forced myself to come to the following conclusions:

1. My friend did not realize the seriousness of Kechi's condition or she would not be making light of it.
2. It was a good thing that the kids in the school could let go of their sorrow and get on with their lives.
3. I was going to write to Fr. Marc and wait for his response before I reached any conclusions. And anyway, responsibility for putting the school back together after the loss of 60 kids at the same time must be a very hard task. I would give them the benefit of the doubt.

I had done the mature, Christian thing and I could only hope that with time, my heart would be more accepting and I could fully let go of the bitterness, with God's help and His grace. I certainly did not want to be estranged from God by harboring negative emotions.

When I got to the hospital, Kechi was doing really well. Her pulse rate and blood pressure were normal and she was awake and fully aware, so I read portions of the bible for her. My Nigerian lady friend came in to visit and pray for her. We also got a visit from Ulo's boss in Microsoft, Gerald. Back at the hotel, Ifeoma and Odi also visited and as usual, Ifeoma brought food for me. We all went from there to the hospital to visit Kechi.

After they left, I noticed that Kechi was wide awake, her lips pressed tight and her upper lip quivering. I asked her if she was in pain and she nodded. I told the sister and she gave Kechi morphine and she soon relaxed, but instead of drifting off as usual after receiving her morphine, she remained wide awake, looking at me expectantly and so I decided to find out if she needed anything.

"Are you sleepy?" She shook her head.

"Are you in pain?" She shook her head.

"Do you want me to sing to you?" She shook her head.

"Do you want me to read the bible to you?" She shook her head.

"Do you want me to just talk?"

Her eyes lit up and she nodded several times.

And so I started talking to her about everything and everyone. I read her letters from her cousins; told her everyone that had called to wish her well, told her how beautiful South Africa was, told her she had slept for more than one month. Her eyes opened wide at that last piece of news and I asked her if that was not unbelievable and she nodded.

I talked and talked until she got that quivering upper lip thing again and I asked if she was in pain. She nodded and I called Hilda in.

At that time, I also noticed that Kechi's right eye was wide open. We asked her to try and close her eyes and she blinked but the right eye remained open. I became worried that her right eyelid had contracted in that position while healing. Hilda said she would keep an eye on it and also inform the plastic surgeon. She gave Kechi a muscle relaxant to help her sleep, saying that another shot of morphine so close to the dose she had barely an hour before would cause her blood pressure to drop. Kechi's lips soon stopped quivering and she dropped off to sleep, both eyelids closing properly. Thank God, the right eye seemed fine.

At the night visit, Kechi was still doing fine. Her vitals were stable and she was awake. She was now staying awake for longer periods. I kept a little distance because I had been feeling quite cold for a while and was not sure if I was getting the flu, so I did not want to take the chance of passing any germs over to Kechi. I used a mask to cover my mouth and nose and stayed within her range of vision, just not as close as I used to be. I resolved to stock up on vitamin C and orange juice and vitamins.

Hilda mentioned to me that evening that with Kechi lying for so long on her back, it would be wise to request an air mattress which will prevent her from getting bed/pressure sores. Already, the back of her head was causing some concern as there was a burn there which had developed into a pressure sore. Hilda said she wanted to put in an order for an air mattress the following morning. She also said that it should actually have been standard for long-term burn patients but was not, because of the high cost. I told her to go ahead and order it. I also made a mental note to call Mike and urge him to go Shell and see Dr. Moses and try and get a feel of whether the company was going to go all the way in terms of paying Kechi's medical bills. By now, I was getting a pretty good idea of just how much it was costing to treat Kechi at Milpark Hospital. So far, Shell was paying all bills without any reference to us and I was thanking God every day for that.

During the night visit, I noticed again that Kechi's right eye did seem to have a problem closing. I called the attention of the night nurse and shift leader and they made a note in her chart to tell her plastic surgeon the next day. Then I noticed that Kechi was doing something strange. She was methodically raising first her hands, then her legs, one at a time, several times each. I asked her, "Are you making sure that all your limbs are intact?" She nodded and just continued. After a while, I told her to also move her feet because I had been a bit concerned that they had tilted to the right, because she favored that side as she lay down. She did so a few times, and then I noticed that her lips were pressed tightly together and I asked if she was in pain. She nodded and I called the nurse. Kechi was given both morphine and Dorminicum, the muscle relaxant, and she slept off, but her right eye remained open. I called the nurse and pointed it out to her. I also ventured to ask her how she would know when Kechi was in pain. She reprimanded me gently, reminding me that they have been trained to look after trauma patients.

On my way to the hotel, Ulo called to remind me that Mom would be coming the following day and that Lanre was arranging to pick her up at the airport. I honestly have no idea what I would have done without the support system I had in South Africa. People really rallied around me when I needed help. I prayed for all of them constantly, asking God to continue to bless them richly.

CHAPTER SIXTEEN

"O LORD, rebuke me not in thine anger, neither chasten me in thy hot displeasure. Have mercy upon me, O LORD; for
I am weak: O LORD, heal me; for my bones are vexed. My soul is also sore vexed: but thou, O LORD, how long?"
Psalm 6 : 1-3 (KJV)

I was so excited that Mum was coming that I barely slept and was up and already downstairs by the time Lanre came at 5.30am. Mom was outside the arrivals section and waiting when we got there. I was very happy to see her. Lanre dropped us off in the hotel and went off to work. I thanked God every day for the concern that Lanre had for us.

Mom took a shower and rested a bit before we left for the hospital.

When Kechi looked up and saw her Grandma, she gave the first smile I had seen on her face since the plane crash.

Then she cried.

Mom could not contain herself as she took in her first sight of Kechi. Hilda led her off into the smaller waiting room and counseled her, telling her that Kechi was doing so much better. I had not really thought of what another person's reaction to Kechi lying there would be. I was so used to seeing Kechi like that, bound from head to toe in bandages, that it did not occur to me that it might be distressing for others to see her like that. Also, I never gave details when asked how Kechi was doing. I just said she was stable, fine or okay. So everyone else, apart from those that had seen her, did not know the magnitude of her wounds.

When Mom pulled herself together, she came back and became a tower of strength, talking to Kechi and reassuring her that she was going to be fine.

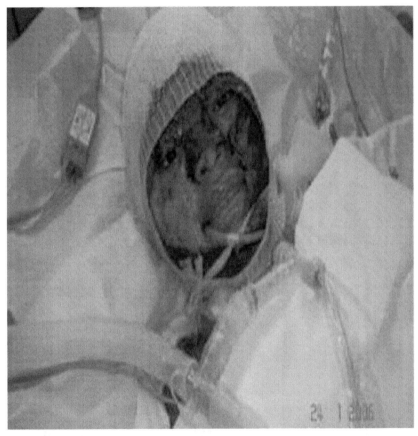

Kechi's first smile.

Kechi just fixed her eyes on Mom, nodding throughout the talk that Mom was giving. Then she raised her hands and legs like before and I joked that she was showing off for her Grandma.

Kechi's temperature was again a source of concern for me. It had inched up to 39 degrees. A high fever worried me because it was a sign of infection, the number one enemy of severe burns. Just then, Dr. Pahad walked in, back from his vacation, and I was very relieved because I trusted him. He prescribed an analgesic for Kechi and changed a few of her other medications. Kechi calmed down after a while and then dropped off to sleep.

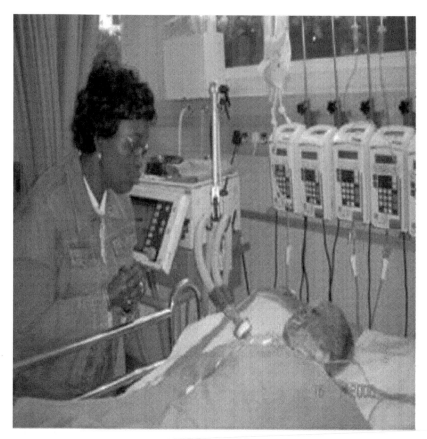

My mother's first visit.

Betty came in after the morning visit to see Mom, and we all went to Sandton to buy a SIM card and fruits for Mom. Back in time for the 4.00pm visit, we found Kechi awake. Hilda gave me the wonderful news that the air mattress had been delivered and in fact Kechi had been transferred to it. Apparently, the hospital called ISOS and was given permission to order it. I examined it closely to see how it worked. The mattress was plugged into a power source and there was a constant flow of air in it, making it firm, but supple and pliable at the same time. That way, there was not enough constant firmness long enough to produce any kind of pressure on any part of the body. And it looked very comfortable too.

Kechi resumed the moving of her hands and legs, and then suddenly, she raised her head. Alarmed, I told her to lower her head. There was a tube in her throat, for crying out loud! She soon started to complain about pain but Hilda was reluctant to give her morphine, as she was concerned that Kechi was becoming addicted to it. She told Mom and I that it was very difficult to stop morphine addiction and it would be better to wean Kechi off it as soon as possible. She advised us to talk to Kechi about enduring the pain for as long as she could. I handed that talk over to Mom and she started to explain everything, with Kechi nodding at intervals. We then prayed for God to remove the pain. It was very hard for me to see her in pain with no immediate relief. Mom saw my distress and tried to encourage me, and Hilda promised to ask Dr. Pahad to recommend another pain killer for Kechi.

During the night visit, we found Kechi asleep, having been given her drugs just before we came. We brought adult diapers for her. Mom suggested it when Hilda said that she had had to change Kechi's dressings because she had a running stomach. I was glad Mom had thought of that because the poop also contributed to the infection of her wounds. With diapers, things were neater, plus it made the job easier for the nurses.

Mom and I started to praise and worship God quietly around Kechi's bed. Betty joined us after a while and this lasted until the visiting time was over.

I had earlier voiced my concerns about Kechi's hands to Hilda after seeing a burns patient in the lobby with fingers all curled up. I remembered that in Port Harcourt, the day of the crash, the skin on Kechi's hands was completely stripped from her fingers. I asked Hilda if she had seen Kechi's hands and fingers and if the skin was completely gone. Then I thought to myself that this was the wrong way to think. I remembered the reprimand in Isaiah 45.

I was once again questioning God's supremacy and power over illness and healing. I was getting petty and taking God for granted once again. He saved

Kechi from death and was healing her and there I was, concerned that the God who plucked her from a fiery tomb could not heal her hands. Even if He chose not to, who was I to doubt Him? I needed to ask for forgiveness. Again.

God help me.

During our morning devotions, Mom and I read Psalm 5:2&3, and also Psalm 6, which is a prayer for mercy in times of trouble. I added a personal prayer for forgiveness for the sins of doubt and lack of trust for Kechi's complete healing regarding her hands and face.

When we got to the hospital, we were told that her surgery was going to be in the late evening. This was kind of good news because it meant that we would get to visit fully with her as opposed to morning surgeries when we missed out on both the morning and afternoon visits.

Kechi was very alert, her eyes bright and she smiled when I made jokes. It was a very pleasant visit as it was clear she was happy to see her Grandma. During the afternoon visit, she was not as bright-eyed and I guessed it was because of the morphine and sedatives she had received over the course of the day. However, she was awake and we still had a good visit. That was until I had the lousy idea to tell her that she was going in for surgery later that day. I figured that since she was now awake, she might be scared when they start to roll her bed out to the OR. I was wrong. I could see the fear well up in her eyes immediately. Then a tear rolled down and my heart broke. I asked if she was crying and she shook her head no. But I had seen the tear drop and knew she was trying to be brave. I started reassuring her that she was going to be fine and to trust that I would always tell her the truth.

I did not do much good, as another tear drop followed the first. I called Mom in and she started to talk to Kechi, calming her down and reassuring her. She succeeded, because Kechi became calmer just before the visit ended.

I read her emails from her best friend, Womiye, as well as a letter from her cousin, Adaugo, and she seemed to receive them well. I was trying to gradually bring Kechi back into the world. I had been praying that all through her coma, the Holy Spirit was ministering to her soul, preparing her for what she would have to contend with when she woke up. But the reality was that Kechi, because of all the morphine in her system, was often confused and disoriented. I was not sure of how much to tell her, but I knew that, being Kechi, she would need to have some idea of what was going on so that she could start to cope in her own way. It was because of this that I goofed earlier by giving her too much information about her upcoming surgery. I should have guessed that she would be burning with questions that she could not ask and would be extremely frustrated by her inability to talk.

I was whipping myself for being stupid and adding to my baby's stress, as if she did not have enough to contend with. I felt so bad, but I kept all these off my face and tried to be upbeat and cheerful until it was time to pray and leave.

When we got back for the night visit, Kechi had still not gone in for surgery. I felt very bad because I had hoped that by then the surgery would have been behind her; instead the poor girl had spent every waking hour since I opened my big mouth dreading the surgery. She was still looking scared and when I asked if she was, she nodded. I sat down and gave her a serious talk, based on my total trust in God and how she needed to trust me when I said that she should not be anxious or scared. I asked her if I had ever lied to her and she shook her head no. I told her that I was not about to start. I assured her that the worst was behind us and that from there on, it was all good.

Just as we were about to leave after the night visit, the OR called for Kechi to be prepped. By that time, Kechi was sedated already and was half asleep by the time we left. I made sure to ask if she was okay and she nodded.

Mom made sure to ask Hilda for some details about the trachea tube. Hilda said that in about two more weeks, if Kechi continued to make steady progress, the tube may be removed and Kechi would be able to sit up, talk, and even feed herself through the mouth. That was so good to hear from someone that we trusted. Hilda had been moved from Kechi to a more serious case. She had told us a couple of days earlier that she was usually sent to take care of the more seriously wounded patients and that since Kechi was making steady progress, it was more than likely she would soon be moved, and she was right.

I had mixed feelings, but on the whole I was glad Kechi was getting better. Mom was so full of expectations that this surgery was going to be the beginning of the end and that some of the bandages would be removed for good. I did not want to rain on her parade, but I knew that the face would probably not be done that day and that after skin grafting, she would probably have more bandages. I had been through this so many times that I knew what to expect. I resolved that after we talked to the surgeon the next day, I would try and tell Mom not to give Kechi a time frame or talk about her going back to school soon because from what I was seeing, it was just possible that God's plan for her future may involve her missing the rest of the school year. I thought it best to focus on her recovery alone - no more talk about school, exams, prom etc., until we were sure that it was going to be possible for her to get back to school. I did not want to raise her hopes only to dash them. It would not be fair to her. She already had so much to deal with. I did not want to say anything, but it was beginning to seem to me that we were going to be in Milpark Hospital for a really long time.

Mom and I started the next morning by sharing thoughts on the need for strength to get through the whole ordeal. Mom had reached the limits of her own strength and now needed God's strength to be made perfect in her. I related my own experience in that regard to her and then we prayed.

At the hospital, Kechi was asleep when we got there and I left Mom with her so I could go and talk with Dr. Edwards and find out Kechi's progress. According to him, Kechi was doing quite well. His partner, Dr. Nel, grafted skin from her right flank to cover her right arm. He also said that the donor sites on her stomach had almost fully healed and this was good news because they had fresh skin to harvest for other areas; he then added that when a patient turned a corner, and started to heal, it was usually at a rapid rate and that Kechi's body had decided to heal. He and his partner were going to examine Kechi that evening and then make a decision as to when the next grafting would be. This was very good news to me.

Back at the TICU, Kechi was awake. She had been propped up for the very first time and Mom was ecstatic about it. We took turns talking to her, and she smiled a lot but was mostly sleepy. She moved her arms and legs from time to time, but I told her not to move her right arm because of the recent surgery. I then put on gloves and a plastic apron to massage her right foot. We left when the physical therapists came to exercise her. This was a very crucial aspect of her recovery, because her muscles could atrophy and wither away if they were not exercised.

Mom, being Mom, bullied the hotel manager into allowing us to buy a small additional fridge for our room, so Betty picked us up and took us to Makro. We bought the fridge, got some groceries and Betty dropped us off at the hotel. After lunch, we headed back to the hospital. Kechi was awake and I left Mom with her while I went to Dr. Pahad's rooms to give his secretary our passports. Our one-month visas had expired and ISOS asked me to get a letter from Dr. Pahad, Kechi's physician, indicating that Kechi was still receiving treatment and thus needed for her visa and mine to be extended. The lady made copies of our passports and asked me to come back at 9.30am the following day.

When I got back to the TICU (Trauma Intensive Care Unit), Mom said that Kechi was drifting in and out of sleep. She began to shiver and I asked if she was cold. She nodded and the sister on duty got another sheet and covered her. The shivers subsided after a while and she began to show off by raising her hands and legs again, though she remembered not to raise her right hand. I could not care less what they said about morphine befuddling people's brains, making them unable to remember anything; Kechi was still as sharp as a whip and did not forget anything I told her. I told her stories of what we had been up to and how Mom bullied the hotel manager into allowing us to get a fridge for the room and she smiled. She knew what her grandma could do.

Then the sister came in with some great news. Kechi was going to be allowed to breathe on her own from the following day to see if she would be able to handle it without support from the machine. At night, the machine would be on standby. If she was able to cope, then the tube down her throat would be removed entirely. This was wonderful news. Steps like this marked progress in the recovery journey and we were very grateful to God. We started telling Kechi not to forget to breathe so that the tube would be removed.

Mom and I were in the lobby waiting for the last visit to start when Bernice, one of the sisters came up to us to say that she was very happy with Kechi's progress and confirmed that they would allow Kechi to breathe on her own to see if she could handle it. She said in the future Kechi was going to need a lot of counseling for her emotional well being, but physically, she was out of danger. I just bowed my head and began to praise God. Mom got up to get a cappuccino at the café within the hospital and she insisted on paying, over Bernice's protests, for what Bernice had bought. Mom insisted that it was the least she could do because she just gave us the best news ever. Bernice told Mom that all the nurses in the TICU were convinced that Kechi was alive because of my prayers.

When we went in to see Kechi, she was awake and very alert.

Her very lively sense of humor was back in full. I said to her, "Kechi, I am bursting with pride over you and how far you have come."

Then I went on,

"Should I go ahead and burst open?" And she nodded, eyes shining.

I said she was a naughty girl and that I was going to beat her, should I? She nodded again. How I loved that child!

Before we left, we reminded her not to forget to breathe so that the tube would be removed and then she would be able to talk and eat with her mouth instead of with a tube down her stomach. Mom and I started to sing and praise God and to pray and she joined in. I knew this because her eyes were fixed on mine throughout, and at the end of the prayer I asked if she said 'Amen' and she nodded.

I believed that Mom was filled with the strength she prayed for because the Holy Spirit was a part of her praise and prayers that night.

Mom and I talked far into the night about God and His faithfulness and grace upon us. The fact that Kechi was alive and actually getting better was more than we could comprehend. We made the decision that whatever it took, we were going to prove ourselves worthy of this immense grace upon our lives. Who were we, that God should pick Kechi out of so many? We were not better or more holy than the rest, it was just the uncommon grace of God and we were going to show our gratitude to God for the rest of our lives, and unto eternity. We sang the following song to end our worship:

> *"Wonderful and marvelous is Jesus to us*
> *Sweeter than the honey in the honeycomb is He*
> *Jesus is real; He will never fail*
> *We will praise Him now, and throughout all eternity"*

The next morning, Kechi was awake and we immediately started chatting to her. She was still on the ventilator, and when we asked, the sister said she wanted to change Kechi's dressings before taking her off the machine. Mom and I told her stories and made jokes and she smiled a lot. I insisted on going back to the hotel after the morning visit because I wanted Mom to rest. Ulo called and we discussed the fact that Loyola Jesuit College had a mass scheduled for the 22nd. I told her to tell Mike to get Menti, his sister residing in Abuja, to attend on behalf of the family.

When we got back to the hospital for the afternoon visit, we were told to wait a bit because they were dressing her face. When we were called in, Kechi was breathing on her own! I just started jumping up and down, shouting "Alleluia, Alleluia, Praise the Lord, the Lord is good, He is an awesome God" over and over again. Our excitement knew no bounds and Kechi just smiled and smiled.

When we finally got ourselves under control, we reminded Kechi that this was the first step towards the removal of the trachea tube, as long as she continued to breathe well on her own. She seemed to understand this and was taking very deep breaths.

I got a lovely surprise when I got a call from a lady named Media. She was member of the South African branch of my fellowship in Nigeria - Sister's Fellowship International. She had been asked to contact me since she lived in Johannesburg. She brought food for me - oha soup and semolina. I was very grateful because I had really started to miss Nigerian food by then. She was such a darling, very caring and friendly. She told me that since I said I missed Nigerian food, she was going to bring food every day for me.

Another lovely surprise was waiting for me that evening. As Mom and I were in Kechi's room that night, Jane walked in. She was a nurse at the Shell Hospital in Port Harcourt, and she was one of the nurses that dressed Kechi's wounds and wrapped her up for the trip to South Africa. In fact, she had ridden in the ambulance with us to the airport that night. It was wonderful to see her. She had accompanied a patient to Milpark Hospital, and came looking for us. She was very happy with Kechi's progress and stayed for a while to chat and then prayed with us. After a while, she called Dr. Moses and I spoke with him. His concern for Kechi was very apparent and he said I should call him any time I had any issues.

That evening, my Mom's friend came from Cape Town and we all visited with Kechi, who was asleep for the whole visit! She was back on the ventilator for the night, as they had said she would be. After the visit, Aunty May took us all for a nice dinner at The Hilton in Sandton, and with the good meal and wine, I fell asleep on the way back.

The next morning, we started our morning devotion with thanksgiving and praise. Mom then shared a dream she had about a beautiful house set on a hill and a tree growing around and encompassing it. She reminded me that in the book of Matthew, it tells of a city set on a hill that cannot be hidden. She was told that hill signifies ascent and that the tree is the love of God encompassing His own. She had been asking for a confirmation of God's covering over Kechi. We also shared from Matthew on the purpose of the coming of Christ.

When we got to the hospital, Kechi was awake and we just spent time talking to her. I told her about the dinner we had and how I fell asleep on the way back because of the wine I had drunk. She was very amused by that. She was off the ventilator for the day, and was lifting her legs even higher, bending her knees, moving her feet back and forth. The girl was in a hurry to move, and talk and walk. Since she was now more awake, I asked her if she wanted me to buy a novel for her so I could read to her. Through a series of questions and nods, she decided on a novel by Nora Roberts, one of her favorite authors. I made her promise to sleep until the next visit.

Betty came to the hotel to take my laundry to wash! To this day, I do not know how to begin to thank her for all she did for me in South Africa. She was simply amazing. She promised to come the following day to take us for a drink and some fresh air.

Sister Chika, the Vice Principal of Loyola called me to say that they were all praying for Kechi and that I should give her the love of everyone in the school. Also, Kechi's former English teacher called from Cote d'Ivoire and asked to speak to Kechi. I explained to him that it was not possible at that time and he promised to call back in two weeks. Also, Kechi's friends, Womiye and Chimdi sent emails for her which I made a note to myself to print later and read to her.

During the 4pm visit, Kechi was alert, eyes bright. She lifted her legs, arms and her head for a bit. I told her some jokes, and read some teenage Christian literature to her sent by her pen pal, Rose-Constance, from America. I also told her of the emails her friends sent. She did not say anything, but I got the feeling that hearing about her school made her sad. I resolved to only read the emails to her once I could ascertain that she was in a good mind frame.

During the night visit, Kechi was fast asleep. The sister on duty was very encouraging. She told us that very soon we would hear Kechi's voice. Then she gave us a shocker - she had heard Kechi's voice! Apparently, she removed the trachea tube briefly and Kechi spoke. She quickly put it back and told us not to say anything because she was not supposed to do that. She said that by the following week, she was sure the tube would be removed. Kechi was put back on the ventilator for the night, but the sister said that even with the ventilator on, Kechi was breathing on her own. The ventilator was on in case of emergency because there was usually no doctor in the night.

Kechi then did something funny. Though she was still asleep, she brought out her tongue and licked her lips for quite some time. Mom was very happy to see Kechi's tongue, for some reason. She had asked me earlier if Kechi's tongue was okay and if the nurses were cleaning it. Well, she saw it that night and she must have been really anxious because she danced and danced with joy. I never got around to asking her the significance of seeing Kechi's tongue.

Aunty May came to our hotel room later that night. She and her friend had gone to the funeral of her friend's child, a six-year-old named Kechi. Strange coincidence in names, we thought. Kechi was not a very common name, the full version, Nkechi, being more common.

It was the morning of Day 41 when Mom received a message for me:
"You are highly favored, dwell in my praises"
I had already woken up with a song of praise in my heart that morning and I resolved to praise the name of the Lord forever for His mercies towards us.

When we got to the hospital, Kechi was awake and very alert. The sister on duty, a Polish lady named Maria told us that they might start feeding Kechi liquids through the mouth that day. We noticed that one of the tubes that fed directly into her stomach had been disconnected. Sister Maria said she was waiting for the doctor to come and take the decision.

Kechi, meanwhile, was all eyes. Very bright and alert. We told her stories and jokes and she was smiling for most of the visit. She included Frank Peretti in the list of books she wanted, as well as CDs of Backstreet Boys and the latest Usher release. Later that evening, we went with Betty to Campus Square Mall but only found Backstreet Boys, no books. We would have to go to a bigger mall the following week.

A friend of Kechi's, a former student of Loyola Jesuit College, called me to say that she was on her way to visit Kechi at the hospital. She had left Loyola to complete her high school in Johannesburg, and when she heard that Kechi was at Milpark Hospital, she decided to visit. By the time we got back from the mall, she and her mother were in the hospital lounge. We sat for a while and I spoke to her on what to expect when she saw Kechi, and the extent of what Kechi knew about the plane crash. By the time I was through, Onyinyechi was quite nervous, and I had to reassure her. I went in with Mom first and told Kechi that her friend was there to see her. I asked if she wanted to see Onyinyechi and she nodded. Mom went out and brought her in and Kechi smiled. I left them for a while to get re-acquainted. After a while, Remi, Lanre's wife, and Ife, Ulo's colleague at Microsoft, also visited. Onyinyechi stayed for the whole visiting period. She had lots of messages and best wishes from their friends in Loyola and took my email address, promising to forward mail from Kechi's friends. She promised to come back again when Kechi could talk. I was glad that Kechi got a visit from someone her age. I also got a list of CDs Kechi liked from her. Onyinyechi's mother told us that she was one of the women whom the Nigerian police tear-gassed in the recent peaceful march by women in protest of the death of children through negligence, greed, selfishness and carelessness in the aviation industry.

Later that day, the nurse took me aside and told me that it was necessary to cut off all Kechi's hair in order to get a good view of all her wounds and make sure they all got properly treated. I tried to explain to Kechi that they needed to cut her hair and her face got stony. I asked her if she didn't want to cut her hair and she shook her head. I tried some more explanations and she still shook her head no and began to get agitated, until the nurse stepped in and told Kechi that no one was going to cut her hair and not to stress herself and she calmed down. Later outside Kechi's room, however, she said that they really had to cut Kechi's hair and I gave her consent to go ahead. I would deal with Kechi's anger later. Her life was more important.

During the night visit, Kechi was awake and I started to read Perretti's Monster to her. After a while, she started to feel pain and was given a shot. Soon after, her lids started to droop and she slept. Mom and I were very tired so we left soon after to get some rest. It appeared that it had become imperative that we got some rest in the afternoon, especially Mom. I resolved that we would do so every day because I also could not afford to break down.

The next morning was Sunday and Layi came to the hotel at 8am to take Mom and I to her church, Rivers Church, in Sandton. I found it to be a very modern church, a bit too fast paced and rushed for me, but the message was real and I enjoyed it. Layi dropped us off at the hospital where we waited about thirty minutes before we could see Kechi because her dressings were getting changed. She looked bright at first, but then after fifteen minutes or so, she started to breathe hard, a sign of pain. The sister gave her a shot of morphine and she relaxed for a while. But then she started to move her arms and legs, started to draw her knees up and at one point she lifted her shoulders so high that her shoulders almost came off the bed. She overdid it, because she started breathing hard from pain again and had to be given more morphine. At this point, the sisters were beginning to get concerned at the high dosage of morphine she had received. They were worried because morphine could drop her blood pressure, and they did not want that. Anyhow, Kechi seemed to be fine and I read some more of the book to her. We got an extra thirty minutes with her because of the time we lost while she was getting her dressings changed. The dressings on her head were changed by the sisters on duty the previous night, so Sister Maria did not know whether Kechi's hair was cut or not.

We got to her room for the evening visit only to hear that Kechi had developed a fever of 38.5°. She had not had a fever that high for a while and appeared to be very uncomfortable. She was feeling sleepy, but fighting it. She was fidgety, trembling, and her mouth was constantly moving as if she wanted to say something. First of all, I spoke to her firmly and told her to calm down. I told her that her body was trying to fight off infection and what she could do in order to make her body win the fight was to sleep. She calmed down and Mom and I began to pray. We began to rebuke the fever and to pray for deliverance from demons and evil spirits in the vicinity. We felt that there was a contrary spirit in that room and cast it out. We pleaded for mercy for any sins we may have committed. We continued to pray in this vein for about thirty minutes and at the end of our prayer, Kechi woke up and was calmer. The fever was still high but I knew that it would go down by the next visit.

Lanre called me from Nigeria and I spoke to Bunmi's mother, who was his Aunt.(Bunmi was the other survivor of the plane crash.) It was an incredible experience. She prayed for Kechi over the phone and said that her family prayed every day for her. I asked her to give Bunmi my love. It then occurred to me that Lanre had a connection to both survivors.

At the night visit, Kechi's temperature was down to 38.1°, and she was more alert. We talked to her until she began to indicate that she was in pain. I learnt from the sisters how to rate her pain from one to ten, with ten being the most pain. I kept raising my fingers until she stopped at eight. She was given a shot and she relaxed. When she started to feel sleepy, Mom and I went into worship by her bedside. Before the worship session was over, Kechi was asleep.

On our way out of the ICU, we noticed that a Mozambican family whose father had been brought in following an accident was looking very defeated and discouraged, so Mom stopped to counsel them, telling them to trust in God and not to lose hope. The man was said to be getting worse. Mom got his name, Evaristus, so we could pray for him, and asked permission to pray by his bedside the next day. We also got the name of the German girl, Dachma, whose Mom had been crying and promised her parents that we would raise her in our prayers. Her parents thanked us and told us she was getting better.

CHAPTER SEVENTEEN

"Be still, and know that I am God: I will be exalted among the heathen, I will be exalted in the earth. The Lord of hosts is with us; the God of Jacob is our refuge."
Psalm 46 : 10&11 (KJV)

On Monday, January 23rd and I woke up with a song on my lips:

"I just want to praise You, Lord
I lift my voice to say I love You
You are everything to me
And I exalt Your Holy name, Oh God".

Mom said we should pray against distractions and we also raised my Dad in prayer, as well as Evaristus, the man from Mozambique, Dachma, and all the other patients in the ICU.

Ulo called to say that there was a mention of Kechi in the Loyola website. They had published an email from Dorothy where she gave an update on Kechi's progress. That went a long way in calming the unease I was beginning to feel on the silence over Kechi and her plight from the school authorities.

Kechi was looking good when we went into her room that morning. We talked with her a bit before I sought out her physician, Dr. Pahad, who reassured me that Kechi was still making steady progress.

When I got back to Kechi's room, Sister Maria said the doctor had authorized giving Kechi small sips of water to see if she could tolerate it. She brought crushed ice, which she said would be better as Kechi could then swallow gradually as the ice melted. She put the first scoop of ice in Kechi's mouth and we all watched, rapt. After a while, she asked Kechi if she had swallowed anything, and Kechi nodded.

Our joy knew no bounds.

Mom started to sing and dance.

The sister asked Kechi if the ice was finished and she nodded. Did she want more? Kechi nodded.

This time, when she was given another scoop of ice, she moved it around her mouth, and then a heard a crunching sound. I grabbed Mom's hand.

'Listen,' I said. 'I think she is crunching on the ice!'

I had to sit down because my legs could literally not hold me up any more. I felt shaky. Mom and I started to give praise to God. We were overwhelmed by God's favors and mercies. Kechi was not only sipping and swallowing; she was also crunching the ice! The girl was in a hurry to show us that she was ready to get out of the hospital.

She then began her 'usual' exercises of lifting her legs and arms. She added a new one today, turning her neck to the left. She had favored her right side since she was admitted, and this had made her neck stiff, so it was a good thing that she was beginning to be able to turn her neck. She soon started to feel pain and was given a shot. I was beginning to make a connection between her exercises and the onset of pain. We were going to have to cut down on the exercises because the medical staff no longer wanted to give morphine so often and I took time to explain this to Kechi so she would slow down.

We left her briefly to pray for Evaristus. He was looking very puffy, and his head was very swollen and bandaged up. We went to his bedside with his son, and his wife joined us in the prayer. I believed that God could bring him back from the brink of death, if He so desired, and we prayed that it was His will to do just that. My heart went out to the family and we prayed for strength for them.

By the time we got back to Kechi's room, the physical therapist had started on Kechi's exercises, and so we left.

When we got back to her room later, Kechi had just been washed and she looked very comfortable. The bandage on her right cheek had been removed and the skin looked pink and new; and she was looking a lot better. Then I noticed that tears were leaking from the corners of her eyes, although she insisted that she was not crying. I just sat beside her and we gazed at each other for a very long time. I would never get tired of looking at this girl, whom God had wrenched out from the hands of death and handed back to me.

'I love you', I told her, and she mouthed 'I love you' back at me. This is what I knew that she had been trying to say for the longest time. I told Kechi that she was going to have to learn how to be very patient. I told her that I had suspended everything to totally focus on God, Whom I believed for her total healing. My job, even Tara, her sister, were on hold for now. I told her that it could only be through the grace of God that I was not climbing walls, missing Tara. This was a girl that I would ordinarily never leave behind even for a day when I had to go out of town. I told Kechi not to worry about school and just focus on getting better.

She nodded, and then tried to start her exercises again and I stopped her. I told her that we were very proud of her progress and the extraordinary efforts she was making, but with her blood pressure low, the nurses would not be able to give her any morphine for now. I persuaded her to rest so that the last dose she was given would last longer. She seemed to agree, but then, when she thought I was not looking, she moved her legs. I caught her and sternly told her to stop, but it had become a game to her, the naughty thing. I reminded her of when she was about two years old and after being repeatedly told not to touch a wall socket, she started to stroke my face with one hand, distracting me, while the other hand was reaching behind her to touch the socket. She found this very amusing, and started to gasp, trying to laugh. I quickly sobered up and told her to stop laughing so we would not get into trouble with the nurses. Needless to say, it was a good visit.

During the night visit, Kechi was asleep for three quarters of the visit. We had just fifteen minutes to go when she woke up. We had been singing in low tones while she was asleep and when she woke up and saw us, she immediately started moving her hands and legs. I reminded her that she was not supposed to do that, and she should rest. She fell back asleep almost immediately.

The next morning, Mom received another message for me,
'I will sustain you'.

This was a confirmation of what we already knew, but it was timely. We prayed for Evaristus, Mimi, (my Nigerian lady friend's daughter), Linda's husband, and the rest of the patients in the ICU. We believed that because of Kechi's presence in that ward, every patient there would leave on his or her own two feet, rejoicing.

Kechi was all smiles that morning. One of the nurse's aides had gone off to bring a television for her. Everyone loved Kechi, and why not? When the TV was brought in, Kechi could not tear her eyes away from it. Suddenly she turned to me and mouthed,

'I love you', then 'I love you, Mommy'. I was so proud of her and asked her, 'Kechi, have you been practicing?' and she nodded. I said to her, 'I love you more' and she shook her head no.

'Is it a competition to find out who loves the other more?' I asked, and she nodded.

'Okay then. I love you more than the whole world,' and she mouthed,

'More than the universe'. And we both laughed. Then she started saying over and over again,

'Mommy I love you, Mommy I love you, Mommy I love you' and then she stared to cry.

I donned gloves and an apron so that I could touch her. I really wanted to gather her up in my arms and hug her tight, but I could not. Her vital signs started to go haywire and I knew that I had to be firm. I looked her in the eye and said to her,

'Kechi, this is not a time for crying, but for rejoicing. The Lord had filled us with joy and laughter and we are happy and dancing with joy. God has restored you from death to life and we will forever give Him praise. The time for crying is long gone.'

She gradually calmed down and I kept talking in the same vein until I coaxed a smile from her. This was the first emotional outburst and I knew there would be more and I prayed that the Lord would continue to give us the wisdom to say the right thing to her. At the end of the visit, we told Kechi that we were going to the mall with Betty to get her CDs. She mouthed, 'books', and I apologized for forgetting. We went to Sandton Mall and every music store had sold out the new Usher CD. We bought Ciara's CD instead and I called Ulo and asked her to buy the Usher CD from Lagos and give it to Lanre to bring back to SA. I also bought a trilogy by Nora Roberts.

Kechi was happy with the purchases and we agreed that we would start on the first book the next day.

For the rest of the day, I was tied up with making arrangements to get our visas renewed. Due to delays by ISOS, who were making the arrangements, I decided to call the Nigerian Ambassador to see if he could facilitate the visa renewal. When I called him, he said he was in Nigeria, but would get his staff to help. A few hours later, I got a call from a lady at the Embassy who said she was coming to the hospital to collect our passports and get the visas renewed. A few minutes later, I got another call from a different lady at the Embassy who told me that she was in charge of visa affairs and gave me a list of things to do.

First of all, I was to get a letter from Kechi's doctor stating how long Kechi would need to stay in South Africa. Then I was to take the letter to the Embassy. Then I was to pay a fee of R850.00, for each of us, to get the visas extended. I told the lady not to bother, I would leave it to ISOS to handle it like they had been doing. I immediately called Heidi from the ISOS office and told her to please go ahead with her arrangements for our visas and she said she would send someone right away to pick up our passports. Then I received a call from the first person that called me from the Nigerian Embassy and she was mortified that I had been asked to pay for the visa. I told her not to bother, everything was under control.

When we came back later for the night visit, Kechi was being prepared for surgery. I felt she was looking a bit scared because her eyes were following every movement the nurses were making and she knew something was up. I asked Mom to tell her she was going in for surgery so she could prepare herself, but instead Mom told her that they were just taking her in to open up her bandages and see what they had done so far. I know Mom trying not to scare her, but then the anesthetist came in and said to me, in Kechi's hearing, that they were going to harvest skin from her back for the grafting she was going in for. He went on to say that they were all very proud of Kechi and she was their star.

After he left, I then had to speak to Kechi about how every surgery was bringing us a step closer to the day she would be fully healed, and how we should be thankful that she even had enough skin for them to harvest and graft with. We stayed with her and prayed until it was time for her to be wheeled in for surgery.

They allowed us to follow her bed to the theater doors where we said goodbye to her before going to wait for the taxi, because she would still be in the OR by the time visiting was over.

The next morning, we prayed for the Holy Spirit to put the right words on our lips when Kechi started to ask questions. Kechi was looking bright that morning and after speaking to the nurses, we were able to tell her that the surgery had gone very well. The nurse told us that the skin taken from her back had been grafted unto the back of her right thigh. Also, the wounds on her right leg and left thigh had been dressed. The nurse was going to dress Kechi's left arm and face later that day.

I told Kechi that her dad said to tell her that he would be coming soon and she mouthed to me,

"Tell him to come now!"

I promised to deliver the message to him. We played the "I- love-you/I-love-you-more "game for a while until my Mom said that the love was equal on both sides. Kechi mouthed, "I don't agree" and I also said I didn't agree and Mom said that when her dad came, he would settle the matter, and we agreed to leave it at that. It was little games like that that really gave me a sense of normalcy in a situation that was very scary and overwhelming. I also liked the fact that it also made Kechi feel a little more normal. I could not even begin to imagine what was going through her mind day after day and night after night, as she lay on that hospital bed alone. At this point I was glad that she was being given drugs that made her sleep most of the time.

She did not want to listen to music or watch TV, she wanted me to talk to her and so I talked about everything I could think of until it was time to go.

Layi picked us from the hospital and stayed to visit with me for a while in the hotel lobby while Mom went upstairs to rest.

When we got back to the hospital, Kechi was dozing on and off, no doubt because of the sedatives she was given before the dressing changes started. I told her that her dad said to tell her that he was going to book his ticket that day to come the following week.

I was getting really good at lip-reading because when Kechi mouthed, "I didn't hear you", I knew what she said. She could not hear because they padded her head dressings around her ears. I asked the nurse about the wounds on her forehead and the back of her neck and she said that they were not very deep. She also said that Dr. Nel had scheduled Kechi for more surgery two days later for more skin grafting. We told Kechi to sleep so that she would be awake when we came back in the night. She was dropping off even before we left.

Later that night, she was in deep slumber when we came, so we just put on her music on low and sat with her, then prayed at the end of the hour and left. We made an appointment to see

Dr. Nel the next morning by 9.30 am to assess Kechi's progress.

We left for the hospital early the next morning and went straight to Dr. Nel's offices. He gave us some good news first. All Kechi's wounds had been fully debrided, which meant that all the dead tissue had been completely removed. The back of the left hand, the right arm, and the front and back of the right thigh had been grafted and the grafts had 'taken' so far. He said he would be taking her to the OR the following day for more grafting. I asked about Kechi's hands and he said they were terrible. I suspected as much because on the day of the crash, I had seen Kechi's hands with the skin hanging off them in strips. Dr. Nel said he would have to do a lot of work on her hands to make sure she had mobility in them. He would have to do contractual release so that her fingers will be separated.

I took a deep breath and said to myself, "It is well". Her hands were now a very specific prayer point.

On her face, he said that he was going to leave that for last because the face had a way of surprising everyone by healing on its own, and that already, parts of Kechi's face had started coming back. He would only graft the face when any part of it showed signs of not recovering on its own.

Second prayer point Kechi's face.

Mom asked about the pain and he replied that morphine took care of that. He suggested that we gave his secretary a list of questions about which parts of Kechi's body we were most concerned about so that when they got Kechi on the operating table, he would look at those specific parts and be able to make notes for us. He went on to say that our greatest enemy was infection, which can cause grafts to fail, and donor sites to deepen and scar.

Third prayer point against infections.

All in all, it was not a bad report. We thanked God and waited patiently for what would unfold next. The doctor stressed that Kechi's treatment was going to stretch out, but who cared? Kechi was alive! God would see us through.

I sent Ulo a text updating her on the doctor's comments on Kechi's fingers. I ended the text by writing,

"It is well, Kechi is alive".

Her reply to that showed that I might have given her the impression that I was full of despair at the doctor's report, because she wrote back,

"Whose report will you believe, the doctor's or God's? Kechi has been restored whole to us"

So I sent her another text message,

"I was not doubting God. I am updating you so all will know the magnitude of this miracle. Remember, I saw those hands in tatters in Port Harcourt."

I must have sounded terse because she responded,

"I was not indicting you. I was strengthening myself by remembering and sharing His promise. You are so right. This miracle was so huge that we would have been grateful for anything. That is why His Word is so powerful because it forces us, especially you, to look beyond what you see. God loves us so very much".

I responded,

"Ulo, that girl was burned from head to toe".

Some of the burns manifested after we got here. I came to understand that with burns, the damage does not end when the fire on the skin is put out. The damage continues inside, under the skin. Burns are really the most terrible of all injuries.

The medical staff in Milpark were excited about Kechi's recovery because they did not expect her to survive. They said she was their star. Kechi was a part of God's plan for that time and we had to seek His face daily.

Every time I looked at Kechi, I marveled at God. At each step of her recovery I saw the hand of God and my gaze was drawn upwards to Him.

Was I worthy? No.

But was I thankful? A resounding YES!

When we went in to see Kechi, she had just been cleaned and was awake. She just wanted to be talked to and when she mouthed, "Talk", I actually heard the 't and 'k' sounds. Her temperature, which had been normal for the last two days, was spiking again, but not too badly.

There was a new sister who appeared to be learning on the job. Mom and I were uneasy because we did not want Kechi to be someone's practice patient. The nursing supervisor came in and started to instruct her on what to do and told her that next time she should come in some hours before time so that she would be acquainted with procedures and be shown where things were kept. After we left, Mom asked me to go back and remind the new nurse to keep asking Kechi if she was in pain. Luckily, I saw one of the older nurses in the room and I begged him to please monitor Kechi for pain and he agreed.

During the next visit, Kechi was wide-awake, eyes darting everywhere. She moved her head and shoulders up almost to sitting position and held that position for a while. Then she shifted her whole body slightly to one side of the bed. Obviously, Kechi practiced when we were not there and when we came, showed off what she had achieved. After we showered her with praises, she wanted to know when the tube in her throat was going to be removed. In fact, she did not even know there was a tube in her throat. She thought that what we meant when we talked about the tube was the one in her mouth. I had to explain the function of the tube in her throat and how it was inserted as soon as we came into the hospital because her throat was swollen and she could no longer get air into her lungs by herself. I went on to tell her that as soon as she could tolerate sipping water, she would graduate to juice, then to light soups etc.

She then mouthed that she wanted juice. I knew she was in a hurry to move on to juice so that the tube would be removed faster. I told her she had to be patient, like we discussed. I reminded her that we had come a long way and now the doctors were saying that the critical time had passed. Now she had to be patient because God promised total recovery, but also said it would take time.

That was when Kechi from nowhere asked me,

"After the plane crash, how did you find me?"

I told her,

"You found me".

I then told her the story of how she had given her name and my phone number to the people that rescued her. Her eyes opened wide as she listened. I then veered off to talk about what my Mom said about Kechi having so much love for me to be able to remember to give such information at a time she was more dead than alive. I quickly started talking about something else, made a joke, and she smiled. That was how far I was prepared to go on that subject just then. Thankfully, she soon drifted into sleep.

The questions I had been dreading were beginning to come. It was amazing how I could read her lips so well. But I decided that when she asked me a question I did not want to answer yet, I would pretend not to know what she was trying to say.

When we got back for the night visit, we saw a different Kechi. She had the feeding tube in her nose instead of her mouth. She was agitated and I asked her why the tube was in her nose. She mouthed that she threw up the one in her mouth because she was coughing. I asked her if she wanted the tube left in her nose and she began to shake her head furiously from side to side. I could see she was in pain and also getting agitated, so I spoke firmly to her to calm down and I would see that it was removed and another one put back in her mouth. She then started to press down the back of her head into the bed and move it from side to side. I asked if the wound at the back of her head was itching and she said yes. It took a while to calm Kechi down and luckily, Primrose, one of the nicer nurses, was on duty, so I got her to give Kechi morphine for the pain.

As soon as she was calm, we started talking to her, but got distracted by sister Veronica who was complaining that the morning staff had not prepared the morphine for the night, nor did they replenish any of the materials used. I also noticed that the pink pad that served as a buffer between Kechi's tracheotomy and her neck was now resting on her chest. Also, her face was not as smooth as it used to be, with dried blood here and there. In fact, it appeared that Kechi was not well cared for during the day. Mom and I decided that if we saw that nurse near Kechi again, we were going to protest.

Before we left, Sister Primrose promised to remove the feeding tube from Kechi's nose and put another one back in her mouth. When we asked Kechi if she was now fine, she nodded yes, and we prayed and left.

Media brought so much food for us in the hotel - three kinds of soup, with semolina, jollof rice with fried plantain, roasted corn, bananas. The girl was a marvel. Mom and I told her that we wanted to start ordering food from her on a regular basis and to pay for it, including delivery charges, but she would not hear of it, so we suspended the discussion. I thought we ought to pay since she actually had a restaurant and cooking was her business but she was vehement in her refusal, so I let it rest.

I was very unsettled that night and I even snapped at Mike when he called. I was filled with thoughts that had not disturbed me since we came to South Africa - who had called, who had not called etc. Ulo called and we discussed what Kechi asked about how I found her after the crash. We started thinking and talking about what to say when she started asking about her friends. Several possibilities were banded back and forth between, Mom, Ulo and I, but we ended up not concluding. I just said that we had to pray for God to take care of that.

I prayed for peace of mind that night.

CHAPTER EIGHTEEN

"Remember the word unto thy servant, upon which thou hast caused me to hope. This is my comfort in my affliction:
for thy word hath quickened me".
Psalm 119 : 49 & 50 (KJV)

The Holy Spirit brought understanding to me on my disquieting thoughts of the previous day. After hearing the doctor's report, being upset by the morning shift nurse, and wondering about how best to deal with Kechi's questions, I started entertaining doubts in my mind without knowing it. And with doubts came a shifting in my trust that God could handle the situation without help from me. With that shifting came a gap, a separation from God, and the enemy pounced. That was the reason for my irritation the night before.

But by the grace of God, because He is so merciful and kind, and because His love for His children knows no bounds, the Holy Spirit ministered to me that morning and it went something like this. Let me point out here that whenever I 'heard' from God, it was not an audible voice in my ears; it was more of an impression from deep inside of me. This is what I got at that time:

I delivered Kechi from death to life,
sent her to the best hospitals, gave her the best doctors and the best nursing care, am healing her wounds, and you doubt whether I can heal her mind and her thoughts?

That was when it hit me, I had doubted God and removed the trust I had in Him. I was stunned, and had no idea how to even start to beg forgiveness. I got up and turned to Mom to tell her what was going on with me and it appeared that the Spirit had been busy, because Mom said she had got a similar message and in fact had been up in the night asking for mercy for doubting. We went into prayers and started to beg God for His mercy. I began to bemoan the weakness of my flesh that I could doubt that God could heal Kechi's mind, in spite of all that He had done for her. I told God that it was indeed like His word said that neither can the clay tell the potter what to do, nor the creature instruct his creator on how to create him. I reminded Him that He had promised to restore Kechi completely, and this included her body, mind and soul and spirit.

We raised Kechi up before God and assured Him that we would no longer go by the doctor's reports or even by what our eyes were seeing, we were holding on to Him and what He promised concerning Kechi.

I resolved to be more careful and to guard my heart better. Trusting God had to be a habit that I should cultivate while in South Africa because when we went back home, there were going to be a lot of distractions. I ended my prayers by saying,

"Thank you, Lord, that I can lay my burdens on You and feel lighter. Thank you, Lord."

Mom said we should read Psalm 17 : 7-9 and Psalm 18 : 1-6, 16- 19 to Kechi when we visited her that morning.

Ulo called to share her thoughts on what we discussed the previous night with me. Apparently, she could not sleep pondering over Kechi's question about how I found her after the crash. She finally came to the conclusion that Kechi must have been thrown out of the plane or jumped out and therefore worried about whether she would be found. I told her that going back to the events of that day was difficult for me and I had buried that day somewhere deep in my mind so that I could fully focus on the here and now.

I told her our experiences that morning and she was overwhelmed, like us, by God's awesomeness. She then added that He knows our frailties and the important thing to understand was that the graph of our upward climb was not straight up. It had some dips here and there, but was ever going up. We should know when to die to self and then continue the journey upwards.

When we got to the hospital, Kechi was awake, alert and happy to see us. She was all smiles, eyes darting all over the place. She mouthed to me that I did not finish telling her the story I was telling her last night. We had by then developed a system for when I could not make out what she said. I would get a pen and paper, and by a process of elimination, hit on what she wanted to say. It would usually start with me going through the alphabets until I hit on the one that began the word she was trying to say, and then we would continue form there. It became a very interesting game that we both looked forward to playing.

I finished the story, which was an Igbo folk tale, and then we began to talk of other things.

Then Mrs. Vessie Marais, whose husband was one of the patients in the ICU gave Kechi a toy stuffed animal which Kechi named Betty. (Betty was thrilled when we told her later). Before we left, I asked if she wanted music and she chose Usher 9010.

When we put it on, my Mom started to dance and Kechi began to smile. Not to be outdone, I joined in and both of us were dancing right there in the ICU to Usher. Kechi could not stop smiling. At one point, my Mom tried to do some of my moves and Kechi shook her head, smiling. Mom pretended to be offended and asked, "What, am I not getting it?" and Kechi shook her head again. We left her to her music, after she asked for the volume to be increased before we left.

Betty picked us up and we went to Eastgate to buy ingredients for vegetable soup, which Mom had promised to cook for Betty. From there we went to Betty's house so we would know where they lived. The estate was lovely and it had a swimming pool, clubhouse etc. From there we went to Sandton Mall because they were having sales. We did not do much there because it was getting close to Kechi's visiting time so we dashed about, picked up a few items and rushed back to the hospital.

We were a few minutes late and Kechi was awake. We talked for a while and Mom reminded me to tell her about the upcoming surgery. I told her that the doctors were going to graft her legs later that day, and asked her if she knew what that meant. She shook her head no. And I explained that they were going to cover the wounds on her legs but not what they were going to cover them with.

Kechi then asked me,

"What kind of accident did I have?"

"You were in a plane crash"

"Was I the only survivor?"

"No, but your injuries were very serious, that's why you were brought to Milpark Hospital".

I did not let her ask more but instead rattled on about how God had used Shell and Dr. Moses and ISOS to bring us to SA for her treatment, and was God not awesome?

She nodded. Then,

"Where was I going?"

"You were coming back from school. Don't you remember?"

She shook her head no. I realized then that the drugs were making her confused.

I asked her, "Do you know where you are?"

She nodded. "Where are you?"

She mouthed, "Johannesburg".

I sighed in relief. At least a few things were clear. It was the actual details of the accident that were unclear. I prayed silently for God's guidance to give the right answers to her question. We read the scripture of the day together and prayed. Kechi mouthed 'Amen' at the end of the prayers.

Mom had been feeling poorly all day. Her stomach was feeling tender and she had the runs. I suspect it was the salad at the hotel restaurant because she also had the runs the last time we ate there.

She looked weak and wanted to go back to the hotel and lie down. I told her not to bother coming back for the night visit since Kechi was going in to surgery.

During the night visit, Kechi was awake, but drifting in and out of sleep. She mouthed that I should talk to her, so I just kept talking. She had already been prepped for surgery and they were waiting on the OR to call for Kechi. The call came at about ten minutes to eight and Kechi was wheeled off. As usual I went with them, walking beside Kechi's bed until they got to the OR doors. It was always a wrench, seeing her being wheeled to the theater, not knowing if she was scared or not, but my trust and my faith were in God and I believed that He would see her through.

The next morning, Mom received a message for the day, 'Who is the Messiah?' and the scripture for the message was from 1 John 5, v 1-12.

After prayers, we got to the hospital and were told that the doctor had ordered that the head and face dressings be changed in his presence so he could assess the progress of the healing. The nurse said she would come and get us after they were through. They came at 12.15pm, fifteen minutes after visiting time was officially over and we insisted on getting our full hour. I knew how much Kechi looked forward to visiting periods, especially the first one, and I was not about to take that away from her. The staff was very understanding, anyway, and always allowed us to make up for any time lost to dressing change or any other thing they had to do to Kechi that coincided with visiting time.

Kechi started to complain about pain almost as soon as we walked in and they gave her a muscle relaxant, Dorminicum, and morphine and she soon felt better, though drowsy. She started to mouth something and then somehow, her voice managed to come through! When she heard the sound of her voice, she stopped mid-sentence, eyes wide.

Then she said in a low wispy voice, "No wonder I'm cold".

I followed her eyes and saw that the fan was on and trained directly on her. The sister on duty said I could put it off and I did. Then I asked Kechi if she heard the sound of her voice and she nodded yes. Mom, as usual, began to dance and to give God the glory. Every new step was a victory for us. We took nothing for granted and every time that we had a breakthrough, we glorified God.

Kechi then asked me to read to her. I took out one of the books to read, but almost as soon as I started the story, she asked me to stop and just talk to her. Today, I have absolutely no recollection of what I used to say when Kechi said to me, 'Talk'. I just know that I rambled on and on about anything and everything.

By the time we left, Kechi was already sleeping. We went with Betty to buy the remaining ingredients for the vegetable soup and then went back to her house where Mom cooked the fastest vegetable soup ever. It was delicious, but we ended up being thirty minutes late for the evening visit. Kechi was awake, but she had a shot for pain soon after we got there and became drowsy, drifting in and out of sleep. I just sat there gazing at her, and talked to her whenever she opened her eyes.

Then she asked a question which I refused to answer, 'Who was in the plane with me?'

I know that when the time came for her to know details of the plane crash, the Holy Spirit would give me the words to use. For that moment, though, it felt right to leave that discussion for another day. And so I told her that because of the drugs she had been given, her lips were not forming the words properly and I could not make out what she was trying to say. Thankfully, she was actually dropping off to sleep even as I was speaking to her and so I told her that we would continue the discussion when I came back for the last visit, hoping that by the time I came back she would not remember the conversation. I told myself that I was not being a coward; I just did not feel as if it was time for her to know the really tragic details of the accident.

We then were asked to leave because they wanted to clean Kechi and change her bed linen. In the waiting room, Uncle Dom, my Mom's relative who lives in Johannesburg, was waiting with his wife, and they had brought food for us. While we were visiting with them, Sister Maureen, one of Kechi's favorite nurses, came to tell us that Kechi was asking for us. Mom and I went in to reassure her that we were right outside the ICU and would come back in as soon as it was visiting time.

Layi visited after Uncle Dom and his wife left, and she brought me a book called 'The Purpose Driven Life', by Rick Warren, a book that was to have a tremendous influence on my spiritual life.

I had seen the book with her during one of her visits and had expressed a desire to buy it. She bought me the keepsake edition, bound in leather. I thanked God for sending her my way. She really was an awesome person and was a source of great comfort to me when I needed it most. She did not stay long, though, because her kids were getting restless and were running all over the hospital.

Kechi was sound asleep when we went in and we were happy because she was resting after the stress of surgery and pain from dressing changes. We worshipped God standing by her bed and it turned into a mini-fellowship with some of the nurses joining in when they knew a song we were singing. The Spirit of God was very present while we sang and prayed.

The next morning, the message received by Mom was on restoration and the main text was from Joel 2 v 25,

And I will restore to you the years that the locust hath eaten, cankerworm, and the caterpillar, and the palmerworm, my great army which I sent among you.

We prayed and thanked God for His mercies. It was a message that filled me with peace and I received it joyfully for Kechi, knowing it was a confirmation of God's promises concerning her. Everything she thought had been lost to her because of the plane crash were going to be restored fully to her - her health, her skin, her body, her looks, even her schooling.

Kechi was as bright as a new penny when we went in for the morning visit. Her eyes were wide open and alert and she gave a big smile when we walked in. We sat and told her stories, made jokes, teased her and she just sat there, smiling. The respirator was now completely removed from her bedside and so Kechi was now fully breathing on her own. She was very happy about that and we took pictures with her. It was a very pleasant visit and by the time we left, we were all in high spirits. We shared the restoration message with her, told her how this was God's promise for her. Mom went on to explain about the different ramifications of restoration and how it applies to every sector of her life.

When we left Kechi, Mom and I headed to Campus Square, the Auckland Park mall, because Mom wanted to buy a few clothes for herself. We had discovered that South Africa had very fashionable clothes, and everyone was well dressed all the time, even older ladies. I bought a new journal, because the one I was using was almost full. Then something unexpected and curious happened.

A few days after we came to South Africa, after I bought my first journal, I received a scripture for Kechi from Jeremiah 29 : 11.

I wrote down the scripture on the inside of the first page of the journal. When I had filled that journal, I had to look for a while for another one, because I could not find any I liked. Finally I found one in a store called PNA. Right there on the front of a journal was the scripture from Jeremiah, printed in full.

At that point, I no longer believed in coincidences. God did have a plan to give Kechi a future and He had nothing but thoughts of good and not of evil for her. The next verse said that she would pray to Him and He would answer her.

We went back to the hotel to eat and rest, and then headed back to the hospital for the 4.00pm visit. Kechi was awake and I just knew that she had been waiting for us to come. She mouthed that she was cold, and I put on gloves and apron and pulled up the sheets to cover her shoulders which were exposed. She soon felt better and we started talking to her telling her that her Dad was coming the following Sunday to visit her, and Grandma was going home when Mike came. She was not happy that Mom was leaving, but we told her that Mom would be back after Mike left. We explained that the hotel room had just two beds and so only one visitor could stay at a time. This led to a discussion of God's love for all of us and then the conversation turned to our recounting of the story of the way God arranged for us to come to Milpark Hospital through Shell. She had never heard this story and was very fascinated, and so we took her through the whole thing.

We told her how Shell was paying for our accommodation as well as her medical bills; how Shell had arranged with ISOS for us to be transported to Milpark Hospital in Johannesburg, the best hospital with the best medical staff and so on. Her eyes just kept getting bigger and bigger as she finally began to understand the grace of God upon her life.

After a while, she began to complain about pain. The sister refused to give her any more drugs, having given her both morphine and Dormicum just before we came. She told us that they were afraid that Kechi was beginning to get dependent on morphine. Also, too much morphine would depress her respiratory system, which would put her back on the respiratory machine. All the sisters on duty chimed in to stress the dangers of morphine and I was thinking, 'so what do we do? The girl is in pain'.

Eventually, she was given a sedative and we asked her to try and sleep. We explained as much as we could about morphine and she seemed to understand and soon drifted off.

Mom and I went to the coffee shop to wait for the next visiting period and while we were there, Ernest Ojukwu, Mike's close friend from Aba, walked in. Mike had mentioned that he was coming to Johannesburg soon, but did not know when. It was great to see him. Then Lanre walked in with Kechi's CDs and we all sat together and talked until it was time for the next visit. I went in with Lanre first, and then with Ernest.

I had told Kechi when Lanre and I were leaving that I had a surprise visitor for her. When Ernest came in, her eyes widened and she gave a huge smile. She and Ernest's daughters had been great friends forever and she was very happy to see him. He gave her get-well messages from his family. Ernest was actually going to Durban for a conference but decided to come into SA a day earlier so he could see Kechi. The goodwill from both friends and strangers was incredible. Ernest told me before he left how much his life had changed since the plane crash, how he no longer took anything for granted. He said that he had never seen a miracle like Kechi's survival in his life and for him, what makes it even more of a miracle was that she did not escape unscathed. She was burnt as badly as other kids, had smoke inhalation and so on, but God still made it possible for her to live through all the injuries, and also put her on the path to recovery.

When he heard the name of the hospital Kechi was in, he had gone to the hospital website and was amazed at how good the hospital was.

After he left, I went back to Kechi's room and shortly after I got there, she started to complain about pain. Sister Veronica gave her 4mg of morphine and after five minutes, she was still complaining that she was in pain. Mom asked her how she got the nurse's attention when she was in pain and Kechi started a tut-tut sound by clicking her tongue against her teeth. As soon as she did this, Veronica came to find out what she wanted. Veronica said the sound was their communication tool.

Ten minutes later, Kechi was still complaining about pain and Veronica gave us the same lecture on too much morphine that we got that morning. We laid hands on Kechi and prayed for her. Veronica told Mom and I that Kechi needed to sleep off the pain, but that as long as we were there, she was not going to sleep. She promised to give Kechi a sedative as soon as we left, and that should make her sleep through the night. We decided to leave at once so that Kechi could get her shot. I did not want her in pain at all. We explained to her why we were leaving and she promised to sleep. We prayed again and left.

Ulo sent me a text message as we were leaving:

"Ije, I came to the conclusion today that you are really blessed of God.

Everything concerning your faith, your search, even your foray into the Grail Message, was part of the search. Then He found you.

Then the miracle of Chizitara. You are indeed blessed among women and among men.

I want you to recognize this oneness with God. Read Genesis 18 again. Like Abraham, You are in a son-ship position to seek His face. Reason with Him, intercede for men, churches, peoples. Seek His Word concerning every situation.

Meditate for others…..You are a prophet."

I replied,
"Ulo, I will not pretend and say that I do not know that the main purpose of my life is unfolding.

Please lift me up daily."
And Ulo responded,
"I will. I do. His yoke is light, Ije.
Just yield yourself as He has been teaching you.
All glory is indeed to our God, Who is able to do just as He says He will do.

He is able, more than able, to make you what HE wants you to be."

Soon after, I received a series of text messages from Betty.

1. Dear Ijeoma, how are you and Mummy? I know Kechi is wonderful. As I send you this text, I have tears running down my face just thinking about the love God has for you. This whole process with Kechi has inspired me greatly, and my belief in Christ is strengthened, because I can see what God is doing in your life.
2. Your faith and confidence in God brought back your daughter to life. Continue to hold on to God and you'll be amazed what He can do. I shall continue to render my support any way I can, don't forget. Someday, I shall testify to the world what I saw throughout Kechi's stay at the hospital, the wonderful work of God.
3. I will always have you all in a special place of my heart. Will be thinking of you. Stay well and tell Kechi I love her so much.

I just bent my head and prayed for God to continue to be my guide. I once more surrendered my all to Him. I prayed for humility from Him to enable me to submit my all to Him. I asked Him to teach me to die to self, every minute of the day.

'Lord', I prayed, 'May I be worthy for your use. Amen.'

CHAPTER NINETEEN

"Have not I commanded thee? Be strong and of a good courage; be not afraid, neither be thou dismayed: for the LORD thy God is with thee whithersoever thou goest."
Joshua 1:9 (KJV)

DAY 50

Mom received a message that morning, *'I have healed Kechi's family because they have obeyed me. My blessings are upon you all this season.*

Ask anything in my name and you will receive it. Remain steadfast.'

I was elated, saying 'Amen and Alleluia' over and over again as I received the message in gratitude. This was a confirmation of all that God had been doing at this time. We began to give Him all the glory, honour, adoration and praise that we could, because He had shown Himself to be more than worthy of our praises. We were humbled by His grace and mercy and we vowed to praise Him from everlasting to everlasting.

We were bubbling over with elation and this was good because we needed all that for the news we were about to receive from Dr. Nel.

I had made an appointment so he could give us the details of the last surgery and also what we could expect from the one scheduled for the next Tuesday. Dr. Nel sat us down and gave us details on what we could expect regarding Kechi's scars.

His revelations shook me up because at that time I had no idea that there was such a large proportion of her skin not yet grafted. I knew there would be scar tissue, but the way Dr. Nel described it, I had a vision of Kechi with thick, horrid scars over her whole body. I was happy and thankful that Kechi was alive, but I could not help thinking of Kechi and how she would feel with her whole body disfigured at only sixteen! I knew it was wrong of me to think that way, as Kechi may well have died along with her school mates, but for the mercy of God and His plan for her life. I told myself to be grateful for her life and not to forget that God had also promised total recovery. Long, but total recovery.

The doctor told us that the back of her head and neck needed to be grafted as well and that work will need to be done to save her left ear. Her forehead and the left side of her face would also require grafting. I had hoped that her face would not need grafting and so be spared of scar tissue. He talked of pressure garments that Kechi would need to wear for between eighteen months and two years on her body which should reduce the scar tissue over time. She would also need a silicone dressing for her face.

This was all very daunting to me. Suddenly a new picture unfolded in my mind's eye of my daughter with a disfigured body and me trying to explain to her how it all happened, and just like that, I gave in to grief. I did not cry, but my heart froze. I had to come to grips with a new reality. I took some time to compose myself before going in to see Kechi. She and I were so close that she usually could tell when I was troubled. In Igbo, there is something that is said about women desiring to have at least one girl child because that is the child that will look at your face and know if all was well with you.

That was Kechi.

When we entered her room, Kechi had just been cleaned up, so she was fresh, but dopey. She had to be given morphine before they started cleaning her so she would not be in pain. We talked a bit with her and left briefly when her physician, Dr. Pahad, came in to examine her. When we came back to the room, Kechi was drifting into sleep so we prayed and left.

During the evening visit, we had to wait a bit because they were changing her bed linen. When we entered, she was more alert, but they were sedating her more than before because of the pain of grafting. I read her some jokes and she smiled. She saw one of her roommates, Mr. Marais, being wheeled out and she asked if it was Tuesday. She knew that she usually went into surgery on Tuesdays. We told her that her surgery was the following day. Mom went on to assure her that surgery was good because every time she went in, a new part of her exposed skin was covered up. Kechi said she was not afraid. Meanwhile, I was thoroughly enjoying the bible passages on every page of my new journal. The passage on the page I was currently writing on is the verse at the beginning of this chapter. As far as I was concerned, the matter was settled. I would be strong and courageous because God was with us every step of the way.

That night, we saw a different Kechi from the one we had left in the evening. She was agitated, her eyes were red and she was sweating on her upper lip. I asked if she was ok. She shook her head no.

'What is it?' I asked.

'I can't breathe'.

There was no nurse by her bed so I went out to the nurse's station and told the first nurse I could see that my daughter could not breathe. One of the male nurses turned to me and said that they were aware of what was happening to Kechi and had made arrangements for an experienced nurse to come and be with her. This calmed me and I went back to tell Kechi to relax, they were aware of the problem and were taking care of it. The male nurse came in and Mom, who was in full panic mode, told him, "She can't breathe, she can't breathe."

The nurse told us to trust that he knows what he was doing, that he had twenty two years of ICU experience. Mom still went on pointing to the breathing machine, saying that Kechi could not breathe. I turned to Mom and told her that she was panicking and scaring Kechi. She calmed down and the nurse explained that they had increased Kechi's oxygen supply from five to ten, her oxygen saturation was 100% and her respiration was fine.

I turned to Kechi and spoke to her calmly and firmly to relax and take deep breaths. I began to breathe in and out with her, deep, slow breaths. I asked if she was scared and she nodded.

"Look at me" I said. "Do I look worried?"

She shook her head no.

"Then why are you scared? If there is something to worry about, should I not look worried?"

She nodded.

"Then stop worrying. Everything is fine."

She began to calm down and mouthed that she was in pain. The sister said she could not give her any morphine, as her blood pressure was too low at that time (78/59). So Mom and I began to pray. Midway through the prayer, Kechi slept off. We prayed also for her blood pressure to normalize, her temperature to come down, her heart rate to stabilize, and for her lungs to function properly.

By the time we left, her blood pressure had come up to 105/65 and her heart rate was at 130, a bit high, but within the normal range. The only abnormal reading was her temperature but they were giving her analgesics every six hours and had taken a blood sample to the lab for investigation. They suspected that she had another infection.

I surrendered everything to God. Kechi was in His safe hands. I refused to give in to worry or panic. Today's events shook me up, but I did not fall because I had built my house on a foundation of rock and though the storms raged, I would not fall, in Jesus's name.

The next morning, Mom and I had a deeply meaningful warfare/praise and worship session. We ejected the spirit of fear from Kechi and went on to adoration and worship from there. We felt the presence of the Holy Spirit and were refreshed at the end of the session and to cap it off, Nkechi sent us a bible message to read- Psalm 65 v 5-8.

This was a very nice way to start the day and when we arrived in Kechi's room, she was alert and bright-eyed. Sister Maria, who was on duty, told us that the night before had been a bit rough for Kechi because of the fever and breathing problems, but that Kechi was fine that morning and we could see that for ourselves, just looking at her. We told her that the experiences of the previous evening were from the evil one who knew what God had in store for her future. We also told her that we had banished the demon of fear from her and she should never give in to it again.

Mom told her of the phone call from my Dad where he had seen a vision of God covering Kechi with His anointing. Dad had fallen on his knees at once, giving God thanks and praise. A little into the visit, Kechi began to retch and was given something to relax her and soon felt better.

She asked if it was Tuesday and we said yes. I know she remembered that she had surgery scheduled. When we were asked to leave so that they could change her bed linen, Betty took us to the mall to buy suitcases for Mom. Traffic delays caused us to be late for the evening visit and by the time we got to the hospital, Kechi was being prepped for surgery. I showed her pictures of the mall I had taken for her and she was pleased. We stayed with her and prayed until it was time for her to go in. She went in around 5.45pm.

Kechi was wheeled back to her room at 7.35pm and we waited about fifteen minutes before we could see her. The sister said that she had just been given 16mg of morphine and she did not want us to excite her. Kechi was obviously in pain, but for the fist time, her forehead and chin were exposed. The forehead had been grafted and heavily bandaged. Her face and lips were swollen form the surgery and she was mouthing, 'pain', 'pain'.

We told her that she has just been given morphine and it would soon take effect as long as she relaxed. We prayed and she drifted off into sleep before we left.

Later that night, as I lay in bed unable to sleep, I started to think about the various problems besetting Kechi - infections, breathing issues, blood pressure etc. I took them all before the Lord in prayer and supplication.

I asked God,

"What is the purpose of all what my baby is going through?"

As sure as if someone was seated beside me, I heard,

"She is consecrated to Me"

Emboldened, I went on to ask,

"Why the pain, why the suffering, the total disruption of her life, all the surgeries? She is only 16!"

"Look at all My prophets. Which one did not suffer? She is being purified. Trust in Me, child."

I opened my eyes, comforted. My heart still broke for my daughter's pain, but I knew that God was in charge and would strengthen her and the rest of us. I knew that He would never give her more than she was able to bear.

Chinedu called to tell me that the church in Lagos had received a prophecy on Kechi from Numbers 23 v19-23.

The passage filled me with joy especially in verse 19 where it said,

"God is not a man, that he should lie; neither the son of man, that he should repent: hath he said, and shall he not do it? or hath he spoken, and shall he not make it good?"

I settled back into sleep, content that God was on top of things and I was going to stop worrying.

I woke up the next day with a certain knowledge that we should pray against evil, particularly from occultists. Psalms 5 talks about God detesting blood-thirsty men.

Mom and I went into prayer of warfare against the enemy and his minions and then Mom prayed for us to continue to follow in the footsteps of God.

When we got to the hospital, Kechi was awake and in a lot of pain. She was given 2mg of morphine. When the pain persisted, she was given two more and she relaxed. Then she turned to me and asked,

"When am I leaving this place?"

I seized that opportunity to tell how serious her condition was when we came; how the doctors and nurses did not expect her to live. That got her attention. I went on to tell her of how she was put in an induced coma for more than a month during which time the doctors and nurses battled to save her life. Now that she was out of danger, they were facing her burns and grafting her skin. I told her that this was the time to wear patience like a garment because, though the worst was behind us, we still had a long way to go in the recovery process. I stressed that she had very severe burns all over her body. Apparently, she had seen her right arm during a dressing change, so she had a pretty good idea of the severity of her wounds. I did not say more at that time. Little by little, we would paint the complete picture of the Grace that saved her life.

I was thrilled that they had exposed more of her face - her eyes, nose and mouth were now visible and her face and lips were no longer swollen. Her face still looked very raw from the debridement, but I had faith that it was going to heal properly eventually, according to the promise of God.

After the morning visit, we went for Mom's appointment with the Orthopedist (back specialist). At the end of the session, she purchased a back brace to support her aching lower back.

During the afternoon visit, Kechi was drifting on and off because she had just received her drugs. The sisters told us that earlier on she had coughed to get their attention, and then she asked what time it was. She knew we came by 4pm and was so obviously fighting to stay awake for our visit, that I told her to go ahead and sleep, we would see her during the last visit. Mom's cousin, Dom came and picked us up to have dinner with his family. He drove through the Johannesburg city center, past the downtown area, and through to the industrial area, where they lived in a nice estate. We got to see the real Johannesburg, not just the quiet suburbs where the hotel and hospital were located. They welcomed us into their home and laid out quite a spread for us.

When we got back for the night visit, Kechi was fast asleep, which was just as well, because there seemed to be a shortage of staff in the unit. It may have been because the unit was very full that day. I recalled that earlier in the day, Mom and I had overheard the sisters complaining about their low salaries and saying that a lot of staff were resigning to go to Europe, USA, and Australia, where nurses were appreciated and paid well. There was no nurse by Kechi's bed when we got there so we waited until someone came in and was assigned to her for the night. She said her name was Faith, and she seemed like a nice person, friendly and experienced. By then I could tell who knew their job and who was new to the job. Kechi's vital signs were fine, her temperature normal, so we prayed and left.

I woke up early the following morning to pain due to a bloated stomach. I was very uncomfortable, so I took some antacid, and laid hands on my stomach and prayed for healing. I got some relief, but not much and started to feel weak. Mom and I prayed again and she laid hands on me again. "God, please I cannot afford to fall ill", I prayed.

Ulo called and told us about the prayers she offered that morning. She said she had no idea what she was praying about because she was praying in tongues, but at the end of the prayers, she got a message,

"In a short time, I will reveal them, then judgment will begin".

She had prayed for the gift of interpretation of tongues. We thanked God for His word and went off to the hospital.

Kechi was awake and very alert when we got there and the sister on duty was a lovely lady whom I had never met. Her name was Patricia, and as an added bonus, she was also a born-again Christian. It was amazing how much all the sisters loved Kechi. Even those that had worked with her earlier stopped by from time to time just to say hello and check her progress. Even the cleaners in the ICU monitored Kechi and rejoiced at every milestone.

The new thing Kechi learnt was to stop anyone passing by her bed to ask the time, so she would know exactly when it would be visiting time. Sister Patricia talked to Mom and I about getting Kechi's school books to her. She said that Kechi's brain was very alert and she needed to be stimulated to keep her that way. I decided I was going to speak with Sister Chika, Loyola Jesuit College Vice Principal, about that. Kechi then chimed in that she all her books had been with her in the plane. She asked what had happened to all her stuff. I told her not to worry about that, I could arrange to get her books from her school sent to the hospital.

Mom and I returned to the hotel room so she could pack. When we returned for the afternoon visit, Kechi's eyes were trained at the door, in anticipation of our visit. Sister Patricia had turned Kechi's head to the left so that her neck would not stiffen in the position she liked so much. She asked us to stay on Kechi's left side so she would be forced to turn her neck that way to look at us. Kechi, of course, preferred to look the other way, but Sister Patricia was firm. Kechi was a bit drowsy, but she asked if she was still going in for surgery the next day. Patricia was not sure, but thought it was unlikely because it was already late in the day and Dr. Nel had not confirmed it. Just then, Dr. Nel walked in and said that the surgery was still on for the next day. He was going to do multiple grafting on both arms. Kechi smiled because she knew that the sooner the grafting was finished, the sooner she could get out of the hospital. On our way out of the unit, one of the nurses' aides came up to tell us that she had a dream where Kechi got up and was walking up and down, going to the restroom by herself. This was very good to hear because at that time it seemed like something that was going to take a while to happen.

On our way back to the hotel, I received a phone call from Sister Chika, the very same person I was going to call for Kechi's books. By this time, God's networking should not have been surprising, but I still marveled at the timing. I wrote down her email address so I could give her details of the books I wanted for Kechi. She sent the love of the teachers and students to Kechi.

That night, Kechi had a male nurse and she was very unhappy about it. She became very agitated and Mom and I had to calm her down. We reminded her to trust that if we thought there was a problem, we would take care of it and she calmed down. We took the nurse aside and told him that Kechi was used to female nurses and he should please be patient with her. He was very understanding and told us not to worry. Kechi's physician, Dr. Pahad, suggested a nose tube for feeding so that Kechi can slowly begin to eat food from her mouth. Kechi vehemently protested and the idea was discarded immediately. When she slept off, we prayed and left.

Mom received a message the following morning,
"I am the God that delivered Israel from her bondage. I have delivered Kechi. I am the Lord. Trust me always."
Kechi was awake and asked what part of her body was going to be covered up that day. I told her that they would work on her arms. She liked my jeans and I told her I would get her the very same type. Sister Patricia was on duty again and she brought us up to date on Kechi's status. The new antibiotic seemed to be working as her temperature had come down. This was very good to hear. Mom and I asked Sister Patricia if there was a way she could be assigned to stay with Kechi regularly, and if it would be possible for Kechi not to have male nurses assigned to her again, and she said we would have to speak with the unit leader.

The unit leader said she would do her best to ensure that Kechi only got female nurses, but informed us that they were seriously short-staffed and, as it was, found it hard to get one on one patient/staff ratio. But she promised to only assign male nurses that she trusted implicitly to Kechi if she could not get a female nurse. There seemed no point after that to request for Patricia on a permanent basis. We went back and told Kechi that we had dealt with the male nurse issue and she nodded.

Betty was late in picking us up and then she had to pick her kids from school, drop them off at home, before taking us to the mall. We got to the mall at about 2.45pm, dashed about madly, and then left the mall at about 3.50pm. Not only were we late, we missed the whole visiting hour, because I had misplaced my handset at Foschini and luckily remembered it while we were in Pick 'n' Pay. We hurried back to Foschini and the phone was there. I had forgotten it in the changing room and they kept it for me. When we eventually walked into the ICU by two minutes to 5pm, we were informed that Kechi had just been taken to the OR. I felt awful.

She came out of the theatre at 6.20pm. When we were allowed in, she was awake. There was gauze covering the back of her right hand, under her left arm, and her upper right arm. The doctor came in to check on her and said they were running out of donor sites, and would have to wait for some of sites they had already used to heal, so they could use them again.

Kechi, meanwhile, was glaring accusingly at us. My hopes that with the sedation she might not remember our absence, were dashed to the ground. Mom also noticed that she was looking upset and asked me to apologize. I asked Kechi if she was upset that we missed her visiting time and her eyes filled with tears as she nodded. My heart melted and we spent the rest of that visit begging for her forgiveness. At the end of the visit, I asked if she had forgiven us and she nodded yes. I still felt terrible and she must have seen that because she then smiled at me and all was right with my world again.

I promised her that I would never miss another visit and she nodded. But when Mom asked if she thought she had been abandoned by us, she shook her head. That meant she knew that I would never leave her alone as long as she needed me, by God's grace.

Media was waiting for us when we left Kechi, with another assortment of meals.

That night I prayed for both her and Betty, for God's blessings and peace upon them and their families.

The next morning, Kechi appeared to be a bit subdued, which was not so abnormal for the day following surgery. She complained about pain and was given something for it. She then asked her Grandma to read the bible for her. Mom wanted to read from the book of Samuel, but Kechi shook her head no, mouthing that she wanted something from the book of Psalms. Mom read and explained Psalm 91 to her. This was the first time Kechi was actually reaching out for spiritual things since the accident. I welcomed this as the working of the Holy Spirit, putting a desire in her heart to hear God's word.

Mom and I left for Sandton Mall after the morning visit so that she could buy some last minute things to travel home with. I bought some undies for Kechi, in anticipation of when she would ask for them.

Back at the hospital, Kechi was in pain and the sisters told us that morphine did not appear to be working on her anymore. They feared that her body had gotten used to it, and was therefore demanding more of it in order for it to be effective. In other words, Kechi had become addicted to morphine. They were waiting for the doctor to come and prescribe another analgesic for Kechi. Meanwhile, because she was obviously in pain, they had given her an extra dose of morphine. With what she had been given so far, Kechi ought to have been knocked out and fast asleep, but she was not. Mom and I began to pray for wisdom for the doctor to prescribe a drug that would work on Kechi. After the doctor saw Kechi, he came out to the waiting room and told us that he had prescribed a different drug for Kechi, since they did not want her to be dependent on morphine.

As we waited for the next visit, we received a call from Mike, who sounded very shocked as he told us of an experience he had earlier that day. Apparently, one of the bereaved parents had asked after Kechi, and when Mike recounted the extent of her injuries, the man remarked that it would probably have been better if Kechi had died with her schoolmates. My initial reaction was shock that anyone would say that, but after thinking about it for a while, I told Mike that he was probably thinking about the pain Kechi was going through every day, not really thinking she was going to survive anyway, so why go through all that only to die in the end?

That may or may not be what he meant, but that is the way I chose to look at it. His bereavement was still very recent, and I was not going to blame him for any reaction.

That night, Kechi was asleep for the whole visit, having at last succumbed to the drugs in her system. We sang softly and prayed by her bedside. We also said a prayer for the man whose utterances had caused us pain and sorrow and asked God to continue to minister comfort to him and his family.

CHAPTER TWENTY

"And it shall come to pass afterward, that I will pour out my spirit upon all flesh; and your sons and your daughters shall prophesy, your old men shall dream dreams, your young men shall see visions."
Joel 2:28(KJV)

Around 3.30am the next morning, I started to have a series of what I will call visions, since I was no longer fully asleep at that time.

Vision Number One

I was seated in place like an airport and people were passing. Suddenly, something stopped and stood there, looking at me. Something, not someone, because it was shaped like a woman, but had an extra eye in its face. I looked up, and it was looking at me. When it noticed I had seen it, it came and stood in front of me and from it emanated anger, jealousy and hate. I immediately started to pray and to plead the blood of Jesus over Kechi and myself. I called on the Holy Spirit to surround us with His fire. I called on the angels to draw their flaming swords and to attack and repel the evil one.

The thing disappeared.

Vision Number Two

Then I found myself in a place like a shop. A hand reached out and gave me two articles of clothing, like sweaters, and a voice said,

"I have clothed you with righteousness and truth, and My truth is your shield and buckler".

Then the voice came again,

"Take up your cross and follow me".

A scripture ran across my mind then 1 John 4 v 1, where it was written,

"Dear friends, do not believe every spirit, but test the spirits to see whether they are from God, because many false prophets have gone out into the world.

This is how you can recognize the Spirit of God: Every spirit that acknowledges that Jesus Christ has come in the flesh is from God".(NIV)

I spoke out loud,
"Did Jesus Christ, the Son of God, die and was resurrected?
Is it You, Lord?"
The answer came, clear as a bell,
"I, child".
The voice came again,
"Nations shall crumble, nations shall fall".
I asked again, "Is it You, Lord?"
"I, child".

Then a resounding chorus started and it was a chorus I knew well:
The cloud of glory is moving
Let us move with the cloud
Move with the cloud
Let our spirits arise
And our strength be renewed

Come, let us move on together
As we follow where He leads
New heights we'll attain
As we move with the cloud
Move with the cloud.

As the chorus became more and more resounding, something started to happen. I tried to reach out to Mom, because I could hear her on the phone with someone, but I could not move physically. I was not frightened, though.

Vision Number Three

The I saw swirling clouds with pinpoints of light in them, rolling and mixing, then the clouds started spinning. They formed a tunnel and at the end of it, forms were taking shape. Then I saw that they were forming words and I paid close attention. While this was going on, I could not move my body, but I was having the sensation of movement and sound, but nothing loud or unpleasant. I will never be able to describe exactly what I saw and felt.

Then I saw that the letter T had formed clearly and as other letters formed, I thought it was going to spell out TRUTH, but what formed was the word TIME.

Then everything faded.

I asked, "What does it mean, Lord?"

He answered, **"It is time for Me to be revealed to My people"**.

At this point, I was able to move and I went across to Mom's bed and told her all I could remember of what had happened. She asked me to write everything down at once, and then she knelt down and began to pray. It was when I was writing things down that I noticed that on the scriptures at the bottom of my notebook had two scriptures about righteousness. (Matthew 5:6 and Matthew 6:33).

I fell down and began to worship God.

After writing all that I have recounted so far, I lay back in bed and started singing in Igbo,

Kedu ihe m g'eji kelee Gi, o Onye Oma?
Ihe I mere di mu mma, Onye Ukwu!

Roughly translated, it means,

How can I possibly thank You enough, Good God?
You have been so good to me, great God!

Then I thought to myself, 'No, it is not enough to sing. I need to act. To sing is lazy and unproductive. I need to find out what God wants me to do. Specific tasks. Is it evangelism? What?

I knelt down and heard the voice again,

"I have given you power far more than you can ever imagine. Go and lay hands on your daughter and see her recover".

I whispered over and over again, "Amen, Lord. I believe, I believe".

And then I actually felt a tingling in my hands!

We eventually went back to sleep, but my experiences were far from over.

Vision Number Four

As soon as I closed my eyes, I saw a man standing in front of a mighty creature trying to subdue it with prayers of warfare. Then the explanation came.

I was told that if I looked closely at the gigantic, fierce creature, more than fifty feet high, I would see that it was really an ant. It represented a problem, a challenge that was very small, and just needed to be crushed underfoot by faith. Instead, fear had come in and the problem, on a steady diet of fear, grew larger and larger until it became gigantic and now could only be subdued and gotten rid of by intense warfare.

I got the message.

Never allow yourself to give in to fear, unless you may find yourself wasting precious time and energy fighting unnecessary battles. By faith, you can nip potential problems in the bud.

Later, I saw Kechi and myself. She was lying on a bed and I was smoothing something that felt like olive oil into her skin. A few parts of her body were still sore and scarred, but her personality was as sunny as ever and she was talking and laughing. I thanked God and drifted off into sleep.

❖

I woke up and went over everything that had happened in my mind. I knew that there was a need to remain very vigilant against the wiles of the evil one, and never to allow fear to get a toe in. I felt very blessed that God had clothed me in His righteousness and truth, even though I still felt unworthy; I mean, who the heck was I to merit such grace? But in retrospect, I realize that on that night, I was given the strength I would need for many years to come, even for the rest of my life.

As for the rest of the vision, I had no clue what it meant at that time, but with the current political, economic and spiritual situations around the world, it is now clear to me that they were prophetic. God is right now being revealed to His people, and even those who do not believe in Him can clearly see that this world is set for major changes, one way or the other.

We woke up a bit late and prayed and laid hands on Mom's hips (she had tried to lift a heavy box the day before, and was feeling the effects of her actions. I had warned her not to, but she went ahead, anyway), then we left for the hospital.

Kechi was bright and wide-awake, eyes sparkling. She smiled when we came in, and I laid hands on her, as I was instructed. Then Kechi started to scratch her stomach with her bandaged hand and said that it was itching. Then she also started to scrunch her face up, saying that her face also itched. Though I did not know it then, itching was going to prove to be even worse than pain.

I showed her the pretty undies and clothes I bought for her, and her eyes shone.

A women's group that Layi belonged to, called Nigerian Daughters, had brought a gift for Kechi the previous day, so I opened it and it was an audio bible on CDs in a lovely case. It was a very thoughtful gift. Kechi asked Mom to read to her again from the bible and she did until it was time for us to leave for the airport. After Mom checked in, I told her to go on and sit in the lounge because I did not want her standing for too long because of her back.

I felt bereft when she left, but I pulled myself together, and went back to the hospital.

Kechi was waiting for me during the next visiting period. I was now certain her internal clock was tuned to visiting periods and resolved again never to miss another one. I told her about the airport trip, and a whole lot of other things. She was in the mood to be entertained, so I just talked and told her stories. She asked about surgery and I said I was not sure. I told her that when her Dad came, we would meet with the doctors and find out more details. She then asked me to slot in the bible CD from Genesis before leaving.

That night, she was drowsy at first, so I just sat there and gazed at her until she woke up around 8.00pm. She immediately asked the time, and I told her we had thirty minutes more. I talked to her, prayed with her and laid hands on her. Before I left, she had slept and I prayed for her temperature to come down, and for her blood pressure to come up within normal range. I committed her sleep to God and left.

What a day it had been! I was totally exhausted and just crawled into bed and was asleep in minutes.

Mike came in around 7. 00 am. I was very happy to see him. My family was trying very hard to make sure there was always someone with me and I really appreciated it and them. Mike brought letters from lots of people - my friends and the Women's fellowship members from Aba. A lot of the envelopes contained money, and I was overwhelmed with all the love, support and good wishes.

Mike and I went to Dr. Nel's office first to set up an appointment because Mike wanted to get an update on Kechi's condition. As it happened, the doctor said he had some free time then, and Mike went in to have the update. I declined. I had had enough of doctor's reports; I only believed God's report.

When we went in to see Kechi, she was dozing, which was very disappointing for Mike. But just then, maybe hearing her Daddy's voice, Kechi opened her eyes, saw him and this huge grin split her face. Mike was not looking at her and when I called his attention, he and Kechi just became lost in each other for a long moment.

Then the dam broke.

Kechi burst out crying. She cried so hard and for so long. Mike was completely helpless and wanted to hold her, but could not. I gave him gloves to wear so he could touch the parts of her body that were not bandaged. He touched her face and her arms, all the while consoling her and encouraging her to be strong. He nearly came undone.

I also put on gloves and held Kechi's head, comforting her. After a while, she calmed down and Mike told her how much he loved her, how proud he was of her, and how much God loved her.

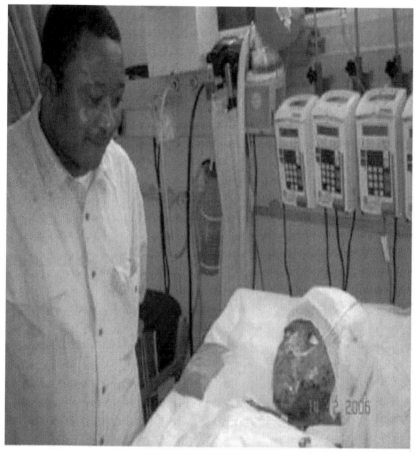

Kechi is awake for her Dad's second visit to Milpark Hospital

Kechi's eyes were trained on her Dad, unblinking.

When she had relaxed, Mike showed her the CDs he had brought for her and she smiled some more. Dr. Pahad came in and he and Mike discussed Kechi's progress. He told us that the tube down her throat would stay on for a while because of her upcoming surgeries. Kechi was not pleased and Mike took time to explain things to her, telling her to be patient. The doctor said Kechi was doing very well. The last infection was sensitive to the antibiotic and was under control. He had booked Kechi into the theater for later that day because they wanted to remove all her bandages and have a look at her wounds; they also wanted to search for a donor site in preparation for her next skin graft.

When we returned at 4.00 pm, she was being prepped for the OR and we stayed until they booted us out. We waited in the hallway so we would see her when she was wheeled out. She was surprised and pleased to see us, and we called out to her that we loved her, and blew kisses at her as she went by, and then we went to the waiting lounge to stay until she came out.

Kechi was wheeled back to her room at 5.30pm, but we could not see her until the visiting time. When we went in, she was awake, but in pain. The sister could not give her anything for pain because she had been given a dose by 7.00pm and it was an hourly dose, the next one due at 8.00 pm. I asked Kechi if the pain was bad and she nodded. I explained to her that the next dose was in 15 minutes and told her that God would never let her experience more than she could handle. She nodded, but monitored the time until 8.00pm, when she got the next dose of morphine. She soon became drowsy but was fighting sleep because we were there. I told Mike that we should leave so we prayed and left.

Mike woke very early after a bad dream and woke me up to ask me to pray. He was very agitated and restless, but after we prayed, he settled down and went back to sleep.

❖

When we woke up again, we did our morning devotions and went in to see Kechi.

She had her eyes trained on the doorway when we entered, and the sister said she had been asking them the time every few minutes. She was in pain, but they were trying to get her to stop on-demand pain medication and stick to a regimen. Since the next dose was just thirty minutes away, I convinced her to bear the pain until then and she agreed. She wanted us to talk to her and I asked Mike to take over since I had been doing all the talking before then. Mike did not waste any time at all and soon he and Kechi were smiling at each other.

At 12.00pm, when sister Veronica began to organize Kechi's drugs, we left, promising to be back at the stroke of 4.00pm.

We headed to the mall to buy some warm clothing for Mike. When we got to Musica, a music store, he went a bit crazy because they had some old CDs he had been looking a long time for. Back at the hospital, Kechi appeared to be in pain again, but the good news was that she was bearing the pain better, knowing that she would be given her medication at a specific time.

Then came the even better news. Sister Veronica told us that Kechi sipped a whole glass of juice with a straw. Then Dr. Pahad came in with the best news of all - since Kechi did so well with the juice, they were going to start reducing the liquid feed so that she would get hungry, start semi-solid food, and eventually will have the feeding tube in her mouth removed. I was concerned about the trachea tube still in her throat and asked if she could still feed with that still attached and he explained that the tube had something that closed off the tube end to prevent food from going into her lungs.

This was such amazing news for us because it signified one more step in Kechi's recovery. We shared the news with Kechi and she gave a huge smile.

When she was given her drugs, she became drowsy and as usual began to fight to stay awake because we were there, so I dragged Mike out after reading Psalms 91 and 118 to her. I had begun to ask the Holy Spirit to minister to me what Kechi needed to hear from the bible, because she now always asked for the bible to be read to her every time we visited.

During the night visit, she was fast asleep. I liked to see her sleeping because it meant that at that point, she was not in pain. Her temperature had gone up a bit from 36.7 degrees that afternoon to 37.8. Mike was starting to worry and began to pace because Kechi's respiration was a bit fast. I was not very concerned, but Mike was a different matter. I tried to calm him down, while sighing inwardly. It was going to be a long three weeks. Mike was a worrier, though he would fight tooth and nail to prove the contrary. With fifteen minutes till the end of the visit, Kechi woke up and we talked with her, prayed and left.

After our morning devotions the next day, I decided to go down to the lobby and check my emails. I had a whole lot of mail, but the server at the hotel was slow and the emails were not loading fast enough, so I just sent an update on Kechi's progress to her best friend, Womiye, knowing she would tell the rest of their friends.

Kechi had a twinkle in her eyes when we got to her room that morning. I found out why when I went to her side and she opened her mouth. 'The tube is gone', I shouted. She nodded vigorously and then began to mouth very fast,

'I'm having potatoes and chicken this afternoon and they said that when you come, you should give me that ice cream.'

I looked on her nightstand beside her and there was a cup of ice cream there. The sister assigned to her that day was not in the room so I went to verify from one of the other sisters nearby and she gave the go ahead.

"Are you ready?" I asked Kechi. She nodded. I wore gloves, and spooned ice cream into her open mouth.

"How does it feel?" I asked.

She closed her eyes in bliss. I gave her about six spoons before she said she had had enough.

She mouthed, "I'm so excited".

I told her that excited did not come close to what I was feeling, and that the family would flip when I told them. Mike was beside himself with excitement. We just began to praise God at this very major step forward.

All the excitement soon got to Kechi and her eyelids began to droop. I told her I was going to go out and buy her a present to celebrate her first meal, and we left her so she could get some sleep. Mike wanted to buy some novels, so we went to FourWays mall where I also bought a lovely pair of closed-toe, Roman-styled sandals with sequins for Kechi.

During the next visit, she was uncomfortable and cross because a pillow had been put under her right side to lift her to another position to avoid pressure sores.

Her face was a thundercloud and nothing her Dad or I said could convince her to leave the pillow there and the nurse had to take it away.

She also wanted the pillow under her head removed; she preferred just the pressure ring she was used to having under her head. After all that was removed, she said she was in pain and was given two pain tablets, which she took with a protein drink. Kechi was now taking pills! I was happy.

When we came for the night visit, I learnt that she had asked the sister to leave her food for me to feed her. It was pasta and mince and she hated it. When I tried to convince her to eat, she told me she would throw it up. When I patiently explained to her that if she did not eat, the feeding tube would be put back, she ate a few bites of the pasta and drank all the juice.

The nurse did not seem very concerned that Kechi did not eat much; maybe it was because she had eaten most of her lunch. She seemed okay after the little she ate, and I was just happy that she was eating at all.

CHAPTER TWENTY-ONE

"Be sober, be vigilant; because your adversary the devil, as a roaring lion, walketh about, seeking whom he may devour:"
1 Peter 5 : 8 (KJV)

Things were getting a bit tense between Mike and I, so much so that he refused to participate in the singing during our morning devotions. We had been having arguments on just about everything, which usually ended with me deciding to be the bigger person and apologize, though I knew I was right. The problem was that with every apology, he felt justified, and convinced that I just liked to criticize everything he did just for the fun of it. At one point, he even said that I was making him uncomfortable and maybe he should not have come to South Africa at all. This just confirmed what I had been feeling since he came that he was not convinced he should have made the trip in the first place.

I was very upset, but could feel the Spirit of God reining me in. I thought to myself that satan must have been enjoying himself, reveling in the clashes between Mike and I, looking to create a rift between God and us.

I was not about to let that happen. I cautioned myself not to respond. I just let him be until we both calmed down. The main problem was that we were used to making decisions regarding the family together and Mike had gotten used to being on his own and doing what he felt was best and did not brook any suggestion that he might have handled things differently. And okay, maybe I should have been more moderate in my criticisms; after all, I was not the only person whose world had been turned upside down. I prayed for direction from God and for the strength I would need to also shoulder this added burden Not surprisingly, I was a little depressed going in to see Kechi that morning, and given the fact that I had no idea how to keep my feelings from showing on my face, I was relieved that Kechi was sleeping. The sister said that she had eaten her breakfast of cereal, scrambled eggs, and juice very well. Kechi slept through the whole visiting hour and while Mike opted to stay behind in the hospital to see Kechi's doctors, I went back to the hotel to wait for the hairdresser that Betty had arranged for me. He came too close to visiting time to do much so we rescheduled for Saturday.

Kechi had just been cleaned and given her pain medications when I arrived for the afternoon visit. She was drowsy and was drifting in and out of sleep, but insisted that we stayed and talked to her. I read Chapter 2 of "The Purpose-Driven Life" by Rick Warren to her. I found that it was quite suited to her own peculiar situation. We left after I promised to come back in time to feed her the night meal.

Mike led the prayers the next morning. I was relieved that he had gotten over yesterday's annoyance.

Kechi was awake and happy to see us. She said she finished her breakfast and I told her that it was because she was hungry, not having eaten her dinner the night before. We discussed the pill taking, which she was not too crazy about, because they were bitter and large, thus hard to swallow. I told her they lasted far longer than the hourly morphine, up to six hours and she reluctantly agreed to continue taking them.

Dr. Nel came in to say that Kechi was going into the OR that day so that all the dressings on her whole body would be removed and the doctors could take a look at all the burns and grafted skin and determine if the donor sites were healed enough to be harvested for grafting. They preferred to do this in the sterile environment of the theater because so much of her body was still raw and prone to infection.

Kechi received the news of going to the OR very well. She was by now very used to the routine. She began to get drowsy and we read Psalm 139 to her before leaving. Mike wanted to go back to the mall to exchange some stuff and I also had a sweater to change. I had bought it in my normal size and it was too big. I had no idea I was even losing weight. Mike bought so much that he exhausted the money he came with and I had to give him some. He promised to send me money as soon as he got back to Nigeria, but I did not mind. It was good to see him having fun after all the stress he had been through. I had my faith to keep me going, but he was still new at the whole faith thing.

Thankfully, we got back in time for the evening visit, and were able to visit with Kechi because she had not yet gone to the OR. She was very alert and feeling naughty. She started to experiment with holding her breath, almost giving me a heart attack when I saw her respiration as a flat line on the monitor. I shook my head at her, telling her I was going to take her over my knee and spank her if she did it again. She smiled and winked at me, then poked out her tongue, blowing me a raspberry. Mike just shook his head at both of us, all the while rejoicing that Kechi was showing echoes of her feisty self.

Meanwhile, she flatly refused for Mike to play his rock CDs on her CD player, even after much begging and cajoling on Mike's part. She was very chatty that evening, telling me to ditch my glasses and get contact lenses because she thought my glasses hid my eyes. Since she had an opinion on everything, I told her I wanted to put in a weave, and did she think that I should have a fringe cut? She thought a fringe would be a different look on me and I should go for it.

Then she asked about school, wanted to know how long we were going to stay in South Africa, and what about the amount of school she had lost. I told her that not to worry about school for now and reminded her that it was the living that went to school. This drew a smile from her. I then showed her the white jeans I had bought for her as promised.

The OR called for her around 5.45pm and Mike and I settled down to wait for her.

She was shivering from cold when we went in to see her. Her temperature was 34.3 degrees! She was also in tremendous pain. The sister informed us that she was given 15mg of morphine in the theater and could not be given any more so soon. I begged Kechi to try and be patient and wait for the drug to kick in and for the warming blanket to gradually warm up, but she was inconsolable and wept from the pain and the cold. My heart was breaking from seeing her in such agony, but I could not let her see how distraught I was. I had to be strong for her.

Mike and I managed to calm her enough to stop crying, but she was obviously in serious pain and I began to pray, to ask God for mercy and remove the pain from her. I reminded Him that He said He would not give us more than we were able to bear. The pain persisted and I finally asked Mike to find out from the nurse if Kechi had been given her analgesic tablets. The nurse brought the tablets and wanted to crush them and mix them with a little water for easier ingestion, but Kechi said she could drink them whole, and we waited for them to take effect.

Meanwhile, Kechi kept asking us if her body was covered, while she had four blankets covering her. I had never seen her take so much time to warm up after surgery. Her temperature had inched up to 34.7 degrees. After some time, she said that the pain had reduced and she was no longer as cold as she was, but she was still shivering. I continued to pray and lay hands on her. She drifted off for a little while, then opened her eyes and complained about pain again. I spoke to the sister on duty, Hannah, but she said there was nothing she could do, they had given Kechi the maximum dosage of morphine they could without shutting down her respiration entirely and killing her. The sister was sounding quite exasperated and told us that she wondered why Kechi did not sleep like other patients who had been administered the same drugs. She complained that Kechi did not sleep for more than three hours at a stretch. I was really shocked at her attitude because she was unsympathetic and never addressed Kechi directly or even went close to her bed to talk to her. When the kitchen staff came to find out if Kechi wanted dinner, she said she did not know and called out to Kechi almost from the door to ask her if she wanted to eat.

I was very upset by this and made a note to complain to the matron the next morning. I was wary of getting on the bad side of those who I would ultimately leave Kechi with, but a line had to be drawn somewhere. Hopefully, my complaint would not be the first and she would be straightened out. I had the greatest respect for nurses, but once in a while, there was one bad egg.

When I ascertained that her temperature was still climbing, and her pain level was tolerable, Mike and I left, thirty minutes after the end of visiting time.

The sister had given her something to make her sleep, and she was drifting off as we left. I told her I had prayed for a peaceful sleep for her.

I pushed a reluctant Mike out of the room, telling him that we have to let God be God. We had done our part; we prayed, laid hands on her, reminding God that the same resurrection power that raised Christ from the dead lay within us, and believed Him for answered prayers. The rest was up to Him. Mike then told me that Dr. Nel had said that some of the grafted skin had become infected and were being cultured so that they could start her on antibiotics. I had also noticed that they had exposed part of her grafted forehead. It then occurred to me that I had not seen Kechi's eyebrows, which had been intact after the accident. They never grew back.

This was one of the down days we had been warned would come. We just had to believe that God was still in control.

I woke up briefly in the night to a reassurance from God that He was still in control. Unfortunately, I did not write down all I heard, in the conviction that I would remember it in the morning. I did not.

A lesson for next time.

Now I know why Mom had insisted I wrote down the vision I had received immediately.

In spite of God's reassurances, I woke up with a heart full of anguish for my daughter's pain. I knelt down and cried out to God for mercy. I poured out all my fears and concerns about Kechi's face and begged for mercy for her. I asked for forgiveness for appearing to doubt His promise for her and asked him to forgive the anguish of a mother that gave rise to such thoughts. For instance, I would look at Kechi's face and wonder how she would feel if the will of God permitted her face to be disfigured. I prayed, "God forgive me for these thoughts, it's a moment of weakness. But your strength is made perfect in my weakness, so that when I am weak, I am strong".

Like I had reminded Mike the night before, we were all also going through the fire.

"Dear Lord", I prayed, "may we all shine forth as gold, in Jesus' name. Amen."

Kechi was very bright and cheerful the next morning, clearly feeling great. I was very thankful to God for the complete change from the previous night. We had a great visit, with me telling her stories and making her laugh. I told her I would wait to feed her lunch to her. She ate all of her mashed potatoes and a few mouthfuls of meat loaf, and juice. As usual, she did not touch the vegetables, but it was a good attempt, and the sister was pleased. We asked Kechi to try and take a nap before we returned for the next visit.

We had to wait for twenty minutes before seeing her because her dressings were being changed. She was still in good spirits, but she had just been given a shot of morphine, and her eyes kept closing so we asked her to get some sleep.

Ade, the hairdresser, came to fix my weave, and he was not very fast, so when visiting time came up, I asked Mike to go ahead, I would meet up with him. Ife, Ulo's friend and colleague, came to the hotel and offered to wait and drive me to the hospital, because she also wanted to see Kechi.

Kechi was waiting for me to feed her, although Mike had persuaded her to eat a few mouthfuls. I fed her three spoons of mashed potatoes and two bites of chicken, her juice cup and protein drink. We stayed with her until 9.00pm, and then prayed with her and told her to sleep. I also told her that she should begin to pray by herself also, that she was very close to God at that time and there was nothing she would ask Him for that He would not give her.

Ulo sent a text later that evening to tell me of her experience with God that morning. She said in the text that "He questioned our love for Him, if it was indeed unconditional".

She called later to give details and said,

"God says we do not know who we are in Him and what tremendous power, resurrection power we have in us. He asks what if He took Kechi home now, will He still be God to us?"

Ulo said she pleaded with Him and reminded Him about Isaac and how God restored him back to Abraham whole, and she asked for mercy on behalf of our whole family.

I told Ulo about my prayer as I laid hands on Kechi that day, how I had reminded God that I had resurrection power in me. Mike also testified that when I was praying, I also touched on several things he had privately prayed about. It was very refreshing to me that we were in sync spiritually. For me it was confirmation that God was present in a very real way in the whole process.

Ulo went on to say that like the bible said, we should just watch and see, that eyes had not seen, ears had not heard and the mind could not even conceive what God had in store for us. She said she had a very strong feeling that God was about to astound us, she did not know how, but was certain that a major miracle was about to enfold. With rejoicing in our hearts, Mike and I sang the following song as part of our worship that night:

"He is able, more than able
To accomplish what concerns me today He is able, more than able
To handle anything that comes my way He is able, more than able
To do much more than I could ever dream He is able, more than able
To make me what He wants me to be".

The following morning, Mike and I obeyed a prompting of the Spirit, and just praised God. We then completed Galatians 6 and the part of the scripture that jumped out was that God is not mocked and whatsoever a man sows, he shall reap. I found myself really hoping that I had not messed up in any way.

We also read Chapter 4 of The Purpose-Driven Life where the lesson of the day was living each day in preparation for eternity with God.

I had received so many emails from Kechi's friends and schoolmates that I made out time to print them out so I could read them to her that morning. She was very thrilled to hear all the school gossip, and asked me to respond and tell them that she loved and missed them, and hoped to be back in time for prom.

I fed her lunch and her appetite had greatly improved. This time she almost finished the mashed potatoes and ate more than half of the chicken. She was in pain and the sister said she was waiting for us to leave so she could turn her and give her painkillers. They were still turning her body from one side to the other so that she did not develop bedsores from being in a position for too long. We left at once so they could get on with it.

Mike, being the friendly person he was, had gotten quite friendly with some white South Africans. One of the men, Owen said he had a relative in the ICU. We later found out it was his wife. They told Mike that they would like to invite us for lunch in their house some day.

When we returned in the afternoon, Kechi had just been given a shot of morphine and was quiet and subdued. Ulo called me and I left the room to answer the phone. All Kechi's friends were on the phone, asking how she was doing. Atuora, Womiye, Somachi, Yimi, Doyin etc. I told them that she was doing well and sent her love. They all asked me to give Kechi their love and to tell her that they missed her and were praying for her.

I went in to tell Kechi, thinking she would be very excited, but she became even more subdued, and in fact remained that way for the rest of the visit. I figured that she was missing being among her friends, and tried my best to distract her with stories, but nothing worked. She soon complained about pain and when she was given another shot, her eyes began to close, so we prayed and left.

The following morning, I printed out some more emails from Kechi's friends, but this time I made sure to ask if she wanted to hear them before I read them to her. She was very agreeable, and laughed over a lot the contents of the mails. Most of it did not make sense to me, as there were many LJC references.

After I put the letters away, I told Kechi we had something to discuss.
I asked her,
"Do you feel sad being in the hospital when all your friends are in school and seem to be having fun?"

I was amazed when she shook her head, but I thought that she was sparing my feelings because she knew that if she said she was sad, then I would be too.
I continued,
"I'm glad you feel that way because it means that you understand that the most important thing now is that God spared your life and you are healing more and more every day. Just continue to take it a day at time, ok?"

She nodded.

I went on to tell her that everything concerning my life in Nigeria, my job in the bank, even Tara, was on hold until she got better, and the same should hold true for her. Nothing, not her school, activities or friends, was as important right then as her journey back to full health.

I told her that God had been in control of the situation from the time of the accident until that day and everything had fit together perfectly because His hand was in it.

Kechi had been listening very intently and seemed to understand. Then she nodded. I hoped I had been able to allay some of her concerns.

Dr. Nel had Kechi down for skin graft surgery that afternoon. I supposed he must have found skin to harvest for grafting. I prayed with Kechi, asking God especially to spare her the excessive pain and cold that had happened after the last surgery. She was not supposed to eat, but she kept yawning and complaining that she was hungry, so the sister, Tchidi, said she would increase her IV fluids so she would not feel hungry.

She left for surgery about 3.50pm and came out at 5.15pm.

She was fast asleep when we peeked in on her at 6.00pm, and was still in deep slumber at 7.30, so we decided to leave because if she heard our voices, she would struggle to wake up. Her face was partially covered by a white linen cloth draped over the top of her face. The sister told us that skin from her inner thighs had been used to graft onto her left thigh.

We prayed over her and left.

The following morning, just when I was struggling to make sense of a dream I had where I had given birth to a baby girl, I received a conference call from my cousins, Chinwe and Francis, from America. It was quite exciting as Francis was sounding very grown up and I had not spoken with him since his Mom, my Aunt's, funeral several years back. They were very concerned about Kechi, and anxious to know how she was doing. We had a nice chat and they asked me to give Kechi their love.

I went back to thinking about my dream. Now more than ever, I believed that Kechi had been restored back from death and the life she had now was a new birth, a second chance, hence my giving birth to a baby girl in my dream. I got up, eager to praise and worship God as usual, but Mike had other plans.

He said he wanted to change the tone of our morning devotions. We would read from the bible first before praying. This meant that we did not sing that morning, and for as long as I had been born again, I always started morning devotion by singing praises to God. But I let him have his way; he was the head of the household, after all.

He chose to read from Ephesians, and then went on to pray. I only joined in to pray for Owen's wife. We went on to read Chapter 5 of The Purpose Driven Life.

Then Mike came up with something that he obviously felt very strongly about. He referred to a comment I had made concerning New Age religion and wanted to set me straight on certain issues.

He told me that my Mom and I, as well as members of our church were guilty of arrogance because we believed that we had found the only path to God. It was his opinion that all religions lead to God.

I asked him what part of "I am the Way, the Truth and the Life. No one comes to the Father except through Me" was ambiguous. This set him off and he ranted about my close-mindedness.

I told him as calmly as I could that he should make sure he did not make himself a stumbling block in our present situation and should wrestle his intellect into submission before it led him astray. I said to Mike,

"If I am arrogant, then like Paul, I will boast in Christ and the message of the gospel. The sum of my beliefs is The Bible, and I simply do not have, nor do I want to have, room for anything else."

He asked what was going to happen to Muslims and Buddhists and by this time I was really exasperated and I told him rather shortly that I did not know, but given what I had said earlier about Jesus being the only Way, they had better look for Him.

This argument had been a long time coming. Mike and I had belonged to the Grail Movement for ten years and after I became born again in a very dramatic way, I left the movement and embraced a new life in Christ. Mike never really left as formally as I did and to this day, he still clings to some of the things he learnt there. For instance, he said then that the Grail Message teaches one to be a better Christian. I took up issues with that because, unlike him, I had read it from beginning to end twice, and I asked him how it was possible for the Grail Message to make people better Christians when the author did not believe in redemption through the blood of Christ. He did not even know this because he never finished reading the book.

I also took the opportunity to caution him about something I had heard him say to one of the nurses. The woman had come to him with questions, intrigued by the way we prayed constantly by Kechi's bed. Mike started to evangelize to this woman, telling her to search both the bible and the Grail Message for answers.

I told him that he had made God a promise to become born-again if his daughter survived the plane crash. He had gone on to give his life, and should be more concerned about learning what it really took to continue his journey to know God better, and stop looking backwards at the life he had left behind. He had been given an opportunity to lead a soul to Christ and he had not done so.

When I saw that the discussion was rapidly deteriorating into a bitter argument, and getting more and more intellectual, I told him we were late for the visit and should get going. But I was very uneasy.

Since October 1998, when I became born again, I had been praying for my husband to also give his life to Christ. Mike is such a wonderful human being, the kind of guy that everyone, both men and women, are drawn to and like. But I knew that it was not enough to have a great personality. You must be born again to enter the kingdom of God. Mike is very cerebral, an intellectual. He questions everything. I had a feeling that now that Kechi was out of immediate danger, he was starting to question if he had even needed to become born again. But no one had pressured him; he had come up with that all by himself, on his way from Aba to Port Harcourt that fateful day.

I resolved to put it away. I would just continue to pray.

When we went in to see Kechi, I stopped in shock by the door. Her face was without the usual bandages, aside from around her forehead. She also had a bandage at the back of her head. She no longer looked like she was wearing a helmet; it was like she was wearing a hat, like the white one Muslims wear. Her cheeks were exposed down to her chin and neck. Her lower left jaw was grafted and healing nicely, and under the scabs, new skin was showing.

While we were drinking in the sight of Kechi's face, the physiotherapists told us that they were waiting for us to leave so that they could block the trachea tube, allowing Kechi to talk. We wanted to leave at once, but Kechi said no, she wanted us to stay till the end of the visiting period. When we left, Mike went outside to stretch his legs and I stayed in the waiting room, also waiting to feed her.

Soon, one of the therapists came in and told me to come and hear my daughter's voice. I rushed into Kechi's room and Kechi said, "Hi, Mom".

I stood stock-still. I could not believe my ears. Kechi's voice after two months! That moment was one of the most incredible ones of my life. I was just jumping up and down shouting, "To God be the glory, to God be the glory". Her voice was more high pitched than I remembered, but I knew it would get back to normal.

Everyone was very excited and then Kechi said, "Mommy, I love you" and they all went, "Oh, shame!", which is something South Africans say when they are touched.

When I could settle down, I fed Kechi her lunch, which was mashed potatoes and fish.

Kechi said, "the fish is nice" in her new high voice.. She was eating better and better and the sister said she had asked for extra eggs after breakfast.

I called Mike on the phone, but did not tell him Kechi was talking. When he walked into the room, Kechi said, "Hi, Daddy", and Mike almost passed out. He was quite overcome and his eyes filled with tears. He gripped my shoulder so tight that it hurt for several hours after that. He thanked God under his breath and then laughed when Kechi asked him, "What's up, Dad?"

It was quite a show as all the nurses and therapists had hung around to wait for Mike's reaction and he got some ribbing from the male nurses he had become friendly with.

Mike was lost for words and we both took a little time to get used to hearing Kechi speak again.

Kechi kept fiddling with the oxygen tube in her nose, insisting that she could breathe well without it. We talked her into getting used to it, and she relaxed for a while. Then she started to complain that air going into her nose was cold. We told the nurse and she attached a humidifier to it, and Kechi relaxed again.

During the next visit, Kechi was holding herself rigidly and I knew this meant she was in pain. The nurse gave her a shot and she became drowsy, but refused to drop off until we promised not to leave her. She however fought sleep and was drifting in and out until it was time for us to leave.

She was fast asleep when we came in for the night visit, and we discovered a new problem, her eyes remained open even while asleep because her upper eyelids had contracted, and also the grafting on her forehead had pulled up her lids. I voiced my concerns to the physiotherapist and she said Kechi must practice closing her eyes fully so that they did not remain open permanently. She also told us to get Kechi to practice deep breathing to expand her lungs, and to turn her neck to the left from time to time, so it did not stiffen in the right position that she favored.

We promised to get Kechi to do all that whenever we visited her, then we prayed and left for the night.

CHAPTER TWENTY-TWO

"Thy word is a lamp unto my feet, and a light unto my path".
Psalm 119 : 105 (KJV)

DAY 66

As I wrote in my journal the night before, I realized it had been sixty-five days since the Sosoliso crash. The days had just flown by and each day merged into the other in an endless stream of hospital visits and total gratitude and submission to God's will. I was far from being the perfect Christian, but at least I was learning to trust God more and more every day. It was really a bit hard not to, given the miracles that came our way every day. Just being able to visit Kechi every day, be with her, talk to her, and now hear her voice as she responded to things going on around her were miracles. God was very close during those days in South Africa, just as if He were sitting beside me, and I often spoke to Him. I realized how blessed I was, and frequently prostrated myself on the floor in my room, crying and thanking Him. I did not know then, and still do not know now, why I was chosen to be the recipient of such immense grace, but I was very grateful, and I made sure He knew it.

Kechi was half asleep when we got to the hospital the next morning. She had just been washed and given a combination of pain and muscle-relaxing drugs. She knew we were there, and she kept drifting between sleep and wakefulness. She whispered, 'Gist me, please', so I sat down and just talked to her. I have no idea what I used to talk endlessly to her about. I just rambled from one topic to another. I know she used to love to hear about some of her antics from when she was much younger. She had always been a very mischievous girl. I told her that the wife of the Nigerian Ambassador had invited me to lunch that day at the embassy in Pretoria. Throughout the time I was talking to her, she was still drifting in and out of sleep. Then she said to me that she had been having some strange dreams.

In the first one, she saw herself all alone in a huge field. Suddenly a beam of light shone down from heaven and surrounded her. Then the light started to go back to heaven and lifted her with it until she got to heaven.

Then she did not remember anything else.

In the second dream, we were all in Ike and Betty's house. She said that there was a party going on and everyone was dressed on retro clothes, and dancing all over the place, on the tables, everywhere, to retro music. She was having a lot of fun watching everyone have fun.

I told her that I was no Daniel, but I would do my best to try and interpret both dreams.

The first one, to me, confirmed what we knew and believed - the presence of God and His anointing had been upon Kechi from the very beginning. I asked if she had been frightened at any point in the dream and she said no. I told her it was God confirming to her that she was bathed in His love and she should bask in it and give thanks.

The second dream, I told her, signified rejoicing at the end of her sojourn in the hospital. I told her that God was very close to her at that point in her life and the Holy Spirit resided in her. I also told her to inquire from God the interpretation of any dreams she had.

When Mike and I went outside to wait for the embassy car and driver, we discussed the dreams, and Mike said he was not surprised that Kechi was receiving visions and dreams, and he had in fact expected it. We also talked about the new skin we could see forming under the scabs on her face and I told Mike that maybe that was the meaning of my dream about having a new baby. Maybe God was telling me that Kechi was going to be reborn and made new. Then he told me about a dream he had just after Kechi left for Johannesburg. He dreamt that he saw a child lying on a bed, and he knew it was Kechi, but the child was younger than Chizitara. He was puzzled by the dream, but now he linked it with my dream and Kechi's recovery and thought that God may have been showing him that Kechi would be reborn after having almost died.

The driver came from the embassy, and I left for Pretoria. The Ambassador's wife, Mrs. Asheru, had invited the wife of the Consul General, Mrs. Bose Kuforiji, and the wife of the former Defense Attaché, Mrs. Egwuonwu. Lunch was lovely and the women were very friendly and put me at my ease. I found Pretoria to be an incredibly beautiful place.

Mrs. Kuforiji dropped me off in the hospital since she lived in Johannesburg.

I rushed in to see Kechi and she smiled when she saw me. She appeared to be drowsy, and Mike confirmed that she had just gotten her drugs. But she opened her eyes then and asked me to tell her anything. I asked her to say something instead and she said,

"I am just lying on this bed, doing nothing, just waiting for the next day to come".

This touched me deeply, and I told her that with each new day, there was more progress in the healing, and that I understood that it was hard for her, lying there, but she should believe that the end was in sight.

I then told her some more stories, gave details of my trip to Pretoria. I resolved to be more entertaining from then on. She got her pain medication and started to drop off and we left, telling her to get some rest, and we would see her in a couple of hours. It was always hard to leave Kechi when she was awake, because her eyes would follow you till you passed out of the door.

While we were in the waiting room, Brother Dotun came to visit. He spoke to Mike at length about accepting that the things of God had nothing to do with logic. Mike's intellect was clinging tenaciously to the way of thinking that he was used to. He told Mike to stop overthinking issues that had to do with faith, and pray for understanding instead.

Kechi was still fast asleep when we came in for the night visit, so we just prayed by her bed and left her to sleep.

That night, I had a dream where I saw Kechi turning over in bed by herself, then getting up and walking around her bed.

After our morning devotions, Mike told me that the songs I raised for worship were tuneless and sounded as though I just made them up. I was not amused at all. The way I saw it, Mike was looking for any excuse not to appear to be fully integrated into a way of life that he had scorned and ridiculed for ages. I tried not to lose my temper, but his constant jibes and criticisms were getting on my nerves, and I prayed for strength.

Kechi had her eyes closed when we walked in, but opened them at the sound of our voices. She informed us that she was going in for surgery the following day, and the doctor said that after her surgery, she would be propped up so she could sit up in bed, and that she was going to start walking also. She was very excited about this. We all rejoiced with her and thanked God that another phase of healing was about to start. I asked if she had any more dreams and she said yes.

She dreamt she was in a crowded room and a nurse came in and gave her something to hold onto. The nurse then used the object they were both holding to lead her from that room into a smaller one filled with cards and colorful things. Kechi sat on the bed, and I came in with another woman, sat on the bed with her and we started to look at the cards, one after the other. At that point, her Grandma came in, saw Kechi sitting up in bed, and started dancing with joy.

Then she woke up.

I told her that God was telling us that the battle had been won and we should rejoice, the end was near.

I then drew up a stool close to her bed and told her we needed to have a serious discussion. I told her I knew she was born-again, and had given her life to Christ at the fellowship in Lagos. She nodded. I told her of the dreams Mike and I had of the babies and that we saw them as a rebirth of her life, physically and spiritually. Because of this, it had been ministered to Uloma, confirming an earlier ministration to me, that she should rededicate her life to Jesus. I asked if she was agreeable and she said yes. I took her through a prayer of rededication and reaffirmation of her faith. She repeated the words after me and then I prayed for her.

Kechi was concerned about the blood she saw in the dressings that came off the back of her head during dressing changes. I told her that she had a very deep wound there. She said that the whole of her upper body was cleaned and redressed the day before, and she saw her hands for the first time. I asked her what she thought when she saw her hands and she said, 'I thought, Wow! Is this how I look?'. I asked her if it brought home to her the seriousness of her accident, and curiously enough, she said no, but went on to explain that after she saw her hands, she thought to herself that she knew that one day she would get her body back, and that it could have been much worse. She could have lost that hand, not just the skin. She went on to say that she now has decided to be patient.

"Sometime yesterday", she went on, "I suddenly felt as if a load was lifted from me and I felt light, and knew that my worries had been taken away and I had been given patience to deal with anything that comes my way from now on.

All the things I used to hate, the spraying of the dressings to keep them moist, the dressing changes that hurt so much, the bathing and so on, I am going to bear them all, knowing that I will just be enduring them for a while. In the next two weeks, I will be out of here.

I have not cried once during dressing changes and I am not going to cry at any of the things the nurses do.

I was no longer scared."

She then shared with us that she used to tell Mom and I that she was not scared before surgeries. She was, but no longer. She now had the patience to bear everything.

I bowed my head and thanked God for what was without doubt a powerful ministration by the Holy Spirit. Then I told Kechi that the patience and new strength she had were a gift from God. I reminded her that ordinarily she had a very low pain threshold, and could hardly bear the slightest pain.

She asked if we knew whether she would be out in the next two weeks. I did not want to burst her bubble, as it was very unlikely that she would leave any time soon, but I told her that if God had made her a promise, then He would keep it.

She told her Dad and I seriously and in calm assurance, "In two weeks I will be able to move this body, and I will sit up", and we said amen to that.

After I fed her, she complained that there was something in her eye. Her left eye seemed a little reddish and I also noticed that she was coughing a lot, trying to bring up phlegm. In addition, she was sniffling. We called the doctor's attention, and he prescribed some drugs for her.

I laid hands on her and prayed for the symptoms to leave. When we got back, the eye was still red, but the sister, Sophie, said that the medication the doctor had recommended had just come in from the pharmacy. She administered eye drops and nose spray to Kechi, and then Kechi asked me to read the bible to her.

I read Psalm 9 first and she found it refreshing. When I went on to my favorite psalm, Psalm 91, Kechi actually said the first two lines with me. She said that I was reading it a lot to her when she was asleep, referring to the coma period. She also recognized the verse; "I shall not die, but live..." from Psalm 118 from that period.

The nurses had been right to tell me to talk to her then. They assured me that she would hear me.

The nurse came in to suction Kechi and to start a blood transfusion, so we left to buy adult diapers from the pharmacy. They had told us earlier that they had run out.

Upon our return, Kechi was now running a temperature of 38.6° and the Unit leader assured us that they would not allow the fever to get up to 39° and there was as yet no cause for alarm. We were asked to leave briefly so they could suction Kechi because she had a lot of phlegm, which she was unable to cough up on her own, and attempting to do so was causing her throat to become sore. We prayed for Kechi, I laid hands on her and we left.

Kechi was looking very dull the following morning. She had been in a lot of pain and was on hourly doses of morphine and dormicum since 7 am. She was unable to sleep in spite of all the medication, and by 11.15am, was complaining about pain. She was very unsettled and told me that she cried in the night because they needed a blood sample and had to prick her. She said she cried so much that the cough became almost uncontrollable and the Unit Leader shouted at her. When she saw the light of battle blaze in my eyes, she quickly added that the lady apologized later saying that she had done so because she knew the cough was worse because Kechi was crying.

I reserved my comments, because Kechi did not have to know that I was going to ask the matron later whether it was permitted for nurses to shout at their patients. My heart went out to my daughter because she was clearly very uncomfortable. She had pain in her hands and in her forehead; she was itching mostly in the bandaged sites, especially on her forehead, and kept squeezing her face to relieve it. Her other eye seemed red also and she was feeling very miserable. I suspected that Kechi had caught another infection.

The nurse said they could not give any more morphine, so I put on gloves, laid hands on Kechi, and prayed for deep sleep to overcome her, and that the drugs would start taking effect so that the pain would lessen.

Kechi started feeling sleepy almost as soon as I prayed but she was fighting it and I told her to go ahead, I would not leave. My presence was all the more reason why she should sleep, secure in the knowledge that her mother was watching over her. I told her I was going to pray, and then read to her from the bible so that the sound of my voice will be in the background while she slept, and when she woke up, there would be no more pain. She obeyed, and went into a deep sleep. When she woke up, after about forty minutes I was still there and she said there was no pain.

Mike, meanwhile, had gone to see Dr. Pahad, to tell him of Kechi's condition, and we left when he came in to examine her.

When we came back, she was calmer. Her eyes had stopped irritating her, her temperature had come down to 37.4° and she was more comfortable. She was still itching, though. I told her that after her wounds were cleaned in the theater, she would feel better. Dr. Pahad was concerned that Kechi was a bit chesty and changed her antibiotics and ordered a vaporizing breathing drug to clear her airways. Just as Kechi began to complain about pain, the theater staff arrived to take her away. I asked if she was scared and she said no. She asked for French fries and minced chicken for dinner and I told her that I doubted whether she would feel much like eating after surgery, but she insisted, so I promised to arrange for that.

She asked if I knew which areas they would be covering, and I told her the consent form I had signed indicated that they would be grafting her legs. I went out to wait while they prepared her for the OR, and to wait in the hallway so that I could see her as they wheeled her by. Ten minutes later, I told her I loved her as she went by on the gurney.

After Kechi was returned to her room, the sister came out to tell us that no grafting had been done because when anesthesia was administered to her, her blood pressure dropped below acceptable levels, so they just cleaned up her wounds, which though clean, bled a lot, further dropping her blood pressure.

She did not know that no grafting had been done and we all agreed not to tell her. She was now on a daily dosage of morphine and dormicum, and she was still in pain. Kechi was really sobbing now, and Mike and I felt so helpless. I prayed, laying hands on her, and committed her to God. She got morphine at 8.00pm and I fed her. After food, she got dormicum and finally calmed down and we left.

The whole experience of today deeply upset Mike, who was scheduled to leave the following day. He said he was leaving on a sour note and I told him it was important that he stayed positive. At this point, Mike snapped at me, saying that I should allow him to feel for his daughter, that not everyone was as strong as me.

I went very still, deeply shocked at his outburst and I kept very quiet because I felt that I might shatter into a million pieces. I felt betrayed and very much alone. Was this what Mike thought of me?

Back at the hotel, I went into the room and bowed down to God, repenting of my lack of faith in His ability to handle Kechi's situation, which was what my brief succumbing to despair and helplessness at the hospital was. I prayed for strength for myself, for Kechi and for Mike. I cried out to God in tears and begged Him for forgiveness for allowing fear to overtake my faith.

When Mike came in, we discussed the events of the day and he confessed that he had been frustrated enough to ask God that if He was going to take

Kechi, then what had the last two months in Milpark Hospital been about? I told him he had to go to God in repentance at once.

At 4.16am, it became apparent to me that sleep was out of the question, so I began to relieve the previous day again in my head. I came to the conclusion that I was clearly in the wrong and again I got down to me knees to beg for forgiveness. Then I got up and began to rebuke the devil.

When I got back into bed, my mind was taken back to what we had read in one of the early chapters of The Purpose Driven Life about life being a test. Mike and I had been tested the previous day and by allowing fear to take hold, we had failed. But I also remembered the scripture in 1 John 1: 8-10,

"If we confess our sins,
he is faithful and just to forgive us our sins, and to cleanse us from all unrighteousness."

This gave me a measure of comfort because I knew that God was not a man that He should lie. If He said He would forgive me when I confess and repent of my sins, then that was exactly what would happen. On that note I fell asleep.

The following morning, Mike woke up before me and was in a very introspective mood when I woke up. I began to tell him of all that had been in my mind earlier. I was reminded of the ant that grew into a monster. If I had squashed the demon of fear like I had been taught in the vision, it would not have grown to take possession of us the way it did. Also, I should have remembered that God had said clearly to me that He had given me the cloak of righteousness to wear. I was tired of my faithlessness. If I had God's righteousness, then why on earth did I have so little confidence in God? When Kechi was doing well, I just coasted along, forgetting that I should also be prepared for trials, which were certain to come.

Mike and I prayed for forgiveness again and resolved to rely on God's strength alone.

Then Ulo called and gave me some good advice. She said that with every new understanding in God, there came a trial. God tests us to be sure that we understand the lesson learnt. She also said that we needed to speak out our faith that the pain was gone and that Kechi's healing had been completed. After speaking it out with our mouths, then we would start believing it in our hearts. She said we needed to speak this out in Kechi's hearing, so that she could see that we were convinced of it and also start to believe.

When we saw Kechi, she was sobbing in pain. We started to talk her through it and eventually she stopped crying, and agreed that she would bear the pain till her next dosage, which was in thirty minutes. We did a crossword puzzle for a while, until the pain became unbearable. Sister Mamsie said we should leave so that she could give her the morphine and then change the dressings on her hands and head. Kechi had wanted me to feed her before leaving, but I persuaded her to do the dressing change first and then let Sister Mamsie feed her. She agreed, but I suspect that by then she was just desperate for the pain medication. We lingered enough to tell her to learn to hand over the pain to God.

Louisa and Digby, the South African couple whose relative, Edwina, Owen's wife, was also in ICU invited us back to their home for lunch. Their home was very lovely with flowering gardens and lots of space. The food was very good too, and Louisa gave me a box of leftovers for Kechi.

Back at the hospital for the afternoon visit, Kechi was once more crying in pain. Sister Mamsie was very concerned by now and wanted to call Dr. Pahad because she thought Kechi needed a counselor, and her pain was more than just physical. At this point, Kechi was getting morphine and dormicum every hour and Sister Mamsie thought it was an overdose. But she was still in pain, so I laid hands on her and reaffirmed our faith in God's word on her healing. I refused to accept the evidence of my eyes or my feelings. I reaffirmed that we believed that the pain was gone because God had declared that her healing was complete.

After the prayer, Mamsie talked with Kechi, telling her it could have been worse. She told her of other cases where burns victims had their noses or lips burnt off.. She told Kechi to have faith that she was going to be fine. Kechi responded that she was trying her best to bear the pain, but it had never been that bad before.

I understood that the main problem was that Kechi was now awake for longer periods than before and the drugs were no longer as effective as they used to be. She bore the pain for thirty minutes before the tears started again I prayed that God would grant her rest so that she slept through the night.

This was a new and painful phase in the healing process for all of us. It tore me apart to see her suffering so much. I started to dread going into her room in case she was crying and I started to cry along with her. But I had faith that God would see us through.

By the night visit, all of us were calmer and Kechi was making a great effort to resign herself to waiting for the designated time for her medication, and she seemed to be able to bear the pain better. By the time we left, she had been given her drugs and was getting drowsy, so we left her after praying. I saw Hilda on our way out and told her about Kechi's insomnia, and she suggested that we should talk to Kechi's doctor about prescribing a sleeping pill for the night.

Mike was leaving, and we prayed and handed over his trip to God. Kechi was awake when we arrived at the hospital. The pain for her was a constant, now just having varying degrees of intensity. She began to cry when Mike said his goodbyes, asking him not to go and getting very worked up and emotional. Dr. Pahad was there and assured Kechi that he was going to take very good care of her, and by the time her Dad came again would probably be taking some steps on her own.

Mike then settled down to talk for a long time with Kechi, telling her never to give up, no matter how bad the pain got. Then Mike got emotional and said to Kechi,

"You are my life. Life without you will be meaningless to me.
Promise me that you will stay strong for me, ok?"

Kechi nodded. "I promise."

She calmed down considerably, but insisted I must stay with her. I had planned to accompany Mike to the airport, but he said I should stay with Kechi, and decided to leave immediately to give himself time to process his VAT returns.

Kechi was probably afraid to let both of us out of her sight at the same time, in case we left her all alone.

Her next dose was at 11.45am, but I kept her busy with crossword puzzles and conversation until 12pm. Her food came at 1.00pm and Kechi had every last morsel of two fish cakes, mashed potatoes, and boiled sweet potatoes in a sauce. She asked for more fishcakes and they gave her two more which she also finished. Kechi's appetite was back with a vengeance which was just as well because she had just about dwindled to skin and bones.

I went to the coffee shop to get some lunch and wait for Media. Kechi had asked for spaghetti for dinner and Media had offered to bring some.

Back in Kechi's room at 4.00pm, she had just been given her pain medication and was drowsy. She was coughing quite a bit and she was given a vaporizer to soften the phlegm. I had to hold it up to her nose because she hated the face mask to which it was usually attached. Then Sister Sophie gave me a nasal spray to spray into Kechi's nose. Soon the phlegm was easier to cough out and she got some relief and wanted to know why she was coughing so much.

I told her that she had a minor chest infection which had been treated with antibiotics and she was getting better. I told her to sleep so that the drugs would take effect. I then laid hands on her and prayed for restorative sleep and the peace of the Lord to come upon her. Before I left, Kechi said she had something to tell me. She said that she was scared of having surgery the following day because of the aftermath of pain; her legs were still painful after the last dressing and she was scared of getting new pain sites.

I prayed and banished the demon of fear, and told Kechi she was going to be fine, God was still in control.

Media brought the spaghetti at 5.30pm and at 6.00pm, I peeked into Kechi's room to see whether she was awake. She was fast asleep, and she slept until 8.00pm. This meant that she was morphine-free for three hours. I was very happy and thanked God for it.

I fed her the spaghetti and chicken Media had brought and she ate very well, then we whiled away the time with crossword puzzles, which had become a huge hit for her. She asked for and was given pain medication and wanted to know when the next dose was going to be. When she was told, she nodded, and said ok. My thinking was that if she knew for sure that another dose was coming, then she bore the pain better. That was her way of coping with pain at that time.

When visiting time drew to a close, I prayed for her and told her to relax and try to go back to sleep. Kechi then asked me to remove the cloth veiling her eyes. I told her that there was nothing over her face and she was probably drowsy from the drugs. I called the sister's attention and she said that the ointment on Kechi's face had probably melted and leaked into her eyes, causing a film. I explained this to Kechi and told her to close her eyes and try and sleep, and she would feel better in the morning.

Leaving it all in God's hands, I left for the night.

CHAPTER TWENTY-THREE

"I beseech you therefore, brethren, by the mercies of God, that ye present your bodies a living sacrifice, holy, acceptable unto God, which is your reasonable service."
Romans 12:1(KJV)

In the tenth chapter of <u>The Purpose Driven Life</u>", surrender to God was ministered to me. I still had a distance to go in totally surrendering myself, but I thought the most important fact was that I was willing to do so and go all the way. I prayed for His grace in order to accomplish this.

I also realized another thing; everything I was doing, reading, even in prayers, I was relating everything to Kechi. I knew I was at that moment completely wrapped up in her, but I also knew that it was not about Kechi it was all about God.

That morning, I looked up and prayed,

"Lord, may I forever realize that, yes, You deserve all my praise and gratitude for saving Kechi, but also that You did it for Your own purpose and to Your own glory!

May I forever look up and see beyond Kechi to Your will and purpose for us all at this time, and may I seek Your kingdom and righteousness always.

Lord, please guide me. It is vital that I do not make any mistake that will take Your Holy Spirit away from me. I want to be led fully by You, Lord. Please help me, Lord".

In that chapter, total surrender meant accepting the pain one was going through as necessary for the fulfillment of God's purpose and glory in that person's life. In linking this with Kechi's life, I realized that we had been wrong all along in asking God to take away Kechi's pain. What we should have been praying was that He should take the glory for giving her the grace to bear it. If it was not necessary for her to have the pain, He would take it away in an instant. With the trial, He had given a way out - ability to bear the pain. I praised Him for this realization and sent Ulo a text at once, asking her to pass it around.

But as soon as I got to the hospital, it was made obvious to me that when God says in the scripture that we should be careful because the devil was going around like a roaring lion, seeking who to devour, He was not playing. There was I, basking in the euphoria of having had a huge breakthrough, meanwhile the devil was also busy.

When I reached Kechi's room, she was crying copiously, telling me that she did not think she could go on. In fact, her words were, "I can't bear it anymore".

I prayed for the Holy Spirit to give me the right words to minister to Kechi. I rebuked the devil and commanded him to flee from the presence of one anointed by God.

I started by reminding Kechi of her promise to her Dad, that she would stay strong for him, that he told her that his life would be meaningless if she was not in it.

"After everything we've been through, we can't get almost to the end of the road and give up. If you give up, what do you want the rest of us to do, especially me?

This pain is part of your healing and don't you think that God is aware of it? If it was not a necessary part of your healing process, and part of the fulfillment of His purpose in your life, then you won't feel it. God has allowed it because He has given you the strength and the ability to bear it.

God has not abandoned you, love, do you not know that His name is at stake?"

When she shook her head no, I explained.

"God cannot allow His enemies to gloat and ask why He brought you back from the brink of death and all the way to South Africa for ten whole weeks, only to call you home. He does not work that way. His name is being glorified for your life all over the world and will continue to be glorified forever."

I went on in this vein for a while and by the time I was through, she was calm. She now knew that the pain would not kill her.

Then came a huge surprise.

Sister Tracy said that Kechi needed to be distracted and was going outside for a while. This was astonishing news both for Kechi and myself. All the wires and leads were disconnected and Sister Tracy and the shift leader wheeled Kechi's bed outside to the front of the hospital, through the same emergency entrance she had been wheeled through, unconscious, ten weeks earlier.

Kechi saw the outside world for the first time in ten weeks and her eyes were popping out, her smile huge. It was thrilling to see her so happy.

I took the opportunity to call home and Kechi was able to speak to Ulo, Mom and Nkechi. I was quite sure I had made their day. Of course, I could not put the phone to her ear for hygiene reasons, but I put it on speaker, so they could all hear her.

The strain of the new experience soon became too much for Kechi, and after about twenty minutes we went back inside. She was very happy to have been outside and asked me to read from the bible to her. She chose Psalm 91.

Sister Tracy was very strict about restricting the use of morphine and Kechi seemed to accept that. I laid hands on Kechi and prayed before leaving.

I had lunch with Jacqui and Naomi, a South Africa mother and daughter that had befriended me at the hospital. They also had a relative admitted into the hospital and we met several times in the waiting room. They took me to a Chinese Restaurant in Rosebank with really good food. It was a good outing and we got back to the hospital well before visiting time, so I had a small nap in the waiting room. I made a note to myself to stop drinking wine when I went out to eat.

When I went in to visit Kechi, she was looking very cross and grumpily told me that she had been waiting for me. I pointed out that it was 4.00pm and

I was exactly on time. The poor thing thought I was late. I started distracting her with stories of my outing and she actually laughed out loud. Small and shaky, but a laugh nevertheless. Then I glanced at the monitor and was shocked to see that her blood pressure was very high at 184/117. I got up and asked the sister whether that was a true reading or if the equipment was defective. She said it was correct and they were keeping an eye on it, and I should find out if Kechi was anxious about anything.

I asked Kechi if she was worried about her upcoming surgery and she said yes. I reminded her about the bible passage we had read earlier and told her to remember that every surgery was a step forward. She asked me for the first time how her face looked and I told her that most of it was still covered, and the opened parts were healing. She was still for a moment and then said she wished they would hurry up and do her hands. I told her that her hands would probably be the last to be done, as the doctor had explained that they would need specialized surgery for her to regain full mobility in them.

We talked about scars and I told her to expect some scarring, but to remember that a lot could be done now with plastic surgery, if not in South Africa, then in America. I told her that most of the scarring was in her hands and legs, but she protested that her stomach looked horrible too. I then explained that her stomach area was the main donor site for skin harvesting and we were very thankful to God that she had a lot of unburned skin there. This led to an explanation of what grafting entailed, and I took the opportunity to slip in that she might have to wear pressure garments for a year or more to flatten the scars and prevent them from growing.

She asked for her pain medication and was given morphine.

Then something interesting happened.

She was not given dormicum, the muscle relaxant which made her sleep, but she soon fell into a short, but deep sleep. The sister pointed this out to me and said it proved that Kechi's pain was mostly in her mind. It was unusual for her to sleep after just a morphine shot. I failed to see how it proved that her pain was in her mind, but I did not argue.

I was still by her bed when she woke up and she insisted that I stayed until she left for surgery. I agreed and told her that we had to present her blood pressure to God so that it would drop before surgery. I laid hands on her and we prayed. Fifteen minutes later, her pressure had dropped to 166/97 and we praised God.

Kechi was taken into the OR at 6.00pm and I settled down to wait. She came out at 8.00pm and when they had put all the leads and wires back, I went in and stayed with her for about fifteen minutes to calm her down. The sisters had noticed that when I came in to see her after surgery, she calmed down faster, so they were now allowing me to come in for longer periods. Kechi never came out well from anesthesia, a trend that has continued till this day.

I kept talking to Kechi, telling her to calm down and let the drugs work. She was given pain medication and she wanted the lights off and more blankets. We dealt with all of that and then I prayed and asked her to go to bed. The sisters told me that Dr. Pahad had called in a cardiologist to look into Kechi's blood pressure.

Before I left, I met with the counselor, Annarie, and told her that Kechi seemed to be getting flashes of recollection because she kept asking me whether she was ever in a van or a bus after the plane crash; and also insisted that she remembered being in a place with other kids. Annarie said that since Kechi was talking now, she would begin to make friends with her and then gradually find out what she could remember.

The following morning, the topic was on being friends with God by having constant conversation throughout the day with Him thereby letting Him into every aspect of my life, and by meditating on His word the whole day. This meant that I could not forget what I had read in the morning as soon as I closed the bible, but I should think about it the whole day, if necessary speak out short memory verses. This way, God would be in my thoughts throughout the day. This sounded very interesting and I resolved to try it.

Kechi was sleeping when I got to her room. Sister Tracy took me aside to tell me that Kechi had been sleeping since morning. She had her last morphine shot by 7.00am and since then when she called for drugs, Tracy would give her sterilized water. Her plan was to regulate morphine intake to three hours. Since she had been sleeping so long and deeply and it had been four hours since her last shot, I was more inclined to believe that a good part of the pain was in her head.

She woke at 11.35am and asked how long I had been there and when I told her I had been there for thirty-five minutes, she asked Tracy for pain medication, and Tracy gave her the morphine she would have gotten at 10.00am. She was determined to wean Kechi from what she was convinced was a morphine dependence, and even though she was thoroughly professional about it, it was obvious she really liked Kechi. She told me that she thought Kechi was depressed that day which was why she was sleeping so much. I disagreed, but decided I would talk to Kechi later.

Kechi wanted to go outside again and after the lengthy process of disengaging her from the machines, we went outside for ten pleasant minutes. Tracy then shooed me out so she could dress the wounds on her arms and face and I told her that I would be in the waiting room so I could come back in and feed Kechi lunch. I noticed that Kechi was a bit dull and I asked if anything was troubling her and she said no. Knowing Kechi, I felt that she might have been protecting me so that I did not get worried about her. I thought it was just as well that the counselor would soon start talking with her. Hopefully, she would find it easier to confide in a stranger.

Kechi's face was looking better after being cleaned and dressed and the whole of her forehead was now exposed. Tracy said that aside from a few spots, her arms were also looking good.

I fed Kechi her lunch and left.

At 4.00pm, Kechi was awake and I read some emails from friends and family to her. Once again, news from her friends about what was going on in school kept her hugely entertained. She was in pain, but said she had been promised morphine at 6.00pm and was going to try and stick it out until then.

I was very grateful for what God was doing with Kechi. For someone with a very low pain threshold to be able to bear the true pain she must be feeling was a miracle straight from God.

Tracy told me that the cardiologist had ordered an EKG just to be sure all was well with Kechi's heart because of the very high blood pressure of the previous day. I was then asked to leave so they could turn her over.

When I came back, I was given the news that Kechi's heart was very fine and her blood pressure had come back to normal. Great news all round and we thanked God for that.

Then Betty came in with the jollof rice and boiled eggs Kechi had requested. I mashed the eggs into the rice as per Kechi's instructions, and fed her. She had seconds, as well as all three eggs and was stuffed by the time I had to leave, so we prayed and I left for the night.

The next morning, Kechi was sleepy and dull again and Tracy said she had been sleeping since morning and the doctor thought it was probably a side effect of a drug they had just started giving her. Kechi insisted on going outside again though her eyes were closed most of the time. We came in after twenty minutes and she complained about pain. Dr. Pahad was there and asked her details about the pain and Kechi said the pain was always there, but sometimes got worse. Tracy gave her a placebo, and I heard her tell Dr. Pahad that she wanted to try and draw the dosage out to four hourly.

Kechi had been started on physiotherapy a few days before, and they usually made sure they did some assisted exercises with her. They would lift her arms and legs so that she could get used to having them move.

When I told Tracy to get me at lunchtime, she said that Kechi was going to be with the physiotherapists for about an hour before eating. I suspected that Tracy gave her a placebo before physio so she could give her the real thing after exercises.

They took so long that I decided to run down to Campus Square and buy some toiletries and rush back. When I came in Kechi pretended to be upset. We did some crossword puzzles together until she complained of pain. Tracy gave her a placebo and she became drowsy. It became clear that for Kechi, drugs had become an escape. As soon as she got it, her mind became relaxed and she went off to sleep, escaping from the pain and reality. I told her I would wait and she slept for about ten minutes. We continued the puzzles when she woke up until she said I should read the bible to her. I read Psalms 33 and 34 to her. I loved reading Psalms because they were very uplifting and I felt that was what she needed then.

Tracy told us she would not be with Kechi the following day and this made us sad, me especially, because I knew no other sister would be as committed to weaning her off morphine as Tracy. When I broached the topic with her, she said she hoped other sisters would continue to do so, because Kechi had only had morphine twice that day, four hours apart. I prayed that sister Maureen would continue to trick Kechi with the placebo.

I was concerned with Kechi's dullness, which had persisted, and Tracy said it was Stillnox, the sleeping pill she got at night. It was good she was sleeping for longer at night, but the downside was that while in the drug-assisted sleep, she did not draw full breaths and did not wake to cough out phlegm when her body needed to. This resulted in a low oxygen blood content of 67% for that afternoon which was not good at all. Her back had to be pounded by the physiotherapist so she could cough up phlegm and she was given an object with balls inside to blow into and make the balls rise; the harder she blew, the higher the balls rose. This was a breathing exercise to strengthen her lungs. She was able to lift just two of the balls and said she was exhausted and I left her to rest.

I went off to the waiting room to wait for the 7.30pm visit. She was still asleep so I laid hands on her and read Psalm 33 in a hushed voice and was quietly singing praises when she opened her eyes at around 8.00pm. She did not want to eat, but I persuaded her to eat a little chicken and some fruit salad and juice. When she began to drift off again, I said good night and left so that she would not struggle to stay awake. I surrendered her to God and left.

The next morning, a song of praise was on my lips after the morning visit,

All heavens declare
The glory of the living God Who can compare
The beauty of the risen God?
Forever You will be
The Lamb upon the throne
I'll gladly bend my knees
And worship You God.

I could see that my daughter was back her impish, mischievous eyes, her pretty face, her sunny disposition!

She was very bright and cheerful, all smiles. The ICU staff were in love with her. She knew all their names and called out to them when they passed by her bed. All, without exception, came by to say hi to Kechi.

We went outside at 1.30pm and she spoke to Mom, Dad, Ned and Nkechi. I had no idea who was more excited, Kechi or my family. She had her first morphine for the day at 10.00am and the second at 2.00pm four hours apart. It was wonderful. But then Maureen gave her 2 mg of morphine at 4.00pm. I did not like that and I explained to Maureen that I had actually endorsed the placebos given by Tracy.

By visiting time, Kechi's eyes were as usual trained at the door as I walked in. We had a lovely time going through three Hello! magazines lent to me by Louisa. She had seen me outside the hospital waiting for a cab, and took me to her car and gave me fruits and a drink for Kechi. She also said she was going to come on Saturday to take me out.

Kechi ate a banana and some blueberries and asked for peaches and more bananas for the following day.

Kechi also, for the first time, offered a glimpse into her feelings. She was keeping so many things inside that I was getting concerned. She was not asking any questions at all regarding the crash and I suspect it was because she did not want to know the answers.

At some point, she looked down at the bruise on her right shoulder and said to me,

"Mommy, look at my shoulder" I looked at said,

"Yes, it's really healing".
"So it was worse than this?"
"Much much worse".
"So I was really badly burned?"
"Yes, baby, you really really were".

"I could never in a million years have imagined that this kind of thing could ever happen to me".

"It's the kind of thing we hear in the news or read in the papers, right?" I asked.

She nodded. And then added, "But it's alright", and I said,

"Yeah, it's okay because we are looking at and talking to each other, right?"

And she nodded. Then she changed the subject. I wished we could have gone further so I could determine whether she was ready to hear the details of just how much had been lost in that plane crash, but she clammed up again and I did not push it, so that the will of God would prevail. After all, He said He would make all things beautiful in His time.

It was a glorious day and I told Kechi to rest before the last visit.

She sent for me to feed her by 6.00pm and ate half of her spaghetti and meat sauce. When I went back to the waiting room to wait for the last visit, Maureen came out to tell me that she was not comfortable about fooling Kechi with the placebo. Apparently Kechi was crying with pain and after the placebo, slept off. Maureen acknowledged that it was good as a way of weaning her off morphine, but was not happy with the deception. But at least she agreed that much of Kechi's pain was psychological.

As for me, I was also feeling slightly guilty, but I knew it was for Kechi's good.

Kechi and I looked through the remaining magazine and then we talked. She got her pain meds at 8.00pm and felt a little drowsy, but refused to sleep so I laid hands on her and prayed, speaking directly to her temperature and blood pressure which were both a little elevated, and then just stood by her bedside, singing praises to God. She joined in after a while and we sang one of her favorite choruses together:

"Awesome God, Almighty God.
We give You praise, You're an awesome God
You are highly lifted up, Awesome God".

I encouraged her to pray in the mornings as soon as she woke up, and then we prayed together, and before I left we both agreed that it had been a great day and we glorified God.

I woke very early the next morning and used the extra time I had after prayers to do some laundry, catch up with my mail and have a full breakfast.

Then Heidi called me from ISOS to say that they had arranged for me to move to Smithfields Cottage, a self-contained apartment home. I had asked for this option since Kechi had started to request her favorite meals and it had become clear to everyone that we were in for a very long stay. Besides, the rent was a fraction of the bill at Garden Court hotel. The proprietress was going to send a car for me the following day, so I had to do all my packing that night.

Kechi started to complain as soon as I stepped into her room. She said she did not sleep a wink all night and she had been itching all over. It was becoming obvious to me that this itching was shaping up to be a problem. Little did I know it was going to become a nightmare, even overshadowing the pain issue!

That morning, though, I told her that itching was a healthy sign of healing and she should be grateful for it.

We started talking and she said that she thought that her survival was really a sign that God wanted us as a family to do something for him, and I agreed with her. Then she went on to say that she did not understand how come she was the only one that got so badly burned; so what happened to the others? Where were they? She knew she was the only patient from the plane crash in that hospital, but was she the only one that survived?

At this point, I knew that I had a choice. I could tell her exactly how terrible the plane crash had been, or I could play hide and seek with the truth. I still did not feel that Kechi was physically strong enough to handle the truth, so I chose to keep my answer short.

I told her that she was not the only survivor, without going into any details, but Kechi continued to probe.

She wanted to know about the others. 'Did anyone die?' I nodded.

'From my school?' I nodded again. Deep, gut-wrenching weeping ensued.

'I didn't think anyone in my school would die. How many people? Any of my friends?'

At this stage, her blood pressure had risen and was at 184/110. The sister had come to see what was going on and I was really regretting having said that much.

I told her to calm down. Her friends were all fine, and only one person died that I knew of. She wanted to know whom, and I said I did not know the name of the person.

She slowly began to calm down. I told her that if she did not relax and let her blood pressure go down, there was no way she was getting surgery that day. I could see the effort it took for her to calm herself, but she did it and her blood pressure slowly came down to 163/84. It was still high, but better than before.

At that point, I was terrified I had made a mistake in telling her anything.

What I found most interesting was that, probably after reading the distress on my face, Kechi said to me that I must have been dreading telling her about the student that died. I agreed, but was thinking in my mind that if she reacted this way to the news that one student died, how would she take the news that ALL the other students had died?

I went out after the morning visit and called my family and related what had happened.

Ulo was of the opinion that I should speak to Kechi's doctors and find out if she could take the full details of the plane crash, from a medical point of view. But she also added that I should know that God was still in control and this was one more test. Now that the questions had started coming, they were likely to continue and so I should surrender the situation to God and tell Him that anything that comes out from my mouth in response to Kechi's questions should be words ordered by Him. That way, she said, God took full responsibility for it.

Nkechi and Dorothy thought Kechi could not handle the news yet and I should keep telling her that her friends were fine.

Mike, like Ulo, said I should speak with the doctors and get their opinion.

I decided I was going to shelve that topic for now and deflect Kechi's questions when they came. It was obvious to me she could not handle it yet.

OR time for Kechi moved from 12.30pm to 5.00pm, and Kechi complained that she was hungry. She had not eaten since the night before, as always before surgery. The doctor said she could have only clear juice and she drank two cups of apple and grape juice. These would have to sustain her until after surgery and she was not amused.

To cheer her up, I told her I was going to Sandton Mall to get her an after-surgery gift, our new tradition. She pouted a little, but said I could go.

To my delight, I saw a shop called Temptation, which carried lovely bras in Kechi's size and came in very soft colors like mint green, pink and coral. I was thrilled, because not only were Kechi's bras a difficult size to find, it was almost impossible to find them in colors other than black, tan or white.

The look on her face when she saw the bras was priceless. She asked, 'Are you sure they are my size?' She kept exclaiming that they were beautiful and called the sister, Rochelle, to come and see. Kechi had really taken to Rochelle and I could see it was mutual.

She was still itching like crazy, though, and said the pain had changed to a deep ache all the way to her bones. I told her that it was because she was tired, not having slept all night, and that she would sleep from the OR till morning and feel refreshed by the next day.

All through the day, I wondered whether I had handled Kechi's questions well and towards evening I remembered that I had surrendered all my words, thoughts and actions to God that morning, and of course this included all my responses to Kechi. How quickly I forgot. But I tried to hold firm and spoke to God several times that day concerning that.

I had spoken to Annarie, the counselor, and she said that if Kechi was asking questions, then she was ready to hear the truth. She said she would be in the following Monday and be with me when I told Kechi. I was still not sure about telling Kechi, so I asked Ulo, Nkechi, Chinedu and Mike to fast with me the next day before enquiring of the Lord if it was time to tell Kechi the whole truth.

Kechi went in for surgery at 5.30pm and came out an hour later. When I went in to see her, she was in pain, cold, the works. She was given morphine and drifted into sleep. I laid hands on her and prayed, then I left for the night.

The next morning, Kechi was crying because of the itching, which she had decided was much worse than pain. I tried to comfort her, but she was inconsolable. She said she was feeling very ill and in fact was too tired to go on.

She had a high fever, and was feeling weak and out of sorts, and just plain tired of being in bed. I sent a text round to ask for prayers to get the fever down.

Rochelle asked me to leave because she wanted to change the dressings on Kechi's face, back and stomach, so I sought out Dr. Opolot to discuss Kechi's condition. He was not worried about her temperature and had ordered another blood culture since the preliminary examination of the previous blood sample had turned up negative. He said Kechi would get something to get her temperature down. It was his opinion that Kechi had a lot to deal with and really needed to speak with a counselor urgently. He felt she was fed up with lying in one place for close to three months, and feeling like wanting to give up at this stage was natural.

This gave me some relief and I decided to get Kechi something that would brighten her day and take her mind off her problems. I found a lovely gypsy skirt for her, and also bought some Barbie movies on DVD for Tara, in preparation for her sixth birthday on March 1st.

When I got back, Kechi was in an itching frenzy and nothing could appease her. She rejected her lunch, rejected the meal that Louisa had brought for her, refused to be comforted by anything anyone said, and generally made it clear to all that she was very unhappy.

I bought chicken and French fries from the coffee shop and she ate a few mouthfuls of it. Then I put on gloves and started rubbing all over her face and any place that itched. This gave her some relief. I tapped the parts covered by dressings on her legs, the top of her head, the edges of the dressing on her forehead, everywhere she said itched. This went on for more than an hour and Kechi kept apologizing for being a nuisance.

I told her that she could never be that to me and to stop apologizing. The itching was really driving her crazy and nothing anyone said about it being a positive sign of healing was making much of a difference to her. When I got up to leave, she wanted to start crying, but I told her to be strong, and she knew I was coming back, anyway.

I was weak with hunger by this time and had to get something to eat.

At night it was the same story. Itching and itching. By 8.00pm the sister gave her morphine and this time I was not anxious about it because it was making her drowsy and I wanted her to sleep.

Her temperature was down and she was calmer. I told her that I had told everyone that she said she was tired and was giving up. She did not like that and said I should not have. I told her that she had frightened me so I had to tell someone. She said she would not give up and I should spread the word.

I laid hands on her and prayed for a deep, restful sleep. The sister said she would give her the sleeping pill in an hour so she would sleep the whole night, and I left.

That day had been a lesson in surrender. I must have surrendered a million times during the course of the draining, emotion-filled day. I thanked God for the day and fell into a deep slumber.

CHAPTER TWENTY-FOUR

"Cast thy burden upon the LORD, and he shall sustain thee: he shall never suffer the righteous to be moved."
Psalm 55 : 22 (KJV)

The next morning, I surrendered all of Kechi's itching, her fingers and her face to God. It was no longer my responsibility, but His. There was definitely relief in trusting Him to make all things right in His time, and I held firmly unto His promise that He would restore Kechi whole and complete to us.

I had almost finished with my packing, having cleaned out the fridge and microwave.

Kechi was fast asleep when I went in to see her and she almost slept through the whole visiting hour. I decided to wait anyway, and feed her lunch. I had also printed out some emails from her schoolmates.

She woke up at the end of the visit and I told her I would stay until they booted me out. She was still very sleepy and I was certain it was the sleeping pill causing that. I was happy that she was not itching, and sat with her until the physical therapist came in for her exercises.

After about fifteen minutes, the therapist came to say that Kechi wanted me to come back in, so I sat with her and fed her when her lunch came. She did not want me to leave but I told her that the staff was being very accommodating, allowing me to stay beyond the visiting period, but we must not abuse the privilege, and besides, I had to eat also.

By the evening visit, Kechi was wide-awake and waiting for me. I read her the emails, and we looked through some more magazines. Two ICU nurses, Rochelle and Sophie came by Kechi's bed and we all started chatting, and they told stories of really bad cases they had seen in the ICU. I believed that this was God's way of preparing Kechi for the shock of the plane crash details. She still had absolutely no memories of it at all.

After the sisters left, Kechi turned to me and said, 'I'm really lucky. Are all my organs fine?' I told her yes.

'Are all my facial features intact, my eyes, nose?' I told her yes, and that not even one single bone in her body was broken.

And she said again, 'I'm so lucky'

Chinedu, my brother, called then to say he had received a word from God that it was time for Kechi to know the truth. He said that I would determine the precise timing, but God said it was time.

Nkechi also called with a similar message. God had revealed to her that it was time and gave this message for me:

"I am the Lord
I sit on the High and Lofty place
I am God
Allow me to be God in this situation
Trust Me."

I did trust Him and prayed that the Holy Spirit would determine the precise timing.

I was in the waiting room, writing in my journal and waiting for the last visit of the day, when the sister came in to say that Kechi wanted me back in her room. She wanted me to feed her and they were really indulging her.

I fed her, rubbed her skin to relieve her itching, and left.

During the night visit, she was once more itching and complaining about pain. Sister Dot, who was on duty, said she had given Kechi pain medication just an hour before and was not giving her anything else. Kechi became upset and started to cry. I tried to calm her down, but I was feeling her pain and was frustrated because I wished I could take away her pain and itching. Kechi must have seen the frustration in my face, and she mistook it for anger at her for not being able to cope with the pain, and said she was sorry. I sat down and explained the reason for my frustration and told her she should never think I was upset with her. I wanted to take away all her pain and take her home, but I could not.

She calmed down and I told her that she would get the sleeping pill again that night so she could sleep. I spent some more time reassuring her that I was not angry with her and that I loved her very much. When I was sure she was completely calm, we prayed together and I left.

I tried to do the rest of my packing, but I was exhausted, so I just ate the food Sister Jane had brought for me, and slept.

The next morning, after surrendering the day to God, I finished my packing and went to the front desk to check out. I printed pictures Obi had sent of his family, which I knew Kechi would enjoy seeing, then I had my last breakfast in the hotel and left for the hospital. I called Diedre, the proprietress of Smithfield Cottages, and she confirmed that she would pick me up at the hotel by 1.00pm.

At the hospital, Kechi was awake and told me she was going to the OR later that day. I had wondered if she was scheduled for surgery, but the previous day, no one had said anything, so I assumed it had been pushed to another day. In fact, she had eaten breakfast before the news about surgery came, so it would have to be much later in the day.

Kechi was in good spirits, and said she had wanted to go outside, but it was raining. She really wanted to speak with her cousins.

I reminded her that I was moving out of the hotel that day, and showed her pictures I had taken of the room where I stayed.

She told me she had a dream where she was wearing a big nightie and walking about in the hospital, dragging her IV lines, and everyone she passed called out to her, 'Hey Kechi, how are you?' I told her it was a prophetic dream and it was going to happen soon.

I went back to the hotel to wait for Diedre. She was late and I waited until 2.00pm. When she came, she had other people in the car and we decided that she would take my stuff on to the guesthouse and drop me off at the hospital. Since Kechi was to have surgery that day, I wanted to stay close to the hospital.

Back at the hospital, Kechi said she was very hungry so I distracted her with some magazines I had brought and showed her the pictures of Obi and his family. I stayed with her until she was wheeled off at 5.30pm. This time, they allowed me to go inside the prep room and sit with Kechi until they took her inside the OR proper at 6.00pm.

She came out forty-five minutes later and when I went in to see her at about 7.30pm, she was still in pain and was given a shot of morphine. It took longer than usual to knock her out, but eventually she got drowsy and I laid hands on her, prayed and left. Deidre picked me up at the hospital. Apparently, transportation was part of the deal at the guesthouse and she catered mostly to people who were there for medical reasons. The cottages were lovely, situated in a hilly area about ten minutes from the hospital. I loved my room, which had a lovely bathroom and kitchenette.

I unpacked a few things, made myself at home, prayed and slept.

I woke up with thanksgiving in my heart, thinking about how good God had been to me. The room was even lovelier in daylight, the surroundings warm and homely.

I had breakfast in the dinning room and met Ann, one of the residents who, while we were talking, revealed that she had cancer. She encouraged me to be strong when she heard Kechi's story.

Nkechi called as I was on my way to the hospital, saying that her boys were anxious to talk to Kechi. I told her the weather had cleared up, and I would see if they would allow Kechi to go outside that morning.

At the hospital, the sisters did not want Kechi going outside because they were afraid of infection. I made a decision, and praying, I went to the nurse's station and asked the unit leader if she would allow Kechi to speak with her cousins. To my relief she agreed and said I should draw the curtains around Kechi's bed. I then called Nkechi and Kechi was able to speak with 'her boys', as she referred to them. There was great excitement on both sides of the phone call.

Then my friend, Chioma's daughter, Adanna, came with some of her schoolmates to see Kechi. They were in South Africa for a program from school and Adanna insisted that she wanted to see Kechi. They brought flowers and a teddy bear, a card signed by the students, and some magazines. Celine Odom's daughter, Oby, and another lovely girl, Sabrina came in with Adanna. I went out to tell them that Kechi still did not know she had lost all her schoolmates, so that they would not talk about it with Kechi.

Kechi was very happy to see them and to chat with people her age, so I left them to have a nice visit, and I put the flowers where Kechi would see them.

After the girls left, Kechi started to complain about being too tired for physical therapy, but I spoke sternly to her, telling her that the doctors and nurses could only do so much; the real work was up to her - how fast she got up from her bed, how soon she moved her fingers depended on her. I told her that if she did not exercise her muscles, they would forget their functions and she would spend the rest of her life depending on people to do everything for her. I told her I would not mind looking after her, but was that what she really wanted? She said no and I left so that the therapists could come in, telling Kechi I would be in the waiting room so I could feed her after the exercise session.

In the waiting room, I met a beautiful South African woman who introduced herself as Gigi, and whose brother was a patient in the ICU. She was also a Christian and we got talking and exchanged phone numbers. She said her brother's name was Clive, and I promised to pray for him.

When I went in to feed Kechi, her left hand was exposed. One of the nails was completely blackened from the fire and the hand itself was covered in black scabs, which would peel away in time. I could already see glimpses of new skin under the scabs.

That evening, Kechi was feeling good, no pain, no itching, and we spent a very pleasant hour just talking. I told her that my sister had said that her son, Nduka, was the tallest boy in his school and for some reason she found that very amusing, saying that in that case, she hoped he had added some weight.

After the visit, I went in to have a chat with Dr. Pahad to see what could be done about the rather frequent headaches Kechi was getting, and also to know the results of the last blood tests.

He said the tests had indicated an infection in the body - septic shock, which may lead to multiple organ failure. I was no doctor, but this seemed to me to be a little extreme, because as far as I knew, none of her organs had failed, and if she had multiple organ failure, would they not have informed me? I decided that this was one of those times I was going to completely disregard what the test results said and stick to my faith in God. I surrendered everything to Him, then went in and laid hands on Kechi and prayed. Then I adjusted the new oxygen contraption they had put on Kechi. I had a feeling that it was pressing on her head and causing the headache.

Kechi was listless and said that for the first time, she felt really ill, her body felt heavy and hot. I told her that she had been battling a fever for several days, but she would be okay. I fed her and left for shift change.

The doctor came in my absence and prescribed new medication based on the lab results and Kechi's headache.

Mrs. Dozie and her son came to visit Kechi that night, and they talked with her, encouraging her to keep her spirits up. She gave me some money to help with expenses and I was very grateful.

Kechi and I went through the "Seventeen" magazine that Adanna brought for her, but she was tired, so I prayed for her and then sat with her until she slept.

Back at the guesthouse, Ngozi Ekechuku, my friend, called to say she was coming to Johannesburg to spend time with us.

I was very grateful, because I was really lonely except when I was with Kechi. I looked forward to her trip.

The following day, March 1st 2006, was my Tara's birthday. She was six years old. I called her first thing in the morning to wish her happy birthday. I had forgotten it was also Uzoma's birthday, but she quickly reminded me. I sent a text to everyone to call both Tara and Uzoma.

We had been in South Africa for eighty days! It did not seem possible that Kechi had been lying down for eighty days. The poor girl.

I had asked Deidre for a bigger room, but she told me that morning that all her bigger units were full. This was disappointing because though my room was charming, it was small, and I knew that once I had visitors, like I surely would, it would be a squeeze. She offered to move me to another facility, but I refused, because I had fallen in love with her cottages and surroundings.

Kechi was asleep when I got there and the sister on duty was concerned that she had been sleeping all morning. I asked if she had gotten the sleeping pill and she checked and said yes. There seemed to be a pattern with that pill. Every time she took it at night, she was very drowsy for most of the next day. I sat down and waited for her to wake up. She soon woke up, complaining that the oxygen mask was pressing into her head, causing discomfort. The sister and I changed the position of the mask, padded the pressure points, and then settled for removing it from time to time to give her relief.

A little drama ensued later when the sister suggested that we cut Kechi's hair to ensure that there were no sore areas that needed to be addressed. Kechi started protesting vehemently and began to cry because she thought it was going to involve more pain. But I saw no way out of it, it was better to uncover any wounds and treat them at once than to leave them to fester. Reason prevailed on Kechi like I knew it would, though she cried for a little while longer before stopping. I thought she had earned the right to cry when she felt like it, so I just comforted her.

At the 4.00pm visit, Kechi's head looked smaller due to the haircut, but the sister said that the top of her head was matted with blood and she recommended that it should be shaved off completely and treated in the OR since it was too painful to touch. She also expressed concern about the wound at the back of Kechi's head. She did not like how it looked, very raw and deep. I remembered that the doctor had said that the back of the head would be grafted, but since they had not done it, I assumed that they were leaving it to heal on its own.

Kechi looked relaxed and was in fact sleeping when I got there. She woke up at the sound of my voice and we looked through magazines together. I fed her when they brought in her food, but she did not eat much, saying her stomach was full. She had not had any bowel movement since the previous day and I told her that she must try, as her stomach was looking distended. Kechi got a little testy and asked how she could go if she did not feel like it. I talked her down and explained that she needed to poo so she would feel more comfortable.

I left for a while so that the sisters could work. They wanted to spray her bandages to help cool her temperature, which had climbed up to 37.9°. As I left, I thought to myself, "God is still in control, that's all I need to know".

We had a visit from Mike's friend, Clement, who was really shocked to see Kechi's appearance. He had no idea she had been so badly burned. He gave me some money before he left.

Later that night, the temperature was only down by a couple of degrees and Kechi was once more itching all over. I smeared an ointment called chloramycetin over all the itchy areas, and it seemed to give her some relief. Then I noticed that in the process of healing, her face seemed to be pulling down towards her left jaw. I told her that she must stop favoring her right side and start looking towards the left more often so that her right neck and jaw muscles would also be strengthened. Also, her eyelids were also contracting even more, pulling her eyes open. She could not shut her eyes fully and this made her uncomfortable, more so when the chloramycetin melted into her eyes, blurring her vision. She also complained about this. In fact, Kechi had so many complaints that day, but I was thankful that she was alive to complain.

Then we had a little scare when I noticed Kechi's blood pressure dropping fast. I called the Sister Sophie's attention and she said that she needed to flush the line in Kechi's groin area. She must have pushed air into the line or something, because Kechi screamed out, saying there was a sharp pain going from her stomach down to her left leg, and that the leg was paralyzed. As I was about to panic, I remembered to trust in God. It was obvious that Sophie was confused, and Kechi's screaming was not helping issues. I calmly asked her to get the doctor and she ran out and came back with the shift leader, Sister Lungi, who soon rectified the problem.

Kechi, who had started asking, with wild eyes, "What's happening, what's happening?" calmed down. I made a note to remember that her reactions fed off mine.

When it was time to leave, she asked me to wait for the nurse to come back in first, and I told her to stop worrying and that if there was anything wrong, I would not leave, I would sleep in the waiting room, if necessary. She nodded, but I gave in and waited until the nurse came back in.

CHAPTER TWENTY-FIVE

"And he said unto me, My grace is sufficient for thee: for my strength is made perfect in weakness. Most gladly therefore will I rather glory in my infirmities, that the power of Christ may rest upon me."
2 Cor. 12 : 9(KJV)

The next day started well. I was still surrendering everything to God every morning and I discovered this made me feel lighter. I knew that God was more than a feeling, but I asked Him to please make me feel Him close to me. I did not ever want His Holy Spirit to be far from me.

Kechi was looking fine and apart from the itching, there were no major issues. I put on gloves and applied the ointment all over her face, but her body began to itch terribly and the nurse, Princess asked me to leave so they could bathe her, which would help with the itching. I went to the store to pick up a few things and went back to the hospital to wait for the next visit.

Princess came to get me long before the visiting time, saying that Kechi had been crying since I left and they thought she might be depressed. When I came in, Kechi's face was red and she burst into tears as soon as she saw me. I sat down and started talking to her. I knew my daughter and I knew that for her, the cup was full to overflowing. She kept things in a lot because she did not want me to worry and now she could not hold back any more. "Kechi", I said, "I'm sure you feel, why me, what sort of life is this, why is all this happening to me?"

She nodded.

"You have every right to feel that way. You are the one lying on the bed with the pain and the itching. If you indulge in self-pity, no one can blame you.

But you should realize one thing some people died in that plane crash. Their relatives left behind would give anything to have an opportunity to sell their houses and all their belongings to have their loved ones recovering in a hospital.

Yes, all these things are happening to you now, and causing you a whole lot of discomfort, but you are alive.

Yes, it's been rough and it's not over yet, but you are alive."

I took her back to where we started from the plane crash, five weeks of complete sedation, doctors not expecting her to live through the night, every night. I took her through the coming- awake stage, the talking stage, each one a milestone.

I told her that God had blessed her greatly in so many ways and each time she felt she could not go on and that life was so unfair, she should remember that some people in that plane did not make it.

She calmed down and nodded, tears all gone now. "I love you, Mommy."

I put on gloves and started putting ointment on the itching parts of her body. Then the itching got unbearable and she started crying again from the frustration of not being able to scratch under the bandages. Dr. Pahad was called in and he prescribed Phenergan. She calmed down about five minutes after she was given the drug and I fed her and left her to rest for a while before the last visit. She was calm when I came back and I put the ointment on a few spots on her face. It seemed the Phenergan worked, because she was quite relaxed and even a bit drowsy. I stayed for a while, and then prayed and left when she started to drift off.

The next morning, I received a text from Nkechi that read,

"Ije, to you, from Him.
'My strength is made manifest in your weakness.
I am the All-Sufficient One.
I AM the ENOUGH.
Wait on Me, child, wait on Me'."

I glorified God for this message to me, thinking, 'who am I to be the recipient of such grace?' Just the previous day I had needed to feel Him close and then He assured me that He always was.

I was humbled.

Kechi was awake and very happy to see me. She was lying on her left side so that by looking to the right, she could exercise her neck muscles. She was full of questions, asking for details of what happened from when I saw her after the crash, to how she came to South Africa. I told her everything, stressing the divine intervention every step of the way. She marveled, shook her head several times and was quiet for a long time, just taking it all in.

She insisted that I must stay until 2.00pm that day, and since the nurses were fine with it, I stayed. She reluctantly let me leave at when the time came, because I told her that I had to go to the store if she wanted to have the dinner she had asked for that night- noodles, egg, and pork chops. When I got back in time for the evening visit, she was being turned and she asked the nurses if I could stay. They acquiesced and I came in and saw that the wounds in her back and bum were looking good, healing nicely. They were donor site wounds, her back having escaped the fire completely. Her upper right thigh was also looking good and the sister felt that the doctors might expose it after the surgery that day.

Kechi and I started to speculate on the time they would take her in for surgery. She said 6.00pm and I said 5.30pm. We were both wrong, as the OR called for her at 4.30pm. As was now our custom, I went into the prep room with her until she was wheeled in at 5.10pm.

She was in the OR for two hours and this was really unusual compared to the one hour or even forty five minutes that were more common. When I finally saw her, she was in her post surgery mode of pain and shivering from cold. The sister said they had given her morphine in the OR, but when she kept complaining of pain, they gave her 2mg more in her room. Kechi kept fretting and crying, saying it made no difference and so I laid hands on her and prayed for sleep to overcome her so that she would no longer feel the pain. She did not want me to leave, but I told her it was way past the visiting period and I had to leave. I made her promise to try her best to relax and let the drugs take effect. I noticed that her forehead had been covered again, and though the staples were out, her eyes were still not closing properly, her eyelids having contracted again as it healed. This would probably require more surgery to correct it. I was also distressed to see that her left ear had lost its shape and was likely going to require elaborate reconstructive surgery. However, I was not going to concern myself with what would probably be cosmetic surgeries; we were still in a fight with numerous infections, which were threatening her life. We would deal with her ear later. The sister said all her wounds were exposed and redressed in the theater and I glorified God that they were all healing well. I prayed for Kechi and left.

The next morning, I woke early so that I could cook for Kechi. I had to use the kitchen in the main house because Diedre was not up and the man who ran the place with her did not seem to know anything about the tabletop stove she had promised me. The staff was making breakfast at the same time I was cooking Kechi's food, so it was not very comfortable, but I went ahead anyway. I had promised Kechi a home cooked meal and she would get it. I resolved, however, to speak with Diedre because the main reason I was in a self-catering apartment was to cook for my daughter.

I hoped the meal would put a smile on Kechi's face, I was really desperate to see her happy. Unfortunately that was not the case that morning.

She was asleep when I got there and the inside of her right eyelid was turned all the way inside out, covering a large part of the eye. The dressings on the forehead from the previous day seemed to have pulled her eyelids even higher. She woke up and started to cry because, as she said, she hated the way her eyes felt. Sister Phil and I tried in vain to calm her down, and Phil said she had tried to clean the film of white covering Kechi's eyes without irritating the eyes even more. Kechi said she could not see me and this made her cry even harder, "I want to see your face".

She did not want her eyes cleaned any further because she said it made no difference. I told her that I could see a white film covering her eye and she would be able to see better if it was cleaned off. She finally agreed and Phil and I carefully cleaned it off with cotton soaked in water. This made a difference and she calmed down when her vision cleared. I showed her an ankle length summer dress I had bought for her and she soon forgot her troubles in the admiration of her dress.

Then the sister took me outside the room and gave me news that knocked me to my knees. Kechi had sat up on her bed that morning, and had actually swung her legs to and fro a few times, and then, supported, stood for a few seconds! After that, exhausted, she had slept.

I was speechless, and then I just started to glorify God, giving Him praise. I recalled that Kechi had told us on February 16th, the day she said she felt a burden lift off her, that she would sit up and move in two weeks, and today, sixteen days after that pronouncement, not only did she sit, she stood up! I was ecstatic, I was weak, I was crying, praising God at the same time. I felt humbled by His greatness and His mercy and grace.

When I composed myself, I went in and playfully asked Kechi,

"So, don't you have some awesome news for me today?"

Her eyes lit up and she very got very excited, giving me details of her great feat of the day.

She said, "Mom, you can't believe how heavy my body felt. After just sitting up and standing for one second, I was so tired that I fell asleep!"

I told her that it would get easier and soon she would be able to walk. I told her I would talk to her doctor about her eyes, but she should also complain to him about it, for emphasis. She did not think that he could do anything about it, but I told her that as her physician, he could tell the plastic surgeon that something needed to be done about it, and she agreed.

By the time I came back from warming up her food, Dr. Pahad had come in and Kechi had spoken to him about her eyes. When I came in, I heard him talking on his cell phone to, first the plastic surgeon, and then an eye specialist. He told Kechi that both doctors would come in to examine her eyes the following Monday and she felt much better. I told her to remember to be patient so that she did not end up being the tortoise in the story that fell into a smelly pit and was there for a very long time with no hope of getting out by himself, yet when rescuers came, he grumpily demanded that they hurry up because he could not stand the smell one second longer. While being amused by the story, Kechi said the analogy did not apply in her case. I begged to differ and we agreed to disagree.

Kechi was moved to tears when I told her of the outpouring of love from her family and the church. I told her how Nduka, my sister's son, had said that he wished that the plane crash had happened to him, and not to Kechi. I always knew they had a special bond, but that moved me. I also told her of how the church had prayed for Kechi's pain to be shared among them. Kechi was overwhelmed. She said she had the best family, natural and church, ever. She said that she loved her grandmother so much and marveled at how my Mom had such a wonderful relationship with all her grandchildren, and how much they all loved her.

When Louisa came for our lunch date, Kechi vehemently refused to let me go. I apologized to Louisa, and she told me not to worry about it. I stayed with Kechi until 2.00pm and then fed her.

By the next visit, Kechi looked dull and when I asked if she was okay, she said her eyes hurt. I consoled her, and told her to be patient a while longer. She soon went into talking mode, and regaled me with stories from school, including when the principal, Fr. Marc spanked her and Emmanuella, her friend, for walking on the lawn.

Thirty minutes past visiting time, I tried to leave, but she was having none of it, complaining that when I was not there, time dragged until the next visit. She confided that she cried when I left after a visit. I was surprised and told her that she must never do that again. Why would she, when she knew that as long as there was breath left in my body, I would be there, come rain come shine? I asked if she ever felt that I would not show up and she said no. But I know that in a secret part of her heart, Kechi always had this fear that one day I was going to disappear. It was a fear I had battled with in her since her childhood. In fact it was so bad that during my sister's wedding, when Kechi must have been around five or six, she held on to my skirt throughout that day as I bustled about busily getting things done. It was funny then, but now I had to wonder whether I had ever given my daughter the impression that I would ever voluntarily leave her.

That day, however, she said that maybe we just loved each other too much. I told her that we must learn to love Jesus more than we loved each other. She was not too sure about that and was shocked and a bit hurt when I told her that I love Jesus more than anyone else. I had to explain to her that He was the reason I was even alive in the first place and that by dying in our place, has taught us that there is a higher, more desirable kind of love. I told her never to forget that this world is just a place of experiencing and refinement in our journey to our real home.

I stopped there, but resolved to throw in nuggets of truth from time to time. I needed for her to see Jesus like I saw Him and to realize that He came first. I would lead her fully to Him, I could not become an idol to her. Jesus had to come first, she had to understand that and I knew that God would help me to teach her full and complete surrender.

When I came back in the evening, Kechi and I just spent long moments staring at each other. Her eyes were still a but blurry from a combination of the ointment on her face that had as usual melted into her eyes, and the fact that she could not shut them fully to blink and clean them in the usual way. Her greatest frustration was that she could not see my face properly and I told her to blink really hard a few times. Luckily, this helped and she could see me. I told her to just hold on for one more day, and on Monday the doctors would find a way.

I laid hands on her and prayed, then told her I was leaving. When she started to protest, I told her that she must learn to let me go, and fully trust that I will be back when I said I would, and she nodded. I blew her a kiss and she blew it back to me and turned her head, following my progress to the door.

'Good night, Mommy'.

I said good night back to her and left.

❖

I woke the next morning feeling optimistic and in my daily bible reading, I read from Hebrews about holding on to my faith, and depending on Jesus, my High Priest in heaven, Who has walked where I walk and therefore knew exactly what I was going through.

Jacqui called to invite me to lunch and I accepted, hoping that I could prevail upon Kechi to let me go. She did not look happy that morning and when I asked if she was okay, she shook her head no, saying that her eyes hurt. I reminded her that the specialist was coming the following day, and a solution was in sight. I continued in the same vein for a while and after a while she calmed down. I saw a film of white stuff over her eyes and I said I would not remove it because her eyes were sore. She started to cry again because she could not see my face clearly. I told her to try blinking hard again and see if the stuff would move to the corners of her eyes, and I could gently remove it. She blinked several times and I was able to remove most of the stuff and she could see better. I left at 12pm because they were ready to bathe her.

When I went back to her room, she was crying again. Her eyes hurt, she was itching, she was cold from being sprayed, she was tired of everything and so on. I talked and talked and eventually she calmed down. Lanre and Remi visited and stayed for a while, then the Ophthalmologist came in and examined Kechi's eyes. He said that she needed contracture releases on both eyelids. This meant that the eyelids would have to be cut open and skin grafted onto them from another part of her body in order for the eyes to close properly. He said that he would push for the procedure to be done later that week. I decided to speak with Dr. Nel so that they would do it very soon.

I left at 2.00pm to have lunch with Jacqui. I did not tell Kechi about the lunch because she was at an all-time emotional low and I did not want to risk her knowing that I was not in the hospital. We went to a Mozambiquan restaurant where we had a marvelous grilled chicken dish. We took a walk after lunch, then stopped somewhere for coffee and talked a whole lot. It felt good to just be with someone and talk about anything but hospital issues.

She took me back to the hospital in time for the 4.00pm visit.

Kechi was in tears when I went into her room. When I asked her what was wrong, the dam exploded, "I'm depressed. Why is all this happening to me? I never imagined my life would turn out this way. I'm always itching all over, my eyes hurt without stopping, I'm always freezing from the constant wetting of my bandages".

I sat down and let her go on and on about all that was wrong in her life. When she was done, I patiently started telling her all that was right in her life. I told her that all my trust was in God who I believed gave her back to me. She listened and calmed down, but not fully. I could tell that she was tired of hearing the same thing over and over again. The climax of her depression came when the sister came in to wet her bandages again. She had been complaining that the last wetting had been excessive and she was cold from it. It was hard to blame her, because the ICU was kept at an almost freezing temperature to discourage the growth of germs, and aside from the bandages, she was naked under the sheet covering her. She protested loud and long, but the nurses insisted on wetting her anyway because the medication in the acticote dressing was only released when wet.

Kechi cried during the wetting of her bandages, deep, heartfelt sobs that tugged at my heart, repeating over and over, "It's not fair, it's not fair". She felt that she was suffering too much, and for the first time, I cried in front of her at the pure misery and anguish emanating from her. She was really depressed that day. I consoled her as much as I could, and left at 6.30pm, one and a half hours after visiting ended, an emotional wreck.

I called Mike and told him to call Dr. Nel from Nigeria and persuade him to do Kechi's eye surgery the next day, so that we would have at least one problem solved. Mike then decided to make a bad situation worse by suggesting that since I was there physically, I was better placed to speak to the doctor. I asked him if he imagined that I had not already done so; I just wanted his call as the father, all the way from Nigeria, to reinforce how anxious we were for the surgery to be done as soon as possible. Mike had no idea the physical and emotional drain the whole situation was for me and he started his usual careless talk and I believe that the loss of phone connection then was God's way of preventing me from saying what I should not say. Mike sent a text asking for

Dr. Nel's phone number, which I gave him. He called me back some time later to say that Dr. Nel promised to see the Ophthalmologist the following morning and then tell me what they decided to do.

I spent the next hour praying in the waiting room, begging God to strengthen Kechi and I. When I went in for the last visit, she was calmer. She had been given morphine and the effects were still with her. I spent the whole hour rubbing her itching areas, which seemed to give her relief. She was much calmer and we both agreed that the bout of tears had relieved much of her tension. By the time I left, I was also calmer and I knew she would be fine.

Hebrews Chapters 5 and 6 were still in the High Priest theme. I thanked God that Jesus was mediating for me before my God. My <u>The Purpose Driven Life</u> reading for the day was about how our becoming like Christ was one of the purposes of our lives on earth. The Amplified version of the bible talked about faith as being a complete leaning upon God, and trusting in His wisdom, knowledge and power - the complete meaning of faith in a God that is all-knowing and all-powerful. It was an awesome start to my day and I wished I could find a way to tattoo this knowledge in my head and in my heart so that I could never forget it.

Ulo called, and after I recounted yesterday's experiences, she suggested again that maybe the time had come to tell Kechi just how blessed she was in being one of the only two survivors. That would surely put an end to her self-pity and she might begin to comprehend the awesome hand of God upon her life. I confessed to Ulo that I had had the prompting to tell Kechi the whole story, but had held back because it was such a huge thing and I was afraid for her state of mind. I think I was being cowardly, but I really wished the Holy Spirit would be more audible in that regard.

Kechi looked bright that morning, but that may have been because her temperature was high. 38.9°! When I exclaimed, Kechi informed me it had been 39° earlier that morning. The doctor had been called and he had prescribed new antibiotics and other drugs. The fan was trained on her, though she was cold. I laid hands on Kechi and prayed, rebuking the fever. Then I surrendered Kechi to God. After about an hour, the temperature started to come down and then she started to shiver violently. I knew this was as a result of the fever, so I stayed calm so that she was not alarmed. She was not hungry, but I persuaded her to eat half of her lunch. When the therapist came in for their exercise session, I left to have lunch.

The Ophthalmologist came in and said he only consulted on Thursdays. This meant it was the earliest Kechi could have the eye surgery and I asked Kechi whether she could wait two more days for the eye surgery and she said yes.

Her temperature continued to come down and she was more comfortable. I left for a bit when they had to bathe her and when I came back in, I did 'itch duty' for a while, fed her a few morsels of food and then went to rest for an hour before the last visit. She was a bit drowsy that night, so I rubbed her in all the usual itching spots and then prayed and left.

Ngozi was coming in the following morning, so I called Franz, the cab guy I used most of the time, and arranged for him to pick her from the airport.

Amechi, Ngozi's husband woke me at 5.30am to ask if she had come in. She came in at about 8.00am and it was really good to see her. We went to the hospital together and we had hardly sat down before every staff that passed by stopped to tell us that Kechi was sitting up in a chair.

This was wonderful news. It was very exciting seeing her sitting in a chair for the first time, though she pressed me into itch duty as soon as we walked in. Ngozi brought lots of get-well-soon cards and letters from her friends in school and I read them to her until the therapist came in and we had to leave.

Kechi was going in for the long-awaited eye surgery later that day. She was a bit nervous because it was her eyes, but I told her not to worry because they knew what they were doing and the eye doctor would be present also. After we went for lunch, Ngozi went back to the guesthouse to sleep, and I did some itch duty before Kechi was called into surgery at 5.30pm.

She came out at 7.00pm and when I saw her thirty minutes later, she was fast asleep. She had been given morphine and was out for the count.

Sister Primrose didn't want me to disturb Kechi, and I agreed with her. I stayed in the waiting room, though, for the rest of the hour, in case she woke up and asked for me.

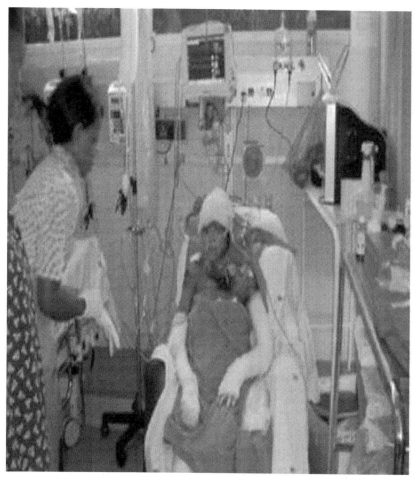

Kechi sits in a chair for the first time – three months after the accident.

I had a visit from some people from the World Burns Foundation - Henry, Bianca, and Lisa. They counseled burns victims and their caregivers, and organized outings for the caregivers to get them out of the hospital for a while. I had no idea then how important that organization would be to Kechi much later in her recovery process.

Kechi's eyes were taped shut when I saw her the next morning and there were tiny white clips holding her upper and lower lids together. She was sitting in a chair again, but did not seem comfortable. She said she was sore and wanted to go back to bed. The sister said that she had only just sat down and they had to train her to go to the general ward. She had to learn to sit and walk or else she could not go to the ward. Kechi started crying and I asked sister Zama to please call the therapists so they could put her back on the bed. They put her through some more exercises before helping her back to the bed. Ngozi and I came back in to see Kechi crying again, complaining that the therapists touched all her wounds while moving and exercising her. Zama gave her some morphine and she calmed down.

After itch duty, I read Psalms 33 and 91 to her. Betty came in with jollof rice for Kechi, but Kechi learnt from school how to eat jollof rice with boiled eggs, and could not eat it any other way, so Betty and I went to her house to boil the eggs. We came back to the hospital late because of traffic, and I was expecting pouting from Kechi, but she was fine, just happy to see me.

After itch duty, I fed her, and then we chatted for a while. She was amazingly calm about her eyes being taped shut, and she said that she had been prepped very well on what to expect by the anesthetist who had seen her before the surgery. I thought also that she finally had relief from the dry and burning sensations caused by eyes that refused to shut.

That night, we all talked at length about celebrities and their antics, and had a good visit. By the time we left, Kechi was relaxed and she had always liked Ngozi's company, so we left on a good note after praying with her.

CHAPTER TWENTY-SIX

"....for he hath said, I will never leave thee, nor forsake thee".
Hebrews 13 : 5(b)(KJV)

Ngozi and I got to the hospital to find that Kechi was sitting in a chair again and not looking too happy about it. I asked if she was uncomfortable, and she said that her knees were killing her. I put a pillow under her feet and her relief was immediate. I went on itch duty while we chatted. After a while, she got tired and wanted to lie down. The physiotherapists, or physio 'terrorists', as Kechi called them behind their backs, came in for her exercises prior to helping her back to bed and we had to leave.

When we got back an hour later, Kechi was back on her bed, crying from pain. Sister Maria gave her morphine and she relaxed and started to drift off. Ngozi wanted to do some shopping and I told Kechi that we were going to the Mall. She demurred at first, but we promised not to be late for the 4.00pm visit. I told her not to fight sleep; it would do her good to rest after her exercises.

Ngozi and I went to Cresta Mall, which was closer than the one in Sandton. I did not want to risk being late for the next visit. Woolworths was having a sale and I picked up a few things for Kechi.

She was in high spirits when we got back to the hospital and took an active part in the conversation, her mind taken off itching, discomfort and pain. After I fed her, she allowed us to leave and get some rest before the night visit. That night, it was more of the same, except that I was pressed into itch duty, but we passed a very pleasant time together until it was time to pray and leave.

Back at the guesthouse, Ngozi gave me a fantastic massage that totally relaxed me. I had no idea I was that tense until I had that massage. I warned her that she had started a precedent, and would have to continue until she left.

Kechi had surgery the next day, and I told the sisters to please inform the plastic surgeon that I was very concerned about the dressing on the wound at the back of her neck, and would really prefer that it be changed.

She was not itching much that morning and Ngozi and I pulled her into our conversation to take her mind off things. She started to complain that she was cold and I noticed that her temperature was inching up. It had gone from 37.5° to 38.1° in the short time we had spent. She was irritable, and complained when her bedcovers were opened for any reason. We left for a while when the therapists came in and when we returned, we talked some more. Then Kechi started to complain about her stomach, she had a pressing, clenching pain. I called Zama's attention to it, but I did not like the way she handled the situation, so I asked her to call the doctor. She replied that according to regulations, she would inform the shift leader, who would make the decision to call the doctor. The shift leader came, listened to Kechi's complaints, and phoned the doctor. This was new to me, because in the past, every time I had asked for the doctor to be called, they usually did so without fail. I refused to get upset, and reminded myself that they were very lenient with me over visiting times, so I was not going to create a ripple that would make them start insisting on my keeping strictly within the visiting times.

The doctor said that the cocktail of drugs she was getting was probably affecting Kechi's stomach, and asked them to give her morphine to relax her, and the pain subsided.

Ngozi and I left to buy foodstuff because Kechi said she wanted to eat rice and gizzard stew. I wondered when she started liking gizzard, but did not argue.

When we came back to the waiting room, there were two priests sitting there already, and one of them asked if I was a Nigerian. When I said I was, he asked if I was Kechi's mother and then introduced himself as the Provincial Leader of North/West African Province of the Society of Jesus, Fr. George Quickly. He introduced his companion as Brother Sam Kojo, both Jesuits. He said they were waiting to see me and had been told that I would come back soon. Brother Kojo had been a math teacher at Loyola Jesuit College, and was completing his studies at Witwatersrand University in Johannesburg.

Fr. Quickly had a very rich and distinctive voice, and a funny thing happened when I took them in to see Kechi. I said to her,

"Sweetie, you have a visitor", and as soon as Fr. Quickly started talking, asking how she was doing, she said, "Father Quickly!"

Kechi's eyes were still taped shut and she could not see, so he was surprised and touched that she recognized his voice. She also recognized Brother Kojo's voice. Fr. Quickly said he brought greetings from the entire students and staff of the school and that Fr. Marc, the principal, and Fr. Peter, the President were going to arrange to send a delegation to see her, but sent goodwill messages through him since he was coming to Johannesburg. Kechi thanked them for visiting her.

She was about to be prepped for surgery, so they left, and shortly after, Kechi was wheeled off to surgery. I sat with her in the theater lobby until she went in. She said she was scared because her eyes were taped shut, how would they know if she had fallen asleep? I assured her that they had monitors that indicate when a patient has gone under, and she should not worry about it. I prayed for her, rebuking the spirit of fear, then I talked to her to take her mind off the surgery until she was taken into the OR.

After she was returned to her room, the anesthetist came to the waiting room to tell me how it went. They grafted skin unto her thigh and changed all the dressings. Her knuckles and scalp were the areas yet to be grafted. The scalp was badly burnt and would be grafted a little at a time. Otherwise, the wounds were fine. Her arms were going to be uncovered so that they could start serious therapy on them.

Kechi was still sleeping off the effects of the sedation, so I prayed over her and left. Back at the guesthouse, I made the stew she requested. I would boil rice in the morning so it would be fresh.

At the hospital the next morning, Kechi was asleep, and the sister said she had been sleeping since that morning, woke briefly for breakfast, again for physio, and then went back to sleep. She slept right through the visiting period, but I knew that as soon as she woke, she would call for me, so I did not leave the hospital, we just stayed in the waiting room. Sure enough, just before 2.00pm, the sister came to get us. I warmed her food and fed her, and she loved every bite of it.

We left at 3.00pm to get something to eat, and when we came back at 4.00pm, she was itchy and a bit uncomfortable. She asked for hot chocolate, which I bought from the coffee shop after making her promise that she would eat her dinner.

Then itch duty started in earnest and nothing I did helped. She started to cry. At this point I had been standing and massaging lotion all over her body for almost an hour, and I was feeling faint, my back was aching from hunching over, and I was physically tired. I sat down and told Kechi that there was really no point in crying. We had both tried our best to overcome the itching and so far nothing had worked, therefore we had to reach out to God to give us the strength to endure for as long as the itching continued. Ngozi started to tell her stories to distract her and it worked, at least until we left.

That night, it was more of the same. I spent the whole hour again trying to rub her itching away, but did not have much success. By the time Ngozi and I got back to the room, I was physically drained and emotionally not doing much better. It had been a discouraging day, but I still thanked God for it.

Saturday, March 12, 2006.

Next morning, I was not doing much better. I was still weak and my face was tired and drawn, no matter how much makeup I slathered on to hide it. I prayed for physical, emotional and spiritual strength to get through the day.

Kechi was crying when we got to the hospital. She was itching and miserable. I told her that she knew I would be there by 11.00am to relieve her itching, so she should stop crying. I put on gloves and went to work and she gradually calmed down. Her blood pressure was going up, and had remained at an average of 164/98 throughout the morning. I asked if she was upset of worried about anything and she said no. I surrendered it to God and left it.

Then something occurred to me. We had been in South Africa for almost three months to the day of the crash, and all along, it had been as if I was on automatic pilot - strength, faith, and grace to bear, all divinely bestowed upon me by God. Now I felt like I was on manual, and had to consciously make the effort to rely on God. The training wheels had come off, and it was sink or swim.

I chose to swim.

I had to surrender to Him, consciously, throughout the day; to let go and let God be God. That was the real testing that built patience and faith in God. I prayed to be worthy of the grace that would follow obedience to His Word. I bowed my head right there and prayed,

'Lord, I surrender entirely to You. Please strengthen me, and may I continually die to self in my journey to become like Christ. Amen.'

Kechi was still crying from pain and itching when we came back in after the therapy. She was given something for pain and I did itch duty until 2.00pm. She wanted to start crying as we left and I gave her a choice. I could stay and never leave her side for hours on end, standing and rubbing all over her body, until I fell ill from lack of rest and would be laid up for days on end; or I could go and have lunch, put my feet up for a couple of hours of rest and come back refreshed. The choice was hers. Not surprisingly, she chose the latter, so Ngozi and I went to Campus Square for lunch, because I was very tired of the food in the coffee shop by then. It was very good food, but after eating it every day for three months, I needed a change.

When we returned, we spent time talking with Kechi and I was tapping on her head dressings to relieve the itching on her scalp. Sister Thandeka told me that the Ophthalmologist had come in to say that Kechi would be going into surgery the following Tuesday to have the eye dressings removed. I was very happy, because Kechi had been extraordinarily patient with basically being blind for a whole week.

We left for her to be washed and when we came back in, Kechi was looking refreshed and feeling wonderful. She said the sisters were very gentle with her and she hardly felt any pain at all, and she was not itching. We had a very nice visit, and then I fed her. She was very fond of the hospital roast chicken and she ate every last bite.

By the night visit, the itch duty reprieve was over and I set to work for the whole hour, after which we prayed and left.

Simone, who worked with Deidre, sent two rough looking young men to take us back to the cottage. I thought about calling Deidre to confirm, but since they came straight to us as soon as we stepped into the hospital lobby and asked if we were waiting for Simone, I decided we should go with them. They blasted the radio, and took a route that we did not recognize. Ngozi and I looked at each other, and I started to have thoughts of theft, rape and murder, and berated myself for not confirming with Deidre before getting into their car. There were countless stories of crimes against women in Johannesburg, committed by both South Africans and immigrants from the Democratic Republic of Congo and other surrounding countries. In fact it was so bad that when we first came and I discovered that the hotel was just across the road from the hospital, a five minute walk at most through a park, I decided to save my money and walk to the hospital one morning. When the security guards at the hospital entrance saw me coming, they rushed to me and asked if I had walked down. When I said yes, they told me never to do so again. Apparently, just the previous evening someone had been shot in that park for her cell phone. So I spent money every morning and evening on a two or three minute ride to and from the hospital.

With all these at the back of my head, I took a moment to bow my head and pray for God's protection over us.

Eventually, I started to recognize the roads. They had simply taken a short-cut. So much for not judging others. I was very relieved when they dropped us off in front of Deidre's guesthouse. I told myself I must remember to tell Kechi this story.

Ngozi gave me another massage that took away most of the kinks in my back.

❖

Kechi was sitting up in the chair again the next morning. She was looking good and was cheerful for the first few minutes. Then she told us that Dr. Nel had ordered a full body dressing change in the ward, and at the thought of the pain that would be involved in the removal of the acticote dressings, she began to cry. She was still crying when Dr. Pahad came in, and sobbing, she begged him to tell Dr. Nel to change her dressings in the OR. Dr. Pahad told her that she was getting spoiled, and teased her, asking 'Where is the sweet girl that used to be in this room? Has she gone back to Nigeria?' His teasing failed to draw a smile from Kechi and when he saw the level of her distress, told her that he would tell the unit leader to call Dr. Nel and tell him the situation so that he could make a decision. Kechi continued her crying and Ngozi reprimanded her for not being fair to her mother.

She nodded and tried to calm herself down. Then she closed her eyes and prayed. I tried to distract her by telling her of the fright Ngozi and I had the previous night, and that worked for a while.

The unit leader for that day, Sister Thandeka called Dr. Nel, and a theater visit was scheduled for later that day for full dressing change.

Kechi's relief was palpable. She heaved a huge sigh of relief and thanked God for answering her prayer. She brightened up immediately and not even the prospect of wetting her bandages and the coming physical therapy fazed her.

She said to Sister Jane, 'You can do anything you want to me, I don't mind. I'm sure you also think I'm spoiled'. Jane replied that she did not blame her; even she, an adult, would behave the same way, or even worse when faced with such pain.

Kechi was noticeably improving, slowly but surely. The pain was lessening daily, and even the itching was either reducing, or was getting more tolerable. When we got back by 4.00pm, however, she was not feeling good. Her temperature was going up rapidly again, going from 37.1° to 39.6° within a space of two hours. In addition to this, her stomach was cramping painfully again. I was beginning to have a serious problem with Jane, the sister looking after Kechi. Apparently, the consensus was that Kechi was spoilt and used to getting her way, and I believe this influenced Jane's behavior and responses towards Kechi's needs. She did not take any of Kechi's complaints seriously and was even reluctant to call the doctor to report Kechi's stomachache. She finally told the unit leader about Kechi's pain when I told her I was going to go to the doctor's office myself.

Dr. Pahad came immediately to examine Kechi and said the stomachache must be related to the fast before the theater visit, since the same thing happened the previous Friday, which was also a theater day. He recommended Buscopan.

Sister Jane was nowhere to be found when the Buscopan was delivered by the pharmacy and for twenty minutes, the drug was lying there on the table while Kechi writhed in pain. By the time Jane finally came in, Kechi was throwing up and coughing and her temperature was still up. Jane administered the drug and sprayed Kechi's bandages to reduce the fever, but it did not help - the temperature remained high at 39.5°.

After all that retching, Kechi's throat was sore, but she said the pressure in her chest had reduced. We now started waiting for the theater to send for Kechi. Meanwhile, her blood pressure, which had been high, stared to drop to within normal range, though her temperature remained high. She was shivering from head to toe due to the fever and I laid hands on her and prayed and after a while, the shivering subsided, except on her feet. At one point, I must have looked worried, because Kechi said to me,

"Mommy, don't worry. You must remain strong for me".

I assured her that I was fine, and had bent my head because I was praying. I told her that she could go on drawing strength from me, because I was drawing strength from God. That just proved to me that Kechi scrutinized my face and demeanor in order to determine the state of her health and well being.

At 8.15pm, she was taken into the OR and came out at 9.30 pm.

We saw her at 9.50pm, and stayed until she got her drugs and drifted off to sleep.

Sister Rose, a wonderful and empathetic nurse, who really liked Kechi, was her nurse for the night, and I was very grateful to God for that, after our experiences with Jane earlier in the day. We prayed and left for the night. It had been a very trying and tiring day and I was glad to go back and get some sleep.

It was now normal to see Kechi sitting up in her chair when we came in for the first visit. She was looking cheerful and her temperature was down, and she participated well in the conversation and jokes. She teased me about my hips, saying I could pass for a South African woman. Then she dropped a bombshell, almost as an after thought. She had walked, assisted of course, halfway to the sink, about ten steps, but could not go all the way because she got tired. She then stood for a few seconds, while still being supported on both sides, and then sat down. She said she stood and walked on her toes and the therapists told her to keep trying to get her heels down, but they were painful and stiff. This was a result of lying down for too long on her back. Her foot had stayed in the pointed-forward position and her ankles had almost locked into that position. They were now teaching her to put her heels down so she could walk again.

The therapists said that I should stop putting a pillow under Kechi's feet to relieve the pressure in her knees because she needed to learn how to bend her knees. This was very painful for her, and we encouraged her to keep trying. She sometimes straightened her legs to relieve the pressure on her knees. She soon got tired and by the time the therapists came back in, she was more than ready to go back to bed. She had complained that getting back into bed after sitting was very stressful because she had to be pulled up, lifted and put in bed, then she had to lift and shift her body into position on the bed. I told her that she had to keep at it until she could do it by herself because she was being prepared to stay in the ward where she would have to get up from the bed and go to the loo by herself.

When we came back in, Kechi was lying on her bed and was looking very relieved to be there, so I reminded her of when she was so tired on lying on the bed; now she could not wait to get back in it.

I fed her and then we told stories about weird stuff and urban legends involving ghosts that supposedly abounded in Nigerian secondary schools. Some of the stories found their way to all secondary schools, like Madam Koi-Koi, whose name was onomatopoeic for the sound her shoes made when she walked by, invisible. Another such tale was the one about the bush baby - an animal that mimicked the sound of a baby's cry and ate whoever came out to investigate. Kechi was fully entertained, and told a few stories of her own.

Back for the 4.00pm visit, Kechi was still looking good, just itching a bit here and there. Then Kechi got mushy, and told Ngozi that she really loved her so much because she was honest, plain spoken and forthright. Ngozi was pleased and so was I.

Her temperature was coming down and by the time we left, it was down to 36.7°, and Kechi was livelier than I had seen her for a long time. She moved the fingers of her left hand for me, actually bent them a little. The doctors had been afraid that that hand would be permanently damaged. The graft on the right hand had failed, and I suspected that it was because the therapists had exercised that hand the day after the grafting, not knowing it had just been done. They would have to repeat that surgery.

That night, Kechi was a bit irritable and I spent the whole hour rubbing at the itchy spots. I did find time, however, to lay hands on her and pray.

The sister for the night was someone I had never seen before and she was a bit hostile, and did not take kindly to our free run on Kechi. She bit Ngozi's head off when Ngozi asked her to straighten Kechi's bed linen, and Ngozi bit right back. I decided not to ask her to do anything, and simply removed the sheet that Kechi was finding irritating. As far as I was concerned, Kechi was in God's hands and not in the irritable nurse's.

Ngozi observed that we really seemed to get saddled with the most unpleasant nurses and I told her that it was because we needed to overcome and rise above the emotions and feelings that their actions generated in us. I was not unmindful of the fact that the whole of my life was a test and a preparation for eternity with God. So I resolved to endure whatever behavior I saw and trust in God.

My bible reading the next morning was from the book of James, addressing how important it was to tame the tongue so that it did not cause destruction. I was going to have to make a conscious effort to learn how to restrict what came out of my mouth.

Ngozi retouched my hair before we left, which was such a relief, because I did not have to bother Betty or anyone else to drive me to the beauty shop.

Kechi was fine that morning, sitting up in her chair, her temperature normal, but she was itching. The hospital had an inspection that morning, and so they insisted that Ngozi and I should wear the full protection - gloves, disposable aprons and facemasks to be with Kechi.

Though she had had breakfast already, Kechi still wanted more of the scrambled eggs she had that morning. The kitchen was already preparing lunch, and could not oblige us, so Ngozi went to get some from the coffee shop while I started itch duty. Kechi enjoyed the eggs and finished every bit of it, rounding it off with a glass of juice. She was getting more comfortable sitting on the chair and her knees only started aching after she had sat for about two hours. We left when the therapists came in and when we returned, Kechi was in bed and her left hand had been exposed and was shedding dried scabs of dead skin, which Kechi found very irritating, and kept asking for me to brush them off her bed.

Ngozi wanted to do some shopping and I told Kechi that we were going to the mall. She was not happy and I cancelled the idea, but surprisingly, she insisted that I should go. I could tell she was trying not to cry and told her the mall was not important, that I would stay. She stuck to her guns and said she would be fine, and it was not as if I would not come back. I left reluctantly, but I knew that I had to have some down time if I did not want to break down.

Ngozi and I decided to go to the Hyde Park Mall, after one of the sisters had said good things about it. It was a bit high end, but very pretty. In Exclusive Books, I found the Narnia series on audiotape and I bought them for Kechi for variety. I also bought a copy of the complete Narnia series all in one book so she could add it to the library she was building.

When we got back to Kechi, we could tell that she was not happy with us for leaving before 2.00 pm, but then I showed her our purchases and she brightened up. We all got talking while I was doing itch duty, and suddenly Kechi wanted to know how Ngozi and I met. This led to the stories of how Ngozi and her husband, Amechi met, how Mike and I met and so on. She was hugely entertained. She began to look sleepy, although she denied that she wanted to sleep when I asked her. We decided to leave at 5.30pm anyway, so we could get some rest before the night visit. We put on the Narnia tape for her, but it did not have any dramatization, and she said she did not like it, so I said I would go and exchange it some other time.

That night and the next morning were pretty much the same. We came in, did itch duty, talked and laughed with Kechi and fed her. There were no nasty surprises in terms of elevated blood pressure, temperature and so on.

Towards mid-morning, Dr. Nel came in and said that Kechi would go in for a full dressing change the next day, and the following Monday, she would be getting a full head grafting. He said he hoped that that would be the last grafting. This was good news and we all rejoiced because suddenly, an end was in sight. After he left, I noticed that the skin on the left side of Kechi's face had contracted and was pulling that side of the face from her left eye to her lips. I made a note to ask the doctor what could be done about that.

Then I mistakenly put my hand on Kechi's right hand, and she said, "Mommy, your hand is on mine'"

Mortified, I snatched my hand away, feeling so bad that I was actually adding to my daughter's pain. I was castigating myself on my carelessness, and Kechi said, "It's alright, Mommy". I nodded, but obviously my expression was not in agreement with my reassurances because Kechi then said, "Smile".

I smiled and felt better. Then I applied the ointment and rubbed it all over her body until the therapist, Romi, came in.

Kechi was sleepy after the physio session and fell asleep before I could ask her if she wanted anything special for dinner. Ngozi and I went back to Hyde Park mall to exchange the CDs.

Kechi was asleep until 4.30pm.

Dr. Pahad came in when I was feeding her and I asked him if Kechi could be taken to the OR earlier in the day since it had been established that the prolonged fasting before surgery caused her stomach cramping. He explained that the plastic surgeons did a lot of cosmetic surgery, and to lower the risk of infection from burns patients, got those ones out of the way before moving on to the higher risk, probably infection-laden burns patients. This made sense to me, and the doctor said he would personally monitor Kechi to prevent a recurrence of her cramping.

Kechi closed up later that day, no smiles, no animation on her face, and insisted that nothing was wrong when asked. I decided that everyone was entitled to an off day once in a while and did not push her for answers. Her face looked good; the graft on her forehead beginning to take on a lighter shade, and to date, remains the best grafting that was done.

The nurse brought in a TV for Kechi, and for the first time, she agreed to watch it, and luckily, there was a show playing which she enjoyed. We fed her and left her with her eyes glued on the screen.

At night, Kechi was still watching TV and she said she had seen three shows already. I did itch duty while she continued to watch TV. I was glad that she was distracted, because it meant that there would be something for her to do when we left.

CHAPTER TWENTY-SEVEN

"He will not suffer thy foot to be moved: he that keepeth thee will not slumber. Behold, he that keepeth Israel shall neither slumber nor sleep."
Psalm 121 : 3&4 (KJV)

Kechi was looking fantastic the next morning. The sass was back in her mouth and the twinkle back in her eyes. I could see the old Kechi peeping through, and even the hospital staff was saying that she was looking better every day. Kechi started sassing me about my clothes, asking me in their teenage slang, 'So what are you feeling like, eh, Mom? You're feeling all fashionable, eh?'

It made me feel so good, because this was the Kechi I remembered. Kechi rarely cried, always saw the good side of every situation, which was why it was so distressing to see her cry so much.

Even the itching seemed to have lessened. Apparently, the night before, they had threatened to restrain her hands if she did not refrain from scratching her body all the time, and this horrified her into striving to endure the itching.

Also the shift leader, Marissa, talked to her and made enough sense to make her decide to try her best to endure the itching.

Ngozi had a trip planned to Soweto so she left at noon, and by 12.20pm, all visitors were asked to leave the ICU. This was so strange because I thought they were used to my being around at odd hours, but they insisted, so I left. I asked the sister if I could return by 1.00pm, and she said she would come by to get me. By 1.20 pm, she came and told me Kechi was asleep, and I was glad because being asleep would take her mind off the fact that she was nil per oral (NPO). This meant she was off food in preparation for surgery.

Ngozi came back before the next visit, and when we went in, Kechi was just waking up and barely ten minutes later, the OR called for her, and as usual, I accompanied her. It occurred to me then that gone were the days of rushing Kechi off to the theater, the staff racing, squeezing the manual air pump. Now we took a leisurely stroll, and after only a few minutes in the prep room, she was wheeled in.

We saw her next at 7.30 pm, when the nurses were still attaching her leads and wires, and they asked us to wait. But I heard some sniffling and I looked round the curtain they had drawn around her bed, and Kechi was crying. I asked her what was wrong, and when she heard the sound of my voice, she started to cry in earnest. It turned out she thought it was close to midnight, and I had left without her seeing me. She began to calm down and then drifted off to sleep. I sat with her and prayed and when she woke up just before 8.30pm, I told her that I would be going, but she would be okay because I had prayed for her. After a token protest, she asked me to hold her and kiss her before leaving and by the time I left, she was calm.

It was a different story the next day.

Kechi was in bed, looking very dull. Sister Primrose said she had been depressed all morning, but had a good breakfast. As soon as Kechi saw us, she set me to work; I had to straighten her bed linen, change the oxygen monitor from her big toe to the next toe, do itch duty, which now included gently beating on the bandages where the skin beneath itched. After all these, she was marginally more comfortable. Then she said she wanted a sandwich, hot chocolate and cake. While Ngozi went off to the coffee shop to get all that, I resumed itch duty, until she got back.

Kechi rejected the cheesecake, but ate the sandwiches with gusto and finished the hot chocolate. She also ate the chicken that came with her lunch, and soon became chatty, and her spirits picked up.

I then asked her why she had been so depressed earlier, and she said it was because she wanted me, to which I replied that if that was the case, she should have brightened up as soon as she saw me. She had no answer to that.

The anesthetist had told me earlier that if I felt that Kechi was depressed, there were mild depression drugs that could be prescribed for her. I decided to hold off on those for the moment.

At 4.00pm, Kechi was awake and relatively peaceful, and I did little to no itch duty. We had a long conversation, though. It all started when Kechi said that the left side of her face felt tight and uncomfortable. I told her that the skin was contracting as it healed and that this was normal for burns victims. Then came the question I had been dreading all along.

"What does my face look like?"

I explained as much as I could, by mentioning specific parts of the face without saying what the overall picture was.

"Was my whole body burned?"

"Sixty five percent of it was burned, from your face to your feet, but your stomach, back and bum were untouched. How does that make you feel?"

"It doesn't make me feel anyhow".

"Well", I said, "If it was me, I would feel blessed and lucky to have survived".

"I don't feel very lucky, after all it's not as if I was the only person that survived. If anything, I seem to have been the worst injured since I'm the only person here".

Again, I felt the nudging to give her the details of the crash if only to emphasize just how blessed she was, but at the same time, I still felt that the time was not right yet. I said instead,

"Kechi, anyone that falls out of the sky and lives to tell the tale is blessed".

She was shocked, because she had thought that the plane had an accident after landing. I told her that I wondered what part of 'plane crash' sounded like an ordinary accident. She wanted to know more, so I gave her a few details and told her that she was the person to tell us more when her brain released the details to her, because she could still not remember anything from after they boarded the airplane in Abuja.

All the time I was talking with Kechi, I was trusting the Holy Spirit to give me the right words, and at the end of our discussion, she said that now she felt blessed and believed that her survival was indeed a miracle.

When I went to the nurse's break room to peel a mango for her, she continued to chat with Ngozi, telling her that she had never questioned God as to why this had happened to her. And Ngozi said she also confided that she knew she had a wonderful mother.

That night was mostly itch duty, and I rubbed and patted for the whole hour. New itching spots kept cropping up and even after we prayed and prepared to leave, I had to keep rubbing until I was halfway out the door.

We came in the next morning as Kechi was finishing her exercises with the therapist, who said she was very pleased with Kechi's progress. She had stood for a while that morning and was feeling pretty smug.

We praised her as she was lowered into her chair and she soon asked for a sandwich and hot chocolate, which she finished as soon as Ngozi came back with them.

Her appetite was not a problem.

The sister said that the physician on duty, Dr. Schleicher, ordered a hypertensive drug to bring down her blood pressure, and it was already working, as I could see that it looked better than the previous day's reading. I was certain that when Dr. Pahad, who was on leave, resumed, he was going to order a round of tests to find out just why it had been rising steadily for the past three days.

We all watched TV for a while, then Ngozi went off to the mall to buy some things that her husband had requested. Kechi asked for potato crisps, which I got for her, and shortly after, when her lunch arrived, polished that off also. I was glad she was eating so well. After lunch, I was allowed to stay with her and we talked, watched TV and the listened to the Narnia tape until 2.00pm when the movie "Beetlejuice" began on TV. I was able to leave knowing she was occupied.

I called Uzoma, and spoke with Tara, who asked to speak with Kechi. I told her not to worry, that she would soon be able to speak with her big sister. Tara sounded well and happy and it was good not to worry about her. She,

Kamara and Dumebie, Uzoma's kids, prayed for Kechi individually over the phone and gave me get-well messages for her, which I promised to deliver. After that, I spoke with Uzoma, and she stressed that I should keep focusing on Kechi and have no worries about Tara at all. After I hung up, I thanked God for Uzoma. What a friend!

By 4.00pm, Kechi was still cheerful, and she was so touched when I recounted the prayers the kids had prayed for her. She wanted to know verbatim what Tara had said, and lamented that she missed her little sister so much.

I did some itch duty, and massaged cream into her left hand. She teased me that I was getting better at massaging. The first time, I was terrified that I was hurting her. We discussed movies, and tried to up each other in the telling of jokes. When I reminded her that Ngozi was leaving in two days, she pouted a bit and protested, but then accepted it, saying how happy she was that Ngozi had come.

During the night visit, Ngozi took over itch duty to give me a break since I was going to be doing it alone after she left. Kechi worked her really hard and she was sweating at the end of the hour. Before we left, I asked Kechi to pray. She thanked God for her healing, for her life, her family and friends. She also gave thanks that she had had a good day that day, and asked for strength to withstand the itching so that it did not ruin her precious visiting hours. She prayed for Ngozi and I to get safely to the guest house, thanked God for the love of her family and friends, and prayed for God's protection of her family back home in Nigeria. She went on to say that she loved God and trusted in Him that her wounds would heal and her body would return to the way it was. And then she concluded by praying for God's protection during the night.

After that, Ngozi prayed that God's purpose for Kechi's life be fulfilled and also for strength for Kechi and I. It was a beautiful time of prayer and thanksgiving. Kechi then had some last minute itch duty requests, and then Primrose distracted her so we could escape.

I received a text message from my friend, Ngozi Nnaji, whose daughter, Chidera, was one of the sixty students from Loyola Jesuit College in that Sosoliso plane crash. The encouragement I had been getting from Ngozi was incredible. The week before, she had sent me a text message from London. She was a great woman, her love for God incredible. I felt blessed to know her and could only hope that I would have been strong enough in my faith to be able to do the same had the situation been reversed. Her text message went thus:

"God can do more than you ever think or ask, He has all the power in His hand. When you cannot see your way, just remember this, He can, because He is able. And her name says it all. "KECHI" "GOD'S OWN". He will see her through".

This gave me great comfort, although I also shed a few tears remembering her sweet daughter, Chidera, a girl that was loved by everyone who knew her in her very short life.

Kechi was sitting up in her usual chair that morning, feeling strong and looking bright. She admired my slippers and my top. I saw Rochelle, and knew why she was feeling so upbeat. Kechi had formed a deep attachment to Rochelle, and it was mutual. Her blood pressure was normal and everything was looking fine.

We asked her to allow us to leave by 1.00pm so that we could go to ABSA and see about opening an account for me. She demurred at first, and then agreed. As we were leaving, she called me back to remind me that she was going in for surgery at 4.00pm that day, and I should come back before then. I promised I would be back and we went off.

The lady at the bank gave me some forms to fill out, and said they would send the forms to my bank in Nigeria, Diamond Bank, and if they got a favorable response, they would open an account for me. I called my friend, Oby, who was the Head of Operations in Diamond Bank, and told her to expect the letter from ABSA. I was glad Ngozi had insisted, because having an account would make a lot of things easier for me. From the bank, we went to Cresta mall for Ngozi to finish her shopping, and for me to buy Kechi's 'theater gift'.

By 3.45pm, we were back in Kechi's room, just in time to see her being wheeled off to the OR. I accompanied her to the prep room and she asked me to pray for her. Her temperature had spiked again to 39.1°, and she was feeling feverish. I rebuked the fever and prayed for peace for Kechi. I asked if she was afraid and she said no. Dr. Nel came in and was very warm and friendly, giving me a hug, and telling me that they were going to graft her left leg and foot. He was going to hold off on grafting the scalp until the results of the tests indicated that there was no longer an infection there.

After he went into the theater, I remarked to Kechi how friendly he was, and she said she gave him no choice because she always sang out 'Hi, Dr. Nel' whenever he came to the ward, even when he was just passing through, or seeing other patients, so he just had to be friendly. I shook my head. That was Kechi, you just had to love her.

The surgery lasted for two hours and I became concerned and went to sit by the theater doors, so I was there when she was wheeled out. At the door of the ICU, I told her I would see her after she was settled in.

As usual, post-op Kechi was sad and tearful. I did my best to cheer her up. Ngozi suggested that I should pray out loud so she could hear me, and when I did, she drifted in and out of sleep. When people came from the radiology lab to do an x-ray, I asked them to be careful, as her back was still sore from being a donor site. Sure enough, she was in pain after that, and Ngozi told her not to try and struggle to wake up, she should remember that we were there with her and just sleep. This seemed to work because it did appear as if she was struggling to keep awake. The sister came in and gave her morphine, and she fell asleep. I asked the sister to please keep an eye on her breathing because she seemed to be straining to breathe.

She reassured me that Kechi's stats were fine, and she would watch her closely. Her temperature was still high, and the sister started an anti pyretic before we left.

Surgery days were always hard, but I thanked God all the same.

Ngozi left early the next morning, and I was a bit teary. I was going to miss her. Coming to be with me, to lend support, meant the world to me. It was the mark of true friendship and I would appreciate it forever.

In the waiting room, while waiting for visiting time to start, Rochelle came in to tell me that Kechi had been crying since morning after being told that she would be having daily dressing changes on her hands. And she cried even more when Rochelle told her that she would be off duty for the next two days.

Kechi's eyes were closed when I went into her room. She said they felt very sensitive that day, and hurt when she opened them. I told her that she could not keep them shut because she had to see me and she opened the left one slightly. She said she was itching all over so I went to work and only stopped briefly to show her the gift I had bought for her the previous day. For the next two hours, I was on itch duty. When I had to leave for dressing change, she was still itching. My helplessness and frustration with the situation surfaced for a second when I blurted out, 'I don't know what else to do, I don't know how else to relieve the itching. I have rubbed you all over your body for two hours, and it has not helped at all. I'm confused. I really am'.

Kechi began to cry again, telling me not be confused. I calmed down and told her that I was not angry with her. All we could do was pray for a solution to the itching problem. She asked if I would come back after dressing change and I assured her I would be in the waiting room and she should tell Rochelle to come and get me when they were through. She was still crying when I left. I felt very bad for letting her see my frustration and making her cry. It was a good thing I had prayed for strength that morning because it was definitely one of the down phases. Her blood pressure was up again, temperature was high, and she was itching all over. My poor baby.

However, there were good things happening too. According to the anesthetist, the previous day's grafting could well be the last major one. Apparently the lab results had come in before the surgery, and since her scalp was cleared of infection, it had been grafted as well as her thigh and foot. Also, her appetite was healthy, and even her irritability was a sign that she was recovering.

I sat down and counted my blessings, and then I prayed about the itching. I asked God to transfer it to me; I could not bear Kechi's suffering any more.

After I was called back in, Kechi said that it had not been so bad because there was no acticote dressing to be ripped off. Rochelle explained further that the doctor used Betidene to dress the wounds and they must be changed daily. Also, Kechi's arms would be exposed soon as they seemed to be healing very well.

Kechi was still itching and she was now upset that I was frustrated. I explained once more that my frustration was aimed inwards at myself and my inability to make a difference to her condition, not at her. When she asked me not to get frustrated, I snapped at her, telling her that she could not control how I felt, but I would try.

Both of us kept quiet for a while because it was out of character for me to snap at Kechi, and she probably felt that she should just leave me alone for a while. As for me, I felt the need to be by myself for a while, so I asked her if she still wanted the McDonalds's burger she had asked for and when she said yes, I went to Campus Square, and sat for a while, getting my composure back.

When I felt at peace again, I bought the burger and went back in time for the 4.00pm visit. She searched my face thoroughly when I went in, and must have been satisfied with whatever she saw because she relaxed and ate her burger. I think both of us came to a silent agreement that day that sometimes, Mom needed to be left alone.

Rochelle wanted to bathe her, and also asked me to buy cotton buds so she could clean Kechi's ears, so I went to the mini drug store in the hospital and bought them, giving them to one of the nurses to pass onto Rochelle.

Kechi sent for me after her bath and I fed her. She was relatively calm and after itch duty, I left at 7.00pm, to return at 7.30pm, the official night visiting time, to pick up from where I had stopped. By this time I was literally swaying from fatigue and feeling low in every way that mattered. For the first time, I actually looked forward to 8.30pm so I could get off my feet. I then made the mistake of telling Kechi that if I had another day like this, I would certainly fall ill. This caused her a lot of distress and she started to cry. I tried to calm her down, and said I did not mean to make her feel bad. All I wanted was for her to join us all in praying for God to show a solution to the itching.

After we prayed and I was leaving, she told me to please try and sleep well, and I felt so guilty for telling her that I may fall ill. It was cruel of me, given what she was going through. When Ulo and Mom called later, I asked them to please pray for strength for Kechi and I.

It was a very exhausting day for me, both physically and emotionally and I was drained by the time I got back to my room. I made some decisions that night, one of them being that I must never again let Kechi see any frustrations I had. It was not fair to her. The second decision was that I had to find a way to plan my days so that I did not get as physically tired as I did that day. If it meant not being with Kechi as much as I was doing, then so be it. It was better for her that she saw a bright and cheerful, well rested mother at different times of the day, than a perpetually tired and frustrated one all day long.

One of the nurses, a different Jane from the other rude one, whom I had become quite friendly with, had made another delicious meal for me, and I ate it gratefully before falling asleep.

CHAPTER TWENTY-EIGHT

"Casting all your care upon him; for he careth for you."
1 Peter 5 : 7 (KJV)

I spent more time than usual on my morning devotions, caught up in praises, and then bowing down to surrender the day and all I might encounter in it to Him. I was led to share the passage above with Kechi for her to cast all her cares on the One that cares so much for her. I was also led to apologize to her for what I had said the night before about falling ill, and also to lead her into a prayer of submission as soon as I got there; a prayer she was to pray every morning to hand herself and her day over to God.

Kechi was asleep when I went in. The sister on duty said that Kechi did not get much sleep the night before because of the itching, and so she was given something to make her sleep. She was out for the whole visiting period and when I left at 12.45 pm, I asked the sister to tell Kechi I would be back by 4.00pm.

On my way out, I decided to ask the Unit leader if Rochelle could be assigned to Kechi when she was on duty, and she said no, they assigned the more experienced sisters to very critical patients and Kechi was on her way out of the ICU because she was doing very well. So instead of being unhappy that she said no, I was pleased that Kechi was being considered well enough to leave the ICU.

I went to the mall to buy some more warm clothes and an apology gift for Kechi, some very pretty sweats, because she would probably only be able to wear very soft fabrics for a while. I also bought her a surprise gift for the day she would leave the ICU for the ward - a digital camera. She had always wanted one, and I knew she would love it.

When I got back to see Kechi, she was not pleased with me for leaving before she woke up. I apologized and asked about the itching. Luckily, it was not so bad that morning. I apologized for the previous night and she said it was okay; I was a human being and had the right to be unhappy sometimes. I told her that I did not know what I did right to deserve her, but I thanked God all the same. I read the scripture for her and it turned out she was well acquainted with it from her Bible Knowledge classes in school. We discussed it at length until I was sure she got it. Then I did itch duty for a while.

Dr. Nel came in and I asked which part of her scalp was grafted. When he said it was about 80% of the scalp, I told him to please tell Kechi to stop moving her head so much to scratch the itching and he said it was fine, since the grafts were stapled, and unlikely to come off.

Earlier I had noticed some pus on the grafting on one of her eyelids, but when I asked the sister to look, she said she saw nothing. So I asked Dr. Nel to take a look. He noticed the pus at once and ordered that a swab be made and sent to the lab for tests. He then told Kechi that she would be going to the OR that Friday for more grafting.

I fed Kechi and left to rest a bit before the last visit. She was in good spirits and actually fooled me into thinking she was crying when I said I was leaving, and was surprised and pleased that her playacting fooled me.

She was asleep for the night visit, and only came awake as I was about to leave. She pouted a little, and then we prayed before I left.

My prayers were a bit jumbled up the next morning, but I offered them up like that because that was the state of my heart at that time. God said we should come as we are and I was doing just that.

It had rained heavily all night and was quite cold, so I dressed very warmly.

Kechi looked drowsy and said she did not get much sleep the night before, but had slept a little that morning. Her head was on a pillow for the first time, and she said it was more comfortable than the pressure ring or the bed, as her scalp was painful. She asked for hot chocolate and when she had finished it, put me on itch duty. Dr. Pahad came in and asked her if she wanted something to help her sleep at night and she said yes. I followed Dr. Pahad out of the room and told her that Kechi was asking for a mirror to look at her face. He spoke to the Unit leader who said she would get Henry from the World Burns Foundation to counsel Kechi first and prepare her to accept what she would see in the mirror. I went in and massaged some aqueous cream into Kechi's right hand. Some of the scabs had softened and she asked me to remove them and then I left for dressings change.

When I was called back in, I fed Kechi lunch before doing itch duty. Kechi loved the chicken and suggested that I got the recipe form the kitchen. Then she asked for KFC! I went to Campus Square to buy it and she ate two chicken pieces and a few fries. Then I felt weak, and remembered I did not have breakfast, so I quickly did itch duty, then put on the TV and left.

At night, it was itch duty for the whole hour. She cried when I had to leave, but we were both glad that she was getting a sleeping pill that night.

She was very bright the next morning, and announced that she slept the whole night through. I was a bit surprised that the drug did not make her drowsy all morning like before, and we concluded that maybe it was a different drug. We had a lovely visit, watched a show together and part of the Commonwealth games, which was on. Kechi was so awake and sharp that morning, laughing uproariously at one high jumper that missed the beam entirely and came back down without jumping over. She laughed so loudly that the nurses came over to see if something was wrong. I did not blame them; they were more used to Kechi's tears.

I left her at 2.00pm after she promised to rest, and by 4pm, she was looking drowsy and said she hoped I did not mind if she slept. Then she said that something in the bed was sticking her bum, and she wanted to be moved up. The sister and I moved her by pulling her up with the bed linen and of course this caused pain and she started to cry. She was given morphine, and just then the OR called for her. I accompanied her and she was wheeled in almost immediately. I barely had enough time to quickly pray with her before she went in.

They were going to change all her dressings and put a special dressing on all the spots that the grafts had failed. These special dressings stayed for two days and this meant that she would go back to the OR on Sunday for another change.

Kechi came out at about 7.00pm and was crying so loudly all the way from the OR to her room that I could hear her from the waiting room. I came out as they were going into the Unit and called out to her to be calm. She turned to me crying' Mommy, Mommy, I can't hear, my ear is blocked. Won't they close the trachea tube?'

I told her to be calm, the sisters would take care of her and I would see her soon. When I went in, the trachea tube had been closed with a plaster and Kechi was not happy. She said she could not get a full breath and could not hear properly. She was very agitated and refused to calm down. I spoke to the sister about the trachea tube cover and she said she was going to get another one since the theater staff seemed to have lost the one Kechi went in with. The sister seemed upset because she muttered that this was the third time the theater staff had lost the tube cover, and replacing it meant opening a new package. She came in with a new cover and closed the tube and Kechi's relief was immediate. I told her that some fluid had probably entered her ear and would likely drain off in the night.

The sister was a very formidable, stern-looking woman and from the way she said that she had already told Kechi that she would replace the cover, I could see that she was exasperated by Kechi's crying. I asked Kechi in Igbo, our language, if any of the staff upset her and she said yes, but not the sister. Apparently, one of the male nurses in the unit had told her to stop crying, it was doing her no good, and had added that she was always crying. I was furious and told Kechi that I was going to report him. My fury must have consoled her because she said he was not important, I should forget it. And anyway, she could not identify him because her eyes were closed.

She took a sip of apple juice, but declined supper, saying she was not hungry. She was more relaxed and we talked for a while before I did itch duty on her leg. She got a bit frustrated when I refused to rub or hit her bandages in full view of the shift leaders because I had a feeling I was not helping the healing process by hitting the wound; but I managed to give her some relief and promised more the next day.

The major highlight of the day was that Kechi put lip balm on her lips by herself by wedging the tube between her left thumb and forefinger and then raised her hand, bending her elbow to apply the balm on her lips.

This was an amazing sight to see.

Then she raised the hand in a salute. She could bend that elbow almost completely. According to her, the therapist said that the grafting on the back of her left hand had healed so tight that the wrist could not bend and the fingers were tight. The surgeons would have to do a contracture release for those fingers to bend and the wrist to relax. As far as I was concerned, it was one step at a time and I was grateful for every progress, no matter how small it was.

The following morning, it was clear that the sleeping pill had gone back to its normal reaction because Kechi was fast asleep. I confirmed with the sister that she had received Stillnox, and settled down to wait for her to wake up. She had some moments of wakefulness and talked aloud in her sleep. At one point she asked a teacher not to send her out from class.

When she heard my voice, she called out 'Mommy', and went back to sleep.

The male counselor, Jappie, came to me and said he was asked to speak to me concerning Kechi's request for a mirror. He felt, like Annarie, that since she had started to ask questions, it was time to tell her the whole story. He then spoke to Dr. Pahad, who assured him that physically, Kechi was strong enough to handle the information and that she should be told so that she could start healing emotionally.

But Jappie was very busy that day because a young girl had been brought into the ICU in a very serious condition and he had a lot to do in addition to dealing with relatives. He was busy up until about 4pm when he came in to tell me he was ready to talk to Kechi. But he was looking exhausted and it was looking to me like Kechi was one more job to get out of the way before going home to crash. I knew how emotional Kechi could get and telling her about something as huge as that could not be a rush job, so I told him to just go in and introduce himself to her first, so that he would not be a complete stranger when he finally told her the news another day. He did this, and told Kechi he was available anytime she wanted to talk or ask questions.

As per Kechi's request, I had bought KFC pop-ups and Magnum ice cream for her for the evening visit, but when I arrived she was in a state of distress. The linen savers on her back were making her uncomfortable, but she understood that they could not be removed or else the wounds on her back and bum would stick to the bed linens and would have to be pulled to remove them. She had all sorts of complaints and I tackled them one at a time and eventually she got comfortable. She then ate her ice cream and nuggets and I did itch duty.

Kechi's godmother's husband, Nnamdi Agbim, visited while I was giving her lunch, and she was pleased to see him, asking after their kids, Obiora and Nneka, who also went to Loyola College. Nnamdi was overwhelmed and visibly shaken to see what he called 'a living miracle' and he thanked God for sparing Kechi. He also gave me some money to help with our upkeep and Kechi gave him some messages to take back to her friends in school.

Betty also visited, making Kechi even happier. She said she would wait for me because she wanted to take me to dinner. As usual, Kechi was reluctant to let me go, but I insisted. Not only had I not eaten all day, I wanted some adult company for a while. Betty took me to Ocean Basket and we had delicious seafood. Her baby, Keanu, had really taken to me and kept reaching out for me to carry him.

It was a welcome break and a well needed rest because when I came back, Kechi was crying. The dressings on her ears were tight, she said, and cutting into her ears. She was in pain; the linens were uncomfortable and so on. I addressed the ones I could and talked her through the rest. The main source of the distress was that her face and neck felt tight. I explained that the skin was pulling as it healed and she was starting to realize that she was going to have major changes in the way her face looked and it scared her. I decided it was time Kechi knew everything. That was the only way she would appreciate the miracle that she was. I was terrified, but I knew the time had come. I saw it would take time to calm her down, so I cancelled my 8.30pm ride home and stayed till 9.10pm, after which I called a cab. I talked extensively with her, while rubbing her legs. I then laid hands on her and prayed, promising to come early the next day so that I would see her before she went into the OR.

The next morning, I was in the hospital before 10.00am, and Kechi was still in her room. I informed the sister, Nthombi, that I was in the waiting room, and she came to get me ten minutes later. Kechi was groggy and she was soon wheeled to the theater. In the prep room, she told me she had been given morphine and Dormicum aside from the Stillnox the previous night. I had wondered she was so groggy. She could barely open her eyes. I prayed, committing the procedure to God. The anesthetist came in to tell us what they were going to do and I told him Kechi's complaints about the tight ear dressings. He promised to mention it to Dr. Nel, and they wheeled her in.

I waited in the hallway outside the OR and a little over an hour later, one of the theater nurses called me into the recovery room where Kechi was crying. She was cold and the warming hose was adjusted to spread the warm air more evenly around her body. I talked to Kechi, trying to get her to calm down and she said she wanted to go back to her room and I told her that Nthombe was on her way to take her back to her room. I walked by her side all the way back to the ICU, then said I would see her later when they had settled her in.

At about 1.30pm, one of the nurses, Lynn came by and told me Kechi was crying, couldn't I hear her? I was startled. Kechi was crying loud enough to be heard outside the ICU? I rushed in and there she was, wailing at the top of her voice. The nurse looking after Mr. Chauke, the patient on the bed next to Kechi, was right there, but was not even glancing in Kechi's direction. Her attitude was appalling and disgusting for a nurse, but I did not spare her a glance. She must have her own problems and maybe she had tried to console Kechi and had given up. Everyone here believed Kechi was spoiled and maybe they had decided they had put up with enough from her. At that moment, though, all I was thinking was, "that is your business, not mine." My business was my daughter, and why she was crying. Bernice also came in, drawn by

Kechi's crying. Kechi said she was in pain and Nthombe had left her. Bernice told Kechi that Nthombe had gone to get her morphine, she had not been abandoned. We talked to her and she gradually calmed down until Nthombe came in and administered the morphine and she fell asleep.

The anesthetist had already told me that he gave Kechi heavy sedation because she came out of anesthesia struggling and very confused, and was likely to sleep for most of the day. This proved to be the case.

By 4pm, she was just starting to struggle her way out of sleep when Layi and her husband came. Kechi wanted a bacon, egg and cheese sandwich with hot chocolate, so I walked to the coffee shop with them, and Layi's husband paid for the meal. They visited Kechi briefly and then left.

Kechi ate the whole sandwich and drank to cocoa to the last drop, and then pressed me into itch duty. I stayed until her dinner was brought, and fed her, then waited for an hour for the last visit.

The shift leader stopped by the waiting room to talk with me before leaving, and advised me to buy vitamin B tablets and take them daily to help my body cope with the stress it was going through. Nthombe, who was passing by, said she had a lot at home and would bring me some when she came back on Wednesday.

At the sight of Kechi shifting from side to side on her bed when I walked in later, I asked her,

'Are you dancing?'. She laughed and seemed to be in good spirits. I got down to itch duty almost at once and this continued for the whole hour. By the time I left, Kechi was not pouting or moaning. She said to me, "Mommy, sleep very well tonight, okay?" I promised to, and reminded her that she had surgery the next day. The equanimity with which she took the news surprised me. Theater two days in a row and she just said, "Really?" Surely such strength could only come from God. She needed that strength because the time was drawing near when she would be told about her friends and schoolmates on that plane. I relied entirely on God for guidance.

Appreciation for God's wisdom, knowledge, power, glory and might filled me the next morning, as I worshipped Him. I was beginning to imagine what it must be like to be with Him in heaven and to behold Jesus face to face, finally coming to an understanding of how it was that He came to die for sinners like me. Not why, but how? My thoughts were beginning to be directed upwards towards heavenly things, and I thanked God for it.

I got up from my devotions knowing it was time to tell Kechi the truth. She was going into surgery that morning, so I was thinking about telling her the next day.

She was very drowsy when I went in, and the sister said she had gotten a sleeping pill the night before. She soon drifted back into deep sleep, so I went back to the waiting room because the ICU was particularly freezing that morning. The sister called me in at about 1.15pm and Kechi was quite cross, telling me not to leave her like that again. She had woken up and I was not there, so she had cried before someone said I was waiting to be called in. I apologized and told her I left because it was so cold in her room.

The worst itching was at the trachea site and I really wished that they would close that hole. Kechi was one of the last patients for theater that day and so we waited.

Chi-Chi, my uncle, Eze's wife, had a conference in Johannesburg, and she had called me to say that she would be coming in that day. She came to the hospital around 4pm and Kechi and I were very pleased to see her.

Chi had the same reaction as everyone that saw Kechi for the first time. She took one look at Kechi, left the room to cry and then came back in when she had pulled herself together. Seeing Kechi lying there with her body so burnt up was a sight that affected everybody. I remembered that even Nnamdi had to sit down for a while after seeing Kechi. I later heard Chi on the phone telling Ulo that Kechi looked a lot worse than she had expected. It was amazing to me how people expected Kechi to look the same after hearing that she was burnt on her face and most of her body. But then I was used to seeing her that way, and I had seen her much worse than she was when Chi came.

Chi and I stayed with Kechi until she was wheeled in at 7pm. At 8.45pm, I was called into the recovery room when she began to wake up. As usual she was confused until I started talking to her. Warmed blankets were put on her and then when she calmed down, she was taken back to her room. I went in to see her at 9pm and she was calm, and on the verge of sleep. I told her that I was proud of her for keeping her promise of not crying as usual after theater. Joyce, the nurse on duty, got her drugs together, and Chi and I left.

The plan was for the cab driver to drop me off first and then take Chi to Sandton, where her hotel was. But the man had a rough look about him and was not familiar with the road to Roosevelt Park.

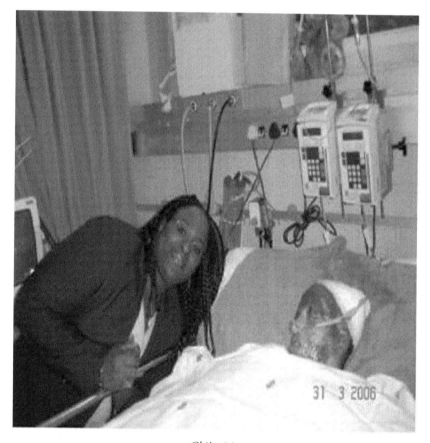

Chi's visit.

In fact at one point he became annoyed with us when he had to stop at a gas station to ask directions. I finally some familiar landmarks and directed him to the guesthouse. I did not like the driver and we decided that Chi would spend the night and leave for Sandton very early the next morning. It was better to err on the side of caution.

She brought a tape made by Kechi's friends in school, and I decided not to play it until Kechi knew all the details of the crash. I would need an arsenal of mood lifters after she knew the truth.

Chi and I ate, prayed and fell asleep.

CHAPTER TWENTY-NINE

"He healeth the broken in heart, and bindeth up their wounds."
Psalm 147 : 3 (KJV)

Franz, my regular cab driver, came at 5.30am and took Chi to Sandton. I slept a little bit more after that before going to the hospital.

Kechi was still a bit drowsy, but I expected her to be after all the drugs of the day before. She told me that the head and hand dressings were going to be changed that morning to acticote dressings and she was dreading it. Acticote dressings have a silver coating that contains drugs which are released only when the bandages are wet. However, they stuck to the wounds, no matter how wet the bandages were, and pulling them away always caused severe pain for Kechi. I told her not to worry about that for now, and then I fed her with the scrambled eggs and hot chocolate she had asked for.

After dressing change, I came back with the food I had cooked in the guesthouse - rice, stew and boiled eggs, black grapes for dessert. She ate very well and when I was leaving at 2pm, she called me before I got to the door. When I turned around she said,

"Mommy, I thank God for giving me a mother like you".

My heart melted and I told her I was blessed to have a daughter like her. It was moments like this that gave me the strength to go on. She asked for a kiss before I left, but I was reluctant because I had not touched Kechi yet without gloves for fear of infection. I could not resist the pleading look on her face, however, and bent down to give her a kiss on her lips, the only uninjured part of her face. A huge smile broke like dawn across her face and this look of wonder and pleasure lit her up. I laughed and told her that that would have to keep her going until I got back by 4pm. I went to the mall in Sandton to get her a combined theater gift for Sunday and Monday. I remembered that she wanted a new watch, so I went to a Swatch shop and got her a really lovely silver watch with a trendy bracelet.

When I returned, Kechi was still drowsy, but she became alert when I spoke to her. I did some itch duty and when she was fully awake, showed her the watch. She loved it and thanked me for it. We talked a bit, watched some TV, and by 6pm I was so tired that I could hardly stand. I told Kechi that Precious would have to feed her, and I left to rest a bit before the last visit.

Chi came in just as I was about to go in to see Kechi and we went in together. Kechi woke briefly to say hi to us before falling back asleep. Chi soon left for a dinner engagement, and Kechi woke again briefly which gave me enough time to pray with her before she slept again and I left for the night.

The next morning, Kechi seemed fine. There was little or no itching and we had a nice chat. She made me promise to get donuts for her later that day.

Jacqui called to ask me out to lunch, and since I really wanted to go, I asked Kechi to take a nap since she was already feeling a little sleepy. I would go and see if I could find donuts for her, and feed her when she woke up. She agreed and asked me to also buy croissants if I found any, and to make sure I was back by 1 pm. I went off to Cresta, and bought croissants and waffles, but did not find any donuts. When I got back, I fed her lunch, one of the croissants, and hot chocolate and she was so full and sleepy that she did not object when I told her to rest until I came back by 4pm.

Jacqui took me to a Chinese place and we had a good lunch and an even better conversation. She told me about how she went to an Eastern medium that told her about reincarnation, and also told her some things in her life that were making her unhappy. I told her about my experience in the Grail movement, which made me familiar with the concepts of karma and reincarnation. I went on to tell her about my conversion experience and how I now knew that true peace could only come from Jesus.

In that morning's reading of The Purpose-Driven Life, it talked about one of life's purposes being to tell people about God. After reading the chapter, I had prayed for strength against two things I knew were limiting me from talking about Jesus to people- timidity and fear of rejection.

As Jacqui talked, I knew it was time to talk about Jesus. I was nervous, and I actually got an opportunity to dump the issue because she had a phone call just as I was going to start talking. But I prayed for strength and the right words and dove right in. She listened attentively to everything I said, and I prayed that the seed had been sown, even if I was not the one to water it. I prayed that I would have more opportunities in the future.

Back in the hospital, Kechi's friend, Onyinyechi came to visit, and they had had fun chatting about any and everything. I had to do itch duty throughout the visit, though. Onyinyechi was so normal and laid back throughout the visit, not seeming to notice Kechi's scars at all. She even laughed when Kechi twitched and squeezed her face in an effort to relieve the itching there. She was such a lovely girl, and promised to try her best to visit Kechi again. After she left, Chi visited with her colleague and insisted that I was going to spend the next night with them in the hotel.

At the last visit, Kechi had just received her drugs and was fast asleep for the whole hour, after which I prayed and left. Nkechi called to say she was planning on coming over to visit the following week, and we were making plans for her to come with Tara. She assured me that she was in touch with Mike and they would sort everything out.

The following morning, Kechi was very sleepy. She complained that she had itched all night and could not sleep, even after getting her sleeping drug. I told her to go ahead and rest, I would sit by her bed for the whole hour. She got her morphine and fell asleep. Dr. Nel came in and said Kechi was going to the OR the next day for them to open up all her bandages to check if there were any more spots to be re-grafted. After that, the trachea tube would be closed and then Kechi could go to the ward as soon as Dr. Pahad gave the go-ahead. I followed him out of Kechi's room so that I could ask him about Kechi's face, since she was bound to ask if anything could be done about it. Dr. Nel said that with silicone pads and pressure garments which she would have to wear for about a year, the scarring on her face should be reduced. He added that reconstructive surgery on the side of her mouth and her left eye to correct the pulling of the skin could only be done a year or so down the line, when healing was complete.

This was a whole new perspective on the whole process because I had not foreseen that the recovery process would be so long and that we would still be talking surgery one year after. I had a lot to learn about burns, and I was a complete novice at that time. Nkechi and Tara were to arrive the following Monday, and I planned tell Kechi the whole truth before they arrived, so that their presence would help with the emotional healing.

Kechi's face was a lot more scarred than I thought it would be and this concerned me a lot because I knew Kechi was very aware of her looks and I was also worried about how others would react to her face when they looked at her. However, I knew God was still in control and knew He would make a way. He did promise complete restoration and He said it would take time, so I was going to leave it all to Him.

The itching that day was unbearable and she was crying. I did my best to rub all the places I could reach. It was not an easy visit and by the time I was leaving she was wriggling all over the bed in an effort to scratch her head and body. I left for a while, so they could put her back in her bed, then I returned to feed her and do some more itch duty.

I finally left at 2.30pm, exhausted and when Mom and Ulo called, I asked for more prayers for the itching.

By 4pm, the itching seemed to have eased up, the worst parts being her scalp and the trachea area. I was very glad that they were going to remove that tube soon.

The nurse on duty, Sophie, and I noticed that when Kechi was focused on something else, she forgot the itching for a while, so we encouraged her to watch TV, and I engaged her more in crossword puzzles, and I constantly told her to pray for strength to withstand and overcome it because if she kept rubbing her head so vigorously on the pillow the way she was doing, she might dislodge the scalp graft and it would have to be redone. That prospect scared her into promising to stop.

At night, I continued itch duty, until a sister came in to tell me that what I was doing was going to make the scarring worse. This gave me pause, but I really hated those who came to give such warnings without a solution. So what could we do to relieve the itching? She did not know and had nothing to add. There was no way I could just sit and watch Kechi going through such discomfort without trying to help.

Kechi was making the effort to keep her head still, it seemed she was all settled for the night.

Chi came to take me to her hotel for the night and we left Kechi watching a movie on TV.

When we got to the hotel room, Chi stunned me with the amount of shopping she had done for Kechi. She even bought a couple of sweaters for me. We spent a pleasant time together, and I almost ate myself into a stupor.

The next morning, I left the hotel and went straight to the hospital with the huge bags of shopping. I did not want to waste time going to the guesthouse first.

Kechi was asleep for most of the day. She had been on dormicum on request. I think the sisters just wanted to give her a respite from all the itching. She went into theater by 4.15pm and came out at about 7pm and it appeared that there had been a need for some grafting on her left leg with skin that was harvested from her right thigh.

When I went in to see her, she was crying from pain, and I asked the sister to please give her something to make her more comfortable. She was given morphine and after she relaxed, I laid hands on her and prayed.

There was heaviness in me throughout that day. I was very low, almost depressed and I knew it was because Kechi had not been comfortable for the past few days. She was depressed and angry and I finally convinced myself that there was no more time to waste. I had to tell her the whole story of the crash so that she could put things in perspective and begin to heal.

I woke up around 4am from a troubled sleep and started to think about Kechi and her scars, her hands, and all she had to deal with. Then I thought of the burden she would have to bear soon, when she knew everything. I knew how emotional Kechi could get and frankly, I dreaded telling her. But I had the full conviction in me that it was time to tell her for the following reasons:

1. So she could grieve and begin to heal.
2. So she could realize how blessed she was and begin to comprehend the magnitude of God's miracle in her life.
3. So she would begin to put things into perspective and if she ever thought 'why me?' it would be for a very different reason.
4. So that her injuries, pain, and discomforts would pale into insignificance beside the fact that so many died that day.

I knew all these in theory, but I was still afraid. I prayed for strength and resolved to tell her that day.

The bible verse from Psalm 61 was my cry that morning as I cried out to God for strength:

"Hear my cry, O God; attend unto my prayer. From the end of the earth will I cry unto thee, when my heart is overwhelmed: lead me to the rock that is higher than I."

Kechi was very moody, upset and irritable when I got there the following morning.

"I can't understand why all this is happening to me. It is beginning to dawn on me that this is my life; it is reality, not a movie.

I touched my face this morning and felt the scars and bumps.

I'm sure I look like a monster."

I sighed.

The day was not starting well I told her that I had never hidden from her that she had scars on her face, and repeated what Dr. Nel had said about silicone pressure garments and returning for surgery after a year. I asked, 'Do you want to see a mirror?'

She said no.

'Kechi, we must count our blessings. You and I will have a talk this afternoon and you will know why you have every reason to thank God'.

I told the unit leader that it was time to tell Kechi everything, and would want an appointment by 4pm with the counselor on duty. She said that if I thought it was time, they would abide by my wishes because I should know better than anyone else.

I fed her, and then left to have lunch with Jacqui, Louise and Nathan, Jacqui's husband. We went to a Mozambiquan restaurant and I was pretty sure the food was nice, but I could not taste anything, I was so very nervous.

Back at the hospital, I met with the counselor and gave him all the background information and details of the crash. He stressed how important it was that Kechi be told and said he would go in alone and break the news to Kechi, and then he would call me in to comfort her.

He went to Kechi's bed and drew the curtains. I paced nervously outside, praying, my heart pounding.

After about fifteen minutes, I heard Kechi screaming, "NO! NO! NO! NO!" and my heart stopped.

After about five minutes of uncontrollable sobbing and screaming from Kechi, he pulled the curtains aside and motioned me to come in. By this time I was a mess. I was crying as I went in and held her shoulders. Her eyes were wide with shock and she fixed them on my face, "Mommy, is it true? Is it true? Toke! Toke!"

I held her shoulders down because she was lurching up from the bed with each scream.

"Yes, baby, it's true".

"NO! NO! NO! NO! NO! NO! NO!" over and over and over again.

I was weeping uncontrollably by then, her pain was way down to the marrow and she was inconsolable.

Then Kechi looked at me and suddenly stopped crying. She said to me, "Mommy, stop crying." I dashed the tears from my eyes at once and said, "I've stopped, see?"

Then Kechi collapsed into tears again. She wept loud and long, calling one of her best friend's name, Toke, over and over again.

I just held her as much as I could, given that she was covered in bandages, while she wept and wept and wept. The counselor left us alone for a while and we grieved and mourned together. Kechi's heart was broken into pieces and I could see it happening right before my eyes. This was one of the hardest things I had ever had to do as a mother - watching my child's heart being torn to shreds.

Kechi turned to me, put one hand on her chest, and said that her heart was hurting. I told her it was okay to weep; we had all done that. I just held her, praying, pouring my strength into her.

She remembered more and more kids form her school and started to call their names Chinenye, Zikora, the Head Boy and his sister, Chinwoke and her sister.

Then she sat up, "Mom, the Ilabors. There were three of them. All dead? All those little JS1 students. It's not fair, it's not fair, it's not fair."

Kechi wept without pause for a whole hour and then the sister came in and gave her a sedative, which calmed her for just a short while. Then she started crying all over again. I asked her what I could do, and she said, "Just be with me, Mom". I asked if there was anyone she wanted to speak with and she said she wanted to speak with her Grandma, my Mom.

I had already told my family I was going to tell Kechi everything and so far Mike had called more than eight times, and Ulo had been calling and texting frantically, so I went out to the nurses' station to get the unit leader's permission to use my phone in the ward to call Mom.

She gave me permission and I called Ulo and told her to call Mike and Mom, and get them to call me right back. Mike called first and attempted to console Kechi, not very successfully, as he failed to hit on the main subject, which was her grief. This was not the moment to tell Kechi how lucky or blessed she was, as she felt neither. It was time to grieve with her.

Mom called soon after and she began to minister to Kechi's heart. She told her to go ahead and grieve because what happened was terrible, and not something that was going to be easy to get over. She told her that the rest of the family were still dealing with the terrible tragedy, and we could not even begin to imagine what the families of those that passed away were going through.

Ulo called after Mom and consoled her, telling her that we were all praying for her, and she would get through this.

Kechi was very depressed and kept calling for Toke. "Mommy, I loved her so much and I never told her. She means so much to me".

I told her that Toke knew that she loved her and that Toke would always be alive in her heart because of that love.

"Toke was so young," she wept, "Two years younger than I. She was so little. My heart hurts, Mom. How can I bear this?"

I talked to her when she was a bit calmer, telling her that we waited to tell her all this when she was stronger, and I hoped she was not upset that I kept it from her. She said she wanted me to know that she did not blame me for not telling her before now. She knew she could not have handled the information before then.

She kept trying to remember all the children on the plane with her that day, until I told her that I had the program from the memorial service held for them, and all the kids had their pictures in it. She made me promise to bring it with me the following day.

My own heart breaking, I held her shoulder, just being with her. I stayed until it was almost 10pm that night, only leaving when they gave her another sedative and she slipped into sleep at last. The whole ward was very quiet that night, everyone feeling so sad on Kechi's behalf, and several of the sisters came round to console her.

On my way home, I gave God all the glory for the day I had feared for such a long time. I felt unburdened, even as I knew that the next few days were going to be tough as she struggled to cope with her grief, but we had God to lean on.

❖

I woke up the next day full of thanksgiving and praise. Deidre insisted on dropping me off a little earlier than usual, so I was at the hospital by 9.30am that Sunday morning. I would have preferred to leave later, but God soon revealed why He had made me come early.

As I walked into the hospital lobby, my phone rang, and it was Sister Maureen, calling to tell me that Kechi was crying and calling for me, could I come at once? I told her I was already in the hospital and hurried to the ICU.

Kechi was still deeply upset, and when she saw me, she apologized for calling for me, but she could not help crying for her schoolmates. I told her it was ok to cry; in fact it was healthy that she grieved for them. I held her as she cried and cried, until she gradually calmed down.

Then she asked me if I remembered to bring the pictures of the children. I asked if she was sure she could handle it and she said yes.

She cried over each of the sixty pictures, and when she got to Toke's picture, she broke down completely, crying over and over, "Toke, Toke, Toke".

My heart broke all over again and I told Kechi that I would always remember Toke the way she appeared in the latest issue of their school magazine, 'Roar', in which Toke wore a traditional outfit made out of blue lace, posing like a model. I showed it to Kechi and after crying for a while she agreed that she also wanted to remember Toke that way.

Kechi then looked at me and said, "Mommy, please don't cry again. I don't like to see you not strong, because I take my strength from you".

I said to her that I could not bear to see her heart breaking like that but I would revert back to the strong Mom she was used to seeing. We talked a little more, and I showed her newspaper reports on the crash, including pictures of the wreckage.

The pictures shocked her into silence. "I came out from that?"

She said she had imagined that the plane would be intact with maybe blackened paint and broken windows, not the total wreck and small pieces.

She said quietly, "Now I know I am blessed." Then she asked me, "Mom, I have never asked this question since I came here, but why me?"

I told her I had no idea, only God knew and He may, or may not choose to reveal the reason to us. All we could do was to thank Him and worship Him with everything we have for the rest of our lives.

She wanted to know the full story of the crash from when I knew the plane had gone down, and I told her everything, up to the day we came to South Africa, and all the miracles along the way.

We spent that whole day talking. She cried several times and told me to pray for Toke's soul. I told her Toke was already with Jesus, and we prayed for comfort for the family.

I had been hoping to surprise Kechi by not telling her that her Aunty was coming the next day, but Mom had already told her while she was comforting her that she should expect a surprise the next day. Kechi, being the smart girl she was, guessed that someone was coming, but I refused to tell her who it was. I also did not mention that Nkechi was coming with Chizitara.

Betty picked me up that night to sleep in her house so that we could leave early for the airport the following day.

CHAPTER THIRTY

"He shall call upon me, and I will answer him: I will be with him in trouble; I will deliver him, and honour him."
Psalm 91 : 15(KJV)

Betty and I were at the airport at 5.30 am the following morning, and the plane had already landed. Nkechi and Chizitara came out about 6.00am. Tara was looking so tall and slim, I could not believe it. She had always been on the chubby side and I could not get used to seeing her that way. Nkechi saw me first and I heard her tell Tara, 'Look, there's your Mom'. Tara looked around, saw me and flew into my wide-open arms. It was glorious to see her and we just held each other tight for the longest time. It was so good to see her.

We all went on to the guesthouse where I made breakfast and then we left for the hospital. The Unit Leader had asked me to tell her when Tara was going to be in the hospital so that she could arrange for the counselor to speak with her first and prepare her for seeing Kechi. Annarie was called in, and she took Tara aside and explained to her how badly injured her sister was, and how her appearance was different. Nkechi and Tara's appearance in the ICU was causing quite a sensation, with almost every nurse coming by to see Kechi's sister, and being told not to tell Kechi, as it was a surprise.

Annarie, meanwhile, showed Tara some pictures of Kechi taken the previous day to prepare her and also stressed that no matter how shocked she was, she should not show it so that Kechi did not panic.

It seemed to me that all that was a bit too much for a six year old to assimilate, but she appeared to understand.

We walked into Kechi's room and Kechi let out a scream, threw her hands up and waved them about, sat up in her bed, and then began to cry. Tara went up to her bed and hugged her. It was so sweet to see how carefully Tara hugged Kechi, not wanting to hurt her. Nkechi went up and also hugged Kechi.

When everyone calmed down, we had a wonderful visit, Kechi talking nineteen to the dozen. She did start to itch at one point, but I jumped into itch duty and it still turned out to be a good visit. Tara was very excited to see her sister and asked her all sorts of questions, was her face painful, why was she looking so thin, and so on, and Kechi answered all her questions patiently.

We went out, had lunch, and came back for the 4.00pm visit and unfortunately, Kechi got one of the bad itching episodes she had dubbed, 'the maddening itch', which always made her irritable and weepy. Tara started to cry, seeing her sister in that state and was still crying when I took them back to the guesthouse for some rest.

I went back alone for the night visit and Kechi was relaxed, happy with the way the day had gone, and I left her happily anticipating the next day's visit. I told her how upset Tara had been and she was contrite, telling me to tell Tara that she would try not to get that way again, and she was getting better everyday.

After our morning devotions the next day, I went to Diedre to clear up some lingering tension caused, I was sure, by my having extra people staying with me. She said that she would have to charge me for the extra person, as only my daughter was covered by her arrangement with ISOS. I told her that everything outside that coverage I would gladly pay out of pocket, and she relaxed. I really wanted to clear the air because Diedre was a very nice person, and I liked her a lot.

Nkechi decided that I should go out with Tara for some time and leave her with Kechi.

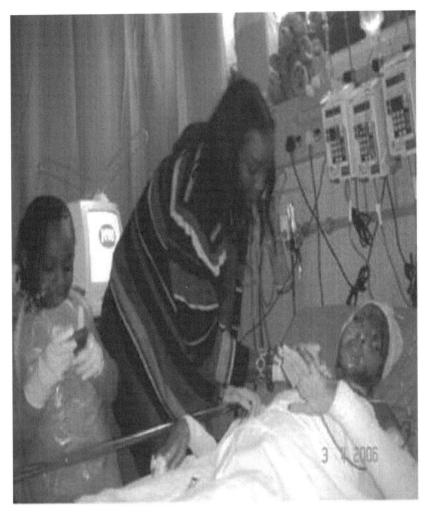

Nkechi and Tara's visit.

It looked like the consensus from Nigeria was that I should rest while Nkechi was here. I found that Tara had outgrown most of her clothes and needed jeans, warm shirts for her stay in SA, vests and socks so I took her to the mall. I also got a Bratz doll and game for her.

We got back in time to see Kechi by 4.00pm and she was fine, having spent a pleasant visit with Nkechi. I did itch duty for a while and Tara enjoyed herself immensely, wearing gloves and a disposable apron, helping to massage Kechi's hands. We were all shocked by her maturity and calm acceptance of the whole situation. She did not flinch for one moment at the sight of her sister's face. She was overjoyed to see her sister and to be with me. She asked Kechi endless questions and listened attentively to the answers.

By the last visit, we took turns staying with Tara in the waiting room because she was getting restless and I could not blame her because the hospital was not really a conducive environment for a six year old and she got bored.

The next morning during devotions, Nkechi had the leading that we were to be full of expectation that day. She thanked God in advance in case we forgot to give thanks when we received the blessings. We also rebuked the spirit of infirmity causing the itching and commanded it to leave Kechi's body.

When we got to the waiting room, Jacqui came in to meet Nkechi and Tara, and told me that she had been rushed to the hospital that morning because she had an allergic reaction to the painkiller prescribed for her. She felt like there were little ants crawling under her skin, she had a headache and palpitations and was very weak.

An alarm went off in my head because Kechi had used that exact analogy of crawling ants to describe her itching. Could she be having the same reaction? I asked Jacqui the name of the drug she took and she said it was Synapforte, the same pain drug Kechi was taking.

Nkechi and I immediately began to praise God, and I told Jacqui that Kechi was taking the same drug and had a very bad itching situation. I thanked God for sending Jacqui to us that morning and she said she was glad that she had been the one sent to make this known to us.

When we got to the ICU, I told Sue, the deputy unit leader what Jacqui had said, and she said that was not the case with Kechi. According to her, Kechi's itching was normal because of new skin growth. She even groused about people who got an allergic reaction to a drug and expected that every other person must have the exact same reaction. I saw that I was not going to get any cooperation from her and decided to reserve further comments for Dr. Opolot.

Kechi was in good spirits and was very pleased to see us. We chatted for a while until she said that she wanted to finish watching the Harry Potter movie she had started. I set it up for her and put it on, and she watched it with Tara. While they watched, I filled in my journal, which had a three-day gap by then, given all the excitement of Nkechi and Tara's visit.

Tara got hungry and I took her to the coffee shop for lunch, and by the time we got back, Kechi's movie was over and Maureen asked us to leave so she could change Kechi's bed linen. I used the time to warm Kechi's lunch up in the microwave, and then fed her when we were allowed back in.

Betty took us to the store after I fed Kechi so we could buy foodstuff, and at the evening visit, Nkechi stayed with Tara in the waiting room while I visited Kechi. We had decided to take turns in visiting Kechi so that Tara would not go into the ICU too often and upset the staff that had already been incredibly accommodating thus far.

However, it was hard to get Tara to understand why she could not be with her sister, and we eventually took her in for a few minutes. Tara had fully acclimatized to her new environment and was her usual restless self, keeping us on our toes, wanting to run around the room, dance and sing. I was exhausted at the end of the visit from just keeping her occupied. We decided that she would definitely sit out the next visit in the waiting room.

That night, Nkechi went in first to see Kechi and stayed for thirty minutes. Before I went in, she said she had been talking to Kechi about her friends, telling her it was okay to grieve. She also told her that she should tell me everything that weighed on her mind, because I felt that she kept things from me in order not to make me worry.

Nkechi also told her that it was clear to everyone that God had a special purpose for Kechi's life, and she should begin to make herself ready for her task, and Kechi said she was ready for whatever God had in plan for her.

When I went in, Kechi was looking somber, and said she had something to say to me. I sat down and she said to me, 'Mom, I'm not keeping anything from you, please don't feel that way. Auntie Nkechi says that you and I have a connection that is awesome, and I agree with her. If there is something I need to tell you, I will. I promise.'

I agreed with her about the connection we had and told her that we would always thank God for it, because it was rare.

'I love you very much, Kechi' I told her.

'And I love you so much, Mom.' Then Kechi began to cry. I comforted her, knowing she was just feeling very emotional.

We prayed together and then Nkechi, Tara and I left for the night.

Kechi was not looking very bright when we got to the hospital the next morning. She said she did not get any sleep the previous night because she was thinking about her friends, and wanted to be given something to help her sleep.

I talked to Sister Zama, who was on duty, and Zama gave me a lecture about how she did not see why Kechi should have been told about her friends and how I should have waited until Kechi got home to Nigeria before being told. She was very accusatory,

telling me that Kechi did not get any sleep the night before, and since that morning had been drifting in and out of sleep, mumbling and obviously having bad dreams.

I told her that we felt it necessary to tell her when we did, and left it at that. Then I asked her to please give Kechi something to help her fall asleep. After Kechi got dormicum, I told her to get some rest, and Nkechi would come in and visit her for the afternoon visit since Tara and I were going to the zoo that afternoon, a trip organized by Henry from the World Burns Foundation. She asked for cocoa and a croissant, and I bought them and fed them to her, after which she dozed off.

Tara and I had a very good time at the zoo, especially when we saw the white lion cubs. We got back at about 3.15pm, had lunch at the coffee shop, and then went into see Kechi at 4pm.

Tara told her about all the animals we had seen, and how she had touched the llama. We showed her all the pictures we had taken. Kechi was hugely entertained, and we gave her some strawberries and chin-chin. The crazy itching of the previous day did not happen and we were all very grateful.

When Tara grew restless, I asked Nkechi to take her out while I fed Kechi. She ate most of her food and was given her drugs after which she dozed off.

Chi, who had gone to Cape Town, came then for a visit, and we all sat in the waiting room until the nurse came to say Kechi was awake and asking for me. I let Nkechi and Chi go in first so that we would not crowd Kechi's room, and also someone had to be with Tara in the waiting room.

The rest of the day passed pleasantly.

The following day, Kechi was in very good spirits because she had a good night's rest. She had Sister Rose as her night nurse, and just that fact was enough to make her relaxed. We had a very nice visit, with Kechi singing along to the Backstreet Boys CD that was playing, and Tara displaying her latest dance moves which had us all applauding and had Kechi sit up in her bed in shock and surprise. She confessed

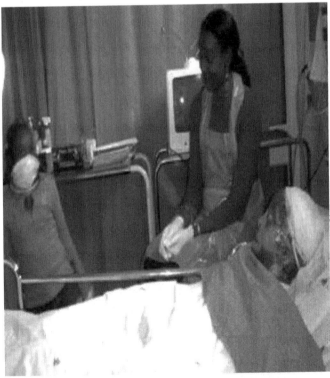

Tara dancing for her sister, Kechi

that she had feared her sister did not have a sense of rhythm, as all Kechi's attempts in the past to teach Tara to dance had not turned out well. Kechi herself was a very good dancer and had always deplored the fact that her sister could not dance.

Betty picked us up to go to the mall because Nkechi wanted to do some shopping. We had lunch at Steers and got back to the hospital forty minutes late. I prayed that she would have gone to the OR before we got back, but she had not.

Kechi was furious, her face a thundercloud.

She would not look at any of us and she soon started to cry. Nkechi and I pleaded with her for a long time before she would even look at us. She finally cheered up and we had a good visit, until she was taken to the OR.

While she was in recovery, Dr. Nel came in to tell me how it had gone. The staples on her legs had been removed, and her legs bandaged because of some slight bleeding. Her arms were now free from bandages and the only two parts remaining to be grafted were her right hand and a section of her scalp, which he said had gone a bit septic. The right hand was going to be grafted the following Monday, and Dr. Nel said he could see no reason why Kechi could not go to the ward very soon.

On the whole, the doctors were very satisfied with her healing, and Dr. Nel said the trachea tube could also come out on Monday, depending on what the physician decided.

When I went in to see Kechi, I looked at her hands and marveled that they were healing. I remembered what they had looked like the day of the plane crash, and I thanked God again. I prayed over Kechi, who was drowsy and sleepy, and then Nkechi also went in and prayed. During the prayer, Kechi asked to feel the presence of God around her so that her faith would be strengthened.

The next day was Saturday, April 8, 2006. We could not see Kechi until 11.45am, because she was sleeping very deeply from the combination of drugs she had received the previous night. In fact, Princess had to wake her so that the whole visiting hour would not go by without us seeing her.

She was still drowsy when we went in, but brightened up a bit to hold up her hands that had been un-bandaged. The hands looked good, with a few scabs here and there. The left hand still had a few sore areas, but the right hand was completely healed.

Sister Maureen said that Dr. Nel had ordered a swab of the part of Kechi's scalp that he feared was infected, and had also said that the trachea tube would be removed the following Monday. He had also ordered that the betidene dressings on her head be changed daily, and we were asked to leave so they could do that.

She was drowsy that evening and night, and I was beginning to suspect that Kechi was getting more dormicum than was wise.

Kechi could be very convincing, and I could see her making her case for the drug with the nurses.

I got her to drink lots of juice, as she was complaining of being constipated, a condition which continued until the next day, when I gave her a lot of fruits and juice. She protested and wanted to eat proper food, but I refused and sure enough, before I left at lunchtime, she felt the need to move her bowels, and I called the nurse.

Betty and her kids came to the waiting room, and Tara had fun getting acquainted with the boys, and this time, when Maureen called me back into Kechi's room, Tara did not complain.

During the 4pm visit, the Nigerian Ambassador's wife came with the wives of the Consul General and one of the attaches to see Kechi. They had some gifts for her and stayed for a while.

Nkechi, meanwhile, had been causing a stir in the ICU, because she had been taking measurements of the sisters who had been nice to Kechi, promising to make Nigerian traditional clothes for them as a sign of her gratitude for their being kind to her niece. There was an air of excitement, because at one point or the other, some of them had complimented me on some of the traditional clothes I wore from time to time, whenever the weather was was not too cold.

Betty (in beige boots), my awesome friend and my rock throughout my stay in Johannesburg, with Nkechi and Tara.

Deidre had moved us into a bigger room that morning, and we had not really had time to do more than throw things into the new place before rushing to the hospital that morning. This meant that after a day of activity and itch duty, we had a lot of unpacking to do before we could relax for the night.

I shook my head at the amount of property I had accumulated in four months. I came to S.A. with just a bag, and now I had so much stuff. At the rate I was going, I was going to have to give away a lot of things before going home.

It was really cold the next morning and we bundled up before going out. We were better prepared to distract Tara, as we had stocked up on games and toys to keep her amused while Nkechi or I went in to be with Kechi. We played cards until it was time to go in.

Kechi was sitting in a chair and was extremely itchy and I spent the whole hour on itch duty. She was not in a very good mood because her exercises had been difficult. In order to get her used to standing up, they had strapped her into a bed-shaped contraption, and then tilted it until she was vertical. This forced her to put pressure on her feet, and she said it was painful. Then she started to complain that her left foot was aching, and when her legs were elevated, she felt better.

I knew that some days would be better than others, and whenever Kechi started to complain, I would spend time comforting her, telling her to hang in there.

Dr. Pahad came in and after looking at Kechi's chart, directed that dormicum should be reduced. I was happy that he did that because I was also concerned that she had been getting a lot of it.

When Kechi got tired of sitting, we left so that they could get her back in bed, but Maureen soon called me in because Kechi was itchy and wanted me to rub her skin. I rubbed and patted for an hour and a half and this time, I was the one that asked Maureen to please give Kechi dormicum to help her relax.

She was soon called into the OR and we walked with her. Nkechi and Tara stopped at the theater waiting room, and I went into the patient waiting area with her. She was wheeled in at 4.30pm and we settled down to wait, playing games with Tara, or taking turns to walk to the different waiting areas around the hospital with her for variety. It was a huge hospital, so there was no shortage of places to go.

Kechi was getting quite a bit of work done grafting on her right hand, dressings change on her head and back, and changing of the CVP line.

She was wheeled out at 6.30pm, and we walked with her to the ICU and went to the waiting area while she was settled in. For the first time, Kechi was calm, not crying, as she was being taken back to her room. I suspected it had a lot to do with Maureen being her nurse that day. Kechi had chosen her favorites among the nurses, and Maureen was definitely one.

When we went in at 7.30pm, she was still calm. We did some itch duty and then left her to rest. Her right hand was so bandaged it looked like a boxer's glove, but she said it was not painful.

Tara led the prayers that night and to hear her ask God in her childish voice to please heal her sister brought tears to me eyes.

Kechi was getting drowsy, so we left for the night.

The next morning, Nkechi and Tara took off with Betty for a day of shopping, and they thought I did not notice that they were planning something for my birthday the next day.

Kechi was having a weepy day. She was sitting up, but complained that her whole body hurt. She was very sad about her schoolmates that had died in the crash, she did not think that her recovery would take so long, or be so painful, she was tired of lying down all the time, of the constant discomfort, the tightening skin on her neck and face and so on.

I told her that she would be a saint if she did not have her off- days, days when she felt bad or sorry for herself.

"But I don't want to feel that way," she said. I told her it was fine. She was just a child and had gone through what would make most adults despair, and she should never feel as though she could not have a crying jag when she felt low. I told her to remember where she had come from, how far she had gone in the recovery process.

"For goodness sake, Kechi," I said to her, "God picked you up from a crashed and burning plane. If what you are going through is the price we have to pay for the gift of your life, please bear it, okay? It is not forever. You WILL get better, in Jesus's name."

She began to calm down, but her spirits remained low for the rest of that day.

Nkechi, Tara and Betty came back tired, and spoke in code around me, amusing me greatly. Tara, obviously sworn to secrecy, was bouncing from foot to foot, and then blurted out, "Mommy, I'm not going to tell you that we bought presents for you".

The ensuing laughter brought Kechi out of her doldrums for a while.

We all visited for a while, then we prayed with Kechi and left for the night.

CHAPTER THIRTY-ONE

*"I will sing unto the LORD as long as I live:
I will sing praise to my God while I have my being."
Psalm 104 : 33(KJV)*

April 12, 2006

My fortieth birthday! I took stock of my life and began to thank God for His mercies and love. It was pretty overwhelming to contemplate His grace over my life and I prayed, as always, to be proven worthy of that privilege.

Nkechi and Tara gave me their gifts while singing "Happy Birthday" to me. I got a bag from Nkechi and a pair of pretty bedroom slippers from Tara. Then my phone started to ring off the hook, Mike, family, friends from everywhere.

Layi came with Francis, bringing a gift, the Ambassador's wife called, and sent flowers. Ulo also sent flowers through Lanre.

Then Nkechi and Betty brought two cakes for the day and night staff of the ICU. I got plenty of hugs from the staff that day. Kechi gave me her own gift to me, a lovely perfume. Apparently she was in on the planning and whispering.

Betty and Nkechi had agreed to drag me away from Kechi for a while, and Betty took Tara and I, and her kids to Gold Reef City, an amusement park, where we had a lot of fun. To this day, I do not know what possessed me to ride a killer rollercoaster known as the Anaconda. I had never been a daredevil, so thinking back, it must have been my own version of buying a Ferrari and wearing leather, which I gather some men do when they turn forty in order to still feel young and hip. Anyway, that day I was feeling fearless and got on that ride, then proceeded to scream my way through the whole ride with my eyes squeezed shut. I still have the photo, and Kechi loved looking at it and laughing at me.

We took in some shows, and the kids had fun meeting characters dressed like cartoon characters.

When we got back to the hospital, Kechi was itching all over, and was miserable and restless. I took over itch duty from Nkechi and did my best to settle her. She apologized for messing up my day by being uncomfortable and making me do itch duty, and I told her to stop being silly. She was upset that she was going in for surgery the next day, because it would lengthen her time in the ICU.

After I made Kechi comfortable and we prayed and left for the night, Betty took us to her home where we had a mini party with cake and finger food. I was very touched at the way they made sure I got a memorable fortieth birthday, in spite of the circumstances.

We spent that night in Betty's house.

Kechi had surgery slated for 4pm the next day. Dr. Nel was going to regraft her eyelids, which had contracted again. She was very itchy and Nkechi and I did what we could to get her comfortable. Just before she went to the OR, I took Tara in to see her, because when she came out, her eyes would be taped shut and she probably would not see Tara again before Tara went back to Nigeria with Nkechi. I had to explain everything to Tara first, so she did not get upset when she saw Kechi after the surgery.

When Kechi came out at 6pm, she was out for the count and did not wake up the whole visiting period, so we prayed by her bed and left.

I was supposed to do some shopping with Tara, since they were leaving on Sunday, but it was public holiday and the banks were closed. That meant I also had to cancel my hair appointment. I had wanted to use the opportunity of having Nkechi keeping Kechi occupied to take the time and braid my hair.

With shopping out, we returned to the hospital to find Nkechi in the middle of serious itch duty. I took over from her and basically did that the rest of the day. By the time we got back, I could barely stand, but I did not want to sleep because I wanted to spend as much time as I could with Tara, whom, with their departure looming, was getting very clingy.

Taye, the braids lady, came at 6.30 am so we could start early and hopefully finish early. Nkechi and Tara left for the hospital at 10am, and we were finished with my braids at 1pm. I met up with Betty at Northgate mall and shopped a lot for Tara, and then we went to her house to pick up the food she had cooked for us, swung back to the guesthouse to drop everything, and then raced for the hospital.

I knew I was in the doghouse with Kechi so I was ready. She would never have given her consent for me to be away for half the day, so I just took off.

She was very upset and would not look at me. Nkechi even faked being upset that her presence was not enough to keep Kechi happy, but Kechi did not even crack a smile. I explained that after getting the braids done, I had to shop for Tara, who was leaving the next day. I kept talking, wearing her down, and eventually she relaxed.

She was also upset that Dr. Pahad was laying down the law about limiting dormicum, with a view to stopping it entirely. To Kechi, that was her only escape from the incessant itching.

I told her that we could not go against the doctor's orders and it had become clear that with the itching problem, doctors, nurses, and drugs had failed, so it was time we offered it up to God to deal with it. Nkechi had already started praying and I joined in. I told God that our own strength had failed, and so we were relying fully on His. Then I told Kechi to talk to her Father and she prayed from deep within her heart.

"Dear Lord", she prayed, "I want to trust You, but I don't know how. I know that though I say I love You and have faith in You, I don't really mean it from my heart, because I don't know how to trust You. I want to know You, trust You and be able to rely on You. Please take this itching away from me, I can't stand it anymore, nothing works, and I don't know what else to do."

It was a deeply moving prayer and we all felt an assurance that it had reached the throne room.

Annarie had spoken to me earlier about referring Kechi to a psychiatrist. She had discussed it with Dr. Pahad and they felt that talking with a professional would benefit her. I agreed readily because Kechi had gone, and was still going, through a lot.

In the car, going home, Tara suddenly exploded into tears. It had finally dawned on her that she was leaving the following day. She cried her little heart out; she did not want to leave her Mom and her sister. I held her and talked to her until she calmed down. I was doubly glad we had made the decision for Tara to remain in Lagos with my family until Kechi and I got back. I noticed that her self-confidence had greatly eroded the last four months without me. Her life shifted on its axis and she needed her family around her to stabilize her.

The dreaded day came. It was amazing how time flew. No one was happy that morning, Tara clinging to me like she was attached with super glue, even after several pep talks. When we got to the hospital, Kechi flatly refused to let me go to the airport with Nkechi and Tara. Nothing I said could make her change her mind, and after a while, I figured she had earned the right to be selfish about our time together.

Luckily, Betty was driving them to the airport, so I felt a little better about not going with them. I talked with Tara and explained to her why I would not be going with them. She was very understanding, and it helped that Betty's kids were coming along for the ride.

Tara kissed Kechi goodbye and Kechi told her how much she loved her and how special she was. Then it was hugs all round before they took off.

It was just Kechi and I again. We spent most of the time just talking, and then I fed her. She got her first dormicum for the day by 2pm and I left her to sleep. While I waited for her to wake, I got permission to call her best friends, Womiye and Atuora. When she woke up, I called her friends and made three teenage girls very happy.

I heard her telling Womiye that she was not going to return until she looked as close to what she looked like before the crash as possible. This worried me because burns take a year or more to heal. I also heard her saying she was not sure she would make it to their prom.

After the call, I told her that I was sure she had realized by now that she would not be graduating with her classmates. She looked surprised until I asked her if she thought she was ready for exams in May/June. She thought about it for a while and then said no, but that she hoped to make it back in time for prom. I thought it was highly unlikely, given the surgeries to come, and the fact that she could not yet stand unassisted, but I did not say anything. I thought it would be better that she came to that realization by herself.

I was asked to leave so that they could give Kechi an aqueous bath. This meant melting the aqueous cream in hot water, then using the water to sponge her body. This was making a huge difference as her skin was softer, not as dry as before, and cleaner.

That night, Kechi and I got into a fight.

She always got very irritable and impatient when I could not get to the exact spot that itched. That night, I did not get to the spot fast enough and when she got irritable, I spoke sharply to her, telling her to stop that at once, to relax and touch the exact place so that I could get to it. I added that I did not like it when she got irritable because it made her tense and worsened her discomfort.

Kechi did not take kindly to being scolded and refused to talk to me or to respond when I called her name. I apologized over and over again until she finally said that she did not usually have to tell me where to pat or rub, and when I tried to say that I was not frustrated at her, she quickly jumped in to say that I obviously was, or else I would not have scolded her.

I did not pursue the issue because I thought to myself that maybe I was a little frustrated with her. I was there for Kechi and only for her and she knew it. I thought she could take a second to say, 'there, not there'. But I also recognized that she must be even more frustrated than I was so I reached deep down and found the reserves of my patience, telling myself that I must never lose sight of the fact that Kechi was carrying much more than she could be expected to handle at her age, and it was only the grace of God that had brought her thus far.

I reminded myself that she was still extremely fragile emotionally and needed to be handled with extreme care and endless patience. I decided that I would apologize again the next day.

When I got back to the guesthouse, I had a few anxious moments when I could not reach Nkechi by phone since, by my calculations, they ought to have landed in Nigeria. I ran out of phone credit and had to wait for Mike's nightly call so that I could ask him to call Ulo and get her to call me. When Ulo called, I told her to keep me informed about Nkechi and Tara's arrival in Lagos. Uloma called back to say that they had arrived safely, and then Nkechi called, and I spoke with Tara. My relief left me wondering if I did not trust God to deliver them home safely. I could see that the events of December 10, 2005 had affected me in more ways than I realized. I went to bed a relieved, if lonely, woman.

I woke up knowing I needed to minister to Kechi on surrender and I decided to take The Purpose-Driven Life with me to the hospital. The chapter on surrender being the heart of worship seemed appropriate to read to her and to show her the importance and necessity of daily surrender.

A few days before, she had alarmed me by saying to me,

"Mom, I'm sorry, but I love you more than I love God", and I said to her, "I do not think that's such a terrible thing for you to say, because you cannot love someone that you do not know. I am going to teach you about the God that I know and have come to love even more than my life and you will begin to know Him in your own way. I believe that everyone knows and loves God according to their nature, personality and peculiarities. We are all made differently, so don't worry about it, okay?"

And she nodded, looking relieved. I was glad that she knew that there was something not quite right about what she had said, but at the same time I was relieved that she was honest and courageous enough to speak what was in her mind.

We had a great visit, and this time, she sat up in her chair for the whole visit without crying to be put back in bed.

She hardly itched and said that Dr. Pahad was pleased with her progress in the reduction of dormicum and had further reduced it to 6mg per day. She had already had a dose that morning and I tried to persuade her to leave the rest for the night when she would need it in order to sleep. But at 2pm, she got agitated and the sister gave her a dose.

When she calmed down, I talked to her about surrendering all that concern her to God on a continuous basis, throughout the day, not just once at the beginning of the day. I also told her that we would be doing some reading and discussion on that later.

In the evening, we had some pleasant conversation. She told me about life in school, her relationships with her friends. Then it was time for Kechi's aqueous bath. When I peeked into her room at about 7pm, she was fast asleep.

She woke up in time for visiting, and things went downhill from there.

She was irritable and itchy and nothing could relax her. At 8pm, I had to ask the nurse to give her dormicum. It was given through a different IV line than she was used to and she claimed not to feel the effects. I told her to relax; I did not see how it would not work since it went into her system, even if it went through another line. This led to long drawn-out wailing, which proved to me how dependent Kechi had become on the drug. She cried, begged, carried on for so long that I asked Sister Fiona to get the shift leader's permission to give Kechi another dose through the normal IV line and this time it worked. Kechi became drowsy and apologized to the sister and I for the way she had carried on.

It was a draining experience for me and not knowing what else to do, I surrendered it to God. I had really reached the end of my own strength and was only surviving through His grace. On my own, I would have broken into pieces a long time ago. Indeed, I thought, His strength was made perfect in my weakness, and His grace was more than sufficient for me.

I thanked God that she slept off before I left that night, because I could not have left her in that state. I decided to lay the drug dependency before God, and also to ask the church family to pray with me.

❖

My heart was heavy the next morning and I unburdened myself before the Lord. I had woken up with my thoughts full of Kechi's itching, her face, hands etc., and it all became too much for me. I found myself wondering again why she had to suffer so much. She had a lot to handle all at the same time, and I felt that she could be spared the itching. No man knew what was in the mind of God and He was under no obligation whatsoever to reveal His mind to any man, so it occurred to me that we may never know why Kechi was being permitted to suffer this itching. When I came to the end of my musings, I came to the conclusion that God was sovereign and I would love and worship Him forever, no matter what came my way, and I was gong to teach my daughter just that.

At the hospital, Kechi was itching as usual, especially around her face and neck and I did my best to make her comfortable, then when she settled down a bit, I bought her hot chocolate and croissants and we talked while I fed her. Then she told me that she had a dream.

In that dream, someone who looked a lot like Harry Potter, from the popular children's series, came to her and said to her, "You and your Mom should stop what you are doing."

Kechi said to the person, "I don't understand, what do you mean?" "Your Mom should stop healing you with her faith. She should leave you to do the work on your own."

Kechi said she asked him to go away, she did not know what he was talking about. And then she woke up.

I told her I would pray about it, and if it was from God, there would be a confirmation one way or the other.

When I was kicked out so they could change her dressings and bathe her, I contemplated going in to Sandton to exchange some dollars into rand, but then Tunde visited with her friend, Jumoke. She remarked on my demeanor, saying I looked tired, and I admitted it had not been very easy the past couple of days with the constant itching. I mentioned that I wanted to change money in Sandton and she offered to take me somewhere closer the next day, and also to give me a loan of R1000 until I exchanged my own money. I was very grateful because it meant I did not have to go anywhere, and I could sit and rest until the next visiting time. They also gave me some fruit juice they had brought for Kechi. I thanked them profusely and thanked God for looking out for me. These were people to whom I was a stranger, but they felt the urge to help because of God's prompting in their hearts.

When I sat with Kechi later, I finally explained in greater detail the issue of surrender. I read out chapter ten of The Purpose-Driven Life to her and I could literally see the words sinking in. She was like a sponge, soaking it all in. This was someone searching for God, trying to make sense of Him. We discussed trust and faith. The way I saw it, Kechi needed to know God first, learn to love him, trust Him, build her faith in Him, and then be able to surrender to Him.

This was an immense responsibility to be the person to lead her to the knowledge of God, but I thought of the scripture that asked that if God be for me, then who or what could be against me? He was going to guide me, give me the right words, and even more beautiful, the more Kechi grew in the knowledge of Him, the more I would grow also. We had a great discussion, as she had some questions, and I stayed until 4.30pm after which I left to eat, then came back to stay till 6pm.

I was back at 7.30pm and Kechi seemed calmer. Then she told me she had had another dream.

This time, she was in a fellowship meeting at my sister, Nkechi's house in Lagos and people were standing with hands joined, praying. She opened her eyes and found that one of the people was staring at her. And the person said to her,

"Why are your eyes open? Do you see how everyone's eyes are closed as they are praying? Why will you not pray like others are praying?"

Kechi said she told the person to leave her alone and the person started to laugh mockingly at her, and then she woke up.

The second dream got me thinking about the first one, and I began to see a connection. In the first dream, she was told to take control of her faith and heal herself by faith. And in the second dream, she was asked why she was not praying like everyone else. As I was thinking of this, Mom called and told me that Kechi had got to start taking responsibility for herself and I should start to teach her the word of God because the rest of her life depended on how she handled what was going on then.

I remembered the scripture from Matthew 18:16b,

"that in the mouth of two or three witnesses every word may be established."

I told Kechi about Mom's call, reminding her of what I had said when she told me of the first dream; that God would confirm if it came from Him. I went on to share the word God had spoken to me when we just came to SA, about righteousness. Then I told her about the vision I had about the ant that grew into a monster because of lack of faith, and how we should see the itching as an ant and deal with it at once with our faith lest it grew into a monster and consumed us.

When we prayed that night, I asked God to begin to fan the tiny fire of the knowledge of Him that had started burning within Kechi into a blazing fire.

Afterwards, I felt the lightness that only came from a successful burden transfer to God, and I glorified Him over and over again.

CHAPTER THIRTY- TWO

"And I say unto you, Ask, and it shall be given you; seek, and ye shall find; knock, and it shall be opened unto you."
Luke 11 : 9(KJV)

The above scripture was at the top of the page of my journal that morning, and I thought it was very apt for Kechi who was beginning to know God.

I decided to start The Purpose-Driven Life again with her from beginning. Together with bible passages, I believed that the lessons in the book would help to build her knowledge of God.

Then Ulo called me. She began the conversation by saying that she got a message for me.

I was to go back to the initial messages I received from God when we first came to SA. Then she went on to say that we should regard the itching against the background of the vision I had received about the ant and faith. She went on to say that there should begin a lessening of Kechi's dependence on me. This was the exact same thing that Mom had said, so I asked Ulo if she and Mom had discussed this, and she said no.

I was humbled. I just sat there with my head bowed, tears streaming from my eyes in gratitude. Ulo was asking me, 'Ije, Ije, are you still there?'

I told her that I was just humbled by God's love and the way He was making sure that we knew that the messages we were getting were from Him.

I told Ulo about Kechi's dreams, and how I had told her that if the dreams were messages from God, He would confirm it somehow or the other. Then

I told her about Mom's call, and how I had already discussed what she herself called me about with Kechi.

I related to Ulo what I had received on surrender and how Kechi and I had begun to study it and about the two dreams Kechi had and we marveled at how God could use anything to reach people. Harry Potter! What better way was there to get Kechi's attention than through a character and a series she loved so much? God had confirmed His word to us and we were on the right path. I glorified and praised Him after Ulo rang off, then I headed out to the hospital.

Kechi was sitting up in her chair and I noticed that she seemed tired. She confirmed it when I asked and said she had walked with assistance to the door and back that morning. She was very pleased with herself but said it had taken a lot out of her.

She was itching, so I went to work, tapping her head, and rubbing her face, which were the itchiest places that morning.

Then I noticed that Kechi looked depressed, and when I asked, said she was tired of the itching. She got very restless, and Rochelle gave her dormicum to calm her down. When she had settled down, I began to minister the word of God to her. With various bible references, I showed her how much God loved her. I told her of the kind of faith God wants us to have in Him by giving her an example from her childhood.

When Kechi was around three years old, she climbed up on the dinning table behind my back and the next thing I heard was, 'Mommy, catch me!' I quickly turned around to see that Kechi had already launched herself off the table and was airborne, in the full trust and conviction that her mother would catch her, and not allow her to fall.

I told Kechi that God was her safety net and she should not be afraid of letting go of a problem and handing it over to God to handle, because He was more than able to deliver her from any situation, as He had proved in her life.

I assured her that the same God who had saved her from a burning plane and arranged for her to be treated at Milpark Hospital could surely relieve her of the itching, but that she must reach out to Him in faith.

I told her that faith was like a muscle, if it is not exercised, it would atrophy and die, and she wanted to know how to do this.

I told her to take any problem she was having to God in prayer and then stop thinking about it, and believe that God will handle it. She said that the problem was that when she handed the problem over, it came right back. I told her to hand - it over again and again until she got used to leaving it in God's hands that was a practical application of faith. By giving the problem over to God, she would be acknowledging that God was bigger than that problem, and if she found herself thinking about the problem again, she should hand it over again. I told her to remember that she had surrendered herself to God and was a living sacrifice. When she let doubts come in, and dwells on them, this is akin to crawling off the altar and she would no longer be in the presence of God. She should immediately ask forgiveness for her doubts and hand over the problem again, and believe that God could handle it. If necessary, she should do this up to a hundred times a day. That was faith-muscle exercising I gave her examples of men of faith in the bible, Abraham, Isaac, and Noah etc.

Then I led Kechi in a prayer of surrender.

I had obeyed the Lord, and I now trusted in Him to do the rest. I prayed that His peace, which she was yearning for, would be hers, and for God to take up His Holy throne deep within her heart.

I had a meeting with Dr. Nel at 3pm and he said they were going to graft Kechi's right hand on Friday, remove the trachea tube, and remove the bandage on her eye. He also said that he would release the contractures on the left hand when he was sure there were no other infections in her body. He said that the damage to the nerves on her right hand was extensive and he did not think that she would ever regain function of that hand. When he said that, I rejected in in my mind, telling myself that he was not God, so he could only talk based on his own human experience.

I asked about the grafted skin, wondering if it was going to remain dry and he said yes, Kechi's grafted skin would need a lot of lubrication for the rest of her life. I asked if the skin would stretch, and if Kechi could add weight again. His answer was not comforting at all. He said the skin could stretch, but not much, and that Kechi would probably remain quite slim because a lot of fat had been scraped off her body. Given how skinny Kechi was at that time, it terrified me that she might remain that size.

I had had enough.

I put my list of mostly unasked questions back into my bag, thanked the doctor, and left. My head was reeling, but I found my center in God. He promised complete healing, and He NEVER lied.

Coming to terms with less doses of dormicum was not easy for Kechi. She thought she was to have four doses of 2mg each, but it turned out to be three doses a day. She had just one dose left for that day and she knew she had to wait and take it as late as she could in the night. She insisted that I stayed with her to take her mind off things until she could take the drug at 8 pm. So I ended up staying with Kechi from 4pm until 8pm.

Rochelle took pity on me, and told me I could help her to bathe Kechi, so that I would at least be doing something. It was a fulfilling experience for me as I got to really touch Kechi, and was able to see, for the first time, the full extent of her wounds and the level of healing.

But by 8pm, both Kechi and I were exhausted, with me standing to rub and tap, and Kechi crying and irritable because of the itching.

It was with great relief that I saw Rochelle come in to give her the drugs. Kechi fell asleep almost instantly.

I woke up the next morning feeling heavy and weak and had a headache. I prayed and surrendered everything to God, and then I rose up to speak life into Kechi's right hand, decreeing in the name of Jesus that she would have full mobility in them.

Kechi was bright that morning, a pleasant change from the past few days, and we joked and laughed together. In fact, Kechi laughed so hard at one point that one of the nurses peeped around the door to find out what was happening.

Kechi was in a good mood and only went back to bed because she wanted to make a bowel movement. Sister Thandi and I tried to put a bedpan under her while she was seated, but it was very painful, so they sent for the therapists to come and take Kechi back to bed.

Kechi told me to wait so I could see her walk. She was helped up, took a few steps to the bed, sat on the bed, and then rolled in, assisted by the therapist.

It was wonderful to behold, though Kechi felt it was no big deal because she was assisted through it all. I told her that seeing her vertical after for months of being horizontal was overwhelming for me.

I fed her after she was done, then it was time for dressings change. Sister Thandi had told me to buy a lanolin-based cream that will help in lubricating Kechi's skin and perhaps reduce the itching. I decided to go and shop in Cresta, as I had groceries and other stuff to buy.

I bought Eucerin, which had lanolin, paraffin, and urea as part of the ingredients. I was running late so I called the hospital and asked left a message for Kechi that I was going to be about ten minutes late. My bags were heavy and I wanted to stop by the guesthouse and drop them off.

When I got to Kechi's room, she said that she was just about to start crying. Sister Thandi approved of the Eucerin and asked me to apply it on Kechi's skin, which I did, but only on her hands, just in case there was an adverse reaction. Kechi refused for me to put it on her face or neck.

I bought ribs from Steers for her lunch and she thoroughly enjoyed them. She had only had one dose of dormicum that day and said she was leaving the other two doses for the night. She then confessed that she had been very restless the previous night and the sister broke the rule and gave her another dose to calm her down.

It was itching galore that night, but luckily Sister Rose was on duty, so I was sure Kechi was going to get a good night's rest. By 8pm, I asked Kechi to have her drug so that she could sleep off, but she wanted to wait until 8.30pm so she could have her full visiting hour. By 8.15pm, she started what I was now calling the full body twitch where she jerked her whole body from side to side in an effort to scratch everywhere at once. I told her to relax and just wait out the next fifteen minutes. I must have spoken sharply because she started to cry uncontrollably and she cried for a long time. I tried to console her, but she refused to look at me and in fact told me to leave her alone. I could see by then that she was very upset and tried harder to calm her down and Kechi refused to be consoled.

"I would have thought," she sobbed, "that you of all people should realize that I cannot possibly be crying or twitching just for the fun of it".

"I'm sorry," I said over and over again with no effect.

"Kechi, I don't know what else to say or do. Do you want me to leave?"

She quieted down and said no. I apologized again and told her she was breaking my heart, and she said I broke hers first.

We both kept quiet for a while, and then I asked if she had forgiven me and she said yes. We prayed together and I left.

I was exhausted by all the activities of the day; dashing about in Cresta and standing almost all day to rub Kechi's body had taken its toll. I was very happy to get to the guesthouse and just lie down and sleep. I needed to be in the hospital earlier the next day so that I could get there in time to see Kechi walk. Maya, the physical therapist had asked me to come if I could.

Kechi was not looking bright the next morning, and complained that she had passed a restless night. She said she could not sleep because the dormicum did not work.

Getting her ready to walk was a very elaborate process. First, Rochelle disconnected every line attached to Kechi, except the central line. Then a gown was put on Kechi, while she was still lying down. Then she bent her knees and helped the therapists to get herself seated by the side of the bed by rocking gently forward and backwards. Maya now had to stand in front of Kechi, with both arms around Kechi and by leaning back, pulled her very slowly, inch by inch, into a standing position.

Then they stood facing each other, Maya's hands on Kechi's waist, and Kechi's hands on Maya's shoulders.

Kechi was then told to gently press her heels to the ground. Lying down so much had caused Kechi's feet to bend forward, and so when she stood, she did so on the balls of her feet, and had to be taught to press her heels down. In order to press her heels down, Kechi pushed her bum out behind her slowly until her heels touched down.

Maya gave her time to recover from the effort and then walked slowly backwards, while Kechi walked slowly forward, one tiny step at a time. They walked to the door of the ICU, about twenty steps, and then back to Kechi's bed twice. They did mini squats and then went back to the bed. There was also a system for getting into bed. Kechi would sit down, then she would sort of fall into bed on her right side, while someone lifted her legs unto the bed, then she would roll onto her back. Then two people would stay, one on each side of her bed, put their hands on her armpits and pull, boosting her up to the top of the bed.

I was very proud of Kechi and told her so. She was also feeling pretty good with herself and smiled. Rochelle had brought a horror movie for her to watch, so I went back to the guesthouse to get my laptop. We watched the horror movie, and then Kechi slept.

When she woke up she asked to watch the show, Friends and we watched it together for a while until she got itchy and I had just started itch duty when the anesthetist came in and said Kechi was going into the OR in fifteen minutes. She was the first on the list that day.

I accompanied her to the OR as usual and she was wheeled in at 2pm. By 4pm, the anesthetist came out to the waiting room tell me they had finished the trachea tube was out, hand was grafted, and eyes were opened. Dr. Nel also came out and said that Kechi's scalp still had a few septic areas, but daily betidene dressings would be continued on it.

They called me into the recovery room to calm Kechi down because she was crying. Then Rochelle came in to wheel her back and she calmed down. I went back to the waiting room, and after a while, Rochelle came in to say that Kechi had been made comfortable and was asleep. An hour later, she came to get me because Kechi had woken up.

She was sitting with the head of the bed a bit upraised and her eyes were finally open. She smiled when she saw me and asked for croissants and cocoa. The coffee shop just had scones and after demurring for a while, Kechi ate them and loved them, washing them down with two cups of cocoa.

We prayed together and she agreed for me to go at the official time because Sister Rose was her night nurse and she was very pleased to see her.

❖

I got to the hospital early the following day and while waiting for the visiting time to start, I was told by one of the passing nurses that Kechi was doing her walking exercises. I rushed to the door to peek in and could see that though it was obviously painful, she was persevering. She caught sight of me and insisted that I stayed, though it was not yet visiting time. She was put back on her bed, not on a chair as usual, because she was post-op. She looked very comfortable, though she soon started to complain about pain all over her body, especially on her face. I went to find Rochelle, who was on her tea break, and she gave Kechi morphine, which made her relax and sleepy. She slept off and was out for two hours.

Rochelle decided to take her lunch break to delay Kechi's dressings change so that we could have time together when Kechi was not itching or in pain.

When she came back, I went to Campus Square to buy croissants so that Kechi would stop crying when they did not have them at the coffee shop. Rochelle had just finished up the dressings change and was about to bathe Kechi when I came back. I joined in and brushed Kechi's teeth myself. We made her comfortable and she was very relaxed, soon dropping into sleep and I went off to have a cup of coffee to fortify myself for the last visit.

It was itch duty galore that night and I was glad when it turned out that Rose was her night nurse once again. She was given morphine for pain and this relaxed her. We prayed and I left, my mind eased by the fact that Rose was with her that night.

Rochelle came to find me in the waiting room almost as soon as I came in the next morning. She said Kechi had asked her to come and see if I had come. When I went in, Kechi was sitting in a chair. She said she slept well, but was looking downcast. I asked her what was wrong and she said, "Everything". I asked her to elaborate.

"I thought that by now I would have made a lot more progress with the itching and pain, but everything seems to have started all over again. I know you said it is always darkest before the dawn and all that, but this is lasting so long.

I don't know why the pain has started again after being manageable for so long, but now I even have pain on my face.

I am grateful to God for saving me, but did He save me to only for me to suffer so much?

I miss Toke so much and I can't believe I'll never see her again. We were sitting together on the bus en route the airport. Chinenye was such a nice, well-behaved girl, while I was always getting into trouble. How come God saved me, and not a better person?

I am so, so sad, and the only bright spot in my life now is you and the fact that you are here with me. If you were not here, there would not be any point in living. I remember my friend, Emeka, who lost his Mom, and I know that I would never have been able to cope if that had happened to me."

I helped Kechi to let it all out and cry. I did not try to stop the tears because I believed that they were cleansing and healing tears.

Dr. Pahad came in while she was crying and I explained that she was depressed because of the friends she had lost, among other things, and he was very sympathetic, telling her that it was healthy and good that she was letting her grief out. Kechi complained about the renewed pain and he prescribed a new drug to replace the morphine. Rochelle explained that the new drug was given to women in labor when they were 3cm dilated, to make them sleep; only waking up when they were fully dilated. Kechi got the drug via a needle in her bum and soon started feeling drowsy, and asked to be put back in bed. She began to itch and Rochelle told me to massage the Eucerin into her skin, and asked Kechi to give it a chance to work.

When she calmed down, I started to counsel her, telling her that only God knows the full answers to some questions. I told her that everyone who knew Toke loved her and though she would always miss her, the pain would lessen with time. I asked her about Emeka, was he not coping well? She answered that Emeka was strong.

"So are you, Kechi," I said. "God has promised that he will never allow us temptation that we cannot bear, and with the temptation, He will give the way out."

I told her that I had asked God once why He was allowing her to suffer so much, someone so young? And God had answered me, asking me to look at all His prophets, which one of them did not suffer?

"Why must they suffer?" Kechi asked.

"Such experiences build character" I explained, "because you learn so much about patience, endurance, love, humility etc. which you can impart to others as you do your own part in building up others for the kingdom of God."

I gave her an example with my barren years. What I learned in those ten years of waiting for another child, I used to counsel other women in a similar situation.

Kechi said that she believed that if she could cast all her cares on God, she would be okay, but she did not know how.

I told her to speak her faith out loud, so she could also hear herself. She could start with an affirmation of her convictions about who God is and what He means to her personally. She could start thus:

"You are God. You created everything. You gave me a wonderful family, and You saved me from death.

Working through Your servants in Shell, You brought me over to Milpark Hospital here in Johannesburg, and You have given me the best doctors and nurses anyone could ever ask for.

I know that You can relieve this itching because You are the same God that gave Abraham a child when it appeared impossible in the eyes of man, You delivered Noah and his family from the flood, You parted the Red Sea, so that Your people would be safe, you have done wondrously great and mighty things throughout the ages. This itching is nothing for You to handle. You have said I should only believe, and I should only ask, and it shall be given to me. I ask now in the name of your Son, my savior Jesus Christ, that this itching be taken away from me. Amen."

Then I told her to close her eyes and imagine a bucket, then I asked her to put in all her fears, doubts, questions, confusion, pain and itching into the bucket, carry the bucket to the foot of the cross, look up at Jesus and tell Him to take it all. Then walk away, leaving the bucket there, and say to Jesus, "Please take my heavy burdens. I give them all to You".

Kechi mumbled something and I realized she was half asleep, so I prayed for her, thankful that she had finally relaxed enough for the drugs to take effect.

Dr. Nel came in while she was asleep and said he would take her in the following morning to expose her hand, and see if her scalp and legs would need more grafting. I prayed that there would be no more grafting. He also said that Dr. Fletcher, an occupational therapist, would come in the following Tuesday to see about getting silicone pressure garments made for Kechi's face to help with the scarring.

Rochelle suggested that Kechi's hair be scraped off in the OR, but the doctor demurred, saying that they were trying to save as much hair as they could, but he would look into the possibility.

When he left, Rochelle confided in me that she had really diluted the morphine and dormicum Kechi was getting, which was why she was not getting the effect she craved from the drugs. She wanted to ease off morphine entirely and believed that between Tramal and Pethidene, the pain should be under control. She believed that Kechi was now using morphine and dormicum as comfort drugs.

When Kechi woke up, she was feeling better and I told her that she fell asleep when we were handing over her burdens to God, and she found that amazing. She said she had been feeling as if nothing would ever be right again, but she felt better and lighter. I was glad that she was getting a feel of the power of God. I had long been praying for her to feel God's presence, and it was slowly starting to happen.

I read the first chapter of The Purpose-Driven Life to her, then after we discussed it, and we read from Luke, and she fell asleep.

I prayed and left, feeling that I had made some progress in getting Kechi's mind focused on God that day.

CHAPTER THIRTY-THREE

"I will lift up mine eyes unto the hills, from whence cometh my help. My help cometh from the LORD, which made heaven and earth."
Psalm 121: 1 & 2 (KJV)

Kechi was calm the following morning, and she had Sister Ancee for the day. She said the ophthalmologist had come earlier and left instructions that Kechi's left eye should be massaged frequently with chloramycetin to avoid another contraction. Also, Kechi should be encouraged to squeeze and hold that eye closed several times a day to encourage the skin to be more flexible.

It was a quiet day, and Kechi slept through most of it.

She was wheeled into the OR about 3pm and was out an hour and a half later. I had to be called into the recovery room to help calm Kechi down. This took some time and a lot of talking and reassuring, but she eventually calmed down and slept. Back in ICU, Kechi was taken to a different room because the other burns patients in her room had infections, which the staff did not want Kechi to catch, since she had been infection free for a while.

It was ironic that it was the same room she had been taken to at the beginning of her stay to isolate her from other patients, and prevent them from getting her infections. This to me was another sign that we were on our way out of the ICU.

She got settled in and sent for me. Sister Anna was her night nurse and she was happy. I was too, because when she got a sister she liked, she relaxed enough to sleep.

They had changed her head and leg dressings in the OR, but there was no grafting, and I was happy because that meant the wounds were healing nicely.

The next morning, Kechi said she slept very well the previous night. I went in early and so I caught the initial physiotherapy when they worked on her fingers and legs. Then Maya came in and they did the walking part. Kechi was really the ICU star, as everyone came out to watch her walking. It occurred to me then that there was really so much about walking that we took for granted. Kechi was learning to put her heels down first and not her toes, as she was inclined to. Then she would bend her knees while taking steps, planting her feet apart so that she did not trip over them.

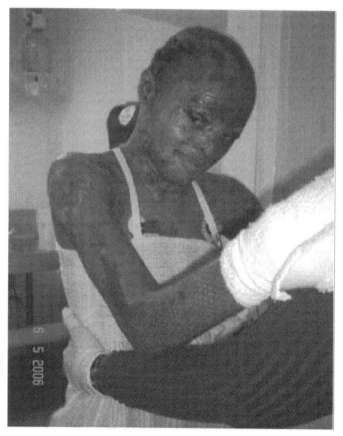

Learning to walk again – Five months after the crash.

After her walk, we watched TV and she told me how she had diarrhea and nausea that morning. The doctor wanted to watch it for a while without giving drugs. I left her at 2pm to get some pajamas, dressing gowns and slippers for her, since she was now ambulatory. When I got back, she was watching TV, quite relaxed. We marveled that she had not itched for two days now, and as if the devil heard us, the full body itch started around 6pm. Nothing anyone did worked for Kechi and she just got more and more twitchy and irritable by the second. After a while, we all just stood by, looking down at her, because nothing was working.

When Maureen came in for the night shift, she gave Kechi dormicum, which worked for all of five minutes before the itching started again. She could not give her anything more after that and Kechi began to cry.

I turned away and began to pray, 'God, if I serve any other god, then do not answer me. You see my heart and You know I serve no one else. Please come to my aid and take this itching from Kechi so that she can sleep. I hand Your daughter over to You. Please take control. Amen.' When I turned back, Kechi had stopped crying and twitching, her eyes heavy with sleep. I held her hand and prayed and she slept off.

I felt burdened and passed a restless night. It bothered me that the itching would not quit and I was not happy about it.

When I got to the hospital the following morning, Kechi told me that she had been restless throughout the night also, and had woken up when I left. She only fell asleep around 4am, but had slept well and had woken up refreshed. She was all smiles that morning, and said she was very happy to see me.

The head dressing had come off entirely in the night with all her twitching, and Maureen had decided to leave it off. I was not sure I liked that because there were still a few sore spots that looked like they could still be prone to infection, and Kechi's hands were never still.

Kechi was like an old man, bald on top and hair around the sides, but she looked beautiful to me. Now that so much of her skin was exposed, I was seeing the full extent of her burns. As Dr. Nel said, the fire was a huge insult to her body. There was obviously still a lot of healing ahead, and a lot of coming to terms with what might not go back to normal.

There was a long road ahead.

Kechi said she was getting impatient and I reprimanded her, telling her that I had never hidden from her that we had a long way to go. I reminded her that I had said from when she came out of her coma, that she should be ready to wear patience like a garment and give herself at least a year to heal. Everything else could wait.

She asked me if the graft on her lower jaw looked like the one at the back of her hand and I said they were similar and could tell she did not like that.

I told her that Dr. Fletcher was making a silicone facemask to help smoothen her face. I promised her then that everything that could be done by medical science would be explored to get her face as close to the way it was as possible.

Then Dr. Pahad came in to decree that morphine and dormicum should be discontinued entirely during the day. This was a blow to Kechi, but Sister Christina, who was on duty, came to talk to me about that, saying that Kechi was hooked to the drugs through no fault of hers, but we must all help her to lose her dependence on the two drugs.

Maya allowed me to walk with Kechi for a while and it was so thrilling to hold my daughter. She was even more thrilled than me, because she had been wanting for months to hug me and hold me. The day we would hug each other tight and never let go was coming closer every day.

I sat with Kechi all day, distracting her from thinking about the drugs, or lack of them. We watched TV, talked a whole lot, ate, and just enjoyed each other's company. Maya had asked me to buy pajama shorts and tops that button in front for easy wearing, so that Kechi would stop feeling like a patient, and start feeling more normal. There was also talk about Kechi walking to the bathroom when she needed to go, so they could remove the catheter. This kind of talk just made my heart sing, because it meant progress and I was all for it.

Since we were a bit shielded from view in the new room, I allowed everyone that called to talk with Kechi - Mom, Ely, Mike, Ulo. There was excitement all round. Then Womiye, Kechi's best friend, sent a text from school with her Mom's phone. I called back and Kechi spoke with Womiye, her Mom, her friend, Dvanhi, and Mr. Paul, a member of staff in Loyola. Kechi was thrilled to bits.

Then she dropped a bombshell on me.

She told me that when she was speaking with her Dad on the phone, she saw her face reflected on the face of my phone. She asked for a mirror so she could see it better.

I told her that she had felt all over her face with her fingers, so she knew her face was rough, and that the healing skin on the left side of her face pulled her eye and mouth on that side slightly, as well as her neck, which was why she could not look up fully. I also told her that the scarring would be taken care of by a combination of prayers, silicone pressure garments, and eventually, reconstructive surgery.

Then I gave her a mirror.

She had obviously expected far worse than she saw and I thanked God that she thought she was really hideous, because everything else was an improvement.

Her expectations made her thankful that her big beautiful eyes were intact, her nose was in place, and her lips were still full and pink. She looked up at me and smiled, 'Mom, I'm still pretty'.

I bent my head and thanked God for the treasure that was this child, and for the spirit He had put inside of her.

When she started to itch later, I spoke to her about taking authority over her body, and told her she was in control of her body and not the other way round. I taught her a relaxation technique my Mom had taught me years ago. Starting at her feet, I told her to tense the muscles and then relax them, then move to the muscles on her calves and work her way to her face. This had always worked for me, and I knew it would work for her too. I told her to force her body to obey her, including the itching.

Then I prayed with her and left her to a new sister who looked motherly and kind.

April 27, 2006

April 27 is a public holiday, Freedom Day, in South Africa - the commemoration of the first democratic elections held in South Africa on 27 April 1994.

I woke up with thanksgiving in my heart and I poured it out to God.

Kechi was asleep when I got to her room and I sat by her bed and waited for her to wake. She said she slept well the previous night and we gave thanks for that. I left the room for dressings change and physical therapy, and when I got back to the room, Kechi was already back in her bed. Apparently, Maya was not around, so the trainee therapists just walked her around the inside of her room a few times. While she was resting, I went to Cresta to buy some more Eucerin cream, as the one we were using had run out. Betty met up with me at the mall, and took me to Mr. Price, where we bought shorts and tops for Kechi to wear in bed.

Kechi was still asleep when we got back, so Betty and I ate the takeout we had bought while we waited for her to wake up.

Sister Ziphora called me in to see Kechi and I fed her with her own share of ribs and fries, then Betty went in to see Kechi, while I stayed with Keanu in the waiting room. Layi also came by with a huge white teddy for Kechi. I asked her to go in and give it to Kechi, who loved the bear and hugged it while exclaiming and thanking Layi.

The full body itch came at its usual time of 6pm, and Layi left while I started to talk Kechi into taking control of her body. Ziphora gave her a shot, and she relaxed. She did not want me to leave that night because she was afraid she would not sleep since she had slept all day. I prayed with her and told her not to worry, as she would definitely sleep. I prayed with her, rebuking the spirit of fear, and told Kechi to remember the bucket and pray when she needed help.

She agreed and was calm when I left.

Nkechi called me and pointed something out to me. Kechi kept talking about the dreams she kept having in which she was with her friends, and while they were all normal, she was the only one that was sick and dressed in a nightie. Nkechi's thinking was that Kechi was in heaven, but my prayers and pronouncements over her at that early stage touched the heart of God and He returned her to me. She pointed out that when Kechi came out of the coma, she said that she was hearing all my prayers and singing while she was under.

Deep gratitude washed all over me that morning while I was praying and I was overwhelmed. I thanked God all over again, weeping, and pledged my life to Him all over again. I was truly ready to do anything God wanted me to do. I also rebuked the spirits of infirmity manifesting in Kechi's high blood pressure and high temperature.

Kechi was bright and cheerful even as she did her exercises and walking. She was tearful at first because the donor site on her bum was still quite painful, but she soon got into her stride and happily walked about. Soon, Maya just rested Kechi's hands lightly on hers, instead of grasping her firmly on her waist like before, and Kechi balanced and walked under her own power.

It was a glorious sight, but she was quite tired afterwards and got a shot for pain.

Dr. Nel came by to take a look at the grafting on the right hand and was happy with it. Kechi asked about her left hand and neck, and was reassured that the contractures would be released as soon as her scalp wounds healed. Then her dressings were changed amidst tears and we put her back in bed.

Womiye called and Kechi spoke to her and to Somachi and Atuora, and this took her mind off her pain for a while. She missed her friends so much and was still holding out hope that she would make it to their prom.

She asked for dormicum to sleep, but both the sister and I said no. She argued and argued and eventually got 0.5mg, which did nothing for her. I reprimanded her for forcing the Sister's hand. I tried to explain to her that as long as she was on dormicum, we would remain in the ICU. It was not given in the ward and the sooner she got off it, the better for her. She needed to find another way to relax without drugs. I explained to her that if she had held out, she would have gotten the full dose of dormicum by 6pm, instead of the tiny bit that did no good. I think she got the message.

I fed her, and after she had a bowel movement, she relaxed and got comfortable. The rest of the day passed comfortably, with just a little complaint about soreness in her shoulders and back. I attributed this to the exercises she was doing, moving parts of her body that had been lying still for so long.

❖

During my devotions the next morning, it was ministered to me to massage Kechi's back and shoulders, so I put the massage oil in my bag.

Kechi was not looking bright. She was dull and listless, and said that she did not feel good. She cried during physio and walking and when she was seated, I massaged as much of her back and shoulders as I could reach, with little relief resulting for her.

Her temperature began to spike and she became feverish and started to demand lots of fluids, but no food. I massaged her neck and shoulders again while she was lying down and this time she got significant relief. The doctor came in and ordered x-rays, blood work and urine tests. He told me not to worry, the x-rays were not bad, and he would prescribe an anti-pyretic for the fever and the soreness, but would wait for the results of the blood work before prescribing antibiotics.

I sent a text to the church to pray with me.

Mom got the ministration that the fever would leave that evening, and I should pray over Kechi and rebuke it, which I did.

Kechi was given Perfalgan and Pethidene, and brightened up as the temperature began to drop to normal range. I massaged her back again and left her watching TV.

Ulo was coming in the next day, so Betty picked me up to sleep in her house so that we could both go and pick Ulo up from the airport early. But en route to Betty's house, Lanre called to say he would be picking Ulo up and bringing her to Betty's house instead.

When I called Lanre at 6.30am the next day, he was already at the airport and called me back at 7.30am to say that Ulo had arrived and they had left the airport. Betty was going to church with her kids, so I told Lanre to go on to the guest house with Ulo, where Betty would drop me off.

We arrived simultaneously at the guesthouse and it was so good to see Ulo, who had been my rock through the whole ordeal.

Betty left and Lanre waited to take Ulo and I to the hospital. Ulo had brought plantains and I fried some to take to Kechi, while Ulo prepared herself for seeing Kechi by looking at some photos I had been taking.

At the hospital, Kechi was sleeping when we got there and Ulo got the chance to look her over for a long time and get used to her. We went to the waiting room until the therapists went in to wake Kechi for her exercises. When we went in, Kechi did not notice Ulo at first and then Ulo asked her, "Kechi, how come you are not excited to see me?"

Kechi turned her head and screamed, "Aunty Uloma!"

She was so happy to see Ulo and had actually forgotten that she was coming in that day.

She did her exercises and walked up and down more confidently, then sat on a chair. She said she had slept well in the night and that the massages had helped, as her back was not as sore as before. Her temperature was fine and had been that way through the night.

We stayed with Kechi until about 4pm, and then I took Ulo back to the guesthouse to sleep off her jet lag and then returned to the hospital to stay with Kechi.

Suddenly, her temperature started to rise very rapidly in spite of the perfalgan and the sister was alarmed enough to ask the shift leader to page the doctor. I began to pray and the temperature eventually came down from 38° to 37.4° and she began to look more comfortable. I gave her another massage and by the time I left, she was watching TV and looking peaceful.

Ulo and I arrived the next morning to find Kechi asleep again.

When she woke up for her exercises, she said she had had another night of uninterrupted sleep. I noticed that the therapist did not take Kechi through the usual leg stretches prior to her standing and walking, and Kechi seemed to be finding it difficult to do both that morning. When I reminded her about the stretches, she did them with Kechi, and her walking became easier and smoother. After a slow start, she was walking better and even when the therapist wanted to take her back to bed, she insisted on walking some more and did two more laps around the unit.

When she got back to her room, she started to itch on her head and all over. I tried my best with itch duty, but nothing helped until she got dormicum and slept off. When she woke up, the full body itch was back and was uncontrollable.

When she started to cry, I told her that she had to take control of her body like we talked about and she got very upset with me, saying that she had been controlling herself since the itching started thirty minutes earlier, and then when she could not stand it any more, I was now talking to her as if she was not making any effort.

She refused to be consoled by me and Ulo tried her best. She eventually calmed down and I told her.

"Kechi, you know I did not mean for you to feel that you are not making any effort. I am the only person who knows how hard you are working, and I never meant to upset you".

After she calmed down, I went to the waiting room to stay with Betty's kids so that she could visit Kechi. When she got agitated again, Ulo sent for me and I went in to find Kechi fretful,

irritable and weepy.

All of a sudden the Lord opened my eyes to what the problem was and I spoke to Kechi.

"Your irritation is not just physical. I know that you are tired of lying down, doing nothing. I am going to ask Dr. Pahad tomorrow to allow us to take you outside in a wheelchair. I will also buy you a portable DVD player so that you can watch movies, since the laptop has packed up."

Kechi was considerably cheered up by this and calmed down.

We prayed with her and then left.

The following morning, Kechi was full of complaints. She had had a very rough night with itching and pain. Also, she had had a bad experience with Sister Dorothy and another sister called Di who was taking care of the patient in the next bed.

Apparently, Dorothy had tried to change the dressing on Kechi's donor site and it was so painful that Kechi started to cry loudly, and Di came round to Kechi's bed and began to shout at her to keep quiet. I could readily believe this because I had noticed that she was a loud person and talked indiscriminately.

Anyway, Kechi was very unhappy and was crying when she was relating what happened. I told her not to pay any attention to those who were unhappy and simply transferring their aggression to her, and she should never forget that she was never alone even when I was not with her - she had Jesus.

The doctor came and okayed the wheelchair idea, and also said that the CVP line should be removed. Apparently that was the source of the infection that had been causing Kechi's fevers.

That meant an end to morphine and dormicum.

The doctor took me aside and told me that I would have to support Kechi through the rough period ahead as her body adjusted to doing without both drugs. Also, the catheter was to be clamped.

Outside in a wheelchair with Aunty Uloma

We dressed Kechi in pink shorts and top, her pink and white dressing gown, and pink bedroom slippers and helped her into a wheelchair. I wanted to cover up her head to prevent stares from people, but she refused, and I persuaded her. We took her through the coffee shop and then outside to the parking lot, and she was so thrilled to see people walking about, cars driving in and out. We stayed outside for a little while until the catheter began to get uncomfortable and we wheeled her back to her room and back to bed.

When we got ready to go to the mall to buy the DVD player, Kechi became weepy and said we should forget it and stay with her. She began to complain about headaches and pain in her back and neck and Sister Ancee said that those were expected withdrawal symptoms.

That night, Ulo had a long talk with Kechi about faith and trust in God. She said that, like Kechi, she too was seeking a closer relationship with God and she was going to join her faith with Kechi's own during that period. She also gave Kechi a bible.

After their talk, Kechi asked to talk to me alone. "Mom, I know I can say anything to you".

"Of course," I said.

"I love you very much, Mom, with all my heart and soul. I also love God, but I know I don't love Him as much as you and Aunty Ulo do, and I know that I love you more than Him".

Trying not to be alarmed, I repeated what I had said to her before. "Sweetie, you cannot love who you don't know, and it is our responsibility to teach you to know God first, as we do, and then to come to love and trust Him, as we do".

Ulo and I began to pray for her, breaking the bonds of dependence and addiction. We told her to speak out her faith with her mouth, even if her heart did not believe it yet.

She did this, and it was a start, even though it was clear to us that she did not believe it. I sent a text to Mom, Ned and Nkechi,

asking them to pray.

Kechi was agitated when we were about to leave and I told her we had prayed for her to sleep well that night.

CHAPTER THIRTY-FOUR

"...but as for me and my house, we will serve the LORD."
Joshua 24 : 15(KJV)

The next morning, when we got to Kechi's room she was fast asleep. The physical therapists woke her soon after we were there and as soon as she saw us, she began to cry.

Apparently the catheter was quite uncomfortable and at a point, she was no longer sure when her bladder was full. First she wanted to pee, then to poo, and before she could call the nurse, she had done both on the bed. Then the two sisters started to yell at her and ask why she did not call them and why she messed up the bed. They would not let her explain what happened and shouted over all her attempts to explain. After she was cleaned up, she cried herself to sleep around 2am.

I saw red! I could actually feel my heart pounding with rage and decided that enough was enough. I marched straight to the Unit Leader, Christina, to make a report and was gratified at her level of shock and horror as she apologized profusely. She promised to speak with both of the sisters and also to make sure neither of them was assigned to Kechi again.

Kechi did four laps around the ward and we dressed her up for going outside. I invited Christina to go to the coffee shop with us and she was delighted to do so. We all sat and had coffee while Kechi had pancakes and hot chocolate, then Christina went back to work while Ulo and I wheeled Kechi around the hospital, showing her the different wards on various floors.

She got tired about half an hour later, and we took her back to her room and got her back into bed where she soon drifted off into sleep.

Ulo and I used the opportunity to go to the mall and buy the DVD player and some DVDs, including Narnia.

She was still asleep when we got back, but the sister woke her up to sit in a chair for a while. She did not complain because we set up the DVD player for her to watch and she settled down happily, watching Narnia, having a marvelous time and smiling. It was like looking at a different person, she was completely transformed.

Sister Ancee removed the catheter at 6pm, and an hour later congratulated her on going for twelve hours without asking for any drugs.

We were largely ignored by Kechi and after we prayed, left her happily watching Friends on her new DVD player.

Ulo and I did a lot of praising God when we got back to the guesthouse that night.

The next morning, we had a particularly lovely praise and worship session, and then something amazing happened. From out of nowhere, Ulo and I started singing the same song,

'Lifted, lifted, lifted by Your word,
out of shame and sorrow
into the presence of the Lord'

It was not one of the songs we had sang that morning, and I had been singing it over and over in my head and when I got to "out of shame and sorrow", I sang it out loud and Ulo looked at me with shock.

"What?" I asked.

"I had been singing that song in my head since after our prayers", she said, "and was just about to sing 'out of shame and sorrow' out loud, when you sang it."

As far as we were concerned, this was a confirmation that God had lifted us into His presence, and we glorified His name even more.

❖

Kechi had already done her exercises when we got to the hospital and had walked five laps that morning. She proudly told us that she had sat on the toilet seat to move her bowels. She then pouted and said she had waited as long as she could so that we could see her.

I explained that we were a bit late because one of the guests had an early appointment, and so was dropped off first at a different hospital. We were thrilled at her achievement and showered praises on her.

First time she used the toilet in five months!

She then confessed to us that she had gone to bed late because she watched movies until 3am. She was still feeling sleepy and soon drifted off, and Ulo and I went to the waiting room.

Kechi woke an hour later and sent for us. She was looking much better that day. The donor sites were not so painful anymore, and she was getting in and out of bed much more easily.

She asked us to put in the Harry Potter DVD for her, and midway through the movie, she felt like moving her bowels, and the sister had gone for her tea break, so Ulo and I helped her out of bed and unto the toilet seat. She then ordered us out while she did the deed.

When she was ready, she called us back into the bathroom and Ulo cleaned her up while I supported her. Supporting her with both my arms, while she rested hers on my shoulders gave us the first opportunity for a full hug, and we made the best of it.

We then walked to her room and she put herself back in bed with very little help from me.

It was an awesome experience seeing a measure of independence from Kechi after so long.

After her movie, she took a nap while Ulo and I had lunch at the coffee shop.

*First mother-daughter hug in five months.
We could not let go.*

For the rest of the day, we talked, and she watched her shows or movies, until it we were well into the night visit. Then I told Kechi it was time for our bible reading and fellowship.

We began with a prayer by Ulo, and then went on to have a discussion about the purpose of our lives and what God expects from us.

This led to a discussion of how Ulo and I became born again. The sharing was deeply meaningful and one of the things that Kechi wanted to know and talk about was what she and her friends always thought about in school - how they should enjoy life, party, have nice clothes, meet boys while they were young, and then when they got older, they would seek God and worship Him.

Ulo asked her, "How do you feel about that way of thinking, especially now?"

Kechi replied, "My thinking has totally changed. We thought we had all the time in the world, and then the plane crash happened."

Ulo and I assured her that changes in her life as a result of a closer relationship with God would be much more profound than the fleeting pleasures of clothes and parties. It had been a beautiful day and we praised God at the end of it.

Kechi was bright and very happy to see us the next morning, had done her exercises and was about to do her laps. I took a video of her walking around so that Ulo could show the family when she went home.

When she got back from her walk, we dressed her up, put her in the wheelchair and went outside. It was a cold day so we did not linger, but went into the coffee shop to sit and chat since she did not want anything. Jacquie joined us for a while before Kechi got tired and we went back to her room. She used the loo, and then we put her back into bed. She was feeling sleepy because she had been up again watching movies, so we made her comfortable and she drifted into sleep.

Ulo and I went to Cresta Mall to buy more movies for her. She was still sleeping when we got back around 3.30pm and the sister told us that she had not fed her, because Kechi so rarely slept well that she had been loath to wake her.

I warmed Kechi's lunch and then woke her up and fed her. Then we showed her the music videos we had bought and she had a wonderful time watching her favorite artistes.

I helped her to the loo again, and then she wanted to have a wash, so I called the sister in, and Ulo and I went off to find food.

When we were called back in, Kechi was clean and fresh, dressed in her pink shorts and top. We spent the rest of the evening talking and listening to music.

Dr. Pahad came in briefly to say that he was very happy with Kechi's progress and that she would be able to transfer to the general ward the following week. He also said that Dr. Nel was waiting for the last few spots to heal before starting the reconstructive surgery on her lips, eyes and neck. Then Dr. Pahad confessed to me that Kechi's situation had given him several sleepless nights and told Kechi that she had come a very long way.

We left at 9pm after prayers.

After praise and worship the following morning, the burden for the day was to speak life into Kechi's right fingers, and we did so at once.

Kechi was asleep, having stayed up until 2am. She was woken up when the therapists came, and she actually raised her upper body off the bed, swung her legs sideways off the bed by herself, before she was helped up to stand. Ulo and I were amazed. It seemed that there was progress every day.

After walking for some time, Kechi went back into bed and I had the pleasure of giving her a thorough wash, supervised by the sister in charge. It was a long process because there had to be two bowls of water, one soapy for washing, and the other clean water for rinsing. I put the washcloth in the soapy water, squeezed out excess fluid, and gently rubbed a particular spot, then squeezed out excess water from the washcloth in the other bowl, and used it to wipe the same area. Then I used a dry towel to blot. This was repeated several times over her whole body, turning her over, one side at a time, to do her back, carefully avoiding the areas with bandages or open wounds.

Needless to say, it was an exhausting process for both of us, but I was so happy to be taking care of her that way.

I put lotion on her skin and dressed her up, and she was so exhausted she decided to forgo her wheel chair ride, so we just stayed in the room and she slept in the middle of watching her musical videos.

That evening, we told stories of home and family, and she talked to Tara when Mom called.

Dr. Pahad came in and confirmed that Kechi would be going to the ward the following Monday. I spread the news and everyone rejoiced.

I looked back at the journey so far and was so very grateful that the day had finally come when Kechi would go to the general ward. What a journey it had been! God had been so very faithful and I knew that would never change.

Morning devotions the next day were full of praises to The Most High God. We just could not stop praising Him for His kindness and goodness concerning Kechi. The burden that day was to lift Bunmi, the other survivor, up to God and we did this, entreating God to be merciful to her and heal her fully.

As was now getting to be the norm, Kechi was fast asleep. The sister said she had had trouble falling asleep the previous night and had finally slept at 5am.

She strenuously resisted getting up for exercises and I had to speak sternly to her. She said she did not want to walk and I told her she had to. She punished me by crying throughout the exercises and walk.

I comforted her, brushed her teeth, and made her comfortable, and she soon went back to sleep.

Ulo and I took off again to find more stuff for her to watch and when we got back at 3 pm, she was still sleeping. I woke her, gave her a wash and then we all watched a movie.

Mom called because Tara wanted to sing a song she had just learned for Kechi. After the song, Kechi spoke with Mom, and also with her Dad.

The next day was going to be a big day in so many ways. It was so hard to put into words just how significant it was. Kechi had spent five months in Trauma Intensive Care Unit, and was finally on her way to the general ward. When she was admitted, she was not expected to survive. Now she was out of danger and well enough to leave 24/7 monitoring. To God be all the glory.

Dr. Nel came in to say that International SOS had called to find out Kechi's progress, and he told them that reconstruction was next, but he was waiting for the remaining sore spots to heal.

I asked him about the soreness of the skin on Kechi's neck and face and he said it was scar tissue and the pressure garments should take care of that.

When the shift leader came in, Kechi requested for Pindi to stay with her that night and Ranee agreed. She also told Kechi that Rochelle would be with her the following day until she went to the ward and Kechi relaxed even more. She was quite anxious about going to the ward, and nobody could blame her because the ICU had been her home for so long.

We sang and prayed and Kechi added a prayer about going to the general ward. She asked God for a smooth transition and that He should also remain with her there. We left her watching a movie.

Monday, May 8, 2006

The big day arrived at last!

Ulo and I glorified God and sang praise after praise to Him.

We saw Rochelle feeding a barely-awake Kechi. Apparently Kechi had slept late again. After breakfast, I took her to the loo and as soon as we got back to the room, the therapists arrived. She walked very well, barely supported, and then she went back to bed where Rochelle and I washed and changed her. She the sat on a chair while Rochelle made up her bed with fresh linen.

Kechi could not wait to get back into bed, and drifted back into sleep the second her head touched the pillow. Ulo took off to do some shopping, and I went to the waiting room.

Kechi woke up around 2pm and asked for a croissant, which I had ready for her. After that, I fed her lunch and we chatted for a while.

Dr. Pahad came in and asked Kechi if she was ready to go to the ward. Kechi said yes. I asked him if she would have a private room and he said she would because of the staph infection she had contracted from the septic CVP line.

I started packing up Kechi's stuff. She was not happy at all and started to cry at the thought of leaving the friends she had made in the ICU, especially

Rochelle. She also started to itch and complain about pain, and Rochelle gave her an injection for pain, which calmed her down.

Around 4pm, Ulo came in just in time for our exit from the ICU.

After five months, Kechi leaves ICU for general ward.
Kechi and the ICU nurses were in tears.

It was a very touching moment. All the sisters on duty gathered around Kechi's bed to wish her well. She was, of course, weeping, Ulo was crying, some of the sisters were crying. I took some pictures to remember the moment, but Kechi's ban on my crying was still in effect, and I held myself together.

Ward 6 was downstairs, and Kechi sat on a chair while her air mattress was transferred to the bed in the room, which was very nice and looked like a hotel room. The room was very cold, though, and I asked the sister to turn up the heat.

I had gotten Kechi a going-to-the-ward gift and she opened it and was very happy to see that I had bought her a digital camera. We took some pictures and Kechi got settled in.

However, when Rochelle left, Kechi's mood went from bad to worse, especially when we discovered that the TV was mounted into the ceiling and therefore, the DVD could not be connected to it. Ulo and I started to make calls at once to find out where we could borrow a TV from, or failing that, buy one. We told Kechi to give us until Wednesday and she nodded.

She had gone very quiet and moody.

The difference between the ICU and the ward was very clear already in the minimal attention that Kechi was receiving. I had to go and let the nurse know that Kechi's drugs were due. Ulo told me later that when I left, she had asked Kechi on her thoughts on her ward experience so far, and Kechi said she did not want to talk about it. Then she turned to Ulo and said she was scared. Ulo tried to reassure her and calm her down, but when I returned to the room, Kechi cried her eyes out. We let her cry to release all that emotion and then we started to minister to her, to remind her that she was never alone - Jesus was with her ALL the time. We told her that we would stay an extra hour that night just to settle her in.

She eventually settled down and we got her comfortable, got the sister to give her something for pain, and then finally left.

It was such a wrench leaving Kechi that night. I felt very depressed, until I received this in the car as we were going home,

"You released her to me when you thought she was dead, why would you not release her to me now that she is alive?"

A weight lifted off me and I relaxed. I knew God was still in charge and Kechi was safe in His hands. It was going to be a tough transition, but with God on my side, I would prevail.

The next morning, we laid all our burdens at the foot of the cross and repented of all our doubts and fears about Kechi's safety in the ward. Ulo received a word that we should be full of expectation and we received it with thanksgiving.

On our way out, Ulo asked Diedre if she had a small TV we could rent, and she said yes, she would take it out of storage that day and we could take it to the hospital the next day. Ask and you will receive, indeed!

Kechi was fast asleep, but woke long enough to reassure us that she had slept through the night. She reluctantly got up for her exercises and walked around the room, as the corridor was quite cold. I wondered why the ward was so cold. It was almost colder than the ICU. Ulo said she was going out to get Kechi some warm clothes; it was that cold.

Kechi slept after therapy until I woke her around 2pm. We ordered Chinese food and it came at the same time Ulo returned. Kechi really enjoyed the sweet and sour pork.

We watched some TV and then Kechi started to complain that her face was really painful. I believed that the skin was still contracting which was causing pulling on her face. She could not bear the pain and was given Pethidene at 4.30pm. The pain was back thirty minutes later, and by 6pm was unbearable. She sat up in bed, wailing uncontrollably. The sister came in and gave her Ativan, which calmed her, though the injection was quite painful being thicker than usual. The pain left and we all watched TV for a while. Ulo and I laid hands on Kechi and rebuked the pain.

Kechi and I began to recollect what had happened in the past. A commercial on TV reminded us of acticote dressing and we remembered how painful it used to be to remove acticote dressing during dressing change. We were amazed that we could now talk about it in past tense. We remembered the full body itch and Kechi also marveled that she could now talk about it in the past tense. She still itched now and then, but nothing close to the full body itch that used to drive her crazy. She said then that she had thought she would itch forever.

We had been through so much, and the road ahead was still long, but we had come along way, by the grace of God.

We dressed Kechi warmly as we prepared to leave her for the night. The neck of the top was tight, so I pulled on it until it stretched, but it was collarless, so it would not irritate her neck. Ulo had also bought socks and a woolen cap.

When Kechi came out from the loo, she said she wanted to try and stand on her own. With Ulo behind her, and my hands hovering around her, she balanced herself and stood for a few seconds on her own!

Her pride in herself was a sight to behold, and of course, Ulo and I showered her with praises and she was still grinning from ear to ear when we prayed and left.

CHAPTER THIRTY-FIVE

"He that dwelleth in the secret place of the Most High shall abide under the shadow of the Almighty"
Psalm 91 : 1(KJV)

Kechi had spent another night tossing and turning, and finally slept at 8am the next morning when she was given an injection to help her sleep. She woke briefly to tell us that she was very uncomfortable in the night and kept calling for assistance. And then the call button controller fell to the floor and she could not reach it, so she kept calling out loudly for the nurses to no avail. She finally gave up and just cried for a long time until she was exhausted and it was only at shift change that a nurse came in and gave her the injection.

Ulo and I decided that we had to find a way to secure the call button control to the bed permanently to prevent this from happening again.

As a result of not sleeping at night, Kechi was asleep the whole day and had to be woken twice to eat. She was ravenous because she had slept through breakfast. She could not be woken for exercises also, and I had to promise the therapist that I would walk her down the corridors myself. Luckily the corridor was a bit warmer that day. The previous day Kechi had bluntly refused to walk there because it was so cold. Kechi's room itself was an arctic zone and we had to bundle up quite warmly just to stay there, though it was warm outside.

Then one of the hospital Administrative staff saw me in the Pharmacy and asked how Kechi was doing in her new warm room. I thought she was pulling my leg at first, until after some confusing conversation, it dawned on both of us that Kechi was not in the room the lady thought she was in. Kechi was supposed to have been put in Room 13, opposite the one she was in, which was much sunnier and warmer. The lady said she would talk to the Unit Manager and arrange for Kechi to be moved.

Kechi finally stayed awake after eating by 4pm and we watched the movie, War of the Worlds, together. After the movie ended, the itching reminded us not to rejoice too soon and attacked in earnest. I began itch duty at once until about 8pm, when I called the sister and asked her to please give Kechi Ativan to make her relax and sleep.

By the time we were leaving at 9pm, she was a lot more relaxed and watching a movie. I told her not to stay up too late or else she would sleep the whole day again. She was a little teary when we left and I prayed that God would see us all through this transition period.

Earlier in the day, something unexpected happened. I had been trying to open an account since I came to South Africa, but to no avail, so I had given up. Then that afternoon, someone called Presh called me from Standard Bank and said he had been inundated with phone calls and emails concerning my account opening. He said that because of my peculiar circumstances regarding our stay in SA, their bank had decided to open the account for me, if I was still interested. He would come to the hospital the next day to see me, then come back the following Friday with the papers I would need to sign. He then asked where I was staying, saying that he would require a letter from my landlady stating how long I had been there for, and also my passport.

I asked if he was the branch manager of the Braamfontein branch I had been to and he said no, he was from the main branch.

Everyone I talked to, especially those who lived in SA, had told me it was impossible to open an account in SA without a work permit. I had doubts myself and only that morning had signed the Standard Chartered Bank, Nigeria form Ulo had come with. But God just shut us all up. Again.

Wearily, I repented yet again of my doubts. When would I ever learn that nothing was impossible for God? The only question I needed to ask was 'Is it in Your will to allow this, Lord'? Period.

I was determined to learn to trust God fully. I thanked Him for everything, and we left for the day.

Ulo had interviews the next morning from 11am to 3pm so she left as soon as we got to Kechi's room. Mamsie, one of the sisters on duty in the ward, told me that Kechi did not sleep well the previous night and was still asleep. This was not good news to me because it meant that for two days in a row, she stayed awake at night.

Dr. Pahad came in when Ulo left and said that Kechi had been itching that morning and he ordered Ativan and Phenergan for her, which was why she was so deeply asleep.

Kechi got up at 11am for breakfast, did her exercises, and then walked around for a bit. Then the therapist raised the bed high and Kechi held on to the bed with her hands and did some stretches. Then the lady removed Kechi's hands from the bed, and Kechi stood, unsupported and unassisted. Then being the daring dare devil she was, she made an attempt to move her foot and the therapist asked if she wanted to walk on her own and she said yes.

And then it happened!

With the therapist hovering behind Kechi, arms outstretched on either side to catch her, and I, rushing to face her, arms reaching out to catch her, Kechi took four steps towards me. When she got to me, we hugged tightly. Then the therapist told me to go and stand by the door and asked Kechi to walk to me. Kechi took fifteen steps to me unassisted, and another fifteen back to her bed. She sat on her bed for a little while, then lay down, exhausted, and was fast asleep in seconds.

While still fast asleep, Kechi was moved across the hall to Room 13. It did get some sun and was warmer than the previous room. Kechi slept through dressing change and woke up at 3.15pm, ravenous.

I had ordered lunch from Spurs, which would come at 4pm, but she could not wait and was crying for food so I rushed off to the coffee shop to get her a sandwich. By the time I came back, the deliveryman from Spurs was there, but Kechi still wanted the sandwich.

After eating, she relaxed again and watched an episode of Friends for a while. Ulo came in with Lanre about 6.30pm and Kechi walked ten unassisted steps for them, thrilling them.

We dressed her in a strapless top so as not to irritate her sore neck and right shoulder, and wrapped her warmly in blankets.

Ulo, Lanre and I prayed with her, and she was feeling sleepy when we left. Ulo gave her a big hug and told her not to forget everything they had talked about. Ulo was leaving the next day.

Lanre dropped us off and we finished Ulo's packing, and then went to bed early because Ulo had to leave at 5am the next morning.

It was exactly five months to the day since we came to Milpark Hospital, and God had been with us every step of the way, through all the different stages.

Ulo left at 5am after our prayers and I went back to sleep. I woke at 7.30am, washed Kechi's nightclothes, and left for the hospital.

Kechi was awake and a huge smile lit her face when I came in. She was looking well rested and said she had slept through the night. Dr. Nel had come in already to tell her she was going to the OR by 2pm that day for her lip contracture release. Also, pillows were banned for her. She was to lay her head flat on the bed so that her neck could stretch. She actually felt much better because her neck had stopped aching since she started lying flat.

Also, Dr. Fletcher had come in with the pressure sleeve for Kechi's left arm. She, however, could not fit the sleeve for the fingers because Kechi had picked at and removed a scab that had not been ready to come off and there was now a sore there. She took back the facemask to adjust the strip under the nose, which was pressing into Kechi's nostrils. She also showed us how to use the gel strip for Kechi's nose since it was too sensitive for a pressure garment. It was pressed directly on the nose and was held in place by a gel substance. It was also very expensive - R800 per sheet!

Maya, the therapist, came in and ramped up Kechi's exercise by adding some really strenuous presses, squats and lunges. With a lot of puffing and panting, Kechi was able to do most of them, and gratefully lay back in bed to rest and watch TV for a while until her neck and the left side of her face started to hurt.

I pressed the nurse call button, and the nurse who came in was more interested in staring at Kechi's face than in asking why we rang. I spoke sharply to her, telling her to please call someone to give Kechi something for pain. She turned to me, looked me up and down, and said that she had to put off the call button first.

I waited an age, with Kechi still crying, and then went out to the nurse's station. Obviously, the nurse who had come in had decided that we could go to hell, for all she cared.

I saw a much nicer nurse who looked at Kechi's chart, saw that she had surgery scheduled for later that day, and said she would call the anesthetist to find out what was safe to give Kechi. I went back and explained all this to Kechi, but she had already cried for about fifteen minutes and was upset at the nurse that came in and at everybody, and I could not calm her down, no matter what I said.

She also said she did not want to get surgery that day because she was not sure about how she would get the sedative since her CVP line had been removed. I told her that she should not worry about that because I was sure that the doctors were experienced enough to know what to do. But Kechi was on a roll and nothing I said worked.

Finally the anesthetist came in and told the nurse to give Kechi Tramal, and then proceeded to calm her fears about anesthesia by telling her he would either put a mask over her nose to put her to sleep, or start another line, if necessary.

Kechi was taken in at 2.15pm and at 4.30pm I was paged to go to the recovery room. I could hear Kechi even before I got inside, wailing loudly. She had just been given Pethidene and was crying for dormicum. The anesthetist asked for her to be given the drug and she slept off shortly after and I was told that they would keep her in the recovery room for a while to keep an eye on her.

At 6.30pm, four hours after she was wheeled into the OR, Kechi was taken back to her room. She was hungry and asked for cocoa and croissants, which I hurried off to get. By the time I rounded the corner heading to Kechi's room, I could hear her sobbing.

Kechi was not a quiet sobber I hurried into her room and saw that Dr. Opolot was there. He told the nurses to give her Pethidene and Ativan, and then he pulled me aside to explain that Kechi was dependent on pain pills and this had affected her pain threshold. They would have to work hard to find a balance between keeping her pain under control, while weaning her from her dependency.

Kechi was given the drugs, and when she calmed down, I fed her, or tried to. She could hardly open her mouth because of the huge bandage running from under her lower lip down to her neck. She tried several times to open her mouth, and when she could not, she was about to start crying again. I told her not to cry, I would find a way.

I compressed the bread until it was almost flat and then pushed it between her lips and she chewed. Thrilled at her success, she ate all three croissants happily until we ran into another snag; she could not open her mouth for the straw. Before she could start crying again, I pressed the tip of the straw flat, and pushed it between her teeth and told her to close her lips around it. Bit by bit, a little noisily, she drank the whole cup of cocoa.

Dr. Nel and the anesthetist came in for a post-op exam of Kechi, and the doctor explained that what they had started on Kechi was reconstructive surgery. They released the contractions on the right side of her neck and her lower lip and covered the sites with artificial skin, which would be integrated into her body. In about four weeks, she would need skin grafts to cover the artificial skin, which was not as soft and pliable as normal skin. He made the decision to start reconstruction because Kechi's neck and lip were causing a functional problem as her mouth was hanging open and she could not straighten her neck, causing her head to be permanently bowed. He said they would probably do the same thing on her cheeks, but reminded us that it was getting very hard to find donor sites; worst case scenario, they would put a balloon under her skin and grow new skin for her cheeks.

He would release the contraction on the other side of the neck later, but for now, Kechi would go back to the theater the following Monday to expose the surgery site and possibly replace the huge bandage currently on her neck with a pressure bandage. He stressed that it was very important for Kechi to begin to wear her pressure garments and splints as often as possible to facilitate better healing.

After the doctors left, I cleaned Kechi up, straightened her bed linen, and tucked her in comfortably, then I prayed and said good night.

Kechi wanted to start crying, but I asked her to please be strong. I stayed for a little while, and when she started drifting off I left, torn. A part of me wanted to stay the night with her, and I had actually put my toothbrush in my bag, but common sense prevailed. If I started now, when would it end? Kechi would expect it every night, and I needed the down time by myself or else I was going to break down. So I forced myself to leave and to trust God to take care of Kechi.

After a largely sleepless night, I got up and threw myself down before God and bared my heart to him, surrendering all my fears, doubts, and worries to Him, and then begged Him to please remove or reduce Kechi's pain, and then I cast out the spirit of fear from Kechi and from me. I felt very tired and achy that morning, and forced myself to eat a bowl of cereal, because I remembered that I had felt faint in the recovery room the previous day.

But then my friend, Nkechi Anyaehie, (now of blessed memory) called me from Aba and told me that she and some of my friends from Aba had contributed $800.00 to help out in our expenses and would give it to Mike to send to me. I was overwhelmed yet again by the love and support being poured on us.

When I got to the hospital, the sister told me that Kechi was finding it hard to find a comfortable position because of her neck and was given something to help her sleep.

She was still sleeping soundly and the bed was in an unusual position with the foot raised and the head lowered and she did look very comfortable.

But when she woke up, the rest of the day was fraught with tension and tears as she was in pain the whole time. But the good thing was that the doctor had left instructions for her to be given pain medication on demand, and no sooner did we call the nurses than they came armed with their syringes of relief!

In spite of the pain medications, though, Kechi was very uncomfortable and could not find a good position to lay her head, flat on her back or on her side. The side was slightly better, though. I decided to give her a treat and ordered lunch from Ocean Basket, because Kechi loved seafood, and she ate every bite.

When it was time for me to leave, she began to cry and I told her that she was not being fair to the both of us, and I would be there in the morning, as always. I told her that I would pray for her to have a very restful night. When I left, she was still crying and my heart was breaking, but I forced myself to go and leave her in the safest hands possible - God's.

That night, I entreated God earnestly from the bottom of my heart to give Kechi rest that night. She really needed to sleep and she was really tired of being awake at night. I prayed that she would sleep and forget her worries, her pain, her neck, everything, and just rest.

The next morning, Kechi was asleep when I got to her room, and my heart sank, thinking she had been awake until late again, but she woke up when she heard my voice and said that she slept well the previous night. And then, smiling, she said that now that I had come, her day could begin.

She had refused to be fed by the nurses, telling them that her Mom would feed her. I warmed her eggs and fed her, after which I had to call the sister to give her something for pain.

She slept until lunch and then asked for ribs, which I had to veto because with the bandages, she would not be able to chew it properly. She opted for fish and I ordered from Ocean Basket again, though she refused to eat the fries saying she was sick of fries.

We spent a very pleasant afternoon, and she told me a lot of stories about some of the antics she and her friends got up to in school. Kechi missed her school and her friends a whole lot. We talked about prom and she said she was still praying hard that she could make it. I knew it was not going to be possible, but I did not want to burst her bubble. Kechi was going to have to reach that conclusion on her own so that it would be easier for her to deal with it. So I let her go on and on about her dress, showing me the sketch Nkechi had made for her when she came, and she worried that there was not enough time to make it. I knew that not making it to her prom would be a major blow because she saw it as the last opportunity to see all her friends together in one place again. She was right, but it was out of our hands.

Through the stories Kechi told, she revealed so much of herself that I did not know, and we drew even closer to each other, if that was possible, given how close we already were.

I told her that I needed her to stop crying when it came time for me to leave for the day because it broke my heart, and left her upset. I explained that I had to leave so I could rest and thus remain strong enough to cater to all her needs the next day. I asked her if she did not realize that it killed me to leave her at night.

I also told her that a few days before, as I was leaving, I called Ulo and asked her to please give me good reasons why I should not just stay back with Kechi at night.

Ulo gave me three reasons:

1. Kechi was not alone.
2. I had to stay healthy to be able to look after her.
3. There was really nothing I could do for her during the night.

I was not fully convinced by what Ulo said, but I did not tell Kechi that.

What I did tell her was that she should not be upset that I did not stay, because ultimately, the fact that I was leaving was for her own good.. I asked her how she would feel if the nurse came one morning and told her that I had called to say I was ill and would be away for several days. I think she got the message because she promised to behave better.

She soon started crying from pain again and was given a shot, which relaxed her and I tucked her in for the night, and after we prayed, put in a movie for her and prepared to leave. She was anxious about going to the OR and only relaxed when I reminded her that she was only going for dressing change, not surgery. I also reminded her that her Dad was coming the following day with his sister, her Aunty Kate, to see her, and she cheered up even more.

CHAPTER THIRTY-SIX

"When thou passest through the waters, I will be with thee; and through the rivers, they shall not overflow thee: when thou walkest through the fire, thou shalt not be burned; neither shall the flame kindle upon thee." Isaiah 43 : 2(KJV)

Mike called from the airport at 5.30am the next morning, and I told him to look out for Franz, the cab driver I had sent to pick them up. They came in about two hours later and it was so good to see them, especially Kate, who had always been not just a sister in law, but also a good friend to me. It was so lovely to have company once again.

After they showered and rested for a bit, we left for the hospital. Kechi was asleep, but she heard her Daddy's voice and woke up with a smile. After hugs all round, she dozed off again until the therapists woke for up. Maya was very insistent on her getting up, though Kechi was dragging her feet, insisting that Kechi had not walked for two days, and they would soon lose all the forward progress if Kechi stopped persevering.

Groaning and moaning, and crying a little, Kechi did her exercises, but soon got into her stride, with encouragement from all of us. She went right back to bed after physio, but soon woke up to pain. She was given a shot and went back to sleep.

She had a theater procedure that afternoon - change of dressing, so she was NPO (nil per oral), which meant she had not had anything but a cup of tea early that morning. Then at about 1pm, Dr. Nel and the anesthetist came in to see her and explain that she would now go in for her procedure at 5pm. Kechi was not happy at all and neither was I. She got something for pain at 3pm and an hour later she was crying again. She cried hard and long, but I knew that she would get nothing more since she was going in at 5pm. The sister on duty took the time to come and explain to Kechi that being so close to theater time, anything she got then would clash with the anesthetics she would get in the theater and she may not wake up after surgery. She calmed down briefly, but then began to wail again from 4.30pm until 5.30 pm, when she was wheeled into OR. Mike left the room, he had never been able to bear Kechi in pain and this was getting to him.

Kechi came back to her room about 7.15 pm, still a little weepy, but hungry. I had anticipated her request for cocoa and croissants, and had them ready for her. She then got her drugs and I made her comfortable, tucking her in, and putting on her show before we left.

Dr. Nel met us outside on his way into Kechi's room and said he was pleased with the healing of the sites they had exposed and that there would be no more surgery for at least three weeks, while it healed. We were exhausted and left at about 9.30pm.

Kechi was groggy when we came in the next morning, and said she had not had a good night because she could not find a comfortable position. Since she was looking sleepy, I encouraged her to sleep, telling her we would be right there when she woke up. Then I rushed off to Campus Square mall and bought two sweaters for Kechi. It was actually the beginning of winter in South Africa, and the temperature had begun to drop.

When I got back, Maya was just getting Kechi out of bed for physical therapy and Kechi was, of course, crying. She cried throughout the walking, the standing and sitting exercises. Maya forced her to straighten her neck and look straight ahead something she had not been able to do before the last surgery. For the first time, Kechi had her head up like a normal person.

Maya put her back in bed, with the back of her shoulders resting on a folded towel to force the neck to stretch. This was very painful for Kechi, but Maya insisted. I fed Kechi her breakfast and she got something for pain, and from there, the day went to pieces.

Kechi pretty much cried for the whole day. First it was because of the pain. Then it was because the pillows had been removed and she could not find a comfortable position that did not strain her neck. Then it was one thing or the other, and in the end she cried so much that she tired herself out. Mike and I left her to cry herself hoarse, and when she could not cry anymore, we started to talk to her about learning to leave everything to God, and reaching out to Him and trust Him with all her problems. We talked at length about how she needed to make the effort to get really close to God and I felt that some of what we said to her that day sunk in.

She got something for pain, but for some reason, the pain medications were not working very well that day. Kechi cried so much that I thought she would make herself ill.

Needless to say I was an emotional wreck. Watching Kechi in so much anguish all day long was destroying me inside, but I had to appear strong, and to comfort her and not let her see what her sorrow was doing to me.

I must have aged ten years that day.

Eventually she got enough drugs to relax her and we tucked her in and had a fervent prayer session around her bed, committing her to God, and banishing pain from her, entreating God to give her a peaceful slumber.

Then we left her in God's hands.

The next day was more of the same. Kechi was asleep until Maya came in for exercises. She cried during exercises and after, until she got something for pain.

Then the bandage on her head started to itch and she began to move her head from side to side, and also to rub her head with her hand.

This distressed Mike and he kept pleading with her to stop, but she did not. Mike kept pacing up and down the room and eventually went outside.

Kechi said that Dr. Nel said she was going back to the OR on Friday for dressings change. I noticed that the swelling on her mouth from the surgery had gone down and the shape of her mouth was more apparent. She was distracted enough to ask for a mirror and was happy at what she saw. Also, she was beginning to look up more, and was gradually getting accustomed to not having a pillow for her neck, though she complained a lot about that.

When the pain started again, Kechi started to wail and thrash about on her bed and Mike and I went through the process of talking to her again. When she calmed down a bit, Mike left the room and I sent Ulo a text, telling her that Kechi was having a bad day. Ulo responded that it was time Kechi realized that I could not be God for her. She needed to know how weak and dependent on God I was, so that she too could start to lean on Him.

I acted on this advice and had a long chat with Kechi, right in the middle of one crying jag. I must have sounded really serious and earnest, because she stopped crying to listen.

When I spoke about how she should try and establish a relationship with God by talking to Him from time to time, she said to me,

"I do. I talk to Him mostly at night when I can't sleep or I'm in pain and He does not answer".

"Listen," I said, "God does not answer us the way we expect. The important thing is to have absolute trust and belief in Him."

I gave her some examples from my life and how I had learnt to depend on God. I told her it was a process and she had to work towards perfecting it. I talked in this vein at length and I believed that some of it got through to Kechi.

After that, the day pretty much ended in pain, tears, injections, and then calm.

When we left, there was no car to pick us up, and when I called Diedre she was angry, and said I had made the others late for their dinner because they had been waiting for us. I was too weary to deal with all that, so we just called a cab. I know there was always a problem when I had more than one person staying with me, but at that moment, I really could not muster the energy to be upset.

The next morning, Kechi was awake and beaming with smiles when we walked in. She had slept well and was full of energy. Needless to say, we all heaved sighs of relief at seeing the Kechi we were more familiar with emerge. Kechi had never been a weepy child. Her sunny disposition had always endeared

her to everyone around her, and that was why I was so distressed at all the crying she was doing. It was not in her nature at all.

She had actually let the nurses feed her with cereal and eggs at the normal early breakfast time before I came, so she was ready for her mid morning snack of croissants and cocoa The upbeat mood continued when Maya came for physical therapy. She took a look at Kechi's face, did a double take and quipped, 'Kechi is back!' This was the Kechi they were used to.

She did her exercises so cheerfully that Kate and I whipped out cameras and took several pictures of her. She stood straight and tall and did all she was asked to do without complaining. After physio, we sat on the patio outside her room for a while until it got chilly.

Some friends of ours, Wangi and Chinenye, had come in from Nigeria for an appointment with Dr. Nel. Wangi had been in a terrible accident and was only alive by the grace of God.

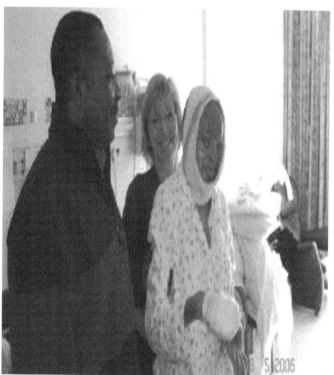

Kechi with her Dad and Maya, the physical therapist.

We all thanked God for saving her life, and then she showed us pictures of the way she had looked just after the crash. They stayed and chatted for a while, and then Mike and Chinenye went to Dr. Nel's offices to get an appointment for Wangi.

That afternoon, we got a visit from a psychiatrist, Dr. Ryan.

Dr. Edwards had called him in since it was being suspected that Kechi's pains were more mental than physical. Indeed I had wondered why, almost a week after surgery, Kechi was still feeling so much pain. I had concluded that it was because this was her first post-ICU surgery without morphine and dormicum.

Dr. Ryan said that Kechi had been on an anti-depressant, which was pretty much standard for patients who had undergone the kind of trauma Kechi had. But he felt that Kechi was a naturally high-spirited and bubbly person and should not be on drugs that made her even higher strung. He believed that the drug was preventing her from sleeping at night. We affirmed that Kechi had the kind of personality he described and he went on to say that the pain-killers were being used too frequently, and had gone ahead to limit the use of Pethidene. In fact, he had stopped the Ativan, but Dr. Pahad, who knew his patient better, prescribed it again.

Dr. Ryan said he was taking Kechi off the anti-depressants and prescribing what he called a mild mood relaxer, starting that night.

As far as I was concerned, Kechi was in God's hands, and He was totally in control and anything she was being given was allowed by Him. Period.

One major cry jag later, an injection, and Kechi got settled for the night. We left at the normal time, which was early for us, so that Diedre did not get angry again.

Kechi was sleeping the next morning when we got to her room, having slept at 1am. Maya woke her, but she was so grumpy and cross that she just walked her around the room a few times, and then made her stand for a short while. After she put Kechi back in bed, she told the sister to inform the night staff to give Kechi the sleeping pill no later than 7pm, since it took three hours to take effect. Kechi had been given the pill at 10pm.

Susan, the Occupational Therapist, came in to measure Kechi for her leg pressure garments, and in her discussion with Maya, I learned that for scars as deep as Kechi's, she would have to wear the garments for two years, because that was how long it would take the scars to mature. Apparently the scars would keep growing and hardening for that period and the garments were supposed to keep them soft and supple so they did not dry out and become permanently raised.

Maya suggested that Susan should talk to Kechi about the importance of wearing the garments all the time so that she would appreciate the seriousness of the whole thing. She had brought a strap thing that Kechi could wear on her hand and put a fork or spoon through it so that she could feed herself.

As she put Kechi back in bed, Maya noticed that she was limping, favoring her right leg. Upon investigation, she noticed a keloid forming at the back of Kechi's right knee, off to one side and very sensitive to touch. She told Susan to make the pressure garment come all the way up, past that knee to press down the keloid. Then she put a towel on the back of Kechi's shoulders to force her head back.

Kechi stayed like this for a while and then she got tired and hungry. Her hunger was a problem because she had an OR procedure that day and for some reason, the sisters did not know this and therefore had not given her the usual toast and tea at 6am which was all she ate on OR days. I asked the sister on duty if she could find out what time Kechi was going in so that we would see if it was going to be possible to give her some clear juice to hold her. The shift leader was a gem, and bumped Kechi to the top of the list when there was a cancellation and Kechi ended up going in at 2pm.

She got out an hour and a half later and slept for another hour before waking up to eat.

There was a pressure garment under her chin, fastening at the top of the head to keep the bandages in place. Kechi said it was really tight and uncomfortable and started to cry. When I undid it, her relief was palpable. I put it back on and called the sister to see for herself how tight it was. She removed it at once and said she would ask for a bigger size in the morning.

❖

Maybe if I had known the drama that would take place the next day, I would have stayed in bed.

It all started when we walked into Kechi's room and she informed us grumpily that the night had been terrible, she had not slept a wink until they washed her that morning. When she dropped off to sleep, I took the opportunity to go out and buy some groceries.

As I walked towards Kechi's room, I noticed movement and activity, and of course, heard Kechi crying. My heart sinking, I rushed in and she was in the middle of throwing a tantrum.

Apparently she had woken up and I was not there, so she refused to be fed by anyone, insisting that she would only eat when I got there and fed her myself.

Kechi was very upset at me and told me that I knew how much she depended on having me nearby all the time. I calmly explained to her that I had other things to do, and always tried to be there for her. After a while she calmed down and I fed her.

When she started to feel pain, they gave her tablets, which took longer to take effect. She rode out the pain for almost an hour waiting for the drugs to take effect, and when she wanted to start crying, I unwisely told her that she knew that crying did not solve anything.

The dam broke, buried feelings coming to the fore.

"You don't know how sad it makes me feel to hear you say that. You know that I don't like to make noise and cry, but that is the only way I can give vent to my feelings. When you and Dad say things like that, or tell me that I can control the pain if I put my mind to it, you hurt me because that tells me that you have no idea how much pain and discomfort I'm going through".

I reassured her that we only said such things because we believed so much in her and her abilities that we sometimes forgot she was only sixteen.

"I have never underestimated your pain, Kechi" I told her. "I'm sorry if we gave the impression that we did." I spent some more time calming her down and then asked,

"Do you feel better now that you have unburdened yourself?" She nodded. We watched a movie while I fed her, and by the time Kate and Mike came in, her mood had improved.

Dr. Opolot and his wife had invited Mike, Kate and I to dinner that evening, but Kechi bluntly refused to let me go, and to forestall tears, I asked them to go on without me.

At the end of the movie, I asked Kechi to pray and she said a lovely prayer about how grateful she was for the strength she had that day to be able to resist the pain for a while, and that she knew that strength came from God. She prayed for a good night's rest and for her Dad to have a safe journey home the next day. She then asked for God's blessings on her family and friends.

She was going to get the new drug that night and it would hopefully make her sleep.

I went back to the guesthouse alone that night because the doctor was going to drop Mike and Kate off later. I packed up my summer clothes for Mike to take home, and as soon as they came in, I fell fast asleep.

We went to the hospital with Mike's stuff, since he was going to leave from there. Kechi looked so peaceful asleep that it seemed a shame to wake her, but I had to feed her. Kechi had now established a routine with the nurses. They only woke her to wash her and change the linen. Her breakfast was left on the stand until I came and fed her.

After eating, she asked to use the loo, and then I walked her up and down the room several times. Her right leg was really becoming a problem. The keloid was tightening up and now, try as much as she could, that leg refused to straighten all the way. She now had a noticeable limp.

After the rest of the exercises, she asked to be taken back to the loo and this time she had the runs. She was so weak after that she almost slumped in my arms. I picked her up and carried her to her bed.

She cried a bit, got her tablets, and then napped for about an hour.

When she woke up, the real action started.

Kechi cried long and hard, thrashing around, sitting up and throwing herself back down, absolutely refusing to be consoled. I just held onto her and let her cry, making sure she did not harm herself as she threw her limbs about.

Kate tried to console her, telling her that God was with her, and she lashed out at Kate yelling, "He is not with me. He doesn't listen to me when I pray".

Putting myself in her shoes, I could understand her frustration, and I was sure God did too, for He saw her heart. But this was now a dilemma for me because I did not know whether to keep talking to her or just stop and leave it all to God.

When the crying was at its peak, Sister Sally came in and asked for Kechi to be given Neurolgin to calm her down. Kechi at first bluntly refused to take the tablets, but then she took them and asked Sister Sally to tell the doctor to give her dormicum. The sister said she would, but then she removed the pillow that Kechi insisted on using and told her that if she did not stretch her neck, it was going to contract again and she would need another surgery.

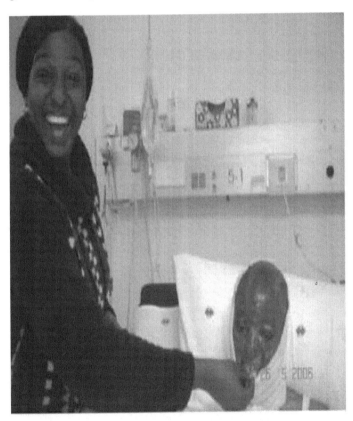

Kechi being fed by her Aunty Kate.

Kechi agreed to remove the pillow in the hope that the doctor would order dormicum for her. She continued to moan and whimper, even when a prayer group came in to minister to her and pray.

After they left, I fed her and she got Tramal and drifted off. She woke up hungry, and Kate went off to buy cocoa and croissants. After eating, we tucked her in, prayed with her and left her watching 'Oceans Twelve'.

Nkechi called at 10.30pm to say that Mike had arrived in Lagos. I thanked her because she knew I would not sleep until I was sure he was home safe.

I woke up feeling lonesome, missing Mike. Kate and I prayed and went off to the hospital, and saw a bright Kechi sitting up in bed. She informed us happily that she slept very well and her eyes were a testament to that, as they were bright and alert. She said she was determined that it was going to be a good day, and no matter what time she went into the OR, she would keep her spirits up.

I was very happy to hear this and we prayed and read the bible together, and when the pain came, she was given Ativan, then it was time for physio. I had earlier massaged behind her right knee where the tight keloid was forming because the leg could no longer straighten fully, and she walked with a noticeable limp. The massage seemed to have helped and the exercises went on smoothly.

We maneuvered Kechi into a comfortable position on her bed, and she relaxed enough to watch a music video. The previous day, Kechi had asked Kate to make puff-puff (fried dough balls) for her, and we told her that she had to let us go to the store and buy the ingredients. So after she had another drug for pain, she asked us to go while she slept.

Kechi actually asking us to leave her? That showed how much she craved the snack.

Just then my Mom called to give me the shocking news that Ngozi's Mom had passed away in Los Angeles. I was stunned, because I did not remember Ngozi ever saying that her Mom was ill, and in fact, she had just been to Nigeria on a visit. I called Ngozi at once and commiserated with her.

Kate and I rushed to the store and were back within the hour. By the time we got back a little before 2pm, Kechi's room was empty. She had been taken into the theater in our absence. I reflected that it was a good thing that we had gone to the store with her blessing, or she would not have been happy with us. She came out at about 4pm moaning a bit with her eyes closed, but when she heard my voice she turned her head and said, 'Mommy'.

We followed her to the room only to discover that Kechi had been moved again to Room 5 because the last rooms were for breast cancer patients. Anyway, Kechi moaned again at changing rooms and insisted that we arranged everything the way it was in the former room.

She was hungry and I was ready with noodles and boiled eggs and after eating, she drifted off to sleep. She slept at 4.30pm, and was still sleeping when we left at 8.30pm. I was a bit apprehensive about leaving while she slept, because of how upset she got when she woke up and I was not there. She looked so peaceful, though, so I decided to risk it. Besides, it had been a draining day and I was exhausted.

CHAPTER THIRTY-SEVEN

"Be of good courage, and he shall strengthen your heart, all ye that hope in the LORD."
Psalm 31 : 24 (KJV)

Kechi was just stirring in bed when we went into her room the next morning. She said she slept through the night from 4.30pm the previous day. In fact, she had slept through her washing, and only woke up just as we walked in. She seemed bright and cheerful, but just as she finished her breakfast, the nurse came in to deliver some news and the day went south from there.

Dr. Nel had ordered daily dressing changes in Kechi's room!

Kechi began to cry as soon as she heard this and proceeded to scream throughout the dressing change. I had to don gloves and assist since it quickly became obvious that the nurse could not cope by herself, because Kechi was making so much noise. I asked the nurse to wet the bandages to make them easier to peel off Kechi's face. We re-bandaged Kechi's face and put back the chinstrap.

Then the next round of crying started when she asked for her pain drugs and was given tablets. The nurse said that Pethidene was now restricted to twice daily and she had already had a dose that morning. Kechi started screaming and crying again, demanding to see the doctor. She carried on for so long that I decided to see the doctor before she made herself ill. Besides, I also wanted to know why they would restrict her pain drugs when she was now getting daily dressing changes in her room.

Sister Helen, whom I had asked to get the doctor, came in to look at Kechi's chart and discovered that the other sister had the chart open to the wrong day, and that the doctor had in fact increased Pethidene to four-hourly. Sister Helen apologized profusely, and Kechi calmed down enough to eat the puff-puffs that Kate had made for her early that morning. She enjoyed them so much that she ate six that morning!

Wangi and Chinenye came visiting after Wangi's appointment with Susan, the Occupational Therapist. She would also have to wear pressure garments, and a splint on her hand.

When they left, Kechi got her shot and relaxed to watch King Kong. Halfway through the movie, she started to itch and to have pain, and got something for it. Towards the end of the movie, close to our leaving time, Kechi got very agitated and started to itch and to cry. I told her to relax because I believed that her itching was a reaction to being left alone. I did my best to calm her down, but she just kept on crying. I was at my wits end, and finally told her that she was going to make me cry. She got even more agitated and gripped my hand,

'Mommy, don't cry. Promise me that you won't cry. I'll be okay.

I'll stop crying, but please don't cry'.

I promised her that I would not cry and she calmed down and allowed us to leave without any more drama. It shook me up to see how disturbed Kechi was at the thought of my crying and I decided there and then that I would never, as long as Kechi was in that hospital, ever give her the impression that I was not strong. I understood now that she was entirely dependent on my strength and until the day that God moved that dependence to Himself, I would not fail her, God helping me.

I left with a heavy heart, after calling the nurse to give Kechi her 8pm drugs.

I was no longer sleeping well. For the past two nights, I had been having meaningless dreams, waking up un-refreshed. I admitted to myself that I was a bit worried about the current stage of Kechi's healing. Aside from the pain and itching, I felt that the constant crying came from Kechi's frustration, rage, anger, grief and so on. Everything was coming to a head inside her and she cried as a release for all the pent up emotions. I did not need to be a psychiatrist to know that the dam had burst. Kechi had always prided herself on her ability to be flexible and adaptable, but she was sixteen years old and had experienced something most people did not experience in their whole lifetime.

All I could do was to continue to intercede for her and hedge her around with prayers.

Mom called very early to tell me that she had received messages for us.

"Kechi is to realize that God has never left her side ever since this whole ordeal and has great plans for her life, but they will not hinder her from being a teenager. She will sing and dance and do what people her age do, but with a lot more maturity than her peers because of her experiences. These months of hospitalization are meant to remind her of the enormity of the miracle He performed on her and to keep Him in the forefront of her mind at all times. His word for her when the accident happened still stands - He will restore her whole."

To me Mom said that God had told her to tell me that I should never waver in my trust in Him for He would continue to strengthen me; I should know that the prayers of my family and brethren from around the world were sustaining me. I was to continue to hold on to God, and would be ministered to from time to time on what to do.

This was a wonderful ministration and had come just when I needed it. I was very relieved, and gave God all the glory before getting up to prepare for the hospital in a much lighter frame of mind.

Kechi was awake, but a bit drowsy. At first she said she had slept well when I asked her, but I saw through the lie and told her to tell me how she really was. She admitted that she did not sleep well, but just did not want me to worry or be sad that she was not feeling okay. I told her to stop protecting me, I was the adult and the one who should be doing the protecting, not her.

She said she was in pain and I went to look for the sister. Annie said she could not give Kechi anything for pain since she had the pills and both injections at 6am. She could only get Tramal and the other analgesic at 12pm. Pethidene was not prescribed at all for that day.

This brought a flood of tears from Kechi. She thought everyone was just being mean to her. I went to enquire how it would be possible to dress her wounds without Pethidene and it turned out there was no dressing change that day, which was why there was no need for Pethidene.

Kechi cried and railed against everyone, but took her pills, and I tried to explain that they were trying to make her stop the shots and rely more on tablets as a way of preparing her for going home. After a while the tablets began to work and she calmed down, then took a nap.

When the physical therapists came in, I persuaded them to give her thirty more minutes to sleep. Still, Kechi was in no mood for them and protested about her lack of sleep the night before. Maya was a no-nonsense person, and soon had Kechi, crying and protesting, out of bed. This was too painful for me to watch so I went off to the coffee shop to get a cup of coffee and calm down.

When I got back, the exercises were over and Kechi, still crying, had been put in a chair to sit for thirty minutes. She was still crying so hard that I helped her up from the chair and back into bed. After a while she calmed down and drifted off into sleep.

Janet came in with the pressure bandage leggings for Kechi and put them on her, as well as the glove for the left hand.

Maya came in to tell me that she had discussed the keloid behind Kechi's knee with Dr. Nel, who said that he did not want to operate on Kechi for now. They decided on a combination of physical therapy, pressure bandage, and a leg brace. If all failed, then he would operate. But he pointed out that in the OR, in a fully relaxed position, the leg straightened fully. Maya said this was because the foot was pointed. When the foot was flexed, the keloid prevented it from straightening. The brace would be brought in later that day.

The previous day, Maya had explained what actually happened during skin grafting in some detail to Kechi and I. The artificial skin grafted into her neck would actually be infused with blood vessels and after healing would require a skin graft from Kechi's own skin on top of it because it was not as malleable and soft as normal skin. The advantage of using artificial skin for contracture release was that normal skin would contract again requiring several more surgeries, while the artificial skin would not contract, and would need just one skin graft to cover it once it had been integrated into the body.

Maya also explained why the grafted skin had diamond shaped markings. Apparently when the skin was removed from the donor site, it was then put in a machine, which rolled and stretched it, and cut little holes in it. These holes allowed the surgeon to stretch the skin to fit the area it was to be grafted unto. That way a small quantity of skin could fit an area larger than it.

It was pretty fascinating.

Kechi was asleep when the leg brace was brought and the man put it on her leg, marked it at various points before taking it away to customize it. When he brought it back a little later, Kechi cried a little at the inconvenience of being woken up, then slept through the rest of the fitting.

Since Kechi had been pleading incessantly for me to spend a night with her, I started to make enquiries about how possible it was. Sister Glen promised to talk to the hospital manager and get back to me. She also said she thought it was a good idea for someone to stay with Kechi at night.

I wondered how this would work out for me in terms of going back at night to unwind from the pressures of the day. But seeing as I had not been sleeping well, it may not be a bad idea to try being with Kechi at night and see if both of us could relax and rest better. My request was approved and the nurse told me that the hospital would provide a roll away bed and blankets. When Kechi started to get tearful as I got ready to leave, I reminded her that she had Friday to look forward to, when I would spend the night with her, and she subsided.

We prayed together and on my way out, I called on the night sister to give Kechi her drugs. I always did this, because the ward nurses were so much busier than the ICU nurses and more than once I had discovered that I needed to direct their attention to Kechi. I did not blame them, they would eventually get to her on their own, but most times reminding them helped, and they did not seem to mind, and Kechi never told me anything about the nurses in the ward yelling at her or being unkind for any reason.

Kechi was tearful when we got to the hospital the next morning. Her call button was not working and she had to yell for the sister when she needed anything. I consoled her and made her comfortable. I was asked to leave at 10am, so that her neck area would be exposed for Dr. Nel to take a look at it.

When he came out, he said that the wound was still a bit septic, but the infection seemed to be under control with antibiotics and the daily betidene dressings. Infection was a problem that ICU patients usually had because of the bugs they picked up from the unit, but he assured me that they were on top of it. He said also that he agreed with Sister Glen, the Unit Manager, that since she was having daily dressings, she still needed to get Pethidene.

When I went in, Kechi's neck was still exposed and I took a close look. The pus I had seen a few days before was gone, and the wound looked dry and clean, and I got to see the artificial skin. According to Maya, a packet of 10 strips of artificial skin cost R50, 000! This was a testimony to the glory of God upon Kechi, because they must have gotten permission from Shell before using such expensive stuff on Kechi. It still blew my mind how much Shell was doing for Kechi. Mike and I had decided long ago that there was nothing we could ever do to repay Shell except to continue to pray for the company and for everyone in it that had a part in making the decision to save our daughter's life. Another thing we could do was to pay it forward, never losing any opportunity to help anyone we could in any way.

Kechi was given Pethidene, and then her dressings were put back.

When she got her tablets, Glen asked me to convince her that they worked because Kechi had no confidence in their efficacy. I told Kechi to remember what we discussed. She had to believe in her heart that the drugs would work, even before her brain moves to ensure that it did.

When Kate went off to do some shopping, Kechi and I told stories and sang a little. It was a good interlude after so many tears and was a welcome change.

Kechi got pain pills at 6pm and decided to wait until 8pm for her Ativan shot. To my amazement, she was able to wait it out, and Kate and I prayed with her, tucked her in and left.

❖

I packed an overnight bag for my sleep over with Kechi at the hospital. She was sleeping very peacefully, so I woke her gently to get permission to quickly go to the bank. She agreed, and I went to Standard Bank in Parktown to get my bankcard set up. I was told that I had to go to one of their Foreign Exchange branches to deposit dollars into my new account, so I left that for another day.

I detoured to Cresta to buy stuff for Tara, as Kate was getting ready to go back home. This wasted a little time and I prepared myself for the cold shoulder I was going to get from Kechi when I got back to the hospital. Surprisingly, she was not upset. She had just finished with her exercises and was resting peacefully. When she woke up because of pain, she got her pills and settled down again. We sat her down in a chair and got fresh sheets to make her bed. Kechi was sweating a lot because with the weather so bitterly cold outside, we had requested for a portable heater for her room, and we also wrapped her up warmly. This made her sweat sometimes and soak the sheets, so we changed it ourselves to save the nurses the extra work.

Kechi was feeling very relaxed, and told me to sing her a song I had sang the previous day about a tree growing by the riverside. When I just got into the song, Kechi suddenly started exclaiming,

"Mommy, I'm getting flashes, I'm starting to remember!"

My heart sank because I knew she was talking about the plane crash, but I asked her anyway,

"Remember what?"

Her eyes very wide and staring into space, she said,

"I remember everything. I remember the plane crash".

I went to her and held her hands, and asked her if she wanted to talk about it. She nodded and kept quiet for a long time, then said,

"The pilot had just announced that we would land in five minutes. I was sitting with Toke. Suddenly the plane jerked violently. Toke grabbed my hand and asked me 'Kechi, what's happening?' I told her I didn't know and that we should pray.

The plane jerked again and there was this ear-splitting noise like you would hear from a plane engine when you went to board, but a hundred times louder.

Toke and I held onto each other with one hand and used our other hands to cover our ears.

Then the plane got unbearably hot, and then there was a loud crash."

She remembered nothing after that.

Then Kechi cried from deep within her soul and I could tell that she was back in that plane. I just held her, opened my mouth,

and God took over. I talked at length and she began to calm down. I told her that the other occupants of the plane were in heaven now, and that Jesus would not have allowed them to suffer before taking then home.

She was not convinced and said she needed to know that Toke was fine, because she had been very frightened and Kechi could remember her eyes, wide and scared. I told Kechi that the fact that she had held onto her friend and at a point when all hope was lost, remembered to reach out to God, told me that Toke was now with Jesus. He chose to take Toke and the others home and to leave Kechi behind for His own purposes, and no one but Him knew why.

I kept on talking in this vein until she calmed down and finally stopped crying. I could see her taking this experience and burying it with the others that she did not want to explore too closely at that moment.

At this point, I was glad that I had decided to spend the night.

This was surely the reason God had arranged it so.

Kate left, and Kechi and I prepared for bed. We watched two movies, and after that, she still could not sleep. I put off the lights and the TV to no avail. Between finding her a comfortable position, bedpan duty and getting up to give her several drinks, Kechi kept me pretty busy. She finally drifted off around 4am and I managed to grab a short nap for an hour or so before Kechi was woken for her wash.

I wondered how I would make do on one hour of sleep.

After being washed, Kechi got a shot for pain and slept until 10am, then wanted her breakfast. I fed her and then we talked for a while. Kate came in with more puff puffs for Kechi and the naughty girl said that she hoped I had learned the recipe, and then Kate left to do some last minute shopping.

Kechi was very restless and cried loudly when she was in pain or itching. Her right shoulder and right ear were sore so she could not lie on that side for long. Her left side was not too comfortable also because the last grafting was to the left side of her neck. As a result, she rotated between both sides and her back and required help to turn over. This kept me busy all day long. I was running on fumes as I had not really slept the night before.

I noticed that aside from being restless and irritable, Kechi was also looking moody, so I asked her if she had anything on her mind. She nodded. Did she want to talk about it? She nodded. Then kept quiet for a long time. I prompted her,

"Kechi, do you want to talk about the flashback of yesterday?" "No". Then she started to cry.

"I am tired. Why is the healing taking so long? It is so slow and frustrating and I'm tired of being in bed. I'm going to miss my prom, my graduation. I miss Womiye, Atuora, Somachi and Yimi. I miss Toke. I miss my cousins."

I sat on the bed and held her and began to talk to her.

"Yes, you will miss your prom and your graduation, but there were sixty students on that plane who will never be graduating or going to the prom. If missing those events is the price we have to pay for God's mercy and grace in giving you back to us, then so be it".

"I'm not saying that I'm not grateful to God for saving me", she replied, "but I wonder, why me? There were many people on that flight who were better human beings than me. I'm always getting into trouble in school. There were little JSS1 kids that had hardly lived on that plane. Chinenye was such a good person."

I told her that I did not know the answer to that question, but I knew that I was grateful to God for her life, and I knew that there were many mothers out there who would willingly sacrifice one of their limbs to have the privilege of being there to nurse their children back to life and health.

"I know Toke is with Jesus and everything, but I'm sure she would not have wanted to go so soon, "Kechi wept.

I assured her that Toke was in a place where she was happy, prom or no prom.

"Kechi, if you have to stay away from school for a year or more to heal and get better, then so be it. I am prepared to put the rest of my life on hold to make the journey back to life with you."

I had no idea then how prophetic that statement was.

Dr. Williams came in and I urged Kechi to tell him how she was feeling and she talked about feeling depressed, the pain and sleeplessness. The doctor wanted to know if the psychiatrist was still seeing her and I told him that we had not seen him in almost a week. Asked about Pethidene, he said that it had been discontinued for Kechi's own good in order to prevent long-term damage to her body. He also said that it was not uncommon for patients who had been in the hospital for a very long time with no physical activities to find it hard to sleep at night because they stayed in one place and did not exert themselves physically enough to make the body tired and in need of rest. He, however, did not prescribe any sleeping pills.

That evening, Kechi received a visit from a nice family - the Galloways - Michelle and her twin daughters, Kirsty and Laura. Harry from the Burns Foundation brought them and you could tell at once that theirs was not a perfunctory, obligatory visit to the sick. They genuinely wanted to help in any way they could, and stayed for almost an hour and promised to come back with movies and other stuff for Kechi.

The visit cheered Kechi up, and she admitted later that her depression lifted with the conversations and that she liked the family because they behaved normally with her and related to her like a normal teenager.

At 5pm, Kechi started to itch all over, taking me back to the 'full body itch' days. I tried my best to help by rubbing Bio Oil all over her body and massaging it in. She then said she had aches and pains because of the way she had been lying on her side and curled into a ball. I massaged all the stiff areas and she began to feel better. Then without warning, Kechi sat up and began to rub all over her body very vigorously. I told her to be calm and tell me where she was itching so I could scratch or rub it, as she was going to break open her newly healed skin. She ignored me and began to cry and to twitch even more, refusing to be consoled.

Suddenly, it got too much for me. I told Kate I was going outside to make a call, and I just went and sat on a bench. I lifted my face to the sky and cried out to God and that I did not know how much more of this I could take. I thought of calling Ulo, but then I remembered that she always said that they drew their strength from me, and changed my mind.

Since I could not rely on anyone, I looked up to God and spoke from my heart.

"Father, you are all I have and there is no other place for me to go. I serve no other God but You. Please strengthen me. I cannot go on this way. My strength has failed me. Help me, Lord."

And sure enough, when my head was bowed, what I call the 'inner knowing' happened. I call it that because I do not hear an audible voice in my ears; I get filled with knowledge that my spirit recognizes comes from God.

"Daughter, I have never left you. Receive the strength that you need."

I got goose bumps all over my body and felt energized.

Bowing my head in gratitude, I received.

I went back to Kechi's room, laid hands on her, and ordered the itching to go away, and spoke out in faith that it should stay away. I just called forth the power within me and banished it, telling Kechi to do the same. She calmed down at once, and we had a good visit.

She got Ativan later in the night for pain and Kate and I made her comfortable, prayed with her, and left her watching a movie.

CHAPTER THIRTY-EIGHT

"Behold, I have graven thee upon the palms of my hands; thy walls are continually before me."
Isaiah 49 : 16(KJV)

Loneliness loomed, as Kate prepared to leave the following morning. We took her luggage with us to the hospital that morning, since her flight was in the afternoon. Kechi was asleep when we walked into her room, but she woke briefly to groggily ask whether Kate had left and Kate asked how she could have left without saying goodbye. Kechi smiled and went back to sleep.

Kate left for the airport at noon, and Kechi woke up at 12.30pm, finally ate her breakfast, and fell back asleep. When the therapist woke her for her daily exercises, Kechi cried and carried on and refused to leave the bed. The lady was quite understanding that Kechi was having a bad day, and led Kechi through some hand, shoulder, and leg exercises while Kechi was lying in bed. Maya would not have taken such rubbish from Kechi and would have dragged her kicking and screaming from bed, but I kept my opinions to myself. I did not have energy for Kechi's tantrums that day.

When she was woken for dressing change, she told me that she was not going to cry. I told her that I trusted her to be brave and left her room to let the sister work. When I returned, the dressings had been changed and Kechi was looking bright and cheerful, telling me with a smug grin that she did not cry, and I told her that I was very proud of her.

She paid the price for not doing her usual walk after dressing change when she agreed to go out in the wheelchair. She could hardly get her legs to support her weight when she stood up.

We first went to the ICU to see her friends and also because the ICU waiting room had a wall dedicated to success stories, with pictures, of those who had also passed through traumatic experiences and were now recovered and leading normal lives. Kechi was very fascinated by the stories. I told her that we had been asked to send pictures of her at the end of her journey to recovery so that they would also put them up on the wall.

We passed through the coffee shop and went outside, took a turn around the parking lot, then went back inside because it was getting nippy. Back at the coffee shop, we ordered pancakes, and when they did not have any, the outing became uninteresting to Kechi because she had been looking forward to having pancakes. She soon began to complain that the fluff on her dressing gown was making her itch so I took her back to the room and settled her comfortably in bed.

I had decided to spend another night with Kechi and she was very happy about it. Kechi fell asleep around 1am and only woke three times for help with bedpan and change of position. The night was very uncomfortable for me because this time I had to sleep on a reclining chair. I could not get comfortable and spent the night shifting from one position to another, but I would not have traded the experience of actually seeing Kechi and taking care of her for anything, so I sucked it up and just reveled in God's mercy.

I woke up stiff and aching the next day when the sister came in to give Kechi a wash. After Kechi was made comfortable, I had a shower and dressed up. Kechi drifted back to sleep and I was catching some well earned sleep myself when Dr. Nel came in. He asked for the neck area to be exposed and said that he had ordered swabs to be taken from the wound area on Kechi's neck to be tested for infection and if there was none, he would graft the neck that Friday, in four days.

I received this news with mixed feelings. On one hand, I was glad that the grafting of the neck area would soon take place as it signified progress and even Kechi saw each surgery as bringing her closer to the day she would leave the hospital. On the other hand, however, surgery meant pain and with Pethidene limited to once a day, I wondered how Kechi was going to cope with donor site pain, which she always said was worse than the pain at the actual surgery site.

After mulling over all this, I realized that there was nothing I could do about the situation and decided to be smart and leave everything to God, as I should.

I went off to the coffee shop to get some breakfast and when I got back, Kechi's neck was still exposed, and Kechi just wanted to sleep. She then fell into this unfathomable deep sleep that neither Dr. Pahad, back from a trip to the States, nor Maya could wake her from. I tried to wake her also, tapping on her shoulder and calling her name loudly, but she slept on, mumbling things no one could hear. I laid hands on her and prayed, then left her to sleep off whatever it was.

When the therapist came back in, I told them to come back later because I wanted her neck wound dressed first. The nurse finally came in and did the dressing and the therapists came back and walked and exercised a finally awake, but very reluctant, Kechi. I left the room for them to work, and when I came back in, Kechi was sitting in a chair and the therapists were telling her that she had done very well.

We spent the day pretty much just talking and watching TV.

Mom called later and said that she had seen Kate and looked at the pictures that Kate had taken of Kechi. Mom was devastated and kept saying over and over that she did not know that Kechi's burns were so bad. This was strange to me because Mom had always been the one to say to me that she knew what burns were like and that Kechi would eventually get back to the way she was before the accident. I asked her what she had expected and she said that she did not expect that Kechi would be so badly burned. I recalled then that when Mom came, Kechi was swathed in bandages all over her body, her wounds hidden.

I assured her that Kechi was better and recovering steadily. I supposed that the way Kechi looked would be a shock to anyone whose memory of her was of before the accident. I had been with her from the beginning of the ordeal and I knew that what I was seeing was better than it was, and getting better every day. I knew that God wanted all of us to see what He had to work with – a disfigured body, which we would see Him transform to its former beauty. I trusted in Him that He would perfect what He had begun.

Mom's call had lowered my mood, though, and I prayed for God to give me the grace to snap out of it. I pasted a smile on my face, and returned to

Kechi's room to talk her out of her own moodiness. She gradually cheered up and when she wanted to get upset that I was leaving, I rebuked her gently and she relaxed.

She had been having the runs all day and the drugs she was getting after every bowel movement were obviously not working, and a stool specimen was sent to the lab for analysis. Kechi said that the bowel actions were not accompanied by stomach cramps, but I limited her juice intake anyway, just to be on the safe side.

I prayed with Kechi and left for the night, quite eager to sleep in a comfortable bed that night. I woke in the middle of the night with severe stomach cramps and the runs, accompanied by dizziness and weakness. I laid hands on my stomach and prayed, went back to bed and woke feeling strong. It must have been something Kechi and I ate, but I could not imagine what it was.

I woke with a positive attitude the next morning, and thanked God for it. My plans for the day included going to the bank to pay in the dollars I had. But first, I went in to see Kechi. She was sleeping, but woke up as soon as I walked in. She said she had slept well, but needed a couple more hours, so I let her sleep until 11am. After I fed her, the therapists came in and with minimal assistance, she managed to walk to the chair and sit down. She was taught a new exercise that day. A towel was looped around her right foot and she had to hold the ends in her hands and pull. This presented a challenge as she could not grip properly with her hands, but she tried the best she could and when she pulled, her leg stretched almost flat. The therapist put her hand under the back of Kechi's knee and told Kechi to press down on her hand. The idea was for Kechi to press down so hard that the therapist's hand would be trapped unless Kechi raised her knee to release it, and as her knee strengthened, it would begin to straighten. She made Kechi promise to continue with the exercise several times a day on her own.

Kechi went back to sleep and I took the opportunity to go to the bank at Killarney Mall. The bank staff made a very big fuss about my paying dollars into my account, asking where I got the money from, asking for details about the names and addresses of the people who gave me money. I had no way of doing this, because half the people that gave me money where people I did not know, and could not reach. God's provision was such that people came up to me saying that they had heard of Kechi's accident and wanted to help by giving me money to offset some of my expenses. I explained our situation to the bank officials and they relaxed a little, but I had to fill a form stating the source of the funds, so I wrote Mike's name. It was really irritating, because I was paying in less than $2000.00 and they were making such a fuss. I understood that the name Nigeria conjured up visions of money launderers and scammers to most people, but the amount I had was negligible. In fact, one of the officers came out to tell me that I must keep all my payment slips intact so that when I was leaving South Africa, there would be the proof that the money belongs to me, and they would be able to change the balance back into dollars for me to take home. She even called me after I left the bank to ask where I intended to run the account from since, according to my visa, I was leaving South Africa in August. I explained to her that I did not know the exact time we were leaving because Kechi still had a number of surgeries ahead, and ISOS usually arranged to have our visas extended when necessary.

At this point, I was getting really exasperated with all the protocol and fussing, and I rather snippily assured the lady that I would withdraw all my money and close the account when I was ready to go back home. This seemed to reassure her and she left me alone.

I went to the mall and got some more tops and DVDs for Kechi, as well as groceries for myself, and when I got back to the hospital Kechi was still asleep.

At 5pm, I woke her, and called the nurse for dressing change, after which I fed Kechi and the showed her the tops I had bought for her.

She was shocked that she had slept through the whole day, and we watched some TV. When it was time for me to leave, she asked to be the one to pray, and she said a beautiful prayer, thanking God for giving her a Mom like me, and praying for Him to strengthen me, and give me good night's rest.

I was so touched.

I made her comfortable, put in a movie for her and left. It had been a relatively good day with not too much pain and itching and I was very grateful to God for that.

Kechi woke up to cry when she heard me come in the next morning. Apparently, Dr. Nel was pretty upset that she was not wearing her pressure garments, brace and splint, and ordered that she should have them on all the time. The nurses had put them on her and she was not happy, especially with the brace. I noticed that it was cutting into her thigh and made some adjustments, which made her feel comfortable enough to fall back to sleep.

I woke her at 11am to feed her, and then Jane, the Occupational Therapist, came in to assess her progress. She was happy with the three fingers after the thumb on the left hand, but not with the little finger. She took the splint with her to make some adjustments, and took measurements for the thigh and stomach pressure garments. She was anxious for Kechi to start wearing something on her right hand and arm, but Kechi's right fingers were so sore that nothing could be pulled up on it like the other hand. She promised to fashion something that closed with a zip or Velcro for that arm.

When the therapists came in, they took off the leg garments and brace so that Kechi would not slip as she walked. I took the opportunity to wash the garments. Kechi was doing better every day with her walking and stood tall and straight as she walked up and down the room by herself as I watched proudly.

But the therapists had something else in mind for that day. They took her out in a wheelchair to the foot of the stairs,
intending for her to climb a few stairs that day.
Kechi surprised everyone, though.
Supported, she climbed one flight of stairs to the landing, rested a bit, and climbed the second flight. She then took a walk down a corridor and then it was time to start the climb down. By this time, she was exhausted, and had to

come down very slowly. By the time we all trooped back to her room, she had just enough energy left to stretch out on her bed and fall asleep.

She woke a little later to complain that her neck felt like it was burning. I went to find the sister on duty, but she was nowhere to be seen, and one of the aides promised to look for her and send her to Kechi's room. I went back in and persuaded Kechi to lie on her side and I placed a pillow directly under her neck to take the pressure off. It worked and she fell back asleep.

I called Mike and Mom to tell them of Kechi's incredible feat of the day and they were thrilled. Mom said she was en route Owerri to attend the funeral of Justice Acholonu. This came as a shock to me because the last time I had seen him in Lagos, he had been looking quite fit and spry.

Kechi woke up and I fed her. I was very grateful for her appetite; she was even beginning to gain a little weight. I started the process of making her comfortable in preparation to leave. We prayed, thanking God for the progress she was making in her recovery, especially in walking. I went back to the guesthouse that night singing songs of thanksgiving and praise to God.

I was thinking back on the first day we arrived in South Africa, and how far Kechi had come, and my heart was overflowing with happiness. I knew I did not deserve this grace, and I also knew that eternity would not be enough to thank God for where He had led us from and where He was going to lead us to.

Kechi opened her eyes with a groan when I walked into her room the next morning. She said she had only fallen asleep after she was bathed by 5.30am that morning so I told her to catch a few winks until I woke her at 11am to eat breakfast and get ready for her exercises. While I was feeding her, the physiotherapists came in and had to wait. Maya was not happy and told us off. She said they had to be in Trauma ICU at 12pm, so we had to be ready for them at 11am. She also said that Kechi had to corporate with everyone so that we could all help her get her body clock back to normal; Kechi should stop sleeping so much during the day, and I was to start taking her for a walk in the evenings, up and down the stairs, and then in a wheelchair all around the hospital, ending with her sitting up for at least an hour in a chair before going back to bed. These new exercises should tire her out if done late enough in the evening and she would be able to sleep earlier, and through the whole night. I promised to do my best and they took Kechi off for her walk. She walked to the stairs, went up and down them, walked back to her room, did some assisted stretches and then she was helped into a chair. I put a book in her lap, and soon she and one of the therapists began to talk about books, and both discovered that they had the same favorite book, Redeeming Love, by Francine Rivers.

Kechi was in a very good mood that day and while she sat in the chair, I made up her bed and then helped her back into it.

When she fell asleep, I dashed over to Killarney to buy groceries and toiletries.

When I got back, she was still asleep, but the sister was already in the room to wake her for dressings change.

After lunch, Kechi's good mood was still holding, so we just spent time together, talking and watching TV. At 6pm, I got her out of bed for her first evening walk. We walked up and down just one flight of stairs because I was afraid she might be too tired, if she went up the second flight, to walk back to her room. After that, I put her in a wheelchair and our first stop was Trauma ICU because she wanted to see her friends, especially Rochelle. Kechi caused quite a stir, as everyone rushed to hug her, exclaim and make a fuss over her. From there I wheeled her around the hospital, up and down the long halls. By the time we got back to her room, she was fagged out.

When I settled her back in bed, she ate some puff-puff while watching TV. She soon started complaining of pain in her back so I sat her up and massaged her back, and then put her through some arm and shoulder stretches. Before she lay back down, she looked down at her body and said, "I was in a plane crash and I survived". I teased her and called her 'the girl that lived' like Harry Potter. I even told her that one of her scars was lightening shaped like Harry Potter's. She laughed and wanted to see, so I brought a mirror and pointed to one of her scars. Of course it was not really lightening shaped, but we had a few laughs all the same.

Kechi and I had really taken to Shakira and Wycleff's new song, 'Hips don't lie', and it was fun for me to see Kechi move her hips on the bed like Shakira. She now listened to the radio at night so that she could keep up with the latest releases. Kechi had no intention of being left behind in knowing the latest trends.

After her snack, we muted the TV and prayed for the next day's surgery. The pain of the last surgery was something else, with Kechi being in excruciating pain for three weeks after the surgery. Our prayer was that the pain should not be as much or last as long as the last time. We banished fear and Kechi prayed for a good night's sleep for both of us.

That day had been a beautiful day and I thanked God for it. Such days were few and far between and I cherished them when they happened.

CHAPTER THIRTY-NINE

"For thou shalt worship no other god: for the LORD, whose name is Jealous, is a jealous God:"
Exodus 34 : 14(KJV)

I woke really early the next morning from a nasty dream where Kechi went in for surgery and did not make it out alive. I leaped out of bed rebuking satan, the father of lies. I banished the spirit of fear he was trying to infest me with after binding it with chains of fire. The devil knew that if he could get me to be afraid each time Kechi went in for surgery, then that would be a significant victory since there was surgery every week. It was a good plan to keep me in bondage, but I refused to be snared. I knew the dream stemmed from my fears concerning the pain that follows surgery, and after praying, the Lord brought to my heart His word from Isaiah 7 v 9b:

"If ye will not believe, surely ye shall not be established."

I knew I had to be steadfast in my faith.

I was planning to spend that night in the hospital, so I packed a bag and left.

Kechi was asleep, but when she heard me say hi to the sister, she woke up and said she had been waiting for me. I told her to go back to sleep and get some rest before the therapists got there.

The nurse came in to take her blood pressure, and Kechi woke up, crying that she had pain in her neck, elbow, behind her knee and her shoulders. I told her that she just needed to do some exercises to stretch out those kinks. She started a new crying jag for hunger. I told her that she had had a lot of time to prepare for abstaining from food that day, and that she should focus on after the surgery, when she would be able to eat. She kept on crying, and I could see it was one of those days, so I stopped trying to console her and just let her get it all out. She calmed down after a while and soon fell asleep.

When Maya came in for physio, Kechi was reluctant to get out of bed and Maya spoke very sharply to her and scolded her, "I can't force you to get up and move, Kechi," she said, "You are old enough to start taking responsibility. If you don't want to get up, then I will go to other patients that are more eager than you to leave this hospital".

Kechi was shocked enough to get up. She liked Maya a lot and did not want her to be disappointed in her. I helped her up from bed and left the room, figuring that if I was not there, Kechi would stop being a baby. I sat on a chair outside her room and they soon came out and walked past me, down the corridor, up and down the stairs, and around the garden section twice. Kechi was walking tall and I was very proud of her.

She sat in a chair when they got back and Maya heaped praises on her. I made Kechi's bed, and helped her back into it. By this time, the nurses in the ward were very used to me and were more than happy for me to take over much of Kechi's care. I used to wash Kechi, feed her, make her bed, take care of her bed pan issues etc.

Kechi was very tired after her exercises, so I made her comfortable and it did not take much to persuade her to sleep, and suggest how wonderful it would be if she could sleep until it was time to go in for surgery. Maya enquired from the nurses, and found out that Kechi was at the top of the list that day, her surgery slated for 2 pm.

She went in at 3 pm and came out at 5 30pm. I was glad when I was not called into the recovery room to calm her down because it meant she woke up without too much pain. The crying soon started, though. When I went in to see her, she said that there were two donor sites on her bum and they were extremely painful, much more than the graft site on her neck.

I had noticed by then that the worst of the pain of surgery usually came from the donor sites, most times overshadowing the pain from the actual surgery. In this case, it was almost a good thing, since the pain from the last neck surgery almost made her crazy.

She was given Pethidene, and as she calmed down, said that the surgery was not as painful as she had feared. I praised God for answered prayers.

Kechi slept off until 10pm. Dr. Opolot came in to see her, and when I told him that I was spending the night, he talked to the sisters about getting in a bed for me. This was marvelous and so thoughtful of him, because as much as I loved being with Kechi at night, the thought of spending the night in that awful hospital chair had been giving me some real concern.

Kechi woke up ravenous. She ate four puff-puffs and four bowls of cereal! I was amazed at her appetite and wondered if I should be worried. However, looking at her emaciated frame, I decided not to worry about it.

She woke four times in the course of the night, twice to change positions, once for pain medication and once for bed pan use. It was not a bad night, in spite of my having to sleep with one ear open.

I thanked God that the day had not been the disaster the devil had planned. God was indeed 'mighty to the pulling down of strongholds' like it said in the bible. I praised Him again and again that night.

The following day, June 3rd, was Mike's fiftieth birthday. I thanked God for Mike's life, rejoiced that he came to know the saving grace of Christ before he turned fifty, and that he was going to celebrate his birthday rejoicing in God's miracle of his daughter's life.

As usual when I slept in the hospital, I got up very early to have my bath and dress up, so by the time the nurses came in at 6am to wake Kechi, I was already dressed. I assisted in bathing Kechi, she got her drugs, and went back to sleep. I waited for Dr. Nel, because the therapist had asked me to find out from him how soon after her surgery she could be mobilized. He usually came in about 8am. I waited until 9am, then left to grab a quick breakfast.

Of course by the time I got back, he had come and gone.

The nurse said that Dr. Nel was very displeased that Kechi was using a pillow, and also about the fact that the brace and pressure garments were not on her. I told the sister to call him on the phone and tell him that her donor sites were bleeding, but he was already in the OR and could not be reached.

While I was having breakfast, the therapists had been, and seeing the bleeding, just did some bed exercises with Kechi. Apparently, Kechi had been quite vocal in her complaints, absolutely refusing to get up and walk, saying her wounds were painful and asking why no one wanted to understand that she was in terrible pain.

I calmed her down and she slept for most of the day. The oozing wounds were bothering me, but the sisters did not seem too concerned about it. The doctor had authorized just one dose of Pethidene for that day and Kechi got it in the evening.

When I was preparing to leave, Kechi started to cry. I told her that this was why I did not want to start staying the night, because of the way she carried on when I had to leave. She said that I could not imagine how hard it was for her to be alone. I told her that she was not alone, God was with her but she insisted that she was alone,

"I am alone, God is not with me, I do not feel Him with me, and He does not answer when I call Him."

I told her, "He is always with you, sweetheart. Do not expect to feel a warm breeze or fire race through your body in order for you to know that He is with you. It is more of a sense of peace deep within you, and a firm belief that He is with you. Never make the mistake of only calling on Him when you need something from Him, like when you want to sleep, or you want Him to take away pain or itching. You should dwell in His presence every minute of the day, calling on Him, talking to Him, just as if He was a dear friend that you love to talk to."

I told her it was not easy for me to leave her, either, and she should remember that. We prayed, and I left.

I was totally exhausted and when I got back to the guest house, I just collapsed into bed. I had to find a way to tell Kechi that spending the night at the hospital was taking its toll on me.

Before I slept, I raised my new concern about Kechi's right eye to God. The eyelid had contracted again and once again that eye remained open while slept. The eye was constantly an angry red and had started to hurt her again. The ophthalmologist was talking about another contracture release on the eyelid.

❖

I woke up the following morning still concerned about Kechi's eyelid and so I took it before God. I told Him that He was the one that created that eyelid and if He wanted it to stretch, then it would. I really did not want any more surgery on that eyelid and would trust Him to heal it.

After saying the prayer and reading some bible passages, I found myself thinking of possible solutions to the eyelid issue. Suddenly it occurred to me that I was trying to be the problem- solver. Obviously I thought God needed my input. Remorseful, I repented of my doubts and lack of trust and, calmer, continued to read the bible.

Then I remembered another burden, that of Kechi feeling all alone, and asking God to deal with her doubts. I began to pray, breaking down the walls of resistance between Kechi and God, until suddenly I heard,

"It is you".

I stopped in the middle of binding and casting, shocked, and again I heard,

"Kechi is looking at me through you".

I sat down on the bed and the meaning began to unfold within me. I was taking God's place in Kechi's life! I had taken the place reserved for God in her life. In other words, I had become Kechi's idol. She had spent the past six months relying fully and depending entirely on my strength and so there had been no need or desire to seek God on her own. That was why, when she desired a connection to God, she failed to get one because she did not know how to do it on her own.

I was shaken to the core, but I knelt back down and repented. "My Father, I'm sure You know that I can never knowingly supplant Your position. You know my heart. Thank You for making me come to this realization. Please give me the grace to do what is right and lead Kechi to You".

When I got to the hospital, Kechi said she had been waiting for me. Apparently, she did not sleep well and only fell asleep after she was washed early that morning. I fed her, and the Ophthalmologist came to take a look at her eye. He said that there was enough skin on her eyelid to cover that eye when she slept, but the skin had not softened enough to be elastic, and he did not think she would need any more skin grafting on that eyelid. He would put a stitch on the lid to keep it closed and also stretched. I was happy at that bit of news.

We allayed Kechi's anxiety at hearing that her eyelid was about to be stitched closed, and she relaxed.

She did some exercises in bed, as she was still in too much pain to move and her donor sites were still oozing. I had hoped to rush out and get some groceries, but Kechi did not want me to go anywhere, so I stayed with her and after a while she managed to nap for a couple of hours.

Ulo called from Abuja where she had gone to Loyola for visiting. Kechi's friends had gathered around Uloma to speak with Kechi and she was very excited. She spoke to Somachi, Sandra, Yimi, Atuora, and many others. Womiye was not there because she had gone home for a college interview.

Kechi was very happy because she had wondered whether her friends missed her. Ulo was leaving that night for South Africa and I was pretty excited.

I was spending that night with Kechi, so she was in a good mood. At nightfall, after I fed her, I knew the time had come to talk with Kechi and I was led to pray.

I began by thanking God for everything He had done so far in her healing. I went on to say that I knew the time had come to relinquish my hold on her and hand her to God. Kechi did not like the sound of that and made a protesting noise. Maybe she thought I was leaving her to go home or something. I told her to listen to what I had to say.

I thanked God for the extraordinary strength He had given me for the past six months, not only for myself, but also for Kechi. Now He had told me that the time had come for me to step aside and let Him have a direct relationship with her. I could not be God to her. My duty was to lead her to God. I prayed for the right words to use in leading Kechi to Him, and then I asked her to talk to God like a child to her father, to place her hand on His knee and talk to Him.

As I prayed, I felt something happen in the room, or was it within me? I got goose bumps and then I broke out in tongues. I told Kechi that I could feel the presence of God in the room, and it was time for her to pray.

Kechi began to pray.

"Lord, I know that I have allowed Mom to take Your place in my life, but I have needed the strength that I know You gave my Mom for both of us.

I know that my Mom really loves You, and You also love her. I want to have that same kind of relationship with You. I have paid lip service to Your love and even in my worship of You and I now want to get serious. I am also scared of the love I have for Mom because I know that one day she will grow old and be called home and I cannot imagine how I will live without my Mom.

I am so tired of the pain and itching, especially the itching. I rebuke it in the name of Jesus. I am putting it in the basket and laying it at the foot of the cross.

I really want to get to know You more, to love You and have a direct relationship with You.

Please show me how".

Kechi went on in this vein for a while, just pouring her heart out to God and I just could not help my tears.

When she finished, I begged God to incline His ear to the plea of His child.

We were quiet for a while and then Kechi said that she had never prayed like that before. I told her that something happened in the room that night and she said she felt calm and at peace.

I told her that I was not about to abandon her spiritually and she said nothing had really changed.

She did not understand that the whole direction of her spiritual life had changed and that I was now merely a support, a guide. She would come to a full realization in due time.

When she started itching that night, I told her to remember that she now had a covenant with God and should reach out to Him I stressed that she should abide or live in God's presence all the time, not visit Him and leave, but remain with Him by praying without ceasing. I explained it did not mean that she would be on her knees all day long. Prayer should take on a different meaning to her. She should think more of prayer as being conversations with her Father throughout the day, talking to Him every time she got a chance.

Eventually she would hear Him reply her. That was being in the secret place talked about in Psalm 91 - a place of worship and prayer.

I thanked God for the day and prayed that His Holy Spirit would help me to lead Kechi into the knowledge of God.

I woke up cramped and stiff from having slept in a chair, and having been awake for most of the night because Kechi only started sleeping at about 5am. Only God could reverse that trend now.

Before the previous Friday's surgery, we had started to tire her out in the evenings by taking her for walks around the corridors and up and down the stairs, and she had actually began to sleep by around 1am. But she was not very mobile since the surgery, because of the grafting and the bleeding of the donor sites. In fact, she was so sore that the nurses decided not to give her a full wash that morning. A few minutes before 7am, I quickly had a shower so that I would be presentable when the doctors came by for their ward rounds.

Kechi woke up itching and I knew this was from not being washed that morning, so I went ahead and washed her, and massaged lotion into her body. She felt a lot better and the itching stopped.

Dr. Nel and Dr. Edwards came in to examine Kechi's right knee and stressed the importance of using the brace, and I promised to make sure she wore it. Dr. Nel said they had run out of donor skin and wanted to save the little remaining for her face. They were not worried when I brought up the bleeding donor sites, saying that it was not unexpected and would stop soon.

When I started feeding Kechi, the eye doctor came in, but said he would come back after she finished her food. He told Kechi when he came back that she would not feel much pain when he gave her a numbing shot on her eyelid prior to putting in the stitch, because the skin on her left eyelid had not softened, meaning that it did not have much by way of nerves. I left the room against Kechi's protests, but I could only take so much.

I heard Kechi yell and I knew she most definitely felt the injection. When I went in, Kechi was crying and said she felt the shots and they were two, not one as the doctor had said. I consoled her and then noticed that he had put in just one stitch at the corner of the eye. She could still see clearly with that eye.

I told the doctor that maybe he should have closed the eye completely, and he said it would not be good for Kechi psychologically.

I wish I had insisted.

Anyway, the eye was closing better than before, and he said I should watch it and see if it would close completely or not.

Then came time for physio. Kechi informed me that she was too tired and did not want to do any exercises that day and that I should back her up. I did try my best to get the therapists to forget about physio that day, but Maya had trained them well, and they refused to take no for an answer. They told Kechi that whether it was that day or the next, it would hurt the first time she got out of bed, so it might as well be that day.

After protesting, Kechi made up her mind and decided to get up. She got out of bed by scooting to the side of the bed on her stomach and then was helped to stand. She was very weak and shaky, and cried for quite a while. Then she firmed her legs and began to walk. She walked down the corridor with assistance, and then back to her room, drooping with exhaustion. She was helped back into bed and when the therapists left I asked her why she was still crying. She said it was because she did so little. She had wanted to do more. I reminded her that she had been lying in bed for almost three days and her muscles had gone slack again. Then I assured her that if she persevered, she would get stronger and be able to do more, and she calmed down.

It had been an eventful morning, and she slept off.

I was tired too, and caught a nap when she slept. When I went to the coffee shop to have lunch, the minister from Tunde's church came in to pray for Kechi. When I came back, she was reading Psalm 91 to Kechi. After the prayers and bible reading, she said that she felt the presence of God very strongly as she read the Psalm. We glorified God, and then she left.

Kechi was in a lot of pain all day, especially when she needed to use the bed pan because that put pressure directly on the donor site areas. I was concerned that the bandages were right up against her crotch and we had to work extra hard to make sure no urine touched the bandages. I was so afraid of infections, so I was very careful to wash the whole area thoroughly, especially after bowel movements, because the bandages were going to stay on until the next theater visit.

I also continued to massage Eucerin lotion into her skin twice daily to soothe her skin and control the itching.

I fed her the ham and egg sandwich I had got her from the coffee shop, made her comfortable for the night, we prayed and then I left to get a good night's rest at the guest house.

CHAPTER FORTY

"For thou, O God, hast proved us: thou hast tried us, as silver is tried."
Psalm 66:10(KJV)

I was running late the next morning as our regular cab driver did not show up, and Tony had to drop off all the guests who were due for hospital runs that morning. Kechi was awake and said she had been waiting for me to feed her. She had allowed the nurse to feed her with cereal and so I only needed to warm her eggs. She decided to catch a nap before physio.

When they came, she was once more reluctant to get up, remembering the pain of the previous day. She started to cry almost at once, scooting over to the side of the bed on her stomach once again.

Her legs were wobbly, almost buckling, and we held her up by her arm pits. After a while, she stabilized and after they put her through some stretches, the therapists walked her out of her room and down the hallway and back to the room. She wanted to walk some more, but her strength failed and she was crying so hard again because of how little she did.

The therapists assured her that she did very well and told her to set herself a goal to walk up the stairs on Thursday, and she agreed.

While she was taking a nap, I rushed to the mall to get some stuff, including socks and slippers for her to walk in.

When I got back, Kechi was still sleeping and I decided to warm her noodles and boil two eggs to mix into it like she liked. I foolishly put the eggs in a bowl of water which I placed in the microwave. It occurred to me that eggs are actually sealed and it may not be a good idea to boil them in the microwave, but I ignored that voice of reason and after a few minutes, there was this loud bang in the microwave and then it stopped. I opened it and there were eggs splattered all over the inside. I tried to turn it on, but nothing happened. I thought to myself,

"O my goodness, I have exploded the microwave in Section 6."

I cleaned up the oven and went to the shift leader to report myself and offer to pay for repairs or replacement. I felt so bad because I had deprived both myself and the sisters of the means to warm our meals. Also I felt pretty stupid for attempting to boil eggs in a microwave oven.

Kechi had fun at my expense when I told her the story, calling me a 'bush' woman, unused to civilized gadgets.

She said she did not mind having cereal that afternoon and she ended up having three helpings!

Her appetite had come back with a vengeance. Kechi had never really been a heavy eater, so I felt that her body just needed to nourish itself.

We began to watch a movie, but halfway through, her pain started so I made her comfortable and she slept until 6pm, when I woke her up and fed her again. Don and Chinyere visited, bringing jollof rice, which was very welcome. When they left, I made Kechi comfortable and reminded her to pray before she slept.

I got home and had a good meal of jollof rice, then I called Uloma and told her of our experiences with letting Kechi find her own way to God.

She said she had sort of figured out the degree of Kechi's dependence on me. Apparently, the family had asked Ulo to make sure that I went out and did other stuff away from Kechi when she visited the first time, but when she came and saw how Kechi was anchoring herself unto me, she knew it was not the time to try and pry me away from Kechi. She also said that after Mike came back from his last trip to visit us in South Africa, he told her that Kechi was staying alive for her mother and for no other reason.

Ulo felt that if God was now intervening in this way, then He felt it was time He did something about it, and thus it had become His thing, not mine.

I released Kechi to Him with gratitude and relief.

❖

I got up early the next morning because I wanted to make puff puffs for Kechi. I mixed the batter and put it into a sink filled with hot water, daring it not to rise this time.

When I knelt to pray, it was mostly songs of praise that I was led to sing and my prayer was one of surrender. Just as I was about to also surrender Kechi, like I was used to doing, I was led to teach her to surrender by herself when I got to the hospital.

I fried the puff puffs, which had risen better than usual, assembled her food and fruits, and got ready to leave for the hospital.

Diedre came to my unit to say that her biggest unit was free and asked if I wanted to stay there since I always had visitors and I seemed to have outgrown my room. It was amazing how much stuff I had accumulated in six months!

I had been wondering how we would cope if Mike should come with Bichu, Kechi's cousin who was eager to see Kechi, and also Mom and Chizitara. I had actually thought about paying for another unit. I thanked God for His provision.

Diedre said she would talk with ISOS and find out if they would agree to pay the R100 difference. I told her that even if they did not, I would pay her the difference in advance. She promised to have my things moved that day, saying that it was a lovely unit that even had floor heating.

Kechi was asleep, but I woke her up to eat before her exercises. She was in a grumpy mood which I believed was because I had interrupted her sleep.

Then the psychiatrist came in to talk with Kechi because apparently, Dr. Nel had been told that Kechi was being uncooperative about wearing her pressure garments. I was very unimpressed with the psychiatrist because we had not seen him for about three weeks. He had come in, prescribed Neurontin, then he had taken off and not come back even once in three weeks to find out if the drug worked.

Kechi informed him that she was not being uncooperative. She had an issue with the night nurse because she had called for her to remove the brace as it was digging into her thigh. Not only did the nurse refuse to remove it, she also refused to get the shift leader so Kechi could explain why she wanted it removed. Maybe that was why she had written that Kechi was uncooperative.

By this time, I was getting really worried about the bandages on Kechi's thighs. They were really beginning to stink offensively, and though I knew that it was a combination of the blood that oozed in the early days and urine that touched the bandages no matter how careful we were, I was concerned that the wounds might become septic.

I spoke to Sister Glen about it and she said that although Dr. Nel said Kechi was going in for dressings change for her face the next day, he had not mentioned her thighs. She did say that he had asked where the smell was coming from, though, but she did not know. She would call and ask him what to do.

Maya came in for physio herself and it was clear that Dr. Nel had told her about Kechi's 'famous uncooperativeness' because she came in with a very aggressive attitude, telling Kechi she was not going to beg her to get better, and if Kechi did not give her a response, she would leave and not return that day.

Kechi started to explain about the pain and how she wanted to do more, but Maya was not listening. She put on the pressure garments and splints in two moves, got Kechi out of bed and standing the next second. She obviously had no time for rubbish and Kechi correctly gauged her mood.

There were no histrionics that morning.

This was what Kechi needed, though it was painful to watch. I knew she was holding everything in, and would unload it all on me the minute Maya left.

Surprisingly, she did not. It seemed that she agreed with Maya that she could take responsibility for her body's healing. They walked all the way to Dr. Nel's rooms and when they got back, Maya sat her down on a chair and said she should sit there for the rest of the day, and feed herself.

I had been introduced to a lady called Lynne by Dr. Nel. Her daughter, Jill, was a burns survivor like Kechi and she was almost fully recovered. They visited Kechi and I and were very encouraging.

Lynne visited again later that day and brought pictures of Jill when she was in the hospital. It was amazing how much like Kechi's wounds hers were and she looked almost normal now. Lynne was full of advice based on her own experiences with her daughter's recovery and she was also really fun to be with.

By the time she left, Kechi and I decided we really liked her. She had invited me to have lunch with her, but Kechi refused. I had thought it was going to be one of those physio-and-back-to-bed days so that I could leave for a couple of hours, but Kechi insisted on sitting up for as long as she could, so I had to stay.

Lynne promised to pick me up one night after 8.00pm and take me to her home for dinner and then drop me off at the guest house. Kechi was tired, but managed to write a few lines in a journal she had started before I took her back to bed. Standing was an ordeal. Sitting on the bed was worse, and I lowered her unto her back so that I could move up her neck and her shoulders. She screamed so loud that I had to speak to her sharply to stop, so that people did not come running thinking that something was seriously wrong.

Kechi took great offence at that and told me that she wished I could feel the kind of pain she was feeling so that I would know if I could bear it. She said that she was very hurt and when I tried to help her turn, she said I should not touch her.

She turned on her own and did not speak to me again except to tell me to raise the bed for her.

I left her to her feelings and just covered her thinking, 'At this rate, how am I going to get her out of bed and into the chair this evening?'

That evening, Kechi and I watched TV together. She was still very upset with me and did not speak to me for a while, but gradually thawed out. After a couple of hours, she began to cry in pain over her donor sites and I convinced her that getting out of bed and walking around a bit would help to stretch out her muscles and do the donor sites some good. She agreed and we got her out of bed fast like I saw Maya do it. Once out of bed, though, her legs buckled and I had to bear her whole weight with my hands under her armpits. After a while, she stabilized and managed to walk up and down her room twice before going back to bed.

Womiye called and they got talking about boy issues with Kechi giving advice. I went out to buy more airtime for the phone and by the time I got back, she was crying in pain. The sister came in and gave her Tramal and then Somkele, one of her classmates from Loyola, called and she started laughing and talking about their school.

After this reprieve, Kechi started to itch and was rubbing really hard on her head. I told her she would really hurt herself, would she try lying perfectly still and ignore the itching?

This set her off again.

"Mom, I want you to get this itching so you can understand what I'm going through! Do you know how it feels to be scratching one itch and another one goes "ping!" and when you leave the first one to scratch it, another one starts? You scratch until you know you are making your skin sore and probably bleed, but you continue because the itch is still there!"

I was helpless, so I did what came naturally when I found myself in a helpless situation. I bowed my head and began to pray. Kechi said I should hold her hand and I did. I began to talk to God.

"There is NOTHING You cannot do, Lord. I beg You to set upon Kechi's heart, Your truth, which will set her free to soar in spirit up to You, to make her yearn and long to be close to You always. Please make her believe that You can help her in every situation she finds herself in, O Lord. In the mighty name of Jesus, I pray. Amen."

After the prayer, Kechi said that when I went to buy airtime, she prayed and nothing happened. I told her once again that prayers were not just for when she needed something from God like relief from pain and itching, she should also just talk to Him even when she has peace and calm within her spirit, and just get used to communing with Him.

She said she did not even know if she was praying right and I told her she should just pour herself out to Him.

I reminded her of what Jesus said about the Pharisees who prayed in the market place where they could be seen. God said that adulation and praise by man was their own reward, and urged us to go into our closets when we pray and He, Who saw us in secret would reward us openly.

I told her not to have any prepared format or chanting, like those Pharisees, but to just speak from her heart.

I reminded her of Psalm 91, how ones 'dwells' in the secret place of the Most High, and 'abides' under the shadow of the Almighty. It is not a place you visit and go. Through praying constantly, you 'live' in God's presence.

I told her to remember to surrender herself as a living sacrifice to God every day, by dedicating everything about her - body, spirit, soul, thoughts, words, actions, the sum total of her being - to God as soon as she woke up every day.

She listened very attentively and nodded several times. I prayed that I made a difference.

Around 8pm, she said that she was not feeling right. I asked if she was feverish and she said no. I was still concerned that the wounds might be infected being surrounded by filthy bandages.

She said the donor sites were really hurting more intensely and her neck was also hurting. I adjusted the bed and she got no relief so I went off to call the nurse. He came back with me to say that he could only give her Lentogesic because Ativan had been stopped.

This news caused Kechi to go off into a paroxysm of grief that cannot be described.

"That is the only thing that makes me relax, and it's only once a day. They want me to die in this hospital. What makes them think I'm so strong? Why are they being so mean to me?"

Kechi went on in this vein and cried so much that she began to hyperventilate. I had initially left her to cry, thinking that the tears had been building since she spoke with her friends and heard how they were done with exams and had gone home to hang out until prom. She must have been feeling left out and very sorry for herself and now the mean doctors had stopped Ativan!

When she began to hyperventilate, I put the back of the bed up to a sitting position, and spoke sharply to her to stop crying and breathe. It took a little time, but she began to catch her breath and began to breathe normally, still crying, though.

At that moment, Rochelle and Maureen walked in. I know in my heart that God sent Rochelle. She began to talk to Kechi, telling her that she was going home soon and had to stop the injections, anyway. She told her that even the tablets would be stopped eventually so that Kechi could start living a normal life without drugs again. She talked and talked, and Kechi began to relax. I stood aside and thanked God for sending Rochelle.

After they left, I told Kechi that she would sleep so deeply that night that she would wonder why she ever needed Ativan in the first place. I told her that would be my prayer that night and I was sure God was going to honor it.

As I was leaving, Kechi's eyes were full of pleading that I should not go. My heart was breaking but I knew I had to trust God to do what was best for Kechi. She started to cry again and I told her not to, kissed her and left.

My heart was breaking into little pieces for my baby and what she was going through. Six months! I knew within me that Kechi was being tried, being refined by God, for His purpose, for His work, but I could not help but pray, "God please, it's enough, surely? Please, please, please let her begin to get better, my Father, please God".

CHAPTER FORTY-ONE

> *"If ye then, being evil, know how to give good gifts unto your children: how much more shall your heavenly Father give the Holy Spirit to them that ask him?"*
> Luke 11:13 (KJV)

Diedre had my things moved into the biggest unit and I slept there that night. I was so tired that I did not even bother to look around.

When I woke up, I rearranged my stuff the way I wanted them and prepared to leave for the hospital.

Kechi was still sleeping and I wondered if she had slept at all the night before. The smell from the bandages was really awful and the poor girl was feeling terrible that she smelled so much. I tried to get the nurses to change the bandages, but Kechi refused, saying she was going to the OR that day, and what was the point of going through all that pain when they would probably change them in there. Sister Primrose agreed with her, so I refrained from insisting.

Kechi was soon in pain and I helped her to turn over to her other side. She said she slept after watching two movies and was asleep until the nurses came in to wash her and I thanked God for that.

I reminded her that the therapists were coming and she should please try and cooperate with them. She got up at once when they came, but was soon crying from the pain. They walked her around up and down the stairs and she came back tired. The anesthetist came in and encouraged her to be strong, telling her she was first on the list and would be sent for around 1.00pm. This made Kechi and I very happy.

They came for Kechi at 12.15pm and at 2pm I was called into the recovery room to see her because she was crying from pain from her donor sites. I asked and was informed that the smelly dressings on the donor sites were not changed. Kechi and I were upset and Kechi cried because she knew this meant they would be changed in the ward with her fully awake.

Back in the ward, she was given her drugs and I fed her. Her appetite that day was awe-inspiring. Kechi ate two croissants, one bowl of noodles with two eggs, and four helpings of cereal. That was one hungry girl.

Since she was not sleepy, as happened sometimes after surgery, I put on a movie for her and we watched it together until it was time for me to go for the day. I gave her the happy news that her Auntie Ulo was coming in the morning, then we prayed, and I left.

Ulo came in and took a taxi straight to the guest house. I was overjoyed to see her. Her support was amazing and I had come to depend on her for advice on everything spiritual.

We got ready and left for the hospital together. Kechi was sleeping and I noticed that the 'Desperate Housewives' DVD in the player was season 7. That meant that Kechi watched from seasons 4 - 7 the previous night.

My heart sank, because this meant that she had not slept at all.

I woke her and asked her what time she slept and she said she only realized it was morning when the nurses came in to wash her. She was very happy to see Ulo and hugged her. I let her sleep until 10.30am and then I woke her and fed her. She said she had been massaging her donor sites and exercising her legs in preparation for physical therapy.

This actually helped because she got up from the bed quite smartly and went off with the therapists, while I stayed back to fix her bed.

She was very tired when she came back, but they persuaded her to sit in a chair for a while. She was still in pain and cried when she had to get up from the chair to get back into bed.

We made her comfortable and when she slept off, we went to Cresta Mall to get a few things, including new episodes of Friends for Kechi.

When we got back at around 4pm, Kechi's wounds were being dressed at last, the smelly bandages removed. Kechi cried, but she was also pleased that she was no longer going to stink. She was given pain medications, and we put in one of the new DVDs for her to watch. Ulo had also brought the newest CD from Styl-Plus, a Nigerian band that Kechi liked, and Kechi had a good time listening to it and getting Ulo and I to dance for her.

She still had a lot of pain turning from side to side while lying down and there were always tears accompanying every change in lying position.

I usually assisted her by putting my hands around and under her waist to lift her and then help her turn. It was very hard to see Kechi in pain each time she needed to turn over.

We made Kechi relaxed and comfortable, prayed with her, and left for the night.

The following morning, Ulo mixed her own puff-puff recipe while I watched attentively, and her own mixture started to rise almost immediately. The result was much lighter and sweeter than what I had been making.

Kechi was sleeping when we got to her room and the rest of the morning went routinely. I woke her, fed her, she went off for physio, came back and sat in a chair and then went back to bed for a nap.

Ulo and I dashed off to Campus Square Mall for groceries.

When we got back, she was still sleeping, and the sister who was going to change her dressings came in to ask for my assistance in changing them that afternoon. I was sure that Sister Olga had related how stressful it was to change Kechi's dressings and how I helped her.

Anyway, I was willing to help in any way that would mitigate Kechi's pain, and removed the Opsite, a transparent plaster, myself amidst Kechi's tears and thrashing around. I had developed a way to dissociate myself from Kechi's tears by impressing it upon myself that this was for Kechi's good. We managed to clean the wounds and then covered them up again. The donor sites were clean, and the grafted sites, while some parts looked a bit raw, were also looking good and free from infection.

Kechi got a shot of Pethidene and calmed down, at least until Ulo started a conversation with her about how often I slept in the hospital. This was because I had packed an overnight bag, since I had promised Kechi I would spend the night with her.

Ulo told Kechi that she was not happy that I was sleeping two days a week in the hospital, and suggested once a month, so that I remained in good health, and all hell broke loose.

Kechi got very upset and said to me that I should have told her that sleeping over would make me ill. She refused to be comforted and did not agree to take part in any discussion about deciding whether or not I should sleep over with her or how often.

She tearfully wept that she just needed me to be around her, but if that would cause me to break down, then I should do whatever I wanted to do.

At that point I would have been happy to promise that I would sleep over every day if it would make her stop crying. I talked and talked to her, trying to calm her down. It took a while, but I finally convinced her that I really did want to stay over from time to time, but it was really uncomfortable sitting up in a chair all night. We all discussed at length and finally agreed on once a week, on Fridays.

Since I was staying over that night, Ulo left for the guest house, and Kechi and I watched a little TV before she slept at 12.30am. She only woke twice to be helped to change positions, so I managed to get some sleep myself, at least until 4.00am when the nurse came in to take Kechi's blood pressure. I drifted on and off until 5.30am and it was time to help the nurse wash Kechi.

I then took a shower and got ready for the day.

The nurse came in to say that Dr. Slabbert, who was on call for Dr. Nel, had asked for the wounds to be exposed by 9am so he could take a look at them. I woke Kechi and fed her, then the nurse removed the bandages. The doctor pronounced the wounds clean and asked that the donor sites be covered with just the Opsite. Betidene and acticote would be continued for the neck sites.

The nurse did the dressing changes immediately and Kechi settled down to rest a bit before physio.

I was not quite sure what happened that day, whether it was because her dressings had just been changed, or because she was feeling particularly weak that day, but Kechi made physio very hard for herself, for me and for the therapists that morning.

She refused to walk, and cried and yelled, but I held firm and insisted that she was going to do it. She dragged herself along, almost resting her whole weight on the poor girls, but I did not want to allow a precedent where Kechi would feel she could get away with being difficult. She had always been a strong-willed child, and I knew I had to put my foot down. Besides, I needed her to get strong so that we could leave.

When they came back to the room, Kechi was almost drooping into the floor with exhaustion. She collapsed on the bed in a heap and just lay there, sobbing. We positioned her more comfortably on the bed and the girls left. That day was their last with Kechi. They were interns and I think they were going back to school after their internship. One of the girls, Natalie, left a really nice card for Kechi in which she had written so many nice things about Kechi.

Kechi fell asleep and had a really long nap. When she woke up, Ulo began to feed her, because I had a lunch date with Jacqui. We went to the Rosebank Sunday roof top market, which was very interesting and featured a lot of local and handmade stuff.

We had lunch at the mall and Jacqui showed a lot of concern about Kechi's situation and told me how it was very important for me to start making plans for the way I would run my family when I got back to Nigeria, knowing that I was going to be pulled in different directions by Kechi, Tara and Mike, and still have to create time for myself.

She also advised me to contact a psychologist that Kechi could see back home.

I was very touched by her concern and she also got me thinking about life back home and how it was going to all play out.

Back in the hospital, Kechi and Ulo were fine. Kechi did not throw a tantrum because of my absence, and Jill had also visited again.

Our sharing that night was wonderful. We sang praises, Ulo ministered, and I thoroughly rebuked the donor site, and commanded it to stop hurting.

Kechi also prayed for Ulo, for me and for herself. It was a great time in the presence of the Lord.

Morning devotion was beautiful the following day. Ulo and I sang praises and worshipped God, and after the prayers, God spoke to Ulo and asked her to impart the Five-Fold Ministry to Kechi.

Ulo sent a text message to Chinedu and asked for directions on how she should go about it. Chinedu called Ulo back and said that it simply meant that Kechi should receive the Baptism of the Holy Ghost by the laying on of hands by Ulo and I. He asked us to prayerfully prepare for the event and also read some relevant scriptures to Kechi to prepare her also. He then sent the following text message:

Baptism of the Holy Spirit
1. The Promise : Matthew 3:11, Mark 1:8
2. The Event : Acts 2
3. The Confirmation : Acts 10: 24-48, Acts 19: 1-7
4. The Gifts : 1 Corinthians 12 :1-11
5. The Fruit : Galatians 5: 22

This was heavy stuff, but it was obvious to us that God was on the move, and we had no choice but to move with Him, however unworthy we thought ourselves to, be to minister such a heavy and serious thing.

Chinedu said the only requirement and condition was that we would have received the Holy Ghost Baptism ourselves and that we were willing to obey God's command

Kechi was sleeping when we got to the hospital, so I woke and fed her and we waited for the therapists. When they had not come by noon, Ulo and I left for Cresta Mall so Ulo could do some shopping. We got back to the hospital at 4pm and Kechi was awake and waiting for us. Apparently the therapists had come at 12.30pm and she had done her exercises and had been waiting for us since then. We apologized and fed her and then we talked for a while.

We started to prepare her for an event that in the earthly realm would look unremarkable, but which would be an extraordinary event in the heavenly realm.

Ulo started by ministering to her about faith.

"Faith is the bedrock of our relationship with God. God can give faith as a gift, but we are also expected to work out our own faith, believing in what we cannot see, and 'foolishly' knowing that what we cannot see has taken place because we believe and have faith that it has. Basically, prayer and belief in God is faith because you are believing in, and praying to What or Who you cannot see."

Ulo went on to scripture, explaining from the bible what the Holy Ghost baptism was all about, talking also about the gifts and fruits of the Holy Spirit.

Kechi already had a good grasp of those portions of the bible from studying Christian Religious Knowledge in school. She remarked that the bible was actually coming to life for her, becoming practical, no longer just theoretical, because we named actual people in our church back home who had some of the gifts we were talking about.

Ulo told Kechi that although one of the outward effects of the Baptism was speaking in tongues, it may or may not happen, but if she felt it bubbling up, then she should by all means give utterance to it. If not, then she should not feel disappointed. I told her it took six months from when I received the Holy Ghost baptism for me to actually speak in tongues for the first time.

She had numerous questions about speaking in tongues, and Ulo answered her to the best of her ability.

Then we began to pray. We began with a prayer of repentance and asked for cleansing by the blood of Jesus. We asked God to purify our hands and invited the Holy Spirit to come and take His place within Kechi. Kechi raised a song:

Let the Spirit of the Lord come down (2ce)
Let the Spirit of the Lord from heaven come down
Let the Spirit of the Lord come down.

We laid hands on Kechi and prayed. It was a significant moment. Very solemn and serious. We all felt that we had just been a part of something serious.

Kechi did not speak in tongues, but this did not bother any of us. We had obeyed God, that was the most important thing.

Afterwards, I fed Kechi. Songs were bubbling up in me and I just kept singing them. What had just happened was extraordinary. God had taken up residence inside Kechi.

Ulo taught Kechi how to test every spirit by asking if that spirit believes in Jesus the Son of God, Who died and resurrected. She felt the need to say this because of a dream Kechi had a few days earlier.

In the dream, a man was calling her to cross over to the other side of a stream where he was. In that dream, Kechi had refused to go with the man, although he looked harmless, telling him that she was waiting for her mother. The man had persisted, telling Kechi he would take her to her Mom, but she refused.

I asked her if the man had seemed threatening in any way and she said she did not think so, but that she did not want to go anywhere with him.

Ulo told Kechi that the bible says in 1 John 4: 1&2,

"Beloved, believe not every spirit, but try the spirits whether they are of God: because many false prophets are gone out into the world.

Hereby Know ye the Spirit of God: Every spirit that confesseth that Jesus Christ is come in the flesh is of God:"

And in 2 Corinthians 11: 13-15

"For such are false apostles, deceitful workers, transforming themselves into the apostles of Christ.

And no marvel; for Satan himself is transformed into an angel of light.

Therefore it is no great thing if his ministers also be transformed as the ministers of righteousness; whose end shall be according to their works."

Ulo told her that if the man intended evil, then she was right in not going anywhere with him, but if he was from God, then maybe he was going to take her and reveal things to her. This was why it was important to test every spirit.

Ulo and I were exhausted in every way and we went home to rest. Ulo was leaving the following day and she began to pack, and then we glorified God for an awesome day.

CHAPTER FORTY-TWO

"Behold, I will do a new thing; now it shall spring forth; shall ye not know it? I will even make a way in the wilderness, and rivers in the desert."
Isaiah 43:19(KJV)

We received a text that morning from Chinedu which he had probably sent the night before:

"What you have done today is a landmark of Kechi's spiritual ascent. And yours!
We are being raised to stand as light-bearers wherever we are. May you reap bountiful testimonies from your experience."

We glorified God once more and Ulo set off for the mall for some last minute shopping while I left for the hospital.

Kechi was asleep and I woke her to feed her. The graft sites had been exposed for the doctor to see. Kechi said that he said they were looking healthy and the nurses were to continue with daily dressings. He also said that the right eye may have to be released again. I hoped not, because I was really believing God for that eye to be corrected without surgery.

After feeding Kechi, Ulo and I went to get something to eat while Kechi's wounds were being dressed and by the time we got back to her room, she had gone off with the therapists. Ulo had to be on her way, so we hunted Kechi down and found her with Maya at the parallel bars where Kechi was exercising. She and Ulo hugged and I saw Ulo off at the reception, waving as she was driven away in a taxi. I was very sad to see her go, especially as it did not seem like anyone else was coming for a while.

While I was feeding Kechi her puff-puffs, we had an unexpected visitor, Mr. Alistair Fraser, the Regional Health Director, Shell Africa.

He was quite pleasant and said he had come to see if he could begin the process of our going home, even if it meant Kechi coming back to S.A. at a later date for more work. He said he was sure we were missing home, and we assured him that we were.

He said he was going to speak with Kechi's surgeons and make sure that we were not staying in S.A. for something that could be done in Nigeria. He asked what they wanted to do next on Kechi and I said that they wanted to do a contracture release on her eyes and do some more skin grafting on her face. He said that contracture release on the hands could be done in Nigeria, but not on the face or eyes - those would have to be done there in Milpark Hospital.

Since Dr. Nel was not around, Mr. Fraser said that when he returned to Nigeria, the Shell surgeons would liaise with Dr. Nel and Dr. Edwards and they would take it from there. We chatted some more before he left, but he made it clear that Kechi would only return to Nigeria when her surgeons decided it was safe for her to travel.

Ulo and I were discussing during her last visit that it had been six months of total care in a very expensive hospital. If Shell had taken stock and decided they had done enough, nobody could fault them.

The visit made us feel at last as if the end was in sight. I was actually beginning to dare to think that we might soon go home. I was still a bit apprehensive because it was obvious that Kechi still needed extensive work, but I left it all to God.

Kechi and I took a stroll down the halls and up the stairs and then to the parallel bars, where she did a few more exercises.

When we went back to her room, she sat in a chair for a while before going back to bed. I made her comfortable, fed her, and then we prayed and I left.

I received a call from my friend, Chioma Brown in Nigeria telling me that one of the members of our fellowship lost her husband to armed robbers and also that one of the other leaders lost her daughter. I was so shocked and I called

Azuka immediately, because she was in the Chapter in which I had been the president. She was devastated and I spent a while, consoling her. I ran out of airtime, and decided to call IC Ify the next morning.

I repeated my mantra to myself before I went to bed,

"I don't know why, but God knows, and that's enough for me."

I woke early the next day because I had a lot of cooking to do - Kechi's puff-puffs and stew. I finished with barely enough time to pack. I was spending that night in the hospital. (Kechi and I carefully kept this nugget of information from Ulo).

Diedre dropped me off that morning and told me that ISOS called her to ask after me. She did not go into detail, and I could only hope that she had said good things about me.

I was very tired that morning, having tossed and turned all night. After our morning routine in the hospital, Kechi went back to sleep and I decided to go to Cresta Mall to buy a few things for myself, especially now that there was talk of our going home. I did not want to be rushed if our return trip was sudden.

Kechi was awake and sitting up when I got back, waiting for her dressing change. I waited outside, and then went in to feed her the puff-puff, of puffies, as she liked to call them. She was itchy and so I massaged lotion into her skin as she watched some music videos.

We got a visit from someone from Children of Fire Foundation, who brought two kids who were also burn victims. One of the kids almost had no face at all, his forehead was kind of melted down and his nose and upper lip were also stretched flat. The other kid had the left side of his face severely burned and also stretched. Both kids each had one hand burned down to stumps.

They brought Kechi flowers and a fluffy toy camel. Kechi was very quiet after they left.

At 6pm, we took a stroll down the halls, up two flights of stairs, and back to the wards and then Kechi sat in a chair for a while.

When she got back into bed, she was hungry and I warmed her food and fed her.

(The microwave was fixed, and they refused to charge me for the repairs, thank God.)

I was very pleased with Kechi's appetite. We watched Friends for a while and then I changed and got ready for the night. Later in the night, Kechi wanted some cereal, so I fed her. We both slept at about 11 pm, and apart from waking two or three times to help her change position, she slept through the night.

It was a different story for me. My night was certainly not comfortable. I had to sleep in a chair and I was cold. I had the whole night to reflect that I really should stop doing this to myself. I still had to spend the whole of that day before going back to the guest house. The nurse had explained that they could not bring in a bed, like they had done once, because Kechi was supposed to be isolated and bringing in a bed from another room would expose the patient who would later use that bed to whatever infection Kechi had. Apparently the scalp wound was not healing well because of the infection Kechi caught in ICU.

Kechi's routine changed a little over the next few days. She now stayed awake all day, no longer taking the little naps here and there.

I decided to take stock of her injuries from head to toe.

On her face, her skin was still pulling and forming keloids across her nose and under her lip. Her eyelids were still scarred and hard to the touch. Her right eye was still not closing well. Dr. Slabbert said that there would definitely have to be a contracture release on that eye.

Her right fingers had movement, although that hand was clenched shut, and I believed she would have use of that hand again. Her left hand was still splayed in an open position, and since she bluntly refused to wear both the gloves and the splint which had rubber bands that force the fingers to bend, I did not have high hopes of her using that hand again.

I talked to Kechi again and again and she knew how important it was to have complete use of that left hand while we waited for the right hand to heal, but she said she found it too painful.

Her thighs and legs were fine, though severely scarred. She wore pressure garments very well on her legs, but there were always wounds from her tight skin opening up at various points which we had to wait to scab over before she could wear the pressure garments.

Most of the time, Kechi's mood was fine, but she still had moments of depression when she asked why Toke and all the others had to die. I tried to reassure her as much as I could and trusted the Holy Spirit to do the rest.

Kechi was still very dependent on me for her strength. I continually stressed to her how vital it was for her to pray and maintain a connection with God on her own. She said she prayed at night, and I tried to turn her mind towards the things of God as much as I could.

She was now staying awake for most of the day and in between catering to her needs and just finding time to sit and relax, there never seemed to be enough time for scripture reading and ministration of the Word. But this was just me being lazy and allowing the 'legitimate' things to distract me from God's work. I made a vow to God that I would tell Kechi of Him every day, and I was determined to keep that vow.

Living conditions were fine. The weather had really cooled. Winter came here in June, it seemed.

God was still providing all our needs. He was touching people's hearts all over the world to send money to us.

I kept a steady stream of prayer going for everyone that was so selflessly providing for us, that God would bless them abundantly.

Kechi's physical therapy had been going quite well, apart from the right leg, which still refused to straighten fully.

The scar at the back of that leg was fighting to bend the leg while we were trying to straighten it with exercise, pressure garments and the leg brace. Of course we were also fighting with Kechi to keep the leg brace on.

At one point I was thinking to myself that the sooner Mom came, the better. She was the only one that could make Kechi behave herself and wear all she should for her own good.

Through this all, how was I ?

Quite frankly, I could feel my strength failing gradually. I was trying very hard to cling to God, but lately it seemed to be taking too much effort. I was beginning to miss Tara so much.

I missed home. I would really have wanted for Kechi and I to go home, but I knew they still wanted to work on her face some more.

I knew that Kechi would not want to go home with her face the way it was now, pulled down to the left.

I prayed and prayed for God to uphold my strength and I knew He could do it.

After all, He was God.

Wednesday, June 21, 2006.

It was bitterly cold that night. There was a power outage and we had to use candles until it was fixed. Diedre arranged for me to have a heater and promised to call the guy who installed the under-floor heating, so that he could adjust it. At that point, there was icy air wafting up from the floor tiles instead of the toasty warmth I had been promised. It was a very chilly night and I was already trying very hard to ward off a cold that was threatening to start. It was Vitamin C to the rescue!!!

I was reading Psalm 42 that morning and thought to myself that David surely had the right approach in appealing to God. In spite of everything he did, he always laid himself bare before God, and God responded by saying of David 'a man after my own heart'. It would not hurt to emulate the ways of David, well, when it came to contrition and repentance, and especially praise.

Dr. Jotham, the Ophthalmologist, came in to examine Kechi's right eye that morning in the hospital. He put a yellow dye in Kechi's eye and said that since the patch in Kechi's pupil did not stain yellow, it meant that it had scarred over and was no longer an active wound. He also said that it was outside the pupil and he did not anticipate any problems with her sight except maybe at night when she may experience glaring. He explained this as seeing a halo around bright lights but said that it was not a problem. He said again that Kechi would need another release on that eyelid because the eyelashes were at an unnatural angle and the eye still did not close properly. He stressed the importance of applying tear gel in both eyes.

I was a bit disappointed about the need for more surgery, and had prayed fervently for it not to be the case, but I submitted to God's will.

Dr. Pahad came in to say that ISOS had called him to ask when Kechi could be discharged. Apparently, they were getting pressure from Shell about our return. He had told them that medically, Kechi was fine (heart, lungs, kidneys etc.), but she still needed a lot of cosmetic surgery, and suggested that they spoke to her plastic surgeon.

This was not unexpected after Mr. Fraser's visit, but it was still a blow. I called Mike and told him to call Dr. Moses and find out what Shell's position was so that we would know what to do. I also sent Ulo a text telling her about the developments. All we knew was that none of us had had anything to do with Shell sending us to Milpark Hospital in the first place. It had all been arranged by God, and His Will would also be done in this new situation. All we needed to do was to trust Him.

Mike promised to see Dr. Moses and get back to me.

I finally succumbed to the flu that seemed to be cruising around Johannesburg and I felt as lousy as only a flu can make one feel.

Kechi's mood was better that day, and after a crying start, physical therapy went well. We watched some TV, and I spent some time reassuring her that God was on top of the situation and she was not to worry about it.

There was a lot of itching that day and I massaged her with the lotion and tried to distract her with TV and music.

Later in the afternoon, she started to complain about a headache and I noticed she was coughing. I prayed that she was not getting my flu.

She was very lazy about getting up to use the loo. The problem was that she knew she could twist me around her little finger to get the bedpan for her. I really needed to be tougher with Kechi, for her own good.

That night she complained that the stitch in her eye was pricking her eye. The doctor was called and he said to pull it out. Nobody knew how to do that and so they left it in. Kechi was very relieved because she was scared it would hurt to pull it out, and happily endured the irritation.

We prayed and I left for the night.

I woke with a very bad case of flu. I knew that being the second day, it was going to be worse than the previous day, so I resolved to get something from the hospital pharmacy when I got there.

I unburdened myself before the Lord and let go of all that troubled me - the Shell issue, Kechi's face, eye and hands, everything. I left it all in God's hands and told Him that I trusted Him to take control.

Kechi was very sleepy that morning, not having slept until 4am. I fed her and she went right back to sleep. As usual, she cried during physio, but at the end of the session she felt much better.

Mike called that afternoon with news from Shell. Dr. Moses said that Mr. Fraser had come to have a meeting with Kechi's doctors to discuss the plan for our return. They wanted to make sure that we were not piling up unnecessary hospital bills for things that could be done in Nigeria, especially now that Kechi was out of the woods. This made perfect sense to me. After all, it was not as if Shell had issued a blank check to Milpark hospital. Dr. Moses also said that since there was the need for more surgery, Kechi would remain until everything was fine. What they required from her doctors was a plan and a time table. He also encouraged Mike to make sure that Sosoliso Airlines paid us all that was due to us.

This was excellent news and I glorified the name of the Lord, Who never forgets or ignores the pleas of His people.

I prayed with Kechi and got her settled and left.

CHAPTER FORTY-THREE

"For he shall give his angels charge over thee, to keep thee in all thy ways. They shall bear thee up in their hands,
lest thou dash thy foot against a stone."
Psalm 91 : 11 & 12(KJV)

I was not feeling too good the next morning, I felt broken up and weak, and my joints ached. I dragged myself out of bed, did my morning devotions and got ready for the hospital. It was clear to me that I would not be able to sleep with Kechi in the hospital that night as I had promised.

When I got to her room, I noticed that the new sleeping pill hat had been prescribed for Kechi was working a bit too well. She fell right back to sleep after I fed her, and was grumpy and tearful when the therapists came. She did not straighten her body for the walk and I was not surprised to see them back in a very short time. Kechi went right back to sleep and I took advantage of that to go to Sandton Mall for some CDs she wanted that I could not find close by. I also found a few hats for her, because Kechi was practically bald and I felt she might be self conscious and want to cover her head at some point.

She loved the movies and hats I bought for her and was very mature about my not spending the night. She said she was sad, but my health was more important.

Dr. Ryan, the psychiatrist, had a session with Kechi, in which he insisted on being alone with her so that she could be frank with him without fearing that some things she says might upset me.

I left the room and came back when he sent the nurse to call me. He felt that Kechi should have a change of scene and recommended that she left the hospital for five hours the next day. He thought I should maybe take her to the mall. He had told Kechi and she was quite excited about it.

Me, I was terrified!

Take Kechi away from the nurses and her drugs?

When I calmed down, I decided that I would take her back to the guest house for a few hours. There I could control the environment to a large extent, and not too many people would stare at her, though she said she did not care about people staring. I really wished that her regular doctors would get back from their vacations and say what they wanted to do about her face. I was trying to keep faith with God's promise for Kechi's total recovery, but it was not very easy when I was looking at her face pulling more and more to the side from the tightening scars and keloids. Even her lip had pulled down again, in spite of the second surgery, and when she looked up, the left side of her face pulled down. And all these were after several contracture releases!

I was constantly repenting for my lack of faith and was always asking God to strengthen me. Kechi believed so much that she would get back to normal, and said to me once that she could deal with the scars on her body, but wanted her face back.

I resolved once more not to be moved by what I was seeing, but by the promises of God.

Kechi was very excited to be leaving the hospital, but I was still nervous the following day, and spent my prayer time handing that day over to God.

In the hospital, everyone seemed to know that Kechi was leaving for a few hours. My intention was to leave by 12pm, by which time she would have finished her physio. When she took her usual nap after breakfast, I rushed to the grocery store to get spaghetti, which I knew she loved, and a few other groceries.

When I got back, the therapists still had not come, so I dressed Kechi in one of the sweat suits Chi bought for her, put a hat on her head, put her in a wheel chair and off we went.

Diedre had offered to come and drive us down to the guest house when I told her the previous day that Kechi was coming for a visit. She was there on time and helped to get Kechi settled in the front seat. I could only imagine what Kechi was feeling, being outdoors after six and half months in the hospital. Diedre was wonderful, chatting with her and pointing out landmarks.

I had noticed people staring at Kechi when we walked or I wheeled her around in the hospital, but the reaction of a woman at a red light brought it home to me. She was openly staring at Kechi, eyes wide and shaking her head. Maybe it was because I was used to seeing Kechi's face, or because I knew her face would come back to normal eventually, but that was really the first time I acknowledged that Kechi's appearance may actually repel people.

But that was their problem, not mine.

We got to the guesthouse and Diedre helped me to get Kechi inside. Kechi loved the place and sat down in the bedroom. After I got our stuff from the car, I helped her into bed and she lay down while I prepared lunch. There was a movie on TV that she liked, and she watched it while I fed her. I lay down beside her and cuddled her, and this made us both feel good. Kechi has always been a 'cuddler,' and growing up did not diminish her need for body contact. Mom, Tara, Nkechi and the boys all called and Kechi was very happy to speak with everyone.

The nurse had given me Kechi's pain meds, so when she needed them, I gave them to her.

Kechi's first outing to the guest house where I stayed in Johannesburg.

When the channel was changed at the landlady's house, Kechi got irritable and itchy and said she wanted to go back to the hospital. All that changed when the movie was put back on.

We left for the hospital at 4pm and, whether we liked it or not, Kechi's room felt like home. I guessed that after almost seven months, it was home!

I undressed her, put her in her nightie and settled her in bed. She had a good time that day and I was happy. I was also spending the night with her, so her day was complete.

For me, it was a magical day and a very significant step forward and I thanked God for it.

I slept surprisingly well, considering that I had slept in a chair, but Kechi was still very sleepy from the new sleeping pill. I woke when the nurse came in to wash her at 5.30am, after which she said she was hungry. I told her it was too early to eat and promised that I would wake her when her breakfast was brought in, and she went back to sleep.

I had a quick shower and dressed up before I prayed. I was led to read the whole of Psalm 18 and I could see that it was because it held a lot of meaning for our situation. I prayed over Kechi, laying hands on her, and read the Psalm aloud to her, even though she was asleep.

She woke at 7am to say again that she was hungry, so I gave her some cereal. Her breakfast came while I was feeding her, and she also insisted on eating it, after which she went back to sleep.

I went to the coffee shop to get some breakfast and when I got back to her room, I walked her around the hallways and up and down the stairs, since I was not sure if the physio therapists would come in that morning. When we got back to her room, she refused to sit in a chair, asking me to help her back into bed. Since she now had full body aches regularly, we asked the nurses to postpone her 6am Lentogesic for just before her exercises. We found that this helped to forestall the onset of the pain, while the Pethidene she got after her daily dressings took care of the rest of the pain.

Kechi started to complain about a headache and the doctor was called, who prescribed an analgesic suppository for her. I suspected that the headache was linked to the cough and cold she had developed. The suppository was inserted and after a while she was more relaxed, and we both rested for a while. When she got restless, I massaged lotion all over her body and she calmed down again.

She was asleep at first when Michelle and her daughters visited, but then she turned over and saw them. The nurses bustled in for dressings change and we left them to it, went upstairs for coffee, while they got on with it.

When we got back, Kechi had just got her Pethidene shot and was pain-free. We all had a very nice visit, and for the first time, Kechi participated in the conversation. They were a lovely family and Michelle really took to Kechi. She said that God had given her a special love for Kechi, and it showed in the way she was relating to her.

After they left, some evangelists came in to pray with us, and one of them kept saying to Kechi that she was beautiful.

Dr. Nel came in the afternoon, and said that a swab would be taken of the neck wound, and further surgery would depend on the results of the lab work.

By the time I left, I was exhausted, but I did not let Kechi see it because I did not want her to worry, or see just how much it cost me to sleep in a chair. I was really looking forward to sleeping in a bed.

I woke up very refreshed and spent quite some time in praise and worship, thanking God for everything He had done so far.

Kechi was not in a good mood that morning. They had exposed her wounds for the doctor to see and she said the doctor had seen them, and the nurses were taking their time dressing them.

I went out and spoke to those involved and they promised to be with Kechi soon.

Kechi cried and carried on, and after trying in vain to calm her down, I just sat beside her let her cry. At one point, I asked her whether it was just the delayed dressing that was making her so cross and irritable and she admitted that she had dreamt of her school and her friends. I put her mood down to depression and tried to talk her out of it by steering her mind to other things.

After the dressing, Maya came in as I was feeding Kechi and said she would come back later. I put Kechi's splints and pressure garments on and we waited for Maya. When she had not come by 12.30pm, Kechi and I walked all the way to Dr. Nel's rooms, then to the parallel bars where Kechi went through all her routines. After that, we walked upstairs to Trauma and then downstairs to her room. She was exhausted, but agreed to sit for a while before lying back in bed.

We watched a movie, had lunch, rested a bit, then took another long walk in the evening. It was an almost stress-free, relaxing day, but by nightfall, her headache came back and she said her head was pounding.

She was given a suppository, but then she had a bowel movement, and the suppository went out.

I laid hands on her and prayed until she calmed down and dozed off. I went and told the nurses about the exit of the suppository and they promised to repeat the procedure.

I made Kechi comfortable, prayed over her, rebuking the evil one for trying to ruin a perfect day, and then I left for the night, and had a very restful sleep.

The next morning, Glen informed me that Dr. Nel wanted me to come to his rooms by 2pm the following day for a meeting. I was taken aback. So formal! A hundred thoughts flitted through my mind. What was happening? Were we about to be sent home? Then I took a deep breath and calmed down, and told myself to remember that God was still in control.

Kechi was in a very sleepy mood, but I woke her, anyway, and fed her, then dressed her in warm pajamas, as it was very cold that day. Maya came in and took her off for physio. When they came in, Maya suggested that Kechi should do more than just lie down and watch TV in bed, she should do some schoolwork, stimulate her brain. I agreed with her that it was a good idea.

After Maya left, Kechi sat up for a while, writing, then she got itchy. I removed the flannel clothes and rubbed her down, then she had to use the loo. She had the runs and was weak after that, sat in the chair for a while, and then used the loo again before going back to bed. She was so weak by then that she could hardly walk to the bed. I had to tell the nurse to call the doctor, and Kechi was given Imodium. She had one more loose movement in the bedpan, because she was very weak, and then her stomach started cramping and she started to cry.

I laid hands on her stomach and prayed and Kechi fell asleep. When she woke up, the cramps had gone and her stomach had settled. She started to itch and I massaged lotion into her skin all over her body, then she started to cry for her dressings to be changed. Thankfully, Primrose came in as I was trying to calm Kechi down and I went outside to wait.

I refused for my joy to be taken away by that day's trials. The previous day had been great and I was determined that that day would be the same. After the dressings change, Kechi began to cry for her dose of Pethidene and I opened her eyes to the fact that she had developed a dependence on the drug, just like she had with morphine. She thought about it, realized it was true, and began to cry. I asked if the pain from her wound was really that unbearable and she said no. I then told her to tell the nurses that she did not want Pethidene any more, but she refused. I called the nurse to give her the drug and she calmed down and watched a movie.

She started to itch and I gave her another rub down. The itching was getting very regular, almost constant. She seemed to be itching all the time, which was very stressful, because it meant that I was standing all day, massaging lotion into her body and rubbing her down all day long. This reminded me of the itch duty days of ICU.

I had been standing for most of that day and I was exhausted. She was in the mood for ribs, so I ordered some from Steers, and we settled down to watch a movie while I fed her. Kechi loved ribs, and I noticed that she was adding some weight. Her boobs were almost back to full size, and her thighs and hips were definitely back to normal.

That evening, when Kechi started to itch, I persuaded her to leave the bed and do something on the laptop - write in her journal or something, anything. She said no, she was not ready. She would rather play a game. I helped her out of the bed and onto a chair, and she played solitaire for about twenty minutes before she insisted that she was tired and wanted to go back to bed. She was not very hungry that night, because she had eaten a lot of snacks.

When it was getting close to the time I usually left, Kechi started getting restless, and soon started to itch. I told her that she could control her itching, if she put her mind to it, because it was becoming obvious to me that the itching was also connected to her emotions. When she was unhappy or uncomfortable, the itching started.

I lifted the itching problem to God in our prayers that night, asking Him to give Kechi the strength to banish it.

Kechi started to cry as I was leaving, saying that she had the feeling I should stay the night. I told her it was the spirit of fear making her feel that way and I laid hands on her, prayed and cast it out and told her that she would soon learn how to silence thoughts and suggestions from the devil.

The next morning I lifted up my meeting with Dr. Nel to God, and asked Him to, as always, take control. I handed over all my apprehension and fear, and prayed for peace.

I believed that His will would be done.

I ran into the Nigerian lady we had met in our early days in the lobby on my way to Kechi's room. She had come back to Milpark with her sister for a check up, and they promised to come and see Kechi.

Kechi was awake and as soon as she saw me she began to cry because the bandage on her donor site had come off and the open wound was hurting. I called the sisters but, as usual, it took a while before they came and Kechi was crying the whole time. I told Kechi she should stop crying for every single thing, and learn how to control herself, because we were going home soon.

The lady and her sister came into see Kechi and they encouraged her to be strong and hold on to God. The change in the lady was remarkable. When last I saw her, she was in a wheelchair and was very disoriented. Now she was walking on her own and was in complete control of her faculties.

I thanked God for healing her.

Kechi fed herself her whole breakfast that morning. I attached the strap to her right hand and she ate on her own- cereal, eggs, and croissants. We had reached another landmark and we praised God for it.

The day deteriorated from there. Kechi began to cry from pain, itching, irritability at the delay in changing her dressings, everything. Not whining, but deep, gut-wrenching, all out sobbing. I tried everything, but nothing worked, so I just sat down and let her get it out of her system. She cried until the dressings were changed and she was given Pethidene.

I left for my meeting with Dr. Nel and he started by saying that ISOS wanted Kechi returned home. They called him to ask whether she was well enough to fly home and he had said yes, but advised that it would be wiser for her to stay and complete her treatment. They told him that the funds allocated for Kechi were depleted and she had to go home. Dr. Nel advised me to call Mike so he could talk to Shell and get them to agree to extend Kechi's treatment.

When I left his office, I called Mike and told him of the situation. He called me back and told me he had gotten an appointment to see Dr. Moses in two days.

Then ISOS called me and asked me to fax the visa pages of our passports so they could process our repatriation. I called Mike back and told him this, and he said he would call Dr. Moses back to see if he could get an earlier appointment. He secured one for the following day and called me back.

I called my family and we all started to pray and lift Mike's meeting before the throne of Grace.

All this was going on in addition to Kechi's crying jag, which I was now thinking was rooted in depression because of everything that she was going through. So between worrying that Kechi would make herself ill from crying, Kechi's now constant headache which Dr. Pahad and Dr. Jotham said was probably as a result of the contractures pulling the eye open and stretching her forehead, and our impending return to Nigeria before Kechi's treatment was complete, I was worn out by the end of the day.

I left that night, exhausted beyond words, knelt down and surrendered everything to God, and poured myself into bed.

CHAPTER FORTY-FOUR

*"Arise, shine; for thy light is come,
and the glory of the LORD is risen upon thee."
Isaiah 60 : 1(KJV)*

Kechi had the blues again the next morning and I, once again, was unable to stop her from crying. It was getting more and more difficult to get Kechi to stop crying. Once again, she was frustrated that her dressings had not been changed, but I knew she was craving the Pethidene she got after dressings change. To be fair to her, the nursing care in the wards was not the best. The nurses were overworked and therefore inclined to take their time doing anything. I had a feeling they felt that Kechi was very high maintenance, but I did not really care because Shell was paying a fortune for her care, and I was going to make sure they got value for their money by demanding that the nurses did their jobs. If they were wishing us gone, then so be it. I was not afraid to demand what was our right.

The psychiatrist came in and discovered that Kechi had not been given the anti-depressant drugs he prescribed for the past two days and he was very upset at the nurses. Kechi told him that she had been telling them that her drugs were not complete and they ignored her because they all thought she was very demanding.

He placed her back on the drugs and I hoped that they would make her feel better, or at least stop crying so much.

ISOS called me again to say that they were trying to contact the psychiatrist to confirm that Kechi was emotionally ready to travel by air soon so that they could continue with their plans to repatriate us. It seemed to me that there was no contact between them and Shell. On the one hand, Shell was asking for the doctor's report to determine whether Kechi needed to stay on for more work, and on the other hand ISOS was telling us to get ready to go home.

My main concern were Kechi's eyelids that needed contracture release so that she could close her eyes. If they could just do that I would be fine and happily take Kechi home. It was agonizing to watch Kechi sleeping with her eyes wide open. I could not even begin to imagine how that felt. It was an immediate problem, while her face could wait. I trusted God to make a way out of the situation.

Meanwhile, Mike had his meeting with Dr. Moses and called me while he was still there so that I could speak directly with him. Dr. Moses said that the position Shell was taking was that Kechi was out of danger, so she could go home and continue her treatment in Nigeria. They had contacted two plastic surgeons based in Lagos who had agreed to come down to Port Harcourt to work on Kechi, but if Dr. Nel wanted more specialized work done on Kechi than could be done in Nigeria, then he should put it in a report and send to Shell. It seemed to me that they should have been talking with Dr. Nel directly, but I promised to go and see him immediately and inform him of the new developments.

Dr. Moses reassured me that Shell was still fully involved in Kechi's treatment and we would come back with club class tickets so that Kechi would be comfortable during the flight home. Also, the connecting flight from Lagos to Port Harcourt would be taken care of. Shell Hospital staff would meet us at the Port Harcourt airport to take us to the hospital.

The two plastic surgeons they had contacted would come down to work on Kechi for as long as she would need. He informed me that Kechi would need plastic surgery for many years down the road because contracture release was an ongoing process and could be done in Lagos. Armed with this information, I went down to Dr. Nel's office, but he had left for the day. I made an appointment to meet with him by 11am the next morning.

Overall, I was joyful and thanked God that it was not as if Shell was saying that they had done enough for Kechi and were pulling their support, as we all feared.

The next morning, I handed over my meeting with Dr. Nel to God, asking Him to take full authority over it.

Kechi looked better that morning and said she slept well. After feeding her, I went to Dr. Nel's office, and while I was waiting for him, Mike called and said he had just spoken to Dr. Nel, who promised to write a full report and send to ISOS. He was reluctant to put a time frame on the rest of the treatment because he said he did not know how fast the wounds would heal and if infections would cause the grafts to fail

When I spoke with Dr. Nel, I put the full picture before him, telling him that I was depending on him to convince ISOS and Shell that Kechi needed to stay to at least do another eyelid contracture release.

He told me that he was committed to seeing Kechi's treatment through and that he knew what Kechi was going through, and since he had kids of his own, he knew what I was going through also. He got a bit emotional at this point, and so did I, and he promised to write the report that ISOS wanted that day. He however, told me he could not state a specific date, which was what ISOS wanted from him. I decided to stop worrying about that God would make a way.

Back in Kechi's room, she was still tearful and crying a lot, but not as much as the previous day. This time she was worried about people's reaction to her. When I pressed her for details, she said that nobody would act 'normal' around her anymore, as she will be "the girl who was in a plane crash". I reminded her of how normal her sister's reaction to her was, and she retorted,

"Tara is a child".

So I asked her about the reaction of her aunties and uncles that had seen her, and she had an answer to that as well,

"They are adults". I gave up.

I knew she was worrying about her friends' reaction to her, and tried to tell her not to worry. I had a feeling that her friends would treat her the same, and I was proved right later.

Because of the possibility that we were leaving the following week, I called Mike and told him to start coming to S.A., because I most certainly would not be able to handle coming back alone with Kechi. He told me that he would have to fix up the house in Aba to get it ready for our return. He said this like it was a done deal that we were coming home the following week and I was upset because if he came away from the meeting with Dr. Moses knowing that we were surely returning the following week, then why did he not tell me the whole story and instead made me think that there was still a chance that Kechi would stay for the rest of her treatment?

I called Ulo and told her that Obichukwu should be sent as planned so that he could be with Kechi while I organized buying boxes and packing our stuff. Ulo went into action at once, called her friend who owned a travel agency, and a ticket was procured for Obichukwu to travel that night or the following night.

The prospect of Obichukwu coming the following night filled Kechi with so much joy that her crying ended at once.

Mom called and insisted that she must also come both to help Kechi beat depression and to help me organize coming home. Plans were made at once for her to leave with Obichukwu on Saturday night. Things were really moving fast. Then I remembered that Tara was supposed to have come with Mom when school closed for the summer, if we were still in Milpark Hospital. It was decided that she might come with Chinedu, who had an impending business trip to Johannesburg.

I sat down and told Kechi what was going on and to make her understand that we might be going home soon. I reminded her that our stay in South Africa had not been of our making, but of God's, and He was still in control.

She was very understanding, but made me promise her that she would get the best plastic surgeon to work on her face, and I did.

I asked if she was concerned that people would stare at her, and she said I knew her better than that. I smiled, happy that there was nothing wrong with her self confidence. I was so proud of her at that moment.

By that night, she was very relaxed, the prospect of Obichukwu coming filling her with so much happiness. It had been an extremely busy day and I spent another uncomfortable night in the hospital chair.

Kechi tossed and turned quite a bit, in spite of the sleeping pill she was given, but she fell deeply asleep towards morning.

Dad called me first thing the next morning to say that Mom would not be coming with Obichukwu that night. She was going to wait for the outcome of the discussion between Dr. Nel, ISOS and Shell. If we were still coming back the following week, then she would come with the next available flight. If Kechi was staying for more surgery, then she would wait and come with Tara. This made sense.

At the hospital, Kechi was excited at the prospect of spending the afternoon in the guest house. I signed her out and called a taxi, and we spent the rest of the afternoon relaxing, eating, and just lying around. Kechi was relaxed, and napped a bit. She was walking mostly unassisted by then and we took slow walks around the compound.

We returned to the hospital at 4.00pm, and spent the rest of the day watching TV and chatting. When I took my leave that night, Kechi did not cry and complain, since she knew she was going to see her cousin the next day. I set my clock for 4.45am, and fell into bed.

I woke up at 2:00 am and tossed and turned until 4.30am when I got up to pray and get ready to leave for the airport.

The pre-arranged taxi came promptly at 5.30am and we left for the airport, getting there at 6am. It was a bitterly cold morning, and the plane had just landed. Obichukwu came out an hour later, looking worn out and cold. He had grown so much taller than the last time I saw him, and I was so happy to see him.

Back in the guesthouse, I fed him and told him to take a nap. I also took the time to rest a bit.

When it was time to leave for the hospital, Obichukwu looked so tired that I told him to stay, since I was bringing Kechi back, then I remembered that I could not disappoint Kechi by coming to her room alone that morning, not after she had been almost giddy with anticipation the previous day. I instead begged Obichukwu to cast aside his jet lag for a couple more hours since we were all coming back to the guest house by 12 noon and he agreed.

I prepared him by showing him recent pictures of Kechi, so that he did not freak out when he saw her. When we were in the elevator going down to Kechi's room, Obichukwu kind of shook out his shoulders as if bracing himself. I asked what was wrong and he said he was psyching himself up before seeing Kechi.

When we got to the hospital, Kechi was asleep and Obichukwu said loudly, "Hey hey, get up!"

Kechi cried out joyfully and stretched out her hands to hug him and within five minutes they were trading insults, normal behaviour for them.

I fed Kechi and signed her out. Ike and his boys also visited as we were getting ready to leave the hospital.

At the guesthouse, Kechi took a little nap while I ordered take out, and when the food came, we all ate and then Kechi and Obichukwu went to the other bedroom, which I had given over to him for his stay.

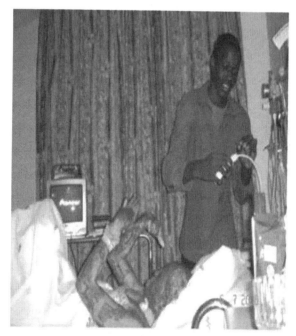

Kechi's cousin, Obichukwu, visits.

After a while, Obichukwu succumbed to jet lag, and Kechi and I just lay around, doing nothing in particular. We left for the hospital at 4.30pm, and spent quality time together, just talking.

When I was about to make Kechi comfortable in preparation for my leaving for the night, she got tearful and told me that she was afraid. When I asked her why she said that she had had a bad dream the night before.

In the dream, she was in her room, on her bed, and was hearing voices whispering close to her bed, but she could not see anyone. Then she heard footsteps in the hallway, which stopped at her door. Then someone tried to open the door to come into the room, and when the door would not open, the person started to bang at the door. The lights went out at that point, and Kechi started to call out for me. I answered her call, but could not find her in the deep darkness. And she woke up, utterly terrified before she remembered to pray.

I reassured her that it was just a dream and explained to her that the name to call was not mine, but the name of Jesus, at the sound of which every knee must bow.

I also told her that she should remember that whatever it was could not come into where she was because she was under the protection of God. Then we prayed, and I cast out the spirit of fear as well as every other contrary spirit hovering around the area.

Kechi calmed down at the calm assurance and authority in my voice and I left for the night, fed Obichukwu, and fell into bed, exhausted.

The next day, after my morning devotions, I woke Obichukwu, we prayed, got ready and left for the hospital. Kechi said she slept very well and as always, I was very pleased to hear that. She was very active and as soon as I fed her, was eager for us to go off for physio, but I insisted on her waiting for Maya, and after sulking a bit she agreed. As soon as Maya came in a few minutes later, Kechi practically jumped off the bed, and shrugged off my helping hand as she hurried, unassisted, to Maya, who was of course very thrilled at this new development.

When they came back Maya was very delighted and said that she was going to tell Dr. Nel that Kechi should be discharged from the hospital and stay with me in the guest house, just coming in daily for dressings change and physio, since all she was basically waiting for was for the infection in her neck wound to heal so that she could have more surgery. She also said she had spoken to Dr. Nel the previous day and he promised to do his best to make sure that Kechi remained until her treatment was complete.

After I got Kechi settled down with Obichukwu, I rushed off to buy groceries for the house since I now had an extra mouth to feed. When I got back, we all watched some movies together, chatted, and just had a really good visit. Mike called to find out the situation with Dr. Nel and I told him we were basically just waiting for the outcome of discussions between him and ISOS.

I was trying my best not to worry about the whole situation, and just kept reminding myself that God had been in control from Day 1, and was not going to let go halfway into the recovery. However it played out was the will of God. Nothing was in our hands, right from the day of the crash, so I was just going to continue to trust God.

One Nadia called me from ISOS to ask if we were comfortable, and if there was anything the company could help us with. I told her that I needed to know exactly what was going on. Were we going home that week, or were we staying for more surgery?

She said that unless Dr. Nel gave them a report, Shell would not disburse any more funds for Kechi's treatment. I asked if ISOS could send a doctor to come and examine Kechi and ascertain that her doctor had in fact done all he said he had done, and then report their findings to Shell. Nadia said she would see what she could do and I asked her to please keep me informed.

Kechi, meanwhile, was starting to complain about full body aches again, this time accompanied by severe headaches. Dr. Pahad said once again that the headache was caused by her eyes staying open. Her right eyelid had contracted so much that the inner lid was visible, the way it had been in the ICU before the second contracture release. That eye was constantly red in spite of the eye ointment and tear gel I was diligently applying. That really worried me, but

Dr. Nel said he could not risk surgery since the infected neck site was very close to eye, and might cause any surgery there to become infected.

Meanwhile the psychiatrist had increased the dosage of Neurontin to help manage the pain, and I really prayed it would help.

The next day, Obichukwu and I arrived to find Kechi fast asleep. I tried to wake her, but she said she slept at 5am, fighting the sleeping pills to watch movies. I fed her, and she went back to sleep. She actually managed to talk Maya out of her physio that morning, but Maya was still pleased about the previous day, so she made Kechi promise to walk later in the evening.

One of the nurses came in to tell me that Dr. Nel asked for me to see him the next day, and I immediately called Mike to ask if he had heard anything. He said he called Dr. Nel, who told him he had spoken with ISOS who in turn said that Shell asked for Kechi to be sent home irrespective of whatever else needed to be done on her. Mike was trying to work out if he could find other sponsors to take over Kechi's treatment, since it seemed as if Shell was done.

I took a deep breath and said to myself, 'It is well'.

I left Kechi for Obichukwu to entertain her, and went off to the mall to buy luggage.

When I got back, Kechi was awake and was watching Narnia with Obichukwu. I fed Kechi and massaged lotion into her skin to stop the itching. She complained about pain and got her drugs.

She complained that the pain was like a burning sensation, and Dr. Pahad said that one of the drugs she was taking - an antibiotic prescribed in ICU to combat the resistant bug - had an unpleasant side effect of making the nerve endings very sensitive. Kechi could not even bear for the bed linen to touch her body. He refused to prescribe any more Pethidene, saying the pain would go away after a while.

It was a pretty miserable day for Kechi and I had to deal with this new pain in addition to every other thing going on.

Obi was very much affected by Kechi's obvious pain and her tears. I felt very sorry for him, but I knew that his presence was helping a lot.

The pain had not lessened by the following day, and we walked in to see Kechi crying. I consoled her and made her comfortable before feeding her. I noticed that her appetite had greatly decreased and I knew that this was because she was focusing on the pain more than any other thing.

Maya came in as she was complaining that her neck was aching badly. She explained to Kechi that the bandages and splint supporting her neck had kind of made her neck muscles lazy, and since they were removed, the muscles have had to work to hold up her head without that extra help. She insisted that Kechi get up for exercises and she did, wobbly and crying. Obi went with them, and I stayed back to change her sheets. She came back feeling better, though.

For some reason, there was an issue with getting someone to change Kechi's dressings that morning, the nurses bickering and quarrelling among themselves about who was to do it. I finally got a break when Joseph came in and said he would do it, and also give Kechi her shot. While he was giving Kechi her shot, Annie came in and proceeded to change the dressings. I wondered briefly what all the fuss was about, but decided not to even worry about it. I had more pressing things on my mind than hospital politics and squabbling.

I went for my meeting with Dr. Nel and he told me that he had faxed a report to ISOS telling them that Kechi required more surgery on both eyes and mouth and had been in discussion with someone called Frank, apparently the person in charge of Kechi's case. He wanted me to rest assured that he was doing everything possible to ensure that Kechi stayed until she was well enough to go.

This was surprising news to me, and I told him that someone called me from ISOS to say that Kechi and I were going home on Sunday. Dr. Nel was shocked, because he had just got off the phone with Frank and had not been told that.

At this point I had no idea what was going on, and was getting a bit weary of the whole issue. Once again, I left it to God to resolve.

Back in Kechi's room, we all watched TV and chatted for a while and when we were about to leave, Kechi reminded me that I had said we would stay an hour longer and leave at 9.30pm.

I had forgotten and she was very upset, but the car was waiting already and we lad to leave. I promised to make it up to her the next day.

It had been an emotionally draining day.

CHAPTER FORTY-FIVE

"Out of the depths have I cried unto thee, O LORD."
Psalm 130:1(KJV)

Things did not get any better the next day.
I was weary of the whole situation, and sent Mike a text first thing in the morning, telling him that I was through with thinking about things I had no control over and was relying on God to resolve the issue. I advised him to do the same.

Mike called back to say that he had been thinking about asking point blank if Shell wanted to pull out. The first time he suggested he was going to do that, I asked him not to. We did not have anything to do with them taking over Kechi's treatment in the first place. Everything was organized by God. So what business did we have with interfering with whatever His next plans concerning Kechi were?

But of course, Mike did not listen to me. What did I know about important stuff, anyway? I was just the wife.

He met with Dr. Moses, who told him that he had received an email from Dr. Nel saying he wanted to insert a balloon under Kechi's skin to stretch out and expand the skin which could then be used for a smoother grafting over her face.

Dr. Moses was not very sure about this, thinking it was a far-fetched idea, but he was going to meet with those who made such decisions and get back to Mike.

I was very nervous because for several reasons:

1. He was going into a meeting about Kechi's continued treatment thinking that the doctor in charge of said treatment was having far-fetched ideas that would probably take two or three more months.
2. Mike had gone ahead and told him that if Shell wanted to pull out, we could handle it.
3. Mike asked him how much Shell had put in so far, and had been told a sum that boggled our minds.

I began to think that a company that had spent this much with no expectation of getting it back surely had nothing but the welfare of the patient at heart. I also remembered that Mr. Fraser had said that Kechi might even come back to SA if necessary after going home.

Then a simple solution presented itself to me.

I would call and speak to Dr. Moses myself and bare my heart to him as the mother of the patient and the person on ground looking after her.

I prayed for the Holy Spirit to give me the words I needed, and called him.

When he answered, I started by asking him to please never imagine that we were in any way against whatever decision Shell took regarding Kechi. I told him that I just wanted to speak to him about Kechi's eyes, because I was the person putting the ointment and drops into the eyes to prevent them from drying out. I told him that her eyes were open all the time, causing headaches and pain. I had only one request, that Kechi's eyelids be grafted one last time before we came home. But if he said it could be done in Nigeria, then we would gladly come home as planned that week.

Very patiently, as always, Dr. Moses explained to me that it seemed that there was a misconception that Shell was raring to go over wanting Kechi home. It was simply that Kechi's treatment was being reviewed and since her doctors said she was able to travel, the general consensus was that she should come home and finish the rest of her treatment in Nigeria. But he added that if there was something that must be done in SA that could not be done in Nigeria, then her doctor had to send a report stating just that. He only just got a report the previous day from Dr. Nel, which was what he needed in order to have a meeting with his superiors, who would take the decision.

I told him that ISOS had called me to say we were going home that week, and he said he would call me back after speaking with them.

I called Ulo and Mom and told them how I had gathered courage and called Dr. Moses, and the details of the call. We all agreed that it was a God-inspired idea, and waited prayerfully for developments.

Two hours later, Dr. Moses called me back to say that he had asked ISOS to suspend our repatriation until Kechi's eye surgeries were done.

I thanked him fervently and as soon as the call was over, I jumped up and down, shouting,

"Alleluia, Alleluia! Our God reigneth forever and ever! Amen and Amen!"

I called everyone and there was jubilation all round. I pondered for a while just how faithful God is. All He ever asked for was our trust. I was very grateful to Him.

Meanwhile, Kechi's pain had not abated. Pethidene was holding the pain at bay, but when it wore out, she would start crying again. But luckily, the doctor had put her back on the drug for the nights also. So that made things a little better.

I woke up the next day still in the mode of thanksgiving and praise to a wonderful God who loved His children so much. I thanked Him again and again for showing Himself strong the previous day, in the way He settled everything.

As soon as Kechi set eyes on us, she started to cry, saying she was in so much pain. I gave her the pain medication the nurse had put on the stand, made her comfortable, and fed her. She calmed down a bit after being fed and fussed over. We had planned a trip to Cresta with Kechi that day, but she said she had changed her mind and did not want to move from her bed just then because she was relatively pain-free. I was of the same opinion, but Maya refused. She said that the pain would come whether we were in Cresta or in the hospital, and she thought it was a good idea for Kechi to go out I could not shield her forever. So we rescheduled for the next day.

❖

Mom and Tara were coming the following week and Kechi and I were thrilled. It was more than likely that we would all be travelling back to Nigeria together.

Then Kechi told us of the dream that she had the previous night.

She had pressed her bell for the nurse and a man came in. She could not see him clearly, it was like he was a silhouette. Then others like him came in after him and they began to whisper to each other. Then the lights went off.

She asked them, "Do you guys believe in Jesus?

The first one began to laugh and said to her, "Are you asking that because your Mom said you should? Do you think it works?"

She asked them again and they all began to laugh.

Then she shouted, "JESUS!" at the top of her voice and they began to drift out of the door like shadows and the lights came back on.

She said she felt very good when that happened, and I thanked God.

I called Dad and told him of the dreams and he explained that hospitals are normal exit points for departing souls, and that many people who die every day do not know Christ, so their naked souls hover around the hospitals where they died. Dad continued to say that whenever a person died, his human spirit returned to God, who gave it, while his physical body is buried in the earth. If he had received Christ while on earth, his soul, which is the real person, would be given a covering and taken home. However, if he rejected Christ while still in the flesh, that soul is naked, and walks to and fro, seeking rest and finding none. So they go to familiar persons and places.

Kechi had been hovering between both worlds for quite a while, and therefore was very sensitive to that realm, which was the attraction for them.

Those who came to her were disembodied spirits who had received no covering from Jesus. They were actually demons and Kechi and I had the authority to rebuke them and cast them out, and he was very glad that we had the knowledge to do both.

I carefully explained all this to Kechi.

The pain came back around 6pm, and soon became unbearable. Kechi yelled so loud that I could not calm her, so I did what I always did when my strength failed. I bowed down my head and prayed. I prayed through the loud cries, and then she began to quiet down.

Then the tempo of the prayer changed and I began to pray with confidence and authority. I was led to pray that the sight of Kechi in pain was never going to make me forget what God did for me on Dec 10, 2005. No matter how bad it got, I would never forget, nor ever question why He had saved her, if He was going to allow her to hurt so much. I would praise Him forever and be forever grateful to Him for His grace upon my unworthy life, saving my child out of so many.

I knew when the Holy Spirit became involved in the prayer, because I was now praying with trust and confidence in who I was in Christ.

I banished the pain and called down the peace and joy of the Lord unto Kechi. I continued to pray and then it happened!

I actually felt an enveloping warmth over me and it was beautiful.

Kechi drifted off into a light sleep. I hugged the feeling to myself, wishing that it would never go away. I knew that God had manifested His presence in the room at that moment.

But I also realized when Kechi woke up after just about twenty minutes that He had sent me His peace to calm me down, and strengthen me, because Kechi woke and started to cry and thrash about in bed, saying that her skin was burning like fire. She was crying out and lamenting, "I can't stand this pain. It's going to kill me. Have I not suffered enough?"

I called Mom and told her what was going on, telling her to pray, because I felt that what was going on was also spiritual. I asked Kechi,

"Do you believe that God can stop your pain?" She did not answer.

I asked again and she said that she did not know. "So you don't believe that God can do it for you?"

Kechi burst out "If He can do it, then why hasn't He done it? I believe that He can do it, so why won't He answer my prayers? He answers yours, why doesn't He answer mine?"

I calmly asked her,

"So God doesn't like you?"

She kept quiet, and I began to minister to her.

"There is NOTHING that God cannot do. You need to hand over all of yourself, and not just your pain to Him. He wants you to have a deep, abiding relationship with Him, not just when you want something from Him.

Have you not had numerous examples of His might and power right here in this hospital"?

She nodded.

"Do not limit God, Kechi. Reach out to Him. God is not Pethidene. Calling on Him just when you need pain relief is an insult and belittles the immense treasures of what you will benefit from having a true relationship with Him. Every aspect of your life will change if you let Him in. Try it, love".

She was listening intently and nodded several times and for the first time, I actually felt that my words were taking root.

Mom called me back and we talked for a while. After the call, Kechi said to me, "I just prayed".

"And...?" I asked.

"The pain is gone."

Apparently, while I was talking with Mom, she prayed to God to remove the pain and He did.

She asked me,

"So He wanted me to pray by myself?"

"Yes", I replied.

"So that's how God is?"

"Yes, you must reach out to Him by yourself".

Kechi was very quiet and contemplative for a long time, and I was quiet because I could see that this was a very significant moment. She had called forth the power of God and seen the first hand results. She was both happy and in awe of God.

While she was thinking, I bowed my head and just let my gratitude flow up to the throne of the Most High God.

Kechi had finally made the connection. Indeed it was true what the bible said in Revelation 3:20,

"Behold, I stand at the door, and knock: if any man hear my voice, and open the door, I will come in to him, and will sup with him, and he with me."

We read Psalm 30 and then Chapter 4 of The Purpose Driven Life, after which we discussed both. It was a beautiful time of sharing, and I gave God all the glory.

I called Mom to speak with Tara, and she was sounding dull. Mom suspected she might be ill.

Obi went back to the guesthouse alone, since I was spending that night in the hospital. Kechi had a restless night, and only fell asleep close to dawn.

Kechi woke up to complain about pain, got her drugs, and went back to sleep. I fed her when she woke again and then she went right back to sleep.

Dr. Nel and Dr. Edwards came in to say that Kechi was getting her eye surgery the next Monday, in two days, and we were all happy.

Then Mom called and said Tara was ill and she was taking her to the hospital., and we began to pray for her recovery.

Sister Chika, Vice Principal in Loyola Jesuit College, then called to say that the principal, Fr. Marc, was coming to visit Kechi. Kechi almost fell out of her bed in shock, I had no idea why.

Mike also called to say that he and Oscar, the MD of Sosoliso Airlines, the owners of the plane that had crashed, were coming together from Nigeria because Oscar wanted to see Kechi.

Suddenly there was so much impending activity, my mind was reeling.

Kechi woke up and insisted that she wanted to go to Cresta Mall as we had planned. Obi had already come in from the guesthouse, so I dressed Kechi up, she got her pain shot, got into a wheelchair, and off we went.

It was a very new experience for her, and I could see that she was getting overwhelmed by the crowds of people there. It was a Saturday, and the mall was full. She did buy some CDs and a lovely pair of white sandals before she got tired. I called a taxi, and we went back to the hospital. She got her pain tablets when we got back and I undressed her and made her comfortable and relaxed on her bed. She was very glad to be back in her room.

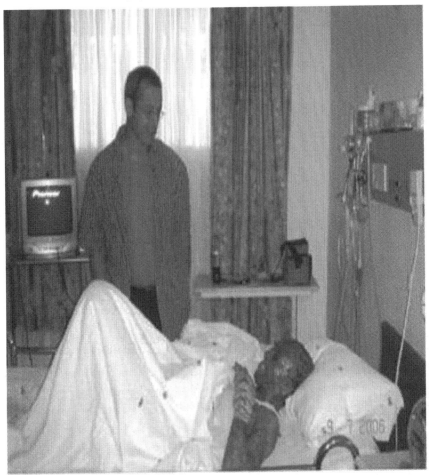

Father Marc, former Principal of Loyola Jesuit College, visits.

We ordered ribs from Steers, which had turned out to be Obi's favorite meal. He could eat it everyday, and he did while he was there.

We then settled in to watch Amityville Horror, which scared us senseless, so much so that we had to watch a couple of episodes of Friends to lighten the mood.

When the pain started, we all prayed against it, and she got some relief. Obi and I then left for the guesthouse where I very happily fell asleep in a proper bed.

The following morning, I lingered in bed, feeling tired and lazy. I did not have to rush about making puff puffs or cook, because Kechi was coming to the guest house that day.

When we finally got to the hospital, Kechi started to cry as soon as we walked in. Her pain tablets had been brought out already so I gave them to her. After feeding her, she said she was ready to go to the guesthouse. She got her shot and I dressed her up, only for the nurse to tell me that her Neurontin had run out and the pharmacy did not have the 100mg tablets in stock and they had to have Dr. Ryan's approval to give Kechi a higher dose. So while Kechi was in the taxi with Obi, the nurses were trying to hunt down Dr. Ryan for the approval.

By the time I got to the taxi, Kechi was crying, frustrated, hot, itchy and very irritable.

She remained in that mood all the way to the guesthouse. After a short nap, she relaxed, and we had a good time chatting and having lunch. Michelle called and when we told her we were at the guesthouse, she and Kirsty and Laura visited with their cat. Kechi, the animal lover, was very pleased and played with the cat throughout their visit.

We returned to the hospital at 4pm, and as soon as I undressed her, put her in her comfortable clothes and tucked her in bed, Fr. Marc visited. He came with Brother Kojo, and another man, whose name I did not catch. He stayed just one hour and promised to return the next day with letters and cards from Kechi's schoolmates, after which they left.

When the pain hit, Kechi submitted herself fully to it and cried inconsolably. I tried to pray, but got nowhere as she just wailed loudly over my prayers and it was clear that she did not want to be a part of it, so I stopped.

I told her that it was obvious that my prayers were getting nowhere and since she was not participating, I was going to stop. The choice was hers she either joined her faith with mine and we banished the pain together, or she wallowed in the pain and continued to hurt. I left the room briefly to give her time to think. When I got back, she cried, but told me that she was ready to pray. After our prayers, she got her peace and we watched some movies before Obi and I left.

EPILOGUE

> *"To every thing there is a season, and a time to every purpose under the heaven: A time to be born, and a time to die; a time to plant, and a time to pluck up that which is planted; A time to kill, and a time to heal; a time to break down, and a time to build up; A time to weep, and a time to laugh; a time to mourn, and a time to dance;"*
> Ecclesiastes 3 : 1-4(KJV)

The day of the eye surgery dawned. Finally.

I raised the day to God and surrendered the surgery to Him. This was going to be Kechi's last surgery in Milpark Hospital, and the end of one chapter of the journey.

For the first time, Kechi did not cry when we walked into her room. Dr. Nel came in and said the surgery would be in the late evening. Kechi was not pleased, but Obi and I tried to distract her. Father Marc came in around 1 pm, and it was a very emotional visit. He was in tears quite a bit and you could see that the tragedy had taken a lot out of him. He spoke a lot about faith and was very much affected by Kechi's survival and what she was still going through. He left about 3pm, after giving us his email address. It was a lovely visit and I was grateful that he had found the time to come.

Kechi went into surgery at 4.30pm, and came out at 6.30pm, crying buckets. I was called into Recovery to calm her down, and they eventually had to sedate her because she was very restless.

Back in her room, she got a shot and fell asleep, so Obi and I left.

Mom and Tara came in on Tuesday morning and it was wonderful to see them. I resolved that Tara was never going to be live apart from me again. She needed me so much. She had never been a clingy child, but she was stuck to my side as if with Velcro as soon as she saw me.

Mom brought traditional clothes that Nkechi had made for the ICU staff she had taken their measurements during her visit, so we went upstairs and handed them out. There was a lot of rejoicing and most of them went to the bathroom to try them out. As usual, Nkechi's measurements were impeccable and they all fit well. Some of them even came down to Kechi's room wearing them to show us how well they fit.

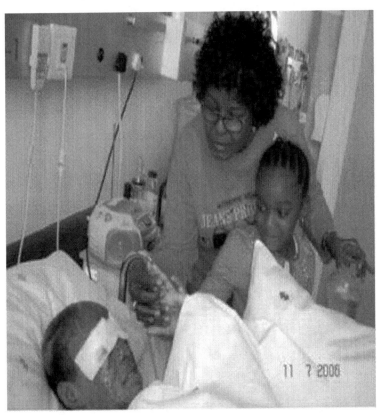

My Mom visits again with Tara.

The rest of the week passed in a blur. Kechi was irritable because a bandage covered her eyes most of the time, and the pain now peaked three times a day morning, afternoon and evening. I was very grateful that Mom was there because she was constantly talking and praying Kechi through the pain, teaching her relaxation exercises to help her cope with pain and also relax her body when she wanted to sleep.

Chinedu and Eze visited us at the hospital. They had business meetings to attend in Johannesburg, and it was good to see them. Chinedu also found time to come again to minister to Kechi on faith, and also to pray for it to be bestowed on Kechi as a gift from God.

Mike arrived with Oscar, the Sosoliso MD. I had mixed feelings when I saw him, but he was a nice young man and so I tried hard to be normal with him.

With Mike, Mom, Tara, Obi and I, the guesthouse was full. But we were all very busy also. We knew that as soon as Kechi's bandages came off, we were leaving, so we started packing up our stuff, mostly Mom, though. I took Obi shopping to buy stuff for him, and Mom also did some shopping. I shopped a lot for Tara and Kechi, and also for myself, whenever I could steal out from the hospital.

I was still spending all day in the hospital because Kechi would not let me out of her sight.

Over the course of the week, the psychiatrist prescribed Pethidene twice a day and Ativan in the afternoon. This calmed Kechi down and made her more settled.

On July 20th, ten days after the surgery, the bandages were removed. We were leaving on the 22nd. Mom, Tara and Obi's tickets had to be confirmed so we could all leave on the same aircraft. I had no idea how it was done, but it was.

Mom had been very busy and we had bought a lot of suitcases.

Between us all, we had thirteen pieces of luggage!

We planned that I would sleep in the hospital that night so that Kechi and I would leave straight to the airport the next morning. I bought a present for

Diedre and went back to give it to her and get clothes and toiletries Kechi and I would need.

Unfortunately she was not in the guesthouse, she had gone out of town and I was sad, because she had been very kind to me and I really wanted to thank her. I called her cell, got voicemail and left a message. I also left the gift behind for her.

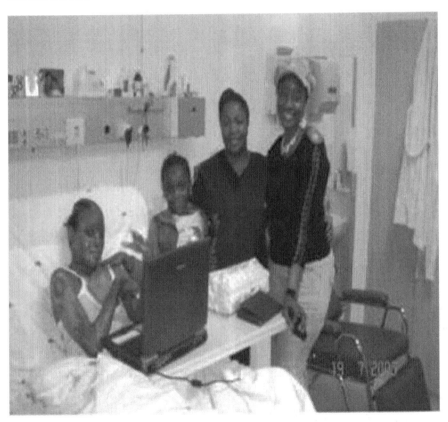

Kechi, Tara and I with Hilda(in scrubs), my absolute favorite nurse who became my friend.

I left Mom, Tara and Obi at the guesthouse. We were all going to meet at the airport in the morning. They were going to leave early so that they could get all the luggage checked in on time.

I went back to the hospital with two large trays of gourmet chocolates I had bought for the staff to say thanks and gave it to them. They were surprised and pleased. Word went round that Kechi was leaving and the ICU nurses going off duty came to Kechi's room to say goodbye.

As Kechi and I were just talking, Diedre walked in. I was so touched that she came. I grabbed her and hugged her, and we both had tears in our eyes. I thanked her for giving me the opportunity to thank her in person for being a lovely human being.

Dr. Pahad came in and gave me his report and that of the psychiatrist and before he left, gave me a warm hug and told me that I was an exceptional mother.

Kechi and I prayed and tried to sleep. I was too keyed up, though, and before I knew it, morning was there.

I showered, gave Kechi a wash before the nurse could even come, and dressed her in comfortable sweats, putting a cap on her head.

The nurse came in and gave me all of Kechi's drugs and hugged both of us, then told us that the driver organized by ISOS was waiting at the lobby.

She wheeled Kechi to the car, and we both helped her in. The driver said that ISOS had made arrangements with the airline to provide a wheelchair for Kechi at the airport, and off we went.

Kechi slept a bit in the car, but all too soon, we had arrived. I went into the departure hall, and Mom and Mike were busy trying to check in the bags. Tara latched herself to me at once and we went to ask for a wheelchair. A staff of airport came with us, pushing the chair, and we settled Kechi in it. Because of Kechi's obvious condition, we were checked in fast and I was told to take Kechi past security so she could rest in a less chaotic environment. I took Tara with us so that Mom did not have to worry about her, and with the staff pushing Kechi's chair, we quickly went to the lounge and settled down to wait for the flight. I was approached by another staff member and was told that Kechi would be boarded first before the boarding announcement was made so that she would not be jostled.

Mom and Obi came into the lounge and we all waited together. We had said our goodbyes to Mike at the departure lounge since he had been unable to change his return date. He was coming in the following day.

Kechi was just about to start fidgeting when the staff member came and told me they were ready to board Kechi and I. We were taken up to the aircraft with a special van which had a lift that raised us to the plane so that Kechi did not have to walk at all. Then she was transferred to a narrower wheelchair that could fit the aisles in the plane up to our seats. We were in business class, I was glad to see, so that meant that Kechi could recline almost immediately.

When others started boarding, Mom and Tara were also in business class, but not near us. Tara was not having any part of it, and started to cry. To my lasting gratitude, a very kind couple seated next to us offered to change seats with Tara and Mom.

I gave Kechi her drugs, enough to make her sleepy, and she slept the entire flight, only waking briefly to eat.

As we approached Lagos, I looked back on the experiences of the past seven months and marveled. We had come such a long way, and yet we still had a long way to go. I had no idea what challenges lay ahead, but one thing I knew was that God, Who had started this good work, was faithful to complete it.

My relationship with God had changed drastically. No longer was He remote, He was very close to me, His Spirit lived in me, and everything about my life had changed because of that. The funny thing was that I thought I knew God, until the accident and events following it showed me that He is so much more than I had ever thought Him to be, and that through His Son, I was so much more than I thought I was.

The flight home. Kechi and I in the airplane on our way back to Nigeria.

Kechi's faith was growing a little at a time, and I knew that it would be a matter of time before she would become an embodiment of the full glory of God. Indeed, as time went on, her faith became the standard by which everyone around her measured theirs. I constantly marveled at the journey of Kechi's faith, and the way it had been forged, right before my eyes, from the fires of affliction into pure gold.

Mom and Tara across the aisle.

I knew the road ahead was going to be rough, but I also had a blessed assurance that God was on our side.

Refined for Rebirth | 469

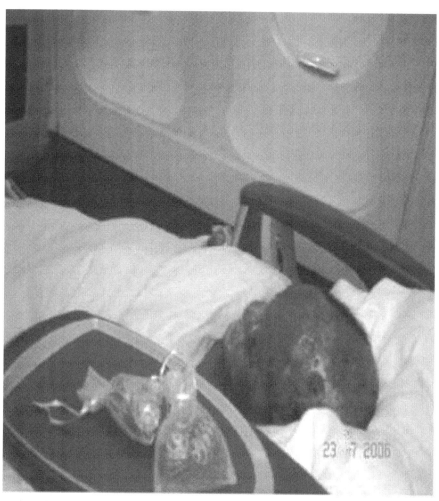

Kechi slept all the way home.

Please turn the page for a glimpse into the next part of the Refined Series, **REFINED FOR SERVICE**, which continues the story of Kechi's amazing journey back to life. This time you get to learn things from Kechi's perspective as she adds her voice to her story.

PROLOGUE

Kechi's story

Before I begin, I would like to inform you, dear reader, that the following are snippets of memories of my healing period in South Africa, a time when things were at their very worst, arranged in chronological order to the best of my ability. It is not my intention to alarm or frighten. I write this because, painful as the experience was, it was those moments that started me on the path I am on today. They redefined me, body and spirit and it is this redefinition that I want to share.

> "My arms feel like they are about to burst! There's so much pressure! Please, help me..."
> This is my very first memory after the plane crash in 2005. I was drifting in and out of consciousness, so the memory is blurry, but I do recall that I was lying down on a gurney, and screaming in pain about the insane pressure in my hands. When I asked, my mom told me later on that my arms were indeed swollen because of the extensive burns, so that explained the pressure.

> The next clear memory following that is the moment I opened my eyes in Milpark Hospital, South Africa after a five-week, hospital-induced coma. I was completely numb and completely exhausted in a way I could not understand; seeing as I had just woken up from a one-month slumber. I was not sleepy at all, and then I heard an unfamiliar voice calling my name, asking me questions.
> "Kechi? Kechi can you hear me?"

My vision was very blurry, and I could barely make out the woman's image. She told me to blink once for yes and twice for no.

I blinked once.

"That's good, honey. Do you know this woman?"

I tried to adjust my sight so I could see the other figure clearly. The figure leaned forward, close to my face.

I knew who she was before she spoke, even through my filmy gaze. "Kechi love? My darling, can you see me? It's Mommy."

Of course I knew it was her; I blinked once. I remember wishing I could see her more clearly. My heart welled up with joy at her presence.

I think I should mention at this point that my condition did not startle me in the least. Why? Well because, I knew what had happened, where I was. I knew I had been in a terrible plane crash, and that I was in a hospital called Milpark in Johannesburg. I knew these things because all through my comatose state, in my subconscious, I could hear my mother talking to me, singing to me. And when her voice stopped, I would hear music, distant, faint music, playing in the back of my mind. Destiny's Child, Westlife, Women of Faith, Don Moen. It was a strange feeling, for even as I was unconscious, information from the world outside of my mind somehow seemed to reach me… and then when the music stopped, it meant my mother's voice would return, telling me repeatedly about where I was and what had happened, or singing to me in her gentle voice. One particular song stuck in my head, one I'd never heard before that time:

> Wonderful and marvelous is Jesus to me
> Sweeter than the honey in the honey comb is He.
> Jesus is real,
> He will never fail
> I will praise Him now and throughout all eternity
> I will praise Him now and throughout all eternity.

It was because of all this that I opened my eyes with complete awareness of the state of things. I heard that many times, people in similar situations rouse from their long sleep in a violent state because they are confused and scared. So my awareness was a true blessing, all because God worked through my mother to prepare me for what was to come even before I had regained consciousness.

Needless to say, the attending nurse was pleased with the situation. I was then asked a number of questions, like 'Do you know where you are?' and 'Do you know what happened?' And 'Are you in any pain?' In response to that last question, I wasn't. The amount of morphine in my system at the time could probably have put down a giraffe.

Refined For Rebirth is simply a mother's diary of the first few months after her daughter's miraculous survival from a deadly plane crash in Port Harcourt, the Southern part of Nigeria.

Kechi Okwuchi, who suffered third degree burns over 70% of her body, may have been the least likely expected to survive since the majority of the less fortunate passengers incurred less burns than she did!

That famous incident was the beginning of a series of less famous, less celebrated experiences that tried every aspect of the lives of mother, daughter and family. In an honest and almost innocent style, Ijeoma Okwuchi allows the world to take a glimpse at the suspense-filled, sometimes grueling, most times extreme, hopelessly diverse experiences that shot both daughter and herself from ordinary, normal existence to frontline spiritual leadership.

Refined For Rebirth exposes the anxiety that was felt in the uncountable surgeries, medical procedures and near-death situations that followed the euphoria of survival. It even decidedly admits the prolonged pains that the family underwent as it fought along with Kechi to really survive, and live again!

Rhema from God said of Kechi on the day of the crash,

"Yes, indeed Kechi is alive. She will be okay. She will be fine, but it will take time. The recovery will be long, but she will be restored fully. It will take time, but it will be complete."

This word has sustained mother, father, daughter and the entire family in a hope that seemed impossible at the beginning.

This book is a celebration of the God's faithfulness and of the true experience and reality of walking with Him, obeying His word and living entirely on trust and dependence in Him.

Author Information

Ijeoma Okwuchi is a Nigerian, born in Lagos.

A graduate of English Language/ Literature in English, she has always loved books and reads voraciously.

She has worked in the Banking industry in Nigeria for most of her adult life, until her life changed forever on December 10, 2005, when the plane carrying her daughter, Kechi, and one hundred and eight other people, including 60 students from Loyola Jesuit College, Abuja, dropped from the sky.

Ijeoma kept a daily journal throughout Kechi's recuperation, which she turned into a book when she was instructed to do so by a word from God.

She currently lives in Pearland, Texas, with her daughters, Kechi and Tara, while Kechi continues the extensive treatments required for her total recovery. Her husband, Mike visits his family twice a year.

Ijeoma is working on her second book, **Refined for Service**, a continuation of the story started in **Refined for Rebirth**.

Made in the USA
Middletown, DE
30 September 2017